Truth Will Prevail

THE NINE APOSTLES WHO WENT TO BRITAIN, 1839-1841

Brigham Young
1801–1877

Heber C. Kimball
1801–1868

Orson Hyde
1805–1878

Parley P. Pratt
1807–1857

Orson Pratt
1811–1881

John Taylor
1808–1887

Wilford Woodruff
1807–1898

George A. Smith
1817–1875

Willard Richards
1804–1854

TRUTH WILL PREVAIL

The Rise of
The Church of Jesus Christ
of
Latter-day Saints in
the British Isles
1837–1987

Editors

V. Ben Bloxham
James R. Moss
Larry C. Porter

The Church of Jesus Christ of Latter-day Saints

751 Warwick Road
Solihull, West Midlands B91 3DQ

Printed in Great Britain by the University Press, Cambridge

ISBN 0 951 2130 08

Exclusive distribution in the United States by Deseret Book Company,
P.O. Box 30178, 40 East South Temple, Salt Lake City, Utah 84130.

Contents

List of Illustrations and Maps

Illustrations were provided courtesy of the LDS Church Archives unless otherwise designated on the individual plates.

Dedication

Father in Heaven who lovest all,
Oh, help Thy children when they call;
That they may build from age to age
An undefilèd heritage.

Kipling

This history is dedicated to
the saints whose lives are chronicled here
and the Latter-day Saints in Britain
who continue to build our heritage.

Foreword

This is a story of strength. It is a true story. It is an unfinished story, related at the time of the 150th anniversary of The Church of Jesus Christ of Latter-day Saints in the British Isles.

In July 1837 two ordained apostles of the Lord Jesus Christ set foot on British soil. They were on assignment from a living prophet of God. The names of the apostles were Heber C. Kimball and Orson Hyde. The name of the prophet was Joseph Smith. Their divine commission was to teach and to baptize, as decreed in both ancient and modern times by the Saviour whom they served. To a world clouded by the darkness of apostasy and innocent ignorance, prophets and apostles had again been ordained by divine direction to bring truth, understanding, love and joy. Elders Kimball and Hyde were part of God's purpose and his plan.

Shortly after arriving in Liverpool, they continued to their destination of Preston, where three forces converged. Their appointment to teach the truth of the gospel of Jesus Christ as it had been restored in the latter days was one of those forces. They were to proclaim the reality that God the Father and His Son, Jesus Christ, personally appeared to the Prophet Joseph Smith in the year 1820 to commence a work that was to fill the earth in preparation for the second coming of the Saviour. A second force was a newly established law, passed in England in 1812, which provided an increased measure of freedom of worship. Subsequent years allowed a marginal cushion of time to assure acceptance of that cherished freedom, even though imperfectly. The third force was a flag – an election banner bearing the motto 'Truth Will Prevail'. This slogan, painted in large gilt letters, was displayed by partisans of one candidate for office. This parliamentary election followed the accession of young Queen Victoria to the throne earlier that year. So impressed were the elders when they saw this banner in Preston that they adopted the motto for their sacred work in Britain.

Thus the title for this book, which is a commemorative review of a remarkable story of strength.

Strength came by another revelation from the God of this earth who, on Sunday, 23 July 1837, declared in Kirtland, Ohio, to his apostles:

> ...whithersoever they shall send you, go ye, and I will be with you; and in whatsoever place ye shall proclaim my name an effectual door shall be opened unto you, that they may receive my word. (D&C 112:19.)

An ocean's breadth away, that very day, that prophecy was fulfilled in Preston, England, as the missionaries occupied a pulpit to proclaim the divinity of Jesus Christ and his atoning sacrifice. A Preston branch of The Church of Jesus Christ of Latter-day Saints was established that year. It has become the oldest continuously functioning unit of the Church in all the world.

Strength came from the character of those who joined the Church. Within nine months of their arrival, Elder Kimball and other missionary companions baptized over 1,000 souls.

Strength came from other apostles when, on 14 April 1840, the Quorum of the Twelve met in Preston – the first meeting of that council outside the limits of North America.

Strength came from the King James Version of the Bible, a British contribution to scriptural understanding for all the world, and from the Book of Mormon, which contains the sacred record of the ministry of the Lord Jesus Christ to his prophets and people of the American hemisphere, broadly between the years 600 B.C. to A.D. 400. A handsome leather-bound copy of the Book of Mormon printed in Great Britain in 1841 was presented to Queen Victoria. This historical document is now in the Royal Library at Windsor. The clarifying concepts contained in that book constituted the great attraction of many people to the Church. As students of that book found it to be true by careful and prayerful study, the corresponding conclusions that God lives, that Jesus Christ is His Only Begotten Son, and that they now communicate with man through a prophet, as in former days, became cornerstones of their faith.

In the year 1850 more members of the Church resided in Britain than in all of North America. The British Isles comprised the springboard for the Church to reach the countries of France, Scandinavia, Italy, Switzerland and Germany. So, in the truest sense, *Truth Will Prevail* commemorates not only one hundred and fifty years of the Church in the British Isles, but also in Europe, the first continent beyond North America to be blessed by the restoration of the gospel of Jesus Christ and the beginning of the promised 'restitution of all things'. (See Acts 3:21.)

This story of strength is punctuated by privation and emigration. Over a period of six decades, tenderly rooted members of the Church in the United States of America were joined by approximately 65,000 saints from the British Isles who added to the stability of the institution of the Church first in Nauvoo, later in Salt Lake City, and then throughout the American West. The eminent English author Charles Dickens described some of these saints as the 'pick and flower of England'. ('The Uncommercial Traveller' in *All the Year Round*, p. 444.)

But it is not just a story of strength from England. The Irish, the Manx, the Scots, and the Welsh all infused power in their unique ways. The now-famous Salt Lake Mormon Tabernacle Choir, for example, grew from Welsh roots and has been led and strengthened by many with ancestral moorings in Wales. Indeed, every country in the British Isles has been represented in the lineages of the prophet/leaders of the Church in this dispensation.

The first edition of the Pearl of Great Price, one of the scriptural standard works of the Church, was published in Britain, as were the *Journal of Discourses* and the *Millennial Star*. Beloved and familiar hymns, such as 'We Thank Thee, O God, for a Prophet', and 'Oh Say, What Is Truth?' and many others come from the inspired compositions of gifted British saints.

This is a story of strength and fulfilment. The Church had come virtually full circle when, in 1958, a holy temple was completed and dedicated on British soil. In the early years, strength from Britain emigrated to the Church in America. A century and a half later, as the Church is officially recognized and established in over a hundred nations of the earth, the 'tent' of the Lord's Church is strengthened by stakes throughout the world. Forty stakes exist in the British Isles, each with powerful leadership provided by local saints in Ireland, Scotland, Wales and England. Chapels dot these lands. Congregations stream regularly into and from these buildings in joyful recognition of continuing growth and blessings. A missionary training centre reseeds the soil enriched by those early missionaries who travelled without purse or scrip, in obedience to their divine commission.

This is a story of strength and sacrifice, not the least of which have been contributed, as a labour of love, by the scholarly authors and editors of this book. Words seem inadequate to express full appreciation. From leaders and readers alike, we extend our heartfelt gratitude.

Truth Will Prevail is a story of strength, a story of commitment, a story of fulfilment, and a story of interaction between our living Lord with his prophets and apostles, with the mighty and the powerful, with the humble and the meek. It is a story of truth – the saga of mankind's struggle in the pursuit of and devotion to truth in the face of challenge and adversity. It is a story of love, unconditional and unchanging, of man for his neighbour and for his Maker. Additional chapters will no doubt be penned by future generations, all to the continuing glory of God and his work.

Russell M. Nelson

Preface

In celebration of the 150th anniversary of The Church of Jesus Christ of Latter-day Saints in the British Isles, we publish this history. Since 1937, when Elder Richard L. Evans wrote *A Century of 'Mormonism' in Great Britain* for the centennial celebration, more LDS history has been made and additional records of early Church history have been discovered. This work is therefore comprehensive, covering the entire 150-year period since the restored gospel was brought to Britain in 1837.

This work was begun when President (now Apostle) Joseph B. Wirthlin and Elder Russell C. Taylor of the Europe Area Presidency commissioned it and Elder Neal A. Maxwell of the Quorum of the Twelve Apostles obtained the First Presidency's approval for the project. James R. Moss, JD, and I were then invited to act as co-editors, and were asked to bring together a group of historians who would write the various chapters. Eleven authors accepted that responsibility, and their efforts have resulted in the fourteen chapters of this history.

To encourage a high standard of scholarship as well as a solid spiritual foundation, editorial review responsibilities were assigned to the Religious Studies Centre of Brigham Young University, Provo, Utah, USA, and Larry C. Porter, Ph.D., as Director of Church History for the Centre, became the third editor of the project. To encourage a similarly high standard of material workmanship, Cambridge University Press was chosen to print the book, and Thomas Kent Hinckley, Ph.D., a post-graduate of the London College of Printing, was appointed as the book's designer. Financial support was provided by the Church, through Brigham Young University and the Europe Area Presidency.

The editors wish to thank, first of all, the First Presidency, the Quorum of the Twelve, and the Europe Area Presidency, for authorizing and underwriting this project. Sincere appreciation also goes to the British Anniversary Committee, to the administration of Brigham Young University, particularly President Jae R. Ballif, Ph.D., to Dean Robert J. Matthews, Ph.D., of the Religious Studies Centre at BYU, and to the administrators and staff of historical societies, libraries, archives, and record offices in Britain and the USA. Special thanks must be given to the LDS Church Archives for the use of documents and photographs.

The authors of the book, whose only remuneration is the knowledge of how well they have performed their assigned tasks, are collectively and gratefully acknowledged, with particular thanks to Richard O. Cowan, Ph.D., and Frederick S. Buchanan, Ph.D., for working under severe time constraints, and to Miss Anne S. Perry, who was obliged to work an ocean apart from the other authors.

Our appreciation is also extended to Daniel H. Ludlow, Ed.D., and the Priesthood Correlation Review Committee of the Church, to the British Review Committee (specifically David Cook and Bryan Grant), and to S. Kent Brown, Ph.D., and the Review Committee of the BYU Religious Studies Centre.

Tamara (Mrs Thomas) Hinckley also deserves mention as the eleventh-hour editorial assistant, who 'took not aught away' but rather improved the final prose and made us all better writers for her efforts. Janiel Lind, secretary to Dr Porter, typed much of the manuscript and lent her much-needed expertise and efficiency to the entire project, for which she has the warm thanks of the editors.

As the anniversary year of 1987 begins, the apostolic keys that were held by Elder Heber C. Kimball in 1837 are held by Elder Russell M. Nelson, MD, Ph.D., who, by authority of the First Presidency, has apostolic appointment for these isles. To him we express great appreciation for writing the foreword to *Truth Will Prevail*, as well as for his support of the work itself. Special gratitude is extended to Elder Joseph B. Wirthlin who, as this history was being written, received a call to become one of the Lord's special witnesses. His love of history and his diligence in helping build the Lord's kingdom in Britain have combined to make this book an important part of the 150th anniversary celebration.

There remain two final expressions of gratitude to be made: firstly, to those faithful saints who have laboured in the Lord's vineyard in the British Isles throughout the history of the Church; and secondly, to the faithful saints who labour there today. May this book now go forth to fulfil its mission: to keep in honourable remembrance our worthy predecessors; to bring new commitment to present-day saints; and to declare to the world that the Lord's kingdom is indeed prevailing in the British Isles.

V. Ben Bloxham, PH.D.

Abbreviations Used in Text

CHC	*Comprehensive History of the Church*
CR	Conference Report
D&C	Doctrine and Covenants
DN	*Deseret News*
HC	*History of the Church*
IE	*Improvement Era*
JD	*Journal of Discourses*
JH	*Journal History of the Church*
MA	*Messenger and Advocate*
MS	*Millennial Star*
NEHGR	*New England Historical and Genealogical Register*
PBO	Presiding Bishopric's Office
PGP	Pearl of Great Price
TS	*Times and Seasons*

Saturday, the 22nd:

We started for Preston in coach. We got there four in the afternoon. Our things was taking off of the coach, Brother Goodson was hunting a boarding-house, [and] Elder Hyde and Brother Snider and myself was standing by our trunks. All at once I looked up, and there was a large flag standing right before us, written on it: *Truth Will Prevail.* We spoke with one voice, 'Amen and amen'.

Heber C. Kimball,
journal entry for 22 July 1837
[spelling and punctuation modernized]

The Apostolic Foundation

WHEN THE LORD began to prepare the world for the restoration of the gospel, he did not set events in motion in the north-eastern USA only; preparations went forward all round the world. The seventeenth-century civil war, for example, displaced thousands – and in the next three hundred years, nearly seventy million people emigrated from Europe to newly discovered lands. Such events not only caused people to break with traditions that might have inhibited their acceptance of the gospel, but also put people in the right place at the right time for the missionaries to find them. In the nineteenth century, the well-developed transportation systems that carried goods and colonists throughout the world just as readily carried missionaries and LDS emigrants.

Perhaps the greatest disruption of all was industrialization. Whereas the average life expectancy for labourers working the land was 38 years, that figure dropped to 19 years for the working classes in the mills. A young girl living in Utah once said to her grandmother, 'It must have been hard for you to give up everything you had to join the Church and come here.' But the grandmother replied, 'Child, you don't understand. In Manchester we had nothing. Here we could have land.' (Effie Kelsey.) The restoration of the gospel offered people a new world, not only eternally but temporally.

There has always been a tendency to think of this period as a sort of 'golden age' of missionary work, when in fact it was an apostolic age. What we have not always understood is that even though the apostles were young, they had been prepared for their tasks before they ever landed in Liverpool. They came not only with experience and discipline, but also with all the keys of their apostolic offices. And as the Lord had prepared them, so had he prepared the people of Britain. The apostles reaped the harvest of the Lord. What happened in Britain in 1840 would happen again under similar circumstances.

1

Beginnings of the Restoration: Canada, An 'Effectual Door' to the British Isles

LARRY C. PORTER

AFTER ALMOST A YEAR of unprecedented success in preaching the gospel of Jesus Christ to the people of Britain (July 1837 to April 1838), Elders Heber C. Kimball and Orson Hyde made final preparations for their return to the United States. In April Elder Kimball made a last tour of Chatburn, Lancashire, and surrounding branches to bid farewell to his friends, many of whom he had baptized. He had first visited that village the previous year, even though he had been warned that the people there would not receive his message because of their 'hardness of heart'. However, Elder Kimball had been blessed with such an outpouring of the Spirit that the 'hard' hearts of the people now held only love – for the Lord, for his gospel, and for his messenger, Heber C. Kimball. Because of this, many of them had joined the Church, and a strong branch had been established at Chatburn.

Now their beloved Elder Kimball had come to give them a parting hand. As he took his leave, most of the saints wept openly, and Elder Kimball himself was deeply affected. He wrote:

> When I left them, my feelings were such as I cannot describe. As I walked down the street I was followed by numbers; the doors were crowded by the inmates of the houses to bid me farewell, who could only give vent to their grief in sobs and broken accents. While contemplating this scene I was constrained to take off my hat, for I felt as if the place was holy ground. The Spirit of the Lord rested down upon me and I was constrained to bless that whole region of country. I

> was followed by a great number from Clithero [*sic*], a considerable distance from the village, who could hardly separate from me. My heart was like unto theirs, and I thought my head was a fountain of tears, for I wept for several miles after I bid them adieu. I had to leave the road three times to go to streams of water to bathe my eyes. (Whitney, *Kimball*, pp. 200–1.)

In Nauvoo the Prophet Joseph Smith responded to Elder Kimball's account of that experience with the enlightened instruction: 'Did you not understand it? That is a place where some of the old prophets travelled and dedicated that land, and their blessing fell upon you.' (*JD* 5:22.) More than 130 years later, President Spencer W. Kimball, grandson of Heber C. Kimball, attended the first British area conference of the Church, where he related that experience from his ancestor's life. President Kimball then affirmed: 'I should like to think that the whole of this great land is blessed and still carrying a blessing from our Heavenly Father from great and holy men who have walked upon its shores.' (British Area Conference Report, p. 21.)

Thus, at some early time now lost to history, the British Isles were frequented by men of God who apparently left a powerful blessing upon the place and its people. Since that time, the spiritual atmosphere of Great Britain has been influenced by many independent thinkers who may well have been inspired by that ancient blessing. For instance, as early as the fourth century a Briton named Pelagius taught that man was not totally depraved, and further, 'that man can take the initial and fundamental steps towards salvation by his own efforts'. (*Oxford Dictionary of the Christian Church*, p. 1058.) This so-called Pelagian heresy was only one of the early traditions that helped prepare the people of Britain for the coming of modern prophets and apostles.

Further manifestations of this independence of thought occurred in the early seventeenth century when Britain began to colonize the New World. Soon the Atlantic coast of North America was peopled by emigrants from the British Isles, many of whom were Puritans and thus had religious as well as economic reasons for emigrating. The Puritans were influenced in varying degrees by the teachings of John Calvin and, though they differed considerably among themselves, most of them were alike in that they were Nonconformists. The Nonconformists' aim was to 'purify' the existing Church of England (though in America they eventually broke

Places of LDS Conversion in Canada 1832–7, and Route of Canadian Missionaries to Great Britain 1837

away completely), while those who preferred to leave the established church altogether were called Separatists. There were also Separatists amongst the early American colonists, but they were in the minority.

Colonial America has often been described as the 'outpost of Europe', and the history of the thirteen American colonies indeed reflects the transplanting of European institutions – including the major European religions – to a primitive frontier. The people who came to America brought with them the Old and New Testaments, the major creeds of Christendom, and the writings of the European apologists. Numbered among those early colonists were Robert Smith of Sutterton, Lincolnshire, who emigrated to Massachusetts in 1638, and John Mack of Inverness, Scotland, who came to Connecticut in 1680. These men were the paternal and maternal great-great-great-grandfathers of the Prophet Joseph Smith – only two of more than 150 of his ancestors known to be British. (J. G. Stevenson.)

At first the early American colonists, somewhat ironically, could not tolerate dissenters in their midst. However, with the passage of time there was a gradual softening of that attitude and a cultural blending took place, old-world institutions and thinking becoming remoulded as they came in contact with a frontier environment now isolated from Europe. Hence a new way of life and a unique religious situation developed in America: the colonies became a melting-pot not just culturally but religiously, and a pattern of religious freedom was created.

As the settlers dispersed, many of them lost contact with organized religion as they found it inconvenient, impracticable or even impossible to attend services. In order to gather these frontier Americans into the Protestant fold, hundreds of preachers began labouring in the backwoods communities. Religion soon became a serious study for most people, and many sought a faith that would encompass the true teachings of Christ. The 'field [was] white already to harvest'.

Amongst the colonial Americans immersed in this religious awakening was Joseph Smith, Sr. In 1791 he moved to the township of Tunbridge, Vermont, coming from Topsfield, Massachusetts, with his father, Asael Smith, Sr. There he helped clear the land and establish a homestead in what was known as the Tunbridge Gore. Then, when visiting the village of Tunbridge, Joseph met a young woman from Gilsum, New Hampshire, named Lucy Mack. Lucy was staying with her brother Stephen, who ran a village shop and tinning business in Tunbridge. Their acquaintance led to matrimony (on 24 January 1796) and over the years eleven children were born to them.

Brigham Young later declared that the fifth child of this union, Joseph Smith, Jr, came through a 'watched bloodline' and that 'Joseph was foreordained in eternity to preside over this last dis-

Joseph Smith, Jr, Prophet of the Restoration 1805–44. (*Courtesy of the RLDS Church Archives.*)

pensation'. (*JD* 7:289–90.) But even earlier, Asael Smith, Sr, Joseph's paternal grandfather, had prophesied 'that there would be a prophet raised up in his family', and just prior to his death in 1830 he declared that Joseph Smith, Jr 'was the very prophet that he had long known would come'. (*MS* 15:174.)

Following a series of family moves, Joseph and Lucy Mack Smith were living in Vermont in 1816 when an 'untimely frost destroyed the crops'. And as this was the third consecutive year that their crops had failed, Lucy declared, 'This was enough; my husband was now altogether decided upon going to New York.' (L. Smith, p. 66.) Hence Father Smith preceded his family to New York and then had them join him in the village of Palmyra. After two years the Smiths acquired a hundred acres of land in what was then the township of Farmington (later Manchester, Ontario County, New York), where they built a cabin and began to clear the land.

As for the local interest in religion, Lucy Mack Smith stated, 'there was a great revival in religion, which extended to all the denominations of Christians in the surrounding country in which we resided'. Continuing, she explained, 'Many of the world's people became concerned about the salvation of their souls, came forward and presented themselves as seekers after religion'. (*Ibid.* p. 68.)

Amongst the 'seekers' were at least four members of the Smith family: Lucy herself and her children Hyrum, Samuel and Sophronia all joined the Western Presbyterian Church in Palmyra; and her son Joseph, then fourteen years old, was no less stirred by this religious fervour. He later wrote:

> ...so great were the confusion and strife among the different denominations, that it was impossible for a person young as I was, and so unacquainted with men and things, to come to any certain conclusion who was right and who was wrong. (PGP, Joseph Smith – History, 1:8.)

Joseph sought for answers in the Bible, and came upon James 1:5: 'If any of you lack wisdom, let him ask of God, that giveth to all men liberally, and upbraideth not; and it shall be given him.' 'Never did any passage of scripture come with more power to the heart of man than this did at this time to mine', Joseph said. 'I reflected on it again and again... [and] came to the conclusion that I must either remain in darkness and confusion, or else I must do as James directs, that is, ask of God.' (*Ibid.* vss. 12–13.)

Finally, Joseph did 'ask of God'. He went into the nearby woods, knelt down, and offered up the desires of his heart. Concerning the miraculous experience that followed, Joseph declared:

> I saw two Personages, whose brightness and glory defy all description, standing above me in the air. One of them spake unto me, calling me by name, and said, pointing to the other – *This is My Beloved Son. Hear Him!*
>
> My object in going to inquire of the Lord was to know which of all the sects was right, that I might know which to join. No sooner, therefore, did I get possession of myself, so as to be able to speak, than I asked the Personages who stood above me in the light, which of all the sects was right... and which I should join.
>
> I was answered that I must join none of them, for they were all wrong... (*Ibid.* vss. 17–19.)

Joseph had seen God the Father and Jesus Christ, and had received the answer to his question; he had learned that all the existing creeds had fallen into error. During that vision he was also told 'that he was called and chosen to be an instrument in the hands of God, to bring about some of his marvelous purposes in this glorious dispensation'. (O. Pratt, *Visions*, p. 7.)

Directed by the Spirit of the Lord, Joseph proceeded to submit himself to the will of God. Throughout the next decade (1820–30) he was tutored by a succession of heavenly messengers, one of whom said that his name was Moroni and, during the night of 21–22 September 1823, told Joseph of the existence of an ancient scriptural record, the Book of Mormon, engraved upon sheets of gold. Four years later, in September 1827, Moroni gave Joseph temporary custody of that singular record during a visit to its repository in a nearby hill.

Joseph then began to translate it, 'through the gift and power of God' and, in the process of translation, discovered many more questions for which he frequently sought answers from the Lord. One of these was the question of proper baptism. Seeking divine guidance, Joseph and his scribe, Oliver Cowdery, found a secluded place and approached the Lord in prayer. In response, another resurrected being, John the Baptist, appeared to them and ordained them to 'the Priesthood of Aaron, which holds the keys of the ministering of angels, and of the gospel of repentance, and of baptism by immersion for the remission of sins'. (D&C 13.) Oliver detailed the event as follows:

> He [Joseph] was ordained by the angel John, unto the lesser or Aaronic priesthood, in company with myself, in the town of Harmony, Susquehannah County, Pennsylvania, on Friday, the 15th day of May, 1829, after which we repaired to the water, even to the Susquehannah River, and were baptized, he first ministering unto me and after – I to him. (Joseph Smith, Sr, 1:8–9.)

During this visitation, John the Baptist instructed Joseph and Oliver that 'this Aaronic Priesthood had not the power of laying on hands for the gift of the Holy Ghost, but that this should be conferred on us hereafter'. The angel also told them 'that he was acting under the direction of Peter, James, and John, the ancient apostles, who held the keys of the higher priesthood, which was called the Priesthood of Melchizedek', and which he said would 'in due time' be conferred upon Joseph and Oliver. (Joseph Smith, *HC 1*:40; see also D&C 13, headnote.) Hence, some time between the 15th of May and the end of June 1829, these ancient apostles of the Lord Jesus Christ also visited Joseph and Oliver, bestowing upon them the promised priesthood of Melchizedek.

Joseph and Oliver finished the translation of the golden plates at the home of Peter Whitmer, Sr, in Fayette, New York, and it was there that the Three Witnesses saw the plates, beheld an angel and, according to David Whitmer, heard the voice of God declaring from the heavens 'that the Book was true and the translation correct'. (*Saints' Herald* 29: 68.) The translation finished, they applied for copyright and by June 1829 were ready to have the Book of Mormon printed. After much discussion, E. B. Grandin of Palmyra, New York, agreed to publish the work.

While the Book of Mormon was still being bound, a man by the name of Solomon Chamberlain, a cooper from Lyons, New York, was travelling to Upper Canada via the Erie Canal. When he neared the village of Palmyra, however, he felt that he should alight there and, having walked three miles further south, he stopped at a farmhouse for the night. Next morning his hosts asked him if he had ever heard of the 'gold Bible'. At the mention of those words, Solomon said, 'there was a power like electricity went from the top of my head to the end of my toes', as some fourteen years earlier *he* had been visited by an angel who told him that 'there would be a book come forth like unto the Bible, and the people would be guided by it, as well as the Bible'. Solomon had been anticipating such a book ever since, and he could not neglect investigating such a claim.

Upon inquiring of his host, Solomon learned that he was less than a mile from the Smith home and the 'gold Bible' itself, and so he quickly made his way 'across lots' to the home of Joseph Smith, Sr. There he met Father Smith, Joseph's brother Hyrum, Christian Whitmer and others, but was informed that the Prophet was at the time in Harmony, Pennsylvania. Solomon then explained his interest to the Smith family, whereupon they proceeded to spend the next two days teaching him directly from the printer's manuscript of the Book of Mormon. He quickly recognized that this was the book he had been looking for.

Hyrum Smith and others then took Solomon to E. B. Grandin's printing works, where he was given 64 unbound, printed pages of the Book of Mormon. Solomon said:

> I took them with their leave, and pursued my journey to Canada, and I preached all that I knew concerning Mormonism to all, both high and low, rich and poor, and thus you see this was the first that ever printed Mormonism was preached

to this generation [in that part of the country]. I did not see any one in traveling for 800 miles, that had ever heard of the Gold Bible (so called) [and] I exhorted all people to prepare for the great work of God that was now about to come forth, and it would never be brought down nor confounded. (Chamberlain, pp. 12–13.)

Unordained, but nevertheless sent with the blessing of those who had charge of the Book of Mormon, Solomon Chamberlain thus preached the restored gospel to anyone who would listen, on his trek through an unspecified part of Upper Canada.

Eleven days after the first public sale of the Book of Mormon, The Church of Jesus Christ of Latter-day Saints was officially organized at the Whitmer home in Fayette, New York, on 6 April 1830. (Joseph Smith, *HC 1*: 77–8.)

Once the Church had been organized, the Prophet could turn his attention to a more expansive proselytizing programme. As a result of this effort, branches of the Church were created at Colesville and Manchester, in addition to the one that had been established at Fayette, New York. Many prospective converts were approached by the newly confirmed saints. Also, events occurred that would soon lead to full-scale missionary work in Upper Canada. For instance, while at the Tomlinson Inn in Mendon, New York, in June 1830, Phinehas H. Young received a copy of the Book of Mormon from Samuel H. Smith. He read it, and then spoke in its defence before a local congregation of Methodists. Two months later Phinehas, a preacher for the Methodist Reformed Church, was asked by his brother Joseph, who was also a licensed Methodist preacher, to go with him to Earnestown, Upper Canada. Phinehas consented. Leaving Mendon about 20 August 1830, the two brothers stopped in Lyons, New York, at the home of an old acquaintance – none other than Solomon Chamberlain. For two solid hours Solomon preached the restored gospel to the Young brothers, then sent them on their way 'pondering upon the things [they] had heard'. (*MS 25*: 374.)

Upon reaching Earnestown, Phinehas and Joseph commenced their labours, but soon Phinehas began to feel dissatisfied with his preaching and decided to return home. On his way he attended a quarterly meeting of the Episcopal Methodists at Kingston, and that evening at his hotel he found many of the Methodists assembled in two large rooms. Greatly moved by the spirit that was working in him, Phinehas stood in the doorway between the two rooms and requested the attention of the group, numbering about one hundred persons. Having asked if anyone present had read the Book of Mormon, and then being invited to enlighten them, Phinehas said:

> I commenced by telling them that it was a revelation from God, translated from the Reformed Egyptian language by Joseph Smith, jun., by the gift and power of God, and gave a full account of the aborigines of our country, and agreed with many of their traditions... I bore a powerful testimony to the work, and thus closed my remarks and went to bed, not to sleep, but to ponder with amazement at the power that seemed to compel me thus to speak. (*Ibid.* p. 375.)

This account by Phinehas Young is one of the earliest references to a discourse on Mormonism being presented in Upper Canada – and this by one who had not yet joined the Church.

That same month (August 1830) other LDS missionaries went into Upper Canada. Anxious to share the restored gospel with his own parents, Joseph Smith, Sr, set out with his son Don Carlos on a mission to St Lawrence County, New York, to visit his father and mother, Asael and Mary Duty Smith, living at Stockholm. In addition to his parents, Joseph hoped to meet his brothers and a sister who also resided in the Stockholm–Potsdam area. Speaking of the course his father took, the Prophet Joseph said that he touched 'on his route at several of the Canadian ports [on the north shore of Lake Ontario], where he distributed a few copies of the Book of Mormon'. (Joseph Smith, *HC* 4:190.) Thus, within six months of its publication, 'a few copies' of the Book of Mormon had been judiciously placed at some unidentified port communities in Upper Canada.

One of the promises in the Book of Mormon was that the Lord would not forget the descendants of the ancient American peoples. (Enos 1:16.) Accordingly, in October 1830 the Prophet Joseph instructed Oliver Cowdery and a small band of elders to go from Fayette, New York, to the 'borders of the Lamanites' (western Missouri and the Indian territory) to preach the gospel to the American Indians. On their way, near Kirtland, Ohio, these missionaries were successful in converting about 127 white people residing there, and two of these, Sidney Rigdon and Edward Partridge, made the journey to Fayette to meet the Prophet that

December. While they were there the Lord revealed the doctrine of gathering, and at a conference of the Church held at the Whitmer home, Joseph Smith pronounced this revelation:

> And that ye might escape the power of the enemy, and be gathered unto me a righteous people, without spot and blameless –
> Wherefore, for this cause I gave unto you the commandment that ye should go to the Ohio; and there I will give unto you my law; and there you shall be endowed with power from on high. (D&C 38:31–2.)

Obedient to this commandment, the Prophet and most of the New York membership of the Church moved to Kirtland, Ohio, in 1831.

Though the headquarters of the Church had moved, proselytizing work in the states of New York and Pennsylvania continued, along with work in Upper Canada. In January 1832 Phinehas Young made a special trip by sleigh to visit a branch of the Church at Columbia, Pennsylvania. Phinehas brought with him a friend, Heber C. Kimball, and his own brother, Brigham Young. After about a week's stay, they returned home convinced that the doctrine of the restored Church was true.

Inspired by this Pennsylvania visit, Brigham Young went to Upper Canada to visit his brother Joseph. While there, Brigham told his brother that he believed the gospel existed in its original purity in Mormonism. Brigham said that Joseph's 'heart rejoiced, and he returned home with me' in March 1832. (Young, 'History', p. 10.)

The following month, back in Columbia, Pennsylvania, for a return visit, Phinehas Young and his father John were baptized on 5 April 1832. Joseph Young, who had left Brigham at home to go with them, was baptized the following day. Brigham Young's baptism soon followed, at Mendon, New York, on 14 April 1832. Referring to his baptism, Brigham wrote, 'I felt a humble, childlike spirit, witnessing unto me that my sins were forgiven.' (*Ibid.*)

Now enjoying the gift of the Holy Ghost and having been ordained to the priesthood, Phinehas and Joseph Young and four of the Pennsylvania elders (Elial Strong, Eleazer Miller, Enos Curtis and an unnamed brother – possibly Alpheus Gifford or Daniel Brown) returned to Earnestown in Upper Canada on the first official LDS mission to that country. Commencing in early June 1832, these elders enjoyed great success in their labours, and in a six-week period established the first branch of the Church in British North America, at Earnestown. (*MS 25*: 376; *Evening and Morning Star*, May 1833, p. 7.)

Members of the Young family continued to take a particular interest in the Canadian proselytizing. In December 1832 Brigham Young returned with his brother Joseph to Upper Canada. Starting from Mendon, New York, they walked through mud and deep snow until they reached Gravelly Point, New York, on Lake Ontario. Here they made a six-mile crossing on the ice to the town of Kingston, Upper Canada. Brigham later recalled that 'the ice was very thin and bent under our feet, so that in places the water was half shoe deep, and we had to separate from each other, the ice not being capable of holding us'. (Young, 'History', p. 12.)

Proceeding from Kingston to West Loughborough, the elders spent one month preaching in that vicinity. They succeeded in baptizing about forty-five persons. A branch was then organized at West Loughborough, along with other branches in the area. In February 1833 Brigham and Joseph returned to their homes in Mendon, again crossing Lake Ontario on the ice.

Not content to remain long separated from his Canadian friends, Brigham soon went back to his former mission-field. Leaving Mendon on 1 April 1833, he crossed Lake Ontario by steamboat from Ogdensburgh to Kingston, then laboured successfully in Earnestown, West Loughborough, and other nearby branches. In July he gathered up the families of Brother James Lake and his son Dennis, who lived at Camden to the north of Earnestown, and helped them prepare to move to Kirtland. In company with Brothers Daniel and Abraham Wood of Loughborough, Elder Young escorted the small caravan to Ohio. (*Ibid.*; McMillan, p. 374.) This group was one of the earliest Canadian emigrations to Kirtland and was in direct response to the doctrine of gathering. (D&C 38: 31–2.)

Then, on 5 October 1833 the Prophet Joseph himself left for Upper Canada, accompanied by Elders Sidney Rigdon and Freeman Nickerson. Arriving at Mount Pleasant, Upper Canada, on the 18th of October, they were welcomed at the home of Freeman's son, Eleazer Freeman Nickerson (who was always called 'Freeman' and not 'Eleazer', which has led to some confusion between father and son in written records). Another Nickerson son, Moses Chapman Nickerson, also lived in Mount Pleasant, where the two brothers had opened a shop in 1830. (Goddard, pp. 2, 5.) For several days the Prophet and his company preached at Mount Pleasant (in the Nickerson brother's shop) as well as at Brantford, Colborne and Waterford.

The Prophet delivered a simple and forthright message to his listeners, bearing a 'faithful testimony that the Priesthood was again restored to the earth, and that God and His Son had conferred upon him the keys of the Aaronic and Melchizedek Priesthoods'. Joseph further proclaimed 'that the last dispensation had come, and the words of Jesus were now in force – "Go ye into all the world and preach the gospel to every creature. He that believeth and is baptized shall be saved; but he that believeth not shall be damned."' (Gates, p. 18.) Many of the people did believe, and the Prophet Joseph himself performed fourteen baptisms. One of these converts, Lydia Bailey, while yet standing in the waters of baptism was filled with the Holy Ghost and exclaimed, 'Glory to God in the highest! Thanks be to his holy name that I have lived to see this day and be a partaker of this great blessing.' (Gates, p. 21.)

A particularly impressive devotional service was held at the home of Eleazer Freeman Nickerson the evening before Joseph Smith, Sidney Rigdon and Freeman Nickerson departed for their homes. With the family seated around the wide, old-fashioned fireplace in the parlour, they listened attentively to Joseph's discourse. Moses Nickerson voiced the wish that the gift of tongues might be made manifest amongst the newly baptized saints as it had been anciently, and the Prophet responded, 'If one of you will rise up and open your mouth it shall be filled, and you shall speak in tongues.' All eyes seemed instinctively to turn towards Lydia Bailey: 'Sister Lydia, rise up.' Lydia did arise and the spirit of tongues came upon her, 'and her mouth was filled with the praises of God and His glory'. (*Ibid.* p. 23.)

A branch of the Church was organized at Mount Pleasant with Eleazer Freeman Nickerson as the presiding elder, and having set the Church in order there, Presidents Smith and Rigdon could return to Kirtland.

While this work was going forward in Upper Canada, proselytizing was also begun in Lower Canada. Elder Orson Pratt, always in the vanguard of missionary endeavour, left Charleston, Vermont, on 19 July 1833, and on the 20th preached in the township of Potton, Stanstead County, Lower Canada (now Brome County). His sermon was, by his own description, 'upon the gathering of Israel and more revelations and miracles, the 29th and 40th chapters of Isaiah and the two sticks'. Although his stay in Canada was but a single day, this event was apparently the earliest excursion by an LDS missionary into Lower Canada. (O. Pratt, journal, 19–21 Jul 1833; *MS 27*: 72.)

During these early years a succession of missionaries proselytized in both Upper and Lower Canada and in what are now the maritime provinces. Of particular significance, however, is the visit of six of the newly ordained apostles in 1835. On the 4th of May the members of the Quorum of the Twelve Apostles set out from Kirtland to perform a special mission amongst the branches of the Church in the east, and after about two months in New York, Elders David W. Patten, Heber C. Kimball, Luke S. Johnson, Orson Pratt, John F. Boynton and Lyman E. Johnson crossed the St Lawrence River into Upper Canada during the latter part of June 1835. A conference was held at Loughborough on Monday the 29th of June, and the six apostles gave valuable instruction to the saints in attendance. In the report of their mission the apostles recorded their experience at Loughborough as follows:

> Here we found a branch of the Saints who not only received us cordially, but also received our teachings with joy of heart. Some were added here also, by baptism, whom we expect to meet on the glorious morn of that day when the dead in Christ shall arise and live. – May God grant that they may all be preserved, gathered to Zion and saved in the celestial kingdom. (*MA 2*: 205.)

In fact, most of the members of the original Quorum of the Twelve Apostles preached in the Canadas either collectively or singly during this formative period.

Although missionary success is not necessarily measured by numbers of converts produced, the work performed by Elder John E. Page deserves mention, as he was the Lord's instrument in bringing literally hundreds into the Church in British North America. Elder Page was called to labour in Upper Canada in May 1836, but, being in poor circumstances, he responded that he was destitute of the clothing necessary to perform such a task. At this the Prophet Joseph 'took off his coat, and gave it to him, and told him to go, and the Lord would bless him abundantly on his mission'. (Young, 'History', p. 212.)

Thus Elder Page, in company with Elder William Harris, left Kirtland on 31 May 1836. On this first mission he was gone for about eight months, labouring in the north-eastern regions of Upper Canada, particularly in the Bathurst and Johnstown Districts. Elder Page described their activities upon reaching Loughborough in the latter part of June:

> We commenced our ministerial labors in [the] township of Loughborough, some 18 or 20 miles north of Kingston, where we added 14 members to the Loughborough branch. From thence we traveled to Leed's [*sic*] Church, distance 20 miles, and baptized 3. – From thence we traveled 25 miles to Bedford, North Crosby, where we planted a church that now numbers 68 members. (*MA* 3:446.)

At this point Elder Harris found it necessary to return to the States, and Elder Page carried on alone, 'preaching and opposing wicked persecutors'. He then left Bedford to work in the South Crosby and Bastard townships, where he was joined in September by Elder James Blakesley. These two elders together succeeded in baptizing 97 people before Elder Blakesley also had to leave. After that, Elder Page continued his labours in the villages of Elgin, Westport, Portland and Perth, and through his diligence 41 more persons were baptized, nine of these being at Perth, Bathurst District. (*Ibid.*)

It is of contemporary interest to note that amongst those brought into the Church through Elder Page's efforts on this first mission were two young brothers in Leeds County, Johnstown District: Arza Erastus and Ira Nathaniel Hinckley. Their great-grandfather, Samuel Hinckley, had come to America from Harrietsham, Kent, two hundred years earlier, and had settled at Barnstable, Massachusetts. His descendants later emigrated to Upper Canada, where Arza and Ira were eventually born at Bastard, Leeds. When their father, Erastus Nathaniel, had been too seriously ill to take care of the family, Arza, still a small child, had gone to live with his maternal grandfather, Arza Judd, Sr, whilst Ira, who was not yet two years old, remained at home with his mother, Lois Judd Hinckley. Erastus Nathaniel Hinckley had died in 1830, and Lois had married her cousin, Evi Judd. Then in 1836, both of these Judd families (Arza's and Evi's) were proselytized by the elders and converted. Ira Nathaniel Hinckley would later become the great-grandfather of President Gordon B. Hinckley of the First Presidency of the Church. (*NEHGR*; L. Hinckley, p. 1.)

Upon his return to Kirtland in January 1837, Elder Page gave the following summary of his proselytizing success:

> Besides all this the elders and priests who have been ordained at the conferences I have held have swelled the number of those baptized to 267 in all added to the church in the bounds of the territory where I have labored over seven months, it being my first mission in the gospel of Christ...
>
> A wide door is opening in that country for preaching; and I humbly trust that my brethren in the ministry will not be slothful in improving the opportunity to promulgate the truth, that the blood of souls may not be found in their garments. Truth is triumphing; error is falling; saints are rejoicing, and Babylon is howling, because of her losses. And for the same let thanksgiving and praise be ascribed to God and the Lamb. (*MA* 3:446–7.)

On 16 February 1837, after a respite of only a few weeks, Elder Page again left Kirtland for his former field of labour. This time, however, his wife and two small children went with him. He said that he took 'all the earthly goods I possessed, which consisted of one bed and our wearing apparel of the plainest kind, to continue my mission in the region of country as before'. (Young, 'History', p. 211.) Once more his labours were blessed with unusual success, and another four hundred souls were converted. Branches were established at Bedford, Bathurst, North and East Bathurst, Leeds, Williamsburg, Bastard and West Bastard. It is estimated that by the conclusion of his second mission Elder John E. Page may have participated in as many as six hundred baptisms in Upper Canada. (Bennett, p. 47.)

These early conversions played an important role in the gospel being taken to Great Britain in June–July 1837. Most Canadians who joined the Church in this formative period were either born in Britain or descended from British ancestors, and many still maintained contact with their relations across the sea. Such associations were indispensable to the success of the Church's proselytizing efforts in Britain, and the Spirit of the Lord carefully directed these preliminary steps.

An example of this fact is an event in the life of Elder Parley P. Pratt. Back in Kirtland, one night in early April 1836, Elder Pratt and his wife Thankful had retired for the evening when a

Parley P. Pratt, who introduced the gospel in Toronto and vicinity, 1836–7.

knock at the door surprised them. Parley arose and opened the door to his fellow apostle Heber C. Kimball and some others who had come to call. Being filled with a prophetic spirit, Elder Kimball blessed both Parley and Thankful, and gave a moving prophecy of singular importance to that household:

> Brother Parley, thy wife shall be healed from this hour, and shall bear a son [ten years of marriage had produced no offspring], and his name shall be Parley; and he shall be a chosen instrument in the hands of the Lord to inherit the priesthood and to walk in the steps of his father. He shall do a great work in the earth in ministering the Word and teaching the children of men. Arise, therefore, and go forth in the ministry, nothing doubting. Take no thoughts for your debts, nor the necessaries of life, for the Lord will supply you with abundant means for all things.

Continuing his prophetic utterances, the gifted elder next pronounced a prediction of monumental significance to the greater Church:

> Thou shalt go to Upper Canada, even to the city of Toronto, the capital, and there thou shalt find a people prepared for the fulness of the gospel, and they shall receive thee, and thou shalt organize the Church among them, and it shall

> spread thence into the regions round about, and many shall be brought to the knowledge of the truth and shall be filled with joy; *and from the things growing out of this mission, shall the fulness of the gospel spread into England, and cause a great work to be done in that land* [my italics].

Elder Kimball concluded with a second assurance of relief from the debts that were then plaguing the Pratts:

> You shall not only have means to deliver you from your present embarrassments, but you shall yet have riches, silver and gold, till you will loathe the counting thereof. (P. Pratt, pp. 130–1.)

Moved by the power of that blessing, Parley began to prepare for his prophesied mission to Toronto, Upper Canada. By the 5th of April his preparations were finished and he took leave of Kirtland, accompanied by his brother Orson Pratt, Freeman Nickerson, and three other elders who were going to Nova Scotia. (*MA* 2:319; O. Pratt, journal, 6 Apr 1836.)

Because Lake Erie was still closed to shipping due to ice, the elders went to nearby Painesville and hired a team to carry the six of them to Erie, Pennsylvania. There the brethren that were going to Nova Scotia left them, and Parley, Orson and Freeman took the stage to Buffalo, New York. After preaching at Black Rock, New York, they crossed the Niagara River into Upper Canada. (P. Pratt, p. 131.)

Walking towards the town of Hamilton, the three elders separated. Orson and Freeman went to keep some appointments they had in the neighbourhood whilst Parley went on into Hamilton. As he contemplated the long, muddy overland road to Toronto, Parley wished he had the two-dollar fare for a steamboat ride across Lake Ontario, which would be considerably faster and less tedious than walking. Musing on that prospect, he retired to a forested place outside the village and prayed for the means necessary to speed him on his mission, then re-entered Hamilton and began to converse with the people he met. He was soon approached by an individual who asked his name and where he was going, then inquired whether he was not in need of money. When Elder Pratt responded that he was, the man gave him ten dollars and a letter of introduction to a Mr John Taylor in Toronto. (John Taylor later said, 'Br. Parley came along and was introduced to me in a letter by Br. Moses Nickerson, a merchant with whom I had a slight acquaintance.' Thus Moses Nickerson may well have been the benefactor who gave Elder Pratt the money as well as that particular letter of introduction.) (Young, 'History', p. 270.)

The time-saving steamboat crossing from Hamilton to Toronto was accomplished on 19 April 1836. (*MA 2*:319.) That same evening Parley presented himself at the Taylor home on Newgate Street (now Adelaide Street) in Toronto. He was greeted at the door by Leonora Cannon Taylor, John's wife, who summoned her husband from his workshop. (John was a turner, and his workshop adjoined the house.) Elder Pratt then informed the couple of his reason for being in that community, but received very little encouragement. He lodged that night at a public house.

The following day he visited each of the clergymen in the city but found them rather hostile; all of them refused him permission to use their houses for preaching or to address their congregations. Undaunted, Parley made application both to the sheriff for use of the court-house and to the city authorities for use of a public room in the market-place, but those applications were similarly denied. Hence, as he had done in like situations, Elder Pratt retired to a pine grove on the outskirts of the city and prayed for assistance, 'asking Him in the name of Jesus to open an effectual door for His servant to fulfil his mission in that place'. Re-entering Toronto, he then went to the home of John Taylor to retrieve the luggage he had left there, intending to 'depart from a place where I could do no good'. While Parley was engaged in a momentary conversation with John Taylor, a Mrs Isabella Walton came to call and went with Mrs Taylor into an adjoining room. (P. Pratt, p. 135.)

Isabella Walton had been widowed almost two years earlier, on 9 August 1834. Her husband Matthew had been the chamberlain of the city of Toronto, and had died quite suddenly of cholera. (*Christian Guardian*, 13 Aug 1834, p. 159.) Since that difficult time, Isabella had received much comfort from her association with the Methodist Church as well as from her participation in an independent scriptural study-group.

Mrs Taylor explained Elder Pratt's situation to Isabella and said that he was about to leave the community, adding, 'He may be a man of God; I am sorry to have him depart'; whereupon Isabella told Leonora that she now knew why she had had the feeling that she should come to the Taylor home and that she should 'go in now'. She then said:

> Tell the stranger he is welcome to my house. I am a widow; but I have a spare room and bed, and food in plenty. He shall have a home at my house, and two large rooms to preach in just when he pleases.... (P. Pratt, p. 136.)

That evening Isabella gathered a small group in her home on Newgate Street to hear Elder Pratt preach. Parley commenced his remarks by bearing testimony that Joseph Smith had indeed been visited by an angel of God and that he had obtained an ancient record written by prophets who had lived on the American continents. He told them that this record contained the history of these early Americans as well as the prophecies and gospel that Jesus Christ had revealed to them. He then bore witness that this same Joseph Smith, with others, had been commissioned by angels and ordained to the holy apostleship, and told them that he himself had been ordained by those apostles.

So powerful were the impressions of the Spirit upon Elder Pratt's hearers that night that, when he finished his discourse, there were immediate requests for baptism. He cautioned them, however, to 'wait yet a little while till I have an opportunity to teach others, with whom you are religiously connected, and invite them to partake with you of the same blessings'. (*Ibid.*)

On the Sunday following his first address at Mrs Walton's, Elder Pratt was invited to the home of Mr William P. Patrick on Bay Street, where there was a meeting of the study-group to which Mrs Walton and the Taylors belonged. Mr Patrick, a wealthy aristocrat, had served as a class leader for the Methodist Episcopal Church and at that time held a position in civic government as clerk of the House of Assembly. (Walton, *York*, p. 122; Walton, *Toronto*, p. 35.) His home was large and fashionable, and a number of well-dressed ladies and gentlemen had assembled there. They had been meeting as a group twice weekly over the past two years, investigating the Bible. Each was seeking truth directly from the scriptures, and their study-group had purposely remained independent of any sectarian organization to which its members might individually belong. (P. Pratt, p. 140.) John Taylor offered the following explanation:

Our investigations were impartially made, and our search for truth extended. We examined every religious principle that came under our notice, and probed the various systems as taught by the sects, to ascertain if there were any that were in accordance with the word of God. But we failed to find any. (*JD 23*:30.)

The meeting began with singing and prayer, after which individuals were free to propose subjects for discussion by the group. John Taylor introduced a reading from the New Testament, the account of Philip teaching in Samaria and the results of his preaching in that land (Acts 8). Then he posed some questions to his friends:

Now, where is our Philip? Where is our receiving the Word with joy, and being baptized when we believed? Where is our Peter and John? Our apostles? Where is our Holy Ghost by the laying on of hands? Where are our gifts of the Holy Ghost? Echo answers, where? (P. Pratt, p. 140.)

After considerable discussion Elder Pratt was called upon to respond. He told them that he was prepared to discuss the subject at length, but, as the meeting had already lasted a long while, he would prefer to do so at another time. The chairman gave him a special appointment for that same evening, and Mr Patrick then offered a benediction, as follows:

O Lord, we have neither apostles, visions, angels, revelations, gifts, tongues, ordinances, nor a Christian ministry; we acknowledge that we are destitute of everything like the pattern of the true Church, as laid down in the holy Word, and we pray thee to send whom thou wilt. (*Ibid.* p. 142.)

Mr Patrick's large rooms were filled for the evening meeting. Elder Pratt introduced the subject of his discourse by stipulating certain basic beliefs of early Christians as found in the Holy Bible, saying:

It appears from our text, as well as from the general tenor of the New Testament, that certain definite principles existed, which, acted upon and enjoyed, constituted the Christian Church, or body of Christ, viz:

First. An inspired priesthood or apostleship, authorized to administer salvation in the name of Jesus.

Second. Faith in their words and testimony, on the part of those who heard them.

Third. Reformation of Life.

Fourth. Obedience to certain ordinances, as baptism and the laying on of hands in the name of Jesus Christ, in order to [obtain] the remission of sins and the gift of the Holy Ghost.

Fifth. The spiritual gifts imparted to the body thus organized, in order to [promote] its edification, growth and perfection.

It may be presumed that every portion of the professed Christian Church, without any exception – I mean those who admit the Scriptures to be a record of things as they existed – will readily agree, that the five principles just named did exist, and did constitute the Christian Church or body of Christ. This, then, constitutes the model or pattern of the object of our present search. (*Ibid.* pp. 143–4.)

Elder Pratt then entered into a detailed comparison of the existing sectarian doctines with the ancient model he had just described, and then concluded his remarks. Naturally his audience wanted to hear more, and asked him to continue his discourse another evening, and still a third. On that third evening he outlined the visions, manifestations and revealed doctrines that had crowned the restoration of the Church of Jesus Christ through the Prophet Joseph Smith; and he later observed: 'The truth was now plainly before this people, who had been in so wonderful a manner prepared for its reception, as predicted by Brother Kimball on my head before leaving home.' (*Ibid.* pp. 150–1.)

At this point Mr Patrick became alarmed at the direction the meetings were taking and refused to open his home to any further discourses by Elder Pratt, an action that created a distinct schism in the study-group. It now became necessary for those accepting Elder Pratt's explanation of the scriptures to move to the home of Isabella Walton, and again many members of that group requested baptism. Isabella Russell Walton, herself a native of Liverpool, was amongst the first to be baptized, along with her sister Sarah Russell Cavanaugh and her niece Ann Wanlass (the daughter of her sister Mary) in the waters of Toronto Bay. (*DN, Church News*, 31 Jul 1937, p. 1.)

Through individuals in that study-group, Elder Pratt was introduced to the writings and publications of a religious group called the 'Irvingites' (after their founder, Edward Irving – whose principal adherents were in Scotland and England. He found that the Irvingites were eagerly searching the scriptures regarding the 'gathering of Israel; the coming of Christ to reign on the earth; the apostasy of the Gentile church; the need of an organization by authority from God; and the restitution of the gifts of the Spirit'. (*MA* 2:318.) Sensing the possibilities for proselytizing such a people in Great Britain, Elder Pratt wrote:

> Tens of thousands are awakened in that land to these subjects, and are sending swift messengers to the nations around them, to teach these things insomuch that the excitement seems to have become general among kings and nobles, priests and people.
>
> I have addressed a letter of eleven pages to that land, giving a sketch of the work of the Lord among us. *Many believers here are late from England, so we may have access to many names in that country; these are already beginning to express desires for their friends in that country to hear these things.* [My italics] (*Ibid.*)

Among the 'swift messengers' sent out by the Irvingites was a Mr William R. Caird. Mr Caird had visited Toronto in May 1834, preached several times and shown great fluency in the scriptures. His doctrinal teachings, however, had worked particular 'havoc' amongst the Methodists of that city. (Shaw, pp. 112, 114.) Mr Patrick and some others of the Toronto study-group had espoused the teachings of Mr Caird and were anticipating his return to Upper Canada in the latter part of 1836. (This was also a key factor behind the rift which developed in the study-group.)

From Toronto, Elder Pratt's work was soon extended into the surrounding country by the influence of his friends in the city. He first visited a farming community known as Charleton (now Downsview), some nine miles north-west of Toronto proper, where Isabella Walton's brother Isaac Russell lived. Isaac was a Methodist class leader and chorister in the little Wesleyan church of that community. Isabella's sister Frances Russell Dawson (wife of John Dawson) also lived at Charleton, and through Sister Walton's persuasion her brother and sister invited Elder Pratt to visit. (*MS* 2:51; *DN, Church News*.)

John Taylor, as yet unbaptized, accompanied Elder Pratt when he fulfilled his engagement at Charleton, and while they were in the vicinity John directed Parley to the home of Joseph Fielding, another of his friends with whom he had studied the scriptures. As the visitors approached the house, Mr Fielding's two sisters, Mary and Mercy, fled to the neighbour's, 'lest they should give welcome, or give countenance to Mormonism'. (P. Pratt, p. 151.) At first, Mr Fielding was opposed to their holding meetings in the area, but when Elder Pratt assured him that he would preach only from the Bible and not from any 'new' revelations, he agreed to attend a gathering scheduled for that evening.

When that was settled, Mary and Mercy were persuaded to come home and prepare a good dinner, after which they all went to the appointed meeting – at the home of John and Frances Russell Dawson. Joseph Fielding later recalled:

> He soon began to open the scriptures to us in a way that we never saw before, reminding us that we had bound him to keep to the word; of this he made a good use, and we could not object to it. (*MS* 2:51.)

At the conclusion of the apostle's sermon Isaac Russell stood and proclaimed, 'This is the Gospel I have been looking for and am ready to live and die by.' (*DN*, *Church News*.)

For the next meeting, an arrangement was made to use the Methodist chapel. However, certain members of the congregation violently objected. Alex McKenzie, John and Edward Boak, William Jackson, John Bull, Thomas Golding and others tried to put Elder Pratt out of the building when he began to preach, whilst Isaac Russell and William Dawson attempted to intervene on Parley's behalf. At that point, Elder Pratt said that rather than cause contention he would voluntarily withdraw and, taking his defenders with him, he moved to the opposite side of the street and convened the meeting in a maple grove on land occupied by Joseph Fielding. (*Ibid.*)

For some time afterwards, a barn served as their chapel (*MS* 2:51), and Mr Fielding recorded his feelings during that period as follows:

> Many strongly opposed the Work, false reports were raised, etc. Sometimes our faith was shaken, but the Word preached came with great Power, in demonstration of the Spirit, so that we could not reject the testimony but to our condemnation. (Fielding, p. 7.)

Many of these people soon saw the need for baptism by the Lord's authorized servant. Samuel Russell (the son of Isaac Russell) gave some details about the baptisms that were then performed in a nearby stream:

> Half a mile west of the meeting house and settlement was a little stream called Black Creek, [and] thither Mr Pratt repaired, baptizing Isaac Russell and ordain-

ing him an Elder at the water's edge, at the same time and subsequent thereto baptizing Mary Russell, his wife, Frances Russell Dawson and John Dawson, his sister and brother-in-law, their son, William Dawson, and their daughters Margaret, Ruth, and Isabella, John Goodson, Joseph Fielding, his sisters Mary and Mercy Fielding, John Taylor, [Leonora Taylor,] John Snider, Margaret and James Wardlaw, Lucy Bridgeland and others. (*DN*, *Church News*; Johnson, p. 4.)

Isaac Russell (who was a native Englishman, having been born at Windy Haugh, near Alston, Cumberland, on 13 April 1807) was baptized some time in the latter part of April 1836. John and Leonora Taylor were baptized later, on 9 May 1836. John Larson and family were also baptized during this same period. (Tagg, p. 10.)

As Parley soon required assistance in his labours, his brother Orson Pratt and Freeman Nickerson took passage by steamboat from Hamilton to Toronto on 20 May 1836, and then travelled to Charleton to see Parley. (O. Pratt, journal, 20 May 1836; *MA* 2:319.) The next afternoon Elder Parley P. Pratt baptized several people from Charleton and also some who had come out from Toronto. (O. Pratt, journal, 21 May 1836.) Parley later described the events that followed, saying:

After I closed my discourse, we went to the water [Black Creek] and I baptized nine persons, who, apparently, came with contrite spirits, believing with all their hearts; expressing a full determination to serve the Lord to the end. – The next day being Sunday, May 22nd, the numbers of those who had been baptized having increased to twenty five, and brethren O. Pratt and F. Nickerson being present and assisting, we laid our hands upon them and confirmed them in the name of the Lord Jesus, for the gift of the Holy Ghost. In the ordinances of the day, we were blessed with joy and peace and with the powers of the Holy Ghost. Thus grew the word of God and prevailed mightily. (*MA* 2:320.)

Joseph Fielding (another Englishman, born at Honeydon, Bedfordshire) identified himself and his sisters Mary and Mercy as being amongst the nine who were baptized in Black Creek on the 21st of May. He likewise recorded their confirmation the next day under the hands of Parley P. Pratt in the chapel in a barn. (*MS* 2:51.) As others in the area requested baptism, Parley stated that they 'organized a branch of the Church, for the people there drank in truth as water, and loved it as they loved life'. (P. Pratt, p. 152.) Joseph Fielding wrote that 'all the members in my neighbourhood met at my House, as their Sanctuary, until I removed'. (He went first to Toronto and then to Kirtland, in March–April 1837.) (Fielding, pp. 8–9.)

One who seemed wholeheartedly converted was Isaac Russell. He soon became influential in the conversion of many people, not limiting his endeavours to the Charleton settlement but also proselytizing in Greater Toronto. His son Samuel later confirmed Isaac's effectiveness by enumerating many of his converts:

> Proclaiming the Gospel first to his brothers John and William and sister Ann [Russell] Gardiner at Millbrook in Durham, they rejecting it, he then preached in Toronto, Scarboro [Scarborough], Esquisinee [Esquesing], Churchville and other places, baptizing some sixty members, among whom were Jacob Scott and family, Theodore Turley [a gunsmith from Churchville], William and Wilson Law, Edward Lawrence, father of Henry W. Lawrence, James Standing and others. (*DN, Church News.*)

These baptisms soon produced a 'ripple effect', as such converts as Theodore Turley began in turn to preach the gospel to their neighbours. Labouring in and near Toronto, Theodore baptized Samuel Mulliner (a Scot, born in Haddington, East Lothian) on 10 September 1837 – and in December 1839 Brother Mulliner and another native Scotsman, Alexander Wright (born in Marnoch, near Banff, Banffshire, and converted to the gospel in Canada in 1836), would become the first LDS missionaries to serve in Scotland. (Evans, pp. 75–6; see Chapter 9 herein.)

During the Sabbath-day confirmation service at Charleton on the 22nd of May, Elder Parley Pratt had announced that he would be returning to Kirtland on personal business as well as to replenish his supply of tracts and other printed items. Following Parley's departure Elders Orson Pratt and Freeman Nickerson continued their ministry in the area. In Charleton, Orson preached at Mr Eaton's barn, and at the school-house near Brother Fielding's residence. He likewise laboured in the city of Toronto, preaching at the home of Isabella Walton, as well as at John Snider's, who was a brickmaker and mason on Berkeley Street. (Walton, *York*, p. 3.) His sermons centred on the first principles of the gospel; the spiritual gifts and officers necessary to constitute the Church of Jesus Christ; the manner in which Joseph Smith found and translated the golden plates; the history and prophecies contained in the Book of Mormon; and the apostasy of the ancient church. He also explained the necessity of the Church being restored as a fulfilment of the revelations found in John 14:6 and Daniel 2. Elder Pratt then left the affairs of the local Church in the capable hands of John Taylor, Isaac Russell and others, and took passage on a steamboat across Lake Ontario to Oswego, where he continued his proselytizing endeavours into Jefferson County, New York. (O. Pratt, journals, 24 May–4 June 1836.)

When Elder Parley P. Pratt returned to Toronto in June 1836, his wife Thankful came with him. Under Parley's direction the Church grew rapidly in Toronto and vicinity, resulting in a genuine outpouring of promised gifts. Elder Pratt specified that 'there were visions, prophesyings, speaking in tongues and healings, as well as the casting out of devils and unclean spirits'. (P. Pratt, pp. 152–3.) The demands upon him soon became so great that he established a regular circuit, moving continually from branch to branch and from one neighbourhood to another.

With this increasing responsibility, Elder Pratt sent a request to Kirtland for assistance from his fellow apostles, and Elder Orson Hyde responded, arriving in Toronto during July 1836. His arrival was so well timed as to involve him immediately in a public debate at nearby Scarborough. There a learned Presbyterian clergyman by the name of Browning challenged the missionaries to a debate on the scriptural validity of the doctrine they were preaching. At first the two apostles declined, stating that they had all the labour they could handle without becoming involved in a debate, but as the minister persisted, they at last consented. Unfortunately, just at the appointed time, Parley was called home to Kirtland as a witness in a legal case, and Elder Hyde was left 'to meet the champion alone'. (*Ibid.* pp. 156–7; Young, 'History', p. 170.) Since there was no building in Scarborough large enough to hold the expected crowd, the meeting was held in the open air. A grove of trees provided the necessary space, and waggons drawn up facing each other supplied the 'pulpits'.

Elder Hyde said that his opponent 'came with some less than a mule-load of books, pamphlets and newspapers, containing all the slang of an unbelieving world'. (Young, 'History', p. 170.) As both sides agreed that the Bible was to be recognized as the standard of truth in the debate, Elder Hyde laid down in his opening statement some specific principles by which the Church of Jesus Christ could be recognized, as outlined in the Bible. He said:

A true Church of Christ is composed of apostles, prophets, elders, teachers and members, who have been baptized [by immersion] in the name of Jesus Christ, and who have received his spirit by the laying on of hands of his apostles, or authorized servants.

A true Church of Christ believed in visions, angels, spirits, prophesyings, revelations, healings and miracles of every kind, as described in the New Testament. Any creed or religious body differing from this New Testament pattern could not be considered the Church of Christ, however sincere they might be. (P. Pratt, p. 156.)

Elder Hyde then called upon his opponent for an affirmation or denial of these premises but, apparently recognizing the implications of either stance, Mr Jenkins would neither confirm nor deny. (Whatever Mr Browning's involvement in arranging the debate, Orson Hyde said that the man whom he actually faced was named Jenkins.) After several such exchanges, as Elder Hyde recalled:

The enemy's fire soon became less and less spirited, until, at length, under a well directed and murderous fire from the long 'eighteens' with which Zion's fortress is ever mounted – to wit: the Spirit of God – the enemy raised his hand to heaven and exclaimed, with affected contempt, 'Abominable! I have heard enough of such stuff.' I immediately rejoined, 'Gentlemen and ladies, I should consider it highly dishonorable to continue to beat my antagonist after he had cried enough.' (Young, 'History', p. 170.)

Elder Hyde said that 'about forty persons were baptized into the church in that place immediately after the debate'. (*Ibid.*)

When Elder Parley P. Pratt returned to Upper Canada he brought Elder Hyde's wife with him, and both elders continued their labours there until the autumn of 1836. Then, as Parley again prepared to return to Kirtland, he was approached by a number of people who were anxious that before his departure he should meet William R. Caird of the Catholic Apostolic Church (Irvingite) who was coming to Toronto from Scotland. It would be Mr Caird's second visit to that city, and he would be accompanied by a fellow evangelist named Cuthbert. (Shaw, p. 112.) Elder Pratt thus explained the circumstances that resulted in his association with Mr Caird:

Many persons greatly wondered that there should arise about the same time one church in America and another in England, both professing apostolic power and universal jurisdiction. Some of those who had heard both of us, tried to think that both systems were one and would run together. Others said they would wait and see which serpent swallowed the other before they would join either. (P. Pratt, p. 160.)

Although Elder Pratt knew that Mr Caird's basic assumptions were erroneous, he had gained a favourable impression of the man through his reputation and felt he might be receptive to the gospel. Thus, when Mr Caird had been detained in Kingston longer than he had expected, Elder Pratt suggested that he should himself take the steamer to Kingston and meet him there. However, that same evening Parley had two dreams in which Mr Caird was revealed not as a man of God but rather as a pretender and false teacher. Accordingly, on the following morning he told Mr Caird's advocates that the man was full of bitterness and would refuse to investigate the Church, and that he therefore had no desire to meet him. They were not to be dissuaded, however, and provided Elder Pratt with his boat fare as well as with a travelling companion, John Goodson.

Once in Kingston, Elders Pratt and Goodson sought an interview with William Caird but received no reply, so they decided to attend the meeting where he was to preach that evening. His sermon was impressive, but Elder Pratt, wishing that the man might reveal his true thoughts, offered a silent prayer that he would 'show himself'. Parley said, 'On a sudden he broke off from his subject, and commenced railing against Mormonism at a most horrible rate...Now all these things were lies. I arose in the meeting and asked to speak, but did not obtain privilege.' (P. Pratt, p. 163.)

Elder Pratt was so concerned about Mr Caird's misrepresentations of the Church that he prepared a handbill reading 'Doth our law judge a man before it hear him?' and distributed hundreds of copies in the streets of Kingston and Toronto. Mr Caird then came to Toronto where he addressed large crowds, first in the courthouse and then in William Lyon McKenzie's former printing office, which he turned into a chapel. His friends urged him to meet Elder Pratt but he utterly refused, choosing instead to continue his assault on Mormonism.

Parley then made application to Mr McKenzie, who was editor of *The Constitution*, for the use of some large rooms above his new printing office in King Street, where he might meet the public and rebut Mr Caird's misrepresentations. Mr McKenzie consented, and

Elder Pratt scheduled meetings on Monday, the 12th of September, and Thursday, the 15th. (*Constitution*, 12 Sep 1836.) The two meetings were well publicized, and drew large and attentive audiences. Elder Hyde acted as chairman, whilst Elder Pratt did the preaching. At the conclusion of the second meeting, Parley stated: 'The truth prevailed over the counterfeit, while the people's minds were settled as to which was the Moses and which was the magician.' Elder Pratt summarized his experience with 'the magician' by saying, 'Mr Caird retired from the country, [and] returned home to Scotland, where I found him ten years afterwards living in private life and of no notoriety.' (P. Pratt, p. 165.)

Having organized a number of new branches and ordained John Taylor as presiding elder over the area, the two apostles and their wives took leave of their friends and returned to Kirtland for the winter. There Elder Pratt witnessed the fulfilment of another part of Elder Heber C. Kimball's prophecy: on 25 March 1837 Thankful Pratt gave birth to a son, whom they named Parley Parker Pratt, Jr. Tragically, however, Thankful herself died soon after the child was born. In sorrowful tones Parley wrote:

> My dear wife had now lived to accomplish her destiny; and when the child was dressed, and she had looked upon it and embraced it, she ceased to live in the flesh. Her death happened about three hours after the birth of this child of promise. A few days previous to her death she had a vision in open day while sitting in her room. She was overwhelmed or immersed in a pillar of fire, which seemed to fill the whole room, as if it would consume it and all things therein; and the Spirit whispered to her mind, saying: 'Thou art baptized with fire and the Holy Ghost.' It also intimated to her that she should have the privilege of departing from this world of sorrow and pain, and of going to the Paradise of rest as soon as she had fulfilled the prophecy in relation to the promised son. (*Ibid.* p. 166.)

Soon after his wife's death, Elder Pratt returned to Toronto 'to confer on the subject of a mission to England'. He explained that 'several of the Saints in Canada were English, who had friends in England. Letters had already been sent to them with information of the rise of the Church, and of its principles. Several of the Canadian Elders felt a desire to go on a mission to their friends in that country.' (*Ibid.* pp. 167–8.)

In March 1837 Joseph Fielding moved with his family from Charleton to Toronto, as an intermediate step in their removal to

Kirtland. When he met Elder Pratt in Toronto, Parley told him that 'the way was opened for them to go to other nations, and it was determined that some should go to England as soon as possible'. (Fielding, p. 9.) Brother Fielding was thrilled with the prospects of such a mission, and wrote:

> It had been my earnest prayer ever since I came into the Church, but especially during the winter, that the Lord would open the way, the glad tidings to go to my native country, particularly to my Brethren in the flesh; my sisters and myself had written to them once on the subject, but I was afraid to write to them more lest I should not do it with that wisdom which the subject required, and so might do harm instead of Good...I also had some desire to be one among those that should go, but felt myself very ill qualified to go on so important [a] mission, and had I not known the Lord takes the weak things of the World to confound the strong I never would have thought of entering on such a work. (*Ibid.* pp. 9–10.)

The Fieldings had many family members in England with whom they were anxious to share the gospel. Among these were their brothers John and Thomas at Bedford; a sister, Ann Fielding Matthews, wife of the Rev. Timothy Matthews, also at Bedford; another brother, the Rev. James Fielding, at Preston; and another sister, Martha Ibbotson Watson, also at Preston. Joseph Fielding asked Elder John Taylor to write to his brother James in Preston. Elder Taylor did so, giving James an account of the restoration of the gospel, and also wrote to Brother Fielding's brother-in-law, the Rev. Timothy Matthews, in Bedford. John Taylor later said that this correspondence was the first announcement of the restoration in England by an authorized servant of God. (Roberts, *John Taylor*, p. 46; *JD 23*:31.)

Moved by the spirit of gathering, Joseph Fielding and his sisters Mary and Mercy moved to Kirtland in the spring of 1837. There they could enjoy the company of the saints as well as the blessings of the recently completed temple. (Later that year, on 4 June 1837, Mercy Rachel Fielding would marry an Englishman who, like herself, had joined the Church in Canada, Robert Blashel Thompson, with the Prophet Joseph performing the marriage ceremony; and the following winter, on the 24th of December, Mary Fielding would marry the Prophet's brother Hyrum Smith, who would by then be a widower with five small children, his wife Jerusha Barden having died in October.)

Upon their arrival in Kirtland, the Fieldings were dismayed to see a situation that was dividing the Church into factions. As part of an attempt to improve the local economy, the establishment of a 'Kirtland Safety Society Bank' had been proposed in November of 1836. Accordingly, Oliver Cowdery had been sent to Philadelphia to acquire some plates for manufacturing paper currency, whilst Orson Hyde went to Columbus to secure state approval for the new bank. Elder Cowdery had been successful, but the Ohio State Senate had rejected Elder Hyde's application for a bank charter. Hence it was decided to establish a joint stock company instead of a bank, and to call the institution the 'Kirtland Safety Society Anti-Banking Company'. The saints were then invited to take stock in the new firm, and many people did so. (Backman, p. 315.)

Unfortunately the new company was started at a very inopportune time, as a financial 'panic' in the United States wreaked havoc amongst banking institutions and their patrons everywhere. As it turned out, 'the country was entering a depression from which it did not fully recover for some seven years.' (Van Deusen, p. 117.) When the panic of 1837 struck, land values in Kirtland and vicinity dropped drastically, and the 'anti-banking company', having very little working capital and plagued with excessive credit buying of its members, was crushed almost before it began. The creditors and some of the shareholders held the Prophet responsible for their losses.

This was a difficult period for the young Church. There were those who lost their faith in the Prophet and in the Church over the matter. Fault-finding, disunity and dissension followed, and apostasy appeared even in some of the apostles. Obviously the situation was intolerable, and about this time the Prophet wrote: 'God revealed to me that something new must be done for the salvation of His Church.' He further stated, 'And on or about the first of June, 1837, Heber C. Kimball, one of the Twelve, was set apart by the spirit of prophecy and revelation, prayer and laying on of hands, of the First Presidency, to preside over a mission to England, to be the first foreign mission of the Church of Christ in the last days.' (Joseph Smith, *HC* 2:489.)

Elder Kimball said that the call came to him on Sunday, 4 June 1837, in the Kirtland Temple. He wrote:

The Prophet Joseph came to me while I was seated in front of the stand, above the sacrament table, on the Melchizedek side of the Temple, in Kirtland, and whispering to me, said, 'Brother Heber, the Spirit of the Lord has whispered to me; Let my servant Heber go to England and proclaim my Gospel, and open the door of salvation to that nation.' (Whitney, *Kimball*, p. 116.)

Overwhelmed by the responsibility, Heber reflected on the magnitude of such an undertaking:

O Lord, I am a man of stammering tongue, and altogether unfit for such a work; how can I go to preach in that land, which is so famed throughout Christendom for learning, knowledge and piety; the nursery of religion; and to a people whose intelligence is proverbial! (*Ibid.* p. 100.)

Keenly aware of his own weakness, Elder Kimball asked the Prophet for permission to take Brigham Young with him, but Joseph responded that he needed Brigham's help in Kirtland and could not spare him. Heber therefore reconciled himself to going to England on his own, and observed, 'The moment I understood the will of my heavenly Father, I felt a determination to go at all hazards, believing that He would support me by his mighty power and endow me with every qualification that I needed.' (*Ibid.* p. 116.)

The Prophet Joseph then called a conference to meet that same Sunday at the home of President Rigdon. Those who attended were Joseph Smith, Sidney Ridgon, Hyrum Smith, Heber C. Kimball, Joseph Fielding, and some others. Elder Orson Hyde also joined them during the course of the meeting. Elder Kimball recorded: 'Joseph and Sidney and Hyrum laid their hands on my head and set me apart for this mission and dedicated me to the Lord.' (*Ibid.* p. 102.)

While they were 'about ordaining' Elder Kimball, as the Prophet later stated, 'Orson Hyde, another of the Twelve, came in, and upon listening to what was passing, his heart melted within him (for he had begun to drink of the cup filled with the overflowings of speculation), he acknowledged all his faults, asked forgiveness, and offered to accompany [Elder] Kimball on his mission to England.' The offer was accepted and Orson Hyde was immediately set apart to be the companion of Elder Kimball, with the added stipulation that the blessings of the Lord should go with them. (Joseph

Smith, *HC* 2: 489–90.) Written credentials were then given to Elder Kimball, in the form of a letter of recommendation admonishing the British people to 'listen with attention to the words of his mouth'. (H. Kimball, *Journal*, 4 Jun 1837, pp. 7–10.)

There were varied reactions to Heber's call in the Kirtland community. Whilst many faithful saints wished him well, some of the apostates attempted to dissuade him from his intended course. John Boynton called him a fool to go at the beck and call of a fallen prophet and told him, 'I will not help you a dime, and if you are cast on Van Diemen's land, I will not make an effort to help you.' In contrast, Lyman E. Johnson (also disillusioned with the Church) urged him not to go 'but [said] if I was determined to go, he would help me all he could; he took his cloak from off his back and put it on mine; which was the first cloak I ever had'. (Whitney, *Kimball*, p. 117.)

President Hyrum Smith was especially supportive, and took every opportunity to strengthen Heber for the experience. Elder Kimball said that when Hyrum spoke to him about his mission he 'wept like a child', and 'was continually blessing and encouraging me, and pouring out his soul in prophecies upon my head; he said: "Go, and you shall prosper as not many have prospered."' Having accepted the responsibility to head the mission, Elder Kimball sought diligently to prepare himself for that task. He wrote: 'I daily went into the east room in the attick story of the temple and poured out my soul unto the Lord, asking His protection and power to fulfill honorably the mission appointed me by his servants.' (*Ibid.*)

Heber had had a premonition that he would be called on this very mission. Some five months before his call, while speaking with Willard Richards in the streets of Kirtland, he had prophesied that he, Heber, would fulfil a mission to Europe. Willard, anxious to know whether Heber perceived that he too would have such an opportunity, asked him, 'Shall I go with thee?' And Elder Kimball had replied, 'Yea, in the name of the Lord, thou shalt go with me when I go.' (*Ibid.* p. 119.)

In spite of Elder Kimball's prophecy, Elder Richards had not been named as one of the missionaries. But on the evening of the 11th of June, Elder Richards went with Brigham Young to the home of President Joseph Smith. There Heber C. Kimball, Orson Hyde and Joseph Fielding were to receive the Prophet's final counsel regarding their mission. As Joseph instructed them, Willard's inner feelings were deeply touched. He said:

> I felt my heart burn within me strongly desiring that I might be one of the number. But I do not recollect that it once entered my mind that it would be possible for me to go for I was deeply involved in the temporal affairs of the Church in company with Brother Brigham and knew not how to extricate myself from the dilemma. So I let my mind rest over night, quite contented with the simple fact I could not go although months before I had entered into a Covenant with Elder Kimball that I should be one of the number to constitute the first mission to a foreign land. (W. Richards, 11 Jun 1837.)

The next day Willard met Elder Kimball on the street, but his greeting was not the usual salutation; Heber said, 'Elder Richards, I am now ready to fulfil my engagement with you. You recollect it, don't you? I start for England tomorrow and I want you with me. Get ready, Sir.' Yet, seeing no way to leave his business obligations or to secure the necessary means to 'go over the great waters', Elder Richards remained non-committal in his response. After conducting some business with Hyrum Smith, however, Willard decided to broach the subject and asked Hyrum if it might not be possible for him to go to England with the others. President Smith assured him that it was if he wished it.

The two of them then called on President Sidney Rigdon and posed the same question, whereupon President Rigdon said that he had 'no objections and did not know why the Lord should have any'. One more conversation, this time with Brigham Young, assured Willard that he would be at liberty to go, as Elder Young agreed to look after all their mutual business affairs while Willard was away. Thus at 6 p.m. on the 12th of June, Elder Willard Richards was set apart as a missionary to Britain, under the hands of Presidents Sidney Rigdon and Hyrum Smith. (*Ibid.* 12 Jun 1837.) President Joseph Smith was absent due to illness.

On the day of departure, 13 June 1837, Elder Robert B. Thompson called on Elder Kimball to ask him when he planned to start out, as Brother Thompson and his wife (Mercy Fielding) were to travel with them for several hundred miles, en route to their own field of labour in Upper Canada. He reported:

> The door being partly open, I entered and felt struck with the sight which presented itself to my view. I would have retired, thinking that I was intruding, but I felt riveted to the spot. [Elder Kimball] was pouring out his soul...While

thus engaged his voice was almost lost in the sobs of those around, who tried in vain to suppress them. The idea of being separated from their protector and father for so long a time was indeed painful. He proceeded, but his heart was too much affected to do so regularly. His emotions were great, and he was obliged to stop at intervals, while the big tears rolled down his cheeks, an index to the feelings which reigned in his bosom. My heart was not stout enough to refrain; in spite of myself I wept, and mingled my tears with theirs. At the same time I felt thankful that I had the privilege of contemplating such a scene. I realized that nothing could induce that man to tear himself from so affectionate a family group, from his partner and children who were so dear to him – nothing but a sense of duty and love to God and attachment to His cause. (Whitney, *Kimball*, 120–1.)

When the missionaries called at the Prophet's home to say their goodbyes, they found him so ill that he was not able to raise his head from the pillow, and they departed lamenting his condition. Several people accompanied Elder Kimball and company as far as Fairport, Ohio.

At Fairport, Mary Fielding gave Elder Kimball five dollars, with which he bought a steamboat passage to Buffalo for himself and Orson Hyde, and Rhoda Greene gave twenty-five cents to Willard Richards, assisting him on his journey. Robert and Mercy Thompson, on their way to Canada, as well as Fitch Brigham, went with the brethren to Buffalo, New York. At Buffalo they had expected to meet either John Taylor or the Canadian brethren who were bound for the British Isles, as Elder Taylor was going to give them a hundred dollars from the saints in Canada, but, disappointingly, the connection was not made.

One reason for this was that the Canadian missionaries (Isaac Russell, John Snider and John Goodson) did not go by way of Buffalo but had travelled directly east from Toronto. Elder Russell then stopped at Kingston to take care of some personal business whilst Brothers Goodson and Snider went on together to Leeds County, Upper Canada. On the 10th and 11th of June, at the time Elder Kimball's party was leaving Kirtland, the two Canadian missionaries apparently were attending a conference of some 300 saints assembled at Portland (a small village north of the township of Bastard, on the south side of Rideau Lake), as Elder Wilford Woodruff mentioned both Brothers Snider and Goodson being present the following day at a meeting in a member's home in the Leeds Branch. (Woodruff, 10–12 Jun 1837.) That evening Wilford Woodruff, John Snider, John Goodson, Milton Holmes, and Jonathan H. Hale 'all bore testimony of the truth of the Book of Mormon and the work that God has commenced in the last days'. Brother Hale further stated that, 'after having testimony we laid our hands on an infant child which was at the point of death to all appearance and by the power of God was restored and returned to its Mother whole'. (Hale, 12 Jun 1837.)

The next day Brothers Goodson and Snider, accompanied by Wilford Woodruff and Jonathan Hale, walked from Leeds to Kingston, where they met Isaac Russell. Then all five made their way by boat through the state of New York, travelling via Lake Ontario to Oswego, then via the Erie Canal to Syracuse, Rome and Utica. A five-hour railway ride then took them from Utica to Schenectady, where Elders Woodruff and Hale 'took the parting hand' with the three Canadian missionaries. Commenting on their mission, Elder Woodruff wrote: 'These brethren were bound for the City of New York to join two of the twelve in leaving New York for England on the 20th day of June AD 1837 to carry glad tidings of Salvation to the inhabitants of Europe...May the God of Israel be with them and make them an instrument in his hands...' (Woodruff, journal, 13–16 Jun 1837.)

Once in New York City the Canadian brethren found themselves in advance of the missionaries from Kirtland, and took quarters at Mrs Fordham's to await their arrival. Meanwhile, finding no one to greet them at Buffalo, Elder Kimball's group continued their journey towards New York City, taking a boat on the Erie Canal. Elders Kimball and Richards then stopped at Rochester whilst Orson Hyde and Joseph Fielding went on, in order to reach New York at the appointed time. Elder Richards invited Elder Kimball to accompany him to his father's home at Richmond, Massachusetts, and the two elders booked a rail passage to Albany. While in Richmond, Willard received forty dollars from his brother William in payment of an old debt – a sum that enabled them to pursue their journey with more assurance.

Returning to Albany, Elders Kimball and Richards took a steamboat down the Hudson River to New York City, where they rejoined their friends on the 22nd of June at Mrs Fordham's. The three Canadian missionaries, as noted, were already there, and were somewhat disappointed at the late arrival of Elders Kimball

The packet-ship *Garrick* carried the first seven missionaries to Great Britain. She had a length of 157 ft 6 in., a beam of 35 ft 4 in. and a depth of 21 ft. (*Courtesy of Peabody Museum, Salem, Massachusetts.*)

and Richards as they had hoped to book passage on the *United States*, which sailed the next day. (W. Richards, 22 Jun 1837.)

On the 23rd the missionaries booked passage instead on the Dramatic Line packet-ship *Garrick*, an 895-ton sailing vessel under the command of Captain Nathaniel Brown Palmer. The *Garrick* was new, having been built at New York City by Brown and Bell in 1836, and was noted for her consistently good times in crossing, her best westward time being eighteen days. ('The Packet *Garrick*'.)

The Garrick was to sail on the 1st of July, and Elder Kimball described their interim lodging arrangements with some irony, as follows:

> We found Elder Elijah Fordham, the only member of the Church in that city, who having no house of his own, we lodged at Mrs Fordham's, Elijah's sister-in-law [at a cost of one dollar per person per day].
>
> Being short of funds we hired a small room in an unfinished store-house [at six cents a week] of Brother Fordham's father [George Fordham], who was very wealthy, as he owned many store-houses and buildings, but he never invited us

John Taylor, born at Milnthorpe, Westmorland, England, 1 November 1808.

Elder Heber C. Kimball, first president of the British Mission, 1837–8

Elder Orson Hyde requested that he be allowed to accompany the first mission, 1837.

Joseph Fielding, born at Honeydon, Bedfordshire, England, 26 March 1797.

Willard Richards, one of the original missionaries to Great Britain, 1837.

John Snider, born 11 February 1800, New Brunswick, Nova Scotia.

into his house to sleep or eat, though he did invite us to assist him two days in raising a building, as a compensation for laying on his store-house floor. (H. Kimball, letter to Vilate Kimball, 27 Jun 1837.)

Despite the inconveniences, the brethren employed this time to prepare themselves. On Sunday the 25th of June, Elder Kimball recorded: 'we fasted, prayed, administered the sacrament, held council for the success of the mission, and had a joyful time'. (Whitney, *Kimball*, p. 123.) The interval before departure also allowed time for those who had insufficient funds to accumulate the twenty-dollar fare for Liverpool and to lay up some provisions for the trip. On this subject, Joseph Fielding wrote: 'The principal provisions were very dear, at least twice the common value; flour $11 per barrel. A great destress [*sic*] was expected the next winter.' (Fielding, p. 14.) And Elder Kimball wrote to his wife about the stores that the missionaries had accumulated by the 27th of June:

We have bought one barrel of Indian meal to make puddings – one hundred pounds of crackers – 40 pounds of rice, 40 pounds of sugar, two gallons of honey, one gallon of molasses, half barrel of flower [*sic*], three hams and got our utencils [*sic*] to cook with and believe we have things plenty to eat. We may have a calm or a wind to blow us off the coast so we got more than we think we shall want. (H. Kimball, letter to Vilate Kimball, 27 Jun 1837.)

The following day they prepared for posting 180 copies of a tract by Elder Orson Hyde entitled 'Timely Warnings' (in some sources referred to as 'Prophetic Warnings'), directing them to the priests and ministers of the respective churches in New York City and carrying them to the post office. They also distributed copies of these tracts to individuals with whom they had had gospel discussions. (*MS 1*: 290; R. B. Thompson, p. 10.) (Although no copies of this edition are known to have survived, it very likely resembled the British edition prepared by Orson Hyde, 'A Timely Warning to the People of England, by an Elder of The Church of Latter-day Saints, Preston, 19th August, 1837'.)

On the 29th of June the brethren boarded the *Garrick* and the crew cast off. They did not actually set sail, however, until two days later, having spent the 30th of June at anchor in the East River. Then, at 7.30 a.m. on the 1st of July the crew weighed anchor and the vessel was towed as far as Sandy Hook by a steamer.

The *Garrick* finally passed out of sight of land at 4.30 p.m. on 1 July 1837. (W. Richards, 29 Jun–1 Jul 1837.)

Reflecting upon his reasons for going to Britain, Elder Heber C. Kimball wrote:

> I was actuated by a different motive than either to please myself, or gain the riches and applause of the world; it was a higher consideration than these that induced me to leave my home. It was because a dispensation of the Gospel had been committed to me; and I felt an ardent desire that my fellow creatures in other lands might hear the sound of the everlasting Gospel, obey its requisitions, rejoice in the fullness and blessings thereof, and escape the judgments which will come upon the ungodly. (Whitney, *Kimball*, p. 126.)

With this determination, a little band of seven Canadian and American missionaries stood on the threshold of 'an effectual door' to 'the salvation of His Church' in Britain.

2

The Setting for the Restoration in Britain: Political, Social, and Economic Conditions

MALCOLM R. THORP

WHEN THE *Garrick* docked at Liverpool in July 1837, the first missionaries from The Church of Jesus Christ of Latter-day Saints to the British Isles were amongst the passengers who disembarked. Although it has often been observed that Great Britain was, at this time, a field 'white already to harvest', the reasons for this readiness have not always been considered. In Liverpool in the 1830s the arrival of missionaries from America was hardly a novel event. Early-nineteenth-century revival movements had often made their way across the Atlantic, bringing with them the most popular preachers of the day (such as Lorenzo Dow, whose revivals in 1805 and 1818 had great effect upon the Primitive Methodist tradition). Beginning in the 1830s, other American evangelists increasingly found Britain to be a fruitful field. In 1831, for example, Asahel Nettleton, one of the greatest popular preachers of his day, came on a successful fifteen-month venture. Nor was it unusual for preachers to come with new gospels of salvation, as did the Millerites and the Campbellites in the 1840s. (Carwardine, pp. 5–7 and *passim*.) But the Latter-day Saint mission of 1837 was something different: Elder Kimball and company ushered in the most spectacular and lasting of the American missionary endeavours in Britain, and the Church became the fastest-growing religious body of that period. (Armytage, p. 260.)

It must have been an exciting experience for these first missionaries to set foot on 'England's green and pleasant land', however tarnished by soot and smoke from belching factory chimneys. At the Liverpool docks the newcomers would have watched bustling humanity bound for all parts of the globe, as well as cargoes from 'the workshop of the world' – exports that had made nineteenth-century British society the wealthiest in history. The industrial production of this island nation was so far ahead of all competitors that Great Britain controlled no less than thirty per cent of world trade.

Whilst the beginnings of Britain's industrial supremacy can be traced to the eighteenth century, the most impressive developments occurred after 1815, when the advent of the steam engine made sweeping changes in the economy, especially in the cotton industry. The magnitude of these changes is indicated by the statistics for raw cotton imports. In 1815, cotton imports stood at 41,000 tons, a figure which in itself was impressive, but by 1860 the industry was using a *half million tons* of imported cotton. Similar statistics were reported in the iron industry, where production increased tenfold during the first half of the century, as well as in the coal industry, where production more than tripled. And this was just the beginning of the industrial revolution in Britain. Many of the developments in heavy industry, in the service industries, and in mass production of consumer goods still lay in the future.

Though industrialization had made a significant impact on the economy by the 1830s, development throughout the country was uneven. Lancashire and the West Riding of Yorkshire were regions where textile industries were predominant. In the Midlands, it was in the metallurgical and engineering industries that most of the new development took place. On the other hand, industrialization had little effect on London, where population more than doubled in size in only fifty years, as a result of the expansion of traditional shipping and service industries. In most regions, however, small-scale workshops and handicraft industries were the rule. Also, farming continued to be important in all areas of the country as the largest single employer of labour (even though the percentage of farmers compared to total population was gradually declining).

For our purposes, however, what was most significant about the industrial revolution was how it affected the lives of the people.

Cotton factories, Preston, *c.* 1840.
(*Courtesy of Central [Harris] Museum, Preston.*)

With so much changing around them – social patterns, working methods, class relationships, even thinking habits – religion began to change, too. There came to be more freedom for individual religious expression, and with this freedom there also came a myriad of new religions.

Several days after their arrival, Elder Kimball and his companions left Liverpool and went north to Preston, and that is where Church history in Britain truly began. Nineteenth-century Preston, Lancashire, a Victorian factory town in all its magnificence and squalor, would play a major role in the early history of the British Mission. It also serves as a fairly accurate model of the industrial and social conditions that helped prepare the British people for the coming of the missionaries.

Despite its many factory chimneys and the bleak-looking aspect of soot-covered buildings, Preston had a pleasing appearance from a distance, being situated on the banks of the River Ribble. On the surface, it might have been the model for 'Cottonopolis', as cotton manufacturing was the principal industry and Preston had earned a particular reputation for fine spinning. With a population of

45,000 inhabitants in 1837, the town had no less than 15,000 cotton-workers, most of them employed in the 38 mills that dominated the urban landscape. (Hewitson, p. 44; Phillips, p. 38.)

Preston was also noted for its early lead in consolidating all the stages of cotton manufacturing into a single factory's operation. Under the leadership of such cotton magnates as John Horrocks, both spinning and weaving were brought together with machinery that utilized steam-driven engines – and this method was quickly copied by other local mills, thus expanding the size and scope of Preston's cotton industry. (Hewitson, pp. 166–73.) Such technological progress did not come without social disruption, however, the most noticeable effect being that Preston's many small hand-loom weavers were being gradually squeezed out of business. In fact, by the late 1830s the formerly prosperous hand-loom weavers were in serious economic trouble, not just in Preston but in most of northern Lancashire.

Even though the name 'Cottonopolis' seemed to fit Preston better than most towns, there is a danger in stereotyping. J. F. C. Harrison has warned against this tendency as follows:

> One of the more unfortunate impressions left by an older generation of historians and sociologists is that all large towns in the nineteenth century were more or less the same – that is, equally smoky, soulless, and horrible to live in. The tendency to lump them all together, ignoring any modifying differencies, was in part derived from contemporary caricatures like Dickens's Coketown and encouraged by references in the 1840s to 'Cottonopolis' and 'Worsted-opolis'. This is very misleading. Quite apart from obvious regional differences in traditional culture and economic and social relationships, the impact of population increase was very uneven. Not all towns were in the position of a Bradford or a Liverpool. Virtually all towns did increase in the first half of the nineteenth century, but in some instances the expansion was relatively modest. Cambridge, Chester, Exeter, and Norwich were of this order. Too often our impressions of urban growth have been derived from an overconcentration on the northern textile towns, although even among them the problems were by no means identical. (J. Harrison, *Early Victorians*, pp. 15–16.)

Whilst Preston was predominantly a cotton town, it also had other industries, including breweries, iron and brass foundries, engineering works, and soap factories. (*Victoria County History*, Lancashire, 7: 92.) Furthermore, as already noted, even within the cotton industry Preston was unique in its speciality of high-quality spinning, which probably developed because the town lacked the natural advantages possessed by other leading manufacturing centres such as Manchester. Although Preston did have coal supplies to power its steam engines, the mines were eight miles away and transportation of the coal was difficult. At first Preston had also been handicapped by its comparative isolation. In the north of England, the town was far from major markets. This problem was soon alleviated, however, by dredging the River Ribble to make it navigable, and by building a dock at Lytham. Moreover, in 1838 the Wigan and Preston Railway brought a new mode of transportation to the city and, in the 1840s, Preston was connected with major rail services in Lancashire and the West Riding of Yorkshire. Far from being geographically isolated, Preston became a major railway junction. (Hewitson, pp. 199–201, 215.)

Preston was also a town with a unusually high level of class tension. (Phillips, p. 61.) Local politics tended to be controlled by an accord between the mill owners and the property owners, which left the working class with very little voice or power. In fact, in November 1836, just months before Elder Kimball's arrival, a protracted strike by 660 cotton-spinners had so disrupted production that 7,840 factory workers were left without employment. The significance of this event was the solidarity of the spinners, even though they eventually had to return to work without gaining their objective. (Hewitson, pp. 175–6.) This was neither the first nor the last instance of working-class dissatisfaction, and it has been said that this hostility between management and labour was a factor in the eventual stagnation of the industry. (*Ibid.* p. 174.)

Like other industrial towns, Preston was a community that was not able to maintain adequate living conditions in the wake of rapid urbanization. From a population of 16,000 at the turn of the century, Preston had increased to 53,400 by 1841. (*Victoria County History*, Lancashire, 2: 334.) By the late 1830s the town was growing at the rate of 1,800 newcomers each year. (Hewitson, p. 44.) Under these circumstances, the local authorities paid little attention to bad housing and sanitary problems in working-class districts, where the typical worker lived in back-to-back row-houses with outdoor toilets that were not connected to sewers. In wet weather sewage would flow into the unpaved streets, creating an unimaginable stench as well as breeding-grounds for disease.

Preston 'Cockpit', Stoneygate.
(*Courtesy of Central* [*Harris*] *Museum, Preston.*)

These conditions undoubtedly contributed to the high death rate, which stood at 28 per thousand in the early Victorian age. (*Ibid.* p. 412.) It was not until 1851 that the city authorities began concerted efforts to improve sanitary conditions, and then their actions were objected to by local advocates of *laissez-faire*.

In fact, the Church's first years in Preston were years of acute economic problems for the people. The railway and shipbuilding boom that had brought prosperity in the early 1830s ended in 1836; the coal-mining, cotton and woollen industries were increasingly pressed for domestic markets; and by the spring of 1837 distress was spreading through the industrial areas of the North and the Midlands. This distress reached its peak in 1842 (the worst year of the century, economically) before conditions improved.

In normal times, the wages paid to factory workers were usually adequate for the necessities of life, if not for much more. This meant that during periods of full employment factory workers were reasonably well off, but during hard times families were pressed to make ends meet. Employers would reduce wages when the economy was bad (as occurred in Preston in 1837) or they would make large numbers of workers redundant. As a result, more than half the working-class population of Preston lived in actual poverty during hard times.

The apostles' journals and letters show an awareness of these problems. One of Heber C. Kimball's first impressions of Preston was that it was a town of unemployment and poverty. Often entire families, including young children and mothers, worked in the factories, and in 1840 Elder John Taylor said he had 'particular feelings' and felt his 'heart break' when he watched a woman leave her children and husband (a shoemaker) to go to work in a factory. (J. Taylor, letter to Leonora Taylor, 30 Jan 1840.) A study for this period in Lancashire, using Preston sources for data, found that about one in four married women with children worked in factories. (Anderson, p. 71.)

Family necessity often meant that children eight or nine years old were also sent to work in factories or fields. And by the age of twelve most children from working-class families had such jobs. (*Ibid*. p. 75.) The autobiography of Thomas Wright Kirby is one of the best LDS accounts of the trauma of a young child in a factory. The son of a farm worker, Thomas was sent to work at the age of seven to help support the family. He wrote of being subjected to physical abuse while working in a silk mill at Ditchingham, Norfolk:

> Most of those who had charge of us younger Children were Ignorent [*sic*] and cruel to us and would whip us for the least little Mishap. One old man by the name of Smith, was an ugly cross old fellow and I shall never forget him nor his ugly features. And another tawl [*sic*] Muscular fellow by the name of Palmer who used to appear to me was always watching to give some poor boys a knock with his big hand. Then there were women under them some of whom were of doubtful morality who were also very tyranical [*sic*] and would Smack us over the head and ears, with their hand or with a stick more because they were cross than for anything else. They [would] follow [us] through the noise and rattle of the machinery and say I'm just in the right temper for you to-day and you shall catch a whiping [*sic*] which we were Pretty sure was true and any being young children would begin crying and then they would whip us because we cried for nothing. (Kirby.)

Though not all factory children were subjected to these petty tyrannies, child abuse occurred with enough frequency to suggest that ill-treatment was a serious problem. And in spite of the Factory Act of 1833 (which relieved some of the worst abuses in employment of young children), conditions remained harsh, as Kirby's account testifies:

> In Winter we worked from 7 a.m. till 8 p.m. They had half an hour Breakfast. [We] used to eat in the 'Breakfast Room' but the small children could seldom get to the fire. At 1 o'clock, dinner one hour. At 5 p.m., 15 minutes for tea as it was called. Then work till 8 p.m. Then I used to hunt up my sister Sarah Ann or Charlotte or both to go home with them. And as they did not work in the same room that I did we often found it very difficult to find each other among the hundreds who flocked out at the gate like so many sheep.... My sisters and I had about 2 Miles to go [home]...and some part being over what is known as Ditchingham Dam. There were then no houses or anything to shelter us from the cold winds and storms and sometimes we did not have very good or warm Clothing or shoes. And sometimes not very Much food as our wages was [*sic*] very low. (*Ibid.*)

Another practice of the time was apprenticeship. Young men would often be apprenticed to a master craftsman for five to seven years, in order to learn a trade. While the system itself was a good one, there were sometimes masters who would abuse their apprentices. In fact, one of the most frequent complaints recorded by early Mormon converts related to this sort of abuse. Edward Ashton wrote that once his master beat him with a stirrup and 'pulled my ears until they were bleeding'. He eventually escaped and went to court, where he was able to break his bond of apprenticeship. (Carter, *13*:420-1.) Similar statements were made by Willson Nowers, who described his apprenticeship as being very irksome and 'a sort of white slavery'; and another convert, William Allen, said that he was arrested and sentenced to one month in gaol for leading his fellow apprentices in protest against the thirteen-hour working day. (Whitney, *Utah*, *4*:421.)

Discontent with the long hours, the boring routine and regimen, the low wages – all these complaints appear with enough frequency in personal accounts to sugest that there was considerable disenchantment with factory conditions. James Bywater stated that after a decade of 'the hateful labors of factory life' he saw emigration as the only alternative to 'white slavery'. (Valentine, p. 8.) But William Gibson was more direct in blaming the mill owners for the inhumanity of the system:

> I have had to labor hard from my boyhood having been left without father, mother, brother or sister. I have often tasted the 'kindness' of the tyrant and oppressor. Some of them cared more for their horses and dogs than for their fellowmen. The first cost them something, the latter, nothing. (Carter, 6:22–3.)

Another class of labourers who recorded severe criticisms about their working conditions were the miners. James Hepworth, for example, wrote a vivid description of mining life, reporting that as a miner he worked 6 a.m. to 4 p.m. six days a week. In the winter, he would see daylight only on Sunday. Food was meagre, yet 'when they returned home at night after a hard day's work and sat down to supper, they would often fall asleep at the table with the meal half finished. They would be so tired that the want of sleep was greater than the want of food.' (Hepworth.) A young Scottish miner, Matthew Rowan, described how he fell sixty-six feet down a shaft, breaking his jaw and ribs and shattering his elbow. The accident left him partially crippled, and he later recalled with some bitterness that the pit owner paid him only a small sum in compensation. (Rowan.) Conditions in the mines prompted one young woman to record how glad she was when she lost her job in a coal mine at the implementation of the Mines Act of 1842, which forbade the employment of women in the collieries. (T. and J. McNeil.)

The early missionaries in Britain were greatly affected by the problems of the working classes. Elder Heber C. Kimball's first exposure to class differences at Liverpool left him distressed. He wrote:

> Wealth and luxury abounded, side by side with penury and want. I there met the rich attired in the most costly dresses, and the next minute was saluted with the cries of the poor with scarce covering sufficient to screen them from the weather. Such a wide distinction I never saw before. (H. Kimball, *Journal*, p. 16.)

In Preston, he wrote in moving terms of the hardships the people suffered during the winter of 1837–8. Because of bad weather, several factories had been closed, leaving the workers out of employment in very harsh conditions. According to Kimball, he was 'credibly informed' that many people had died of starvation during the winter. He wrote:

Market-place, Preston, Lancashire.
(*Courtesy of Central* [*Harris*] *Museum, Preston.*)

Oh! When will distress and poverty and pain cease, and peace and plenty abound? When the Lord Jesus shall descend in the clouds of heaven – when the rod of the oppressor shall be broken. 'Hasten the time, O Lord!' was frequently the language of my heart, when I contemplated the scenes of wretchedness and woe, which I daily witnessed, and my prayer to my Heavenly Father was, that if I had to witness a succession of such scenes of wretchedness and woe, that He would harden my heart, for those things were too much for me to bear. This is no exaggerated account; I have used no coloring here. They are facts which will meet the Elders of Israel when they shall go forth into that land [Britain], and then I can assure them they will not be surprised at my feelings. (*Ibid.* pp. 44–5.)

This was but the beginning of the apostles' negative social commentary. The arrival of the Quorum of the Twelve in 1840 was likewise accompanied by lamentations of what they saw as economic exploitation and needless class antagonism. (See Allen and Thorp.) Elder Wilford Woodruff wrote, 'The poor are in as great bondage as the children of Israel in Egypt.' (Kenney, p. 405.) And Elder George A. Smith, in the Staffordshire Potteries, recorded:

> So many of the poor are begging that it would astonish the Americans. England is in distress and I pray to the Lord for deliverance of the Saints from the coming ruin...
>
> Of the more than 450 Saints in this District not more than one third of them have full Employment. Many of them Rest Not more than two or three Days per Week and Many have no work at all. Times are growing harder Every Week. Some are turned out of Employ because they have been baptised by the Latter Day Saints. (George A. Smith, 15 Feb 1840, 5 Dec 1840.)

During his second mission in 1840, Elder Heber C. Kimball wrote of the economic distress in Manchester:

> I was asking some of the brethren what made the people look so bad. They said because they ware [*sic*] famished for the wont [*sic*] of food. Say they to me thare [*sic*] are hundreds that are starving for the wont of food and other things. I thought thare was misery enough in Preston. It is nothing to compare with Manchester. I asked them if they thought the brethren went hungry. Yes many of them have [nothing] to eat. Times are so hard they can't quit work. Therefore they have to go hungry. Thare has been such a change here in two years as never known by the oldest men in this land. (H. Kimball, letter to Vilate Kimball, 27 May 1840.)

Wilford Woodruff's reflections on the Malvern Hills in May 1840 were prompted in part by his experience in industrial England. Among other things, he wrote:

> God...will soon level all hills, exhalt all valies [*sic*] & redeem the earth from the curse of sin & prepare it for the abode of the Saints of the MOST HIGH....[But] the rise, progress, decline & fall of the empires of the earth...must still transpire before the winding up scene & the comeing [*sic*] of Christ. (Woodruff, journal, 11 May 1840.)

In spite of the wealth and splendour of early Victorian society, it was described by early Church leaders as a Babylon that was on the verge of destruction. The apostles' compassion for the plight of the working classes played an important role in the Church's success amongst these groups. Whereas most sects refrained from open criticism of British society, the missionary apostles condemned its evils. Their message to the saints was to flee those evils and build up Zion in America.

From his first arrival in Britain in 1837, Heber C. Kimball was immediately aware of many differences from his own experience. Not only did the wide discrepancy between social classes shock him, as he recorded in Liverpool, but he was also interested in the process of political change that was taking place as Britain made the transition from the reign of King William IV to that of the young Queen Victoria, then a girl of seventeen. In fact, one of the first impressions of Preston recorded in Elder Kimball's journal related to the beginnings of a parliamentary election made necessary by the accession of the new queen. (H. Kimball, *Journal*, p. 17.)

The election of 1837 was the third since the passage of the Reform Act of 1832, which had brought two major changes in British politics. Firstly, it allowed those owning or renting property worth £10 or more to vote – meaning, in practical terms, that the upper-middle class could now vote. Nationally this raised the percentage of the voting population from five per cent to only seven per cent, but in towns like Preston even fewer new voters qualified, the number being increased by only one per cent. (Hewitson, p. 137.) The second change was more far-reaching for Britain in general but did not affect Preston specifically: seats in Parliament were redistributed to give representation to many of the industrial cities of the North and the Midlands. (Since Preston was already represented in Parliament by two members, this change made no difference there.) Still, the end result of the Reform Act of 1832 was the continued dominance of the aristocratic class, a dominance that was maintained for many years in both houses of Parliament.

The 1837 Preston election took place soon after Elder Kimball's arrival. Such occasions in the past had been violent affairs, and this election was no exception. The winners were two Tory gentlemen, Mr Hesketh-Fleetwood and Mr R. Townley Parker, a fact that illustrated both the conservative nature of Preston politics and the political influence of the landed class. (B. Harrison, p. 117.) But the election culminated in a riot, as Irish labourers and hired bullies (called 'bludgeon men') went on a rampage. Many people were injured; property was damaged; and it was necessary to call in soldiers to restore order. (*Ibid.* p. 139.) Because of the intense class antagonism, violence was always near the surface in Preston.

For the majority of Preston citizenry, however, there was no vote for parliamentary candidates, and the election must therefore have been of only marginal concern to them. No doubt many working people harboured bad feelings for this exclusive political establishment. Indeed, prominent amongst the Preston working-class critics were the Chartists, whose political programme included such principles as annually elected parliaments and universal male suffrage.

In the 1837 election the Chartist agitator Fergus O'Connor, who was to become famous as an advocate of violence, was nominated for a parliamentary seat. Obviously he had no chance of winning, but the election at least gave him a platform from which to take his brand of politics to the people. (*Ibid.*) In addition to the political goals of Chartism, the movement also preached some religious rhetoric aimed at the Christian element in the working class. In fact, they even borrowed songs from the evangelists, and one favourite contained the line, 'Jesus Christ was the first Chartist'. (Gash, p. 202.) Like many other northern industrial towns, Preston was subject to occasional riots. Following the one after the elections of 1837, there was another, inspired by the Chartists, in 1839, and in the summer of 1842 Chartist militancy coupled with local labour disputes incited the mob not only to riot but also to pull the plugs on the factory boilers, thus stopping production. (Hence this came to be known as the 'Plug Riot'.) On this occasion a mob of over five hundred angry demonstrators had to be controlled by the combined forces of the police and the military. (Mather, pp. 15, 21.)

While there is no evidence that Church members participated in these disturbances, the Church did attract a smattering of ex-Chartists, such as the former Christian Chartist, John Freeman, who converted to Mormonism in Manchester in 1840. (Freeman.) In general, however, in accounts of their lives written by LDS converts from this period, what stands out as a common thread in all is their apparent lack of concern about politics. To be sure there were occasional references to trade-union participation, even some references to fellowship in friendly societies and, as we have seen, there were also complaints about low wages and hard times. But there was virtually nothing except the occasional Chartist experience that indicated any significant pattern of political involvement. There was, in other words, a pronounced other-worldly dimension to the accounts left by early members, suggesting that

Table 2.1, Member occupations in the Preston Branch

Shopkeepers	2	Winders	3
Ass't shopkeeper	1	Thrasle daffer	1
Doctor	1	Cotton frame tender	1
Total middle class	4	Wool washer	1
		Hand-loom weaver	2
Dandy foreman	1	Policeman	1
Foreman of looms	1	Blacksmith	1
Bootmaker	1	Moulder	1
Power loom weaver	3	Mechanic	1
Steam loomweaver	2	Corkscrewmaker	1
Dandy weaver	1	Laborer	2
Weavers	3	Collier	1
Cottonspinners	1	Total working class	29

in some significant ways they were not 'average' working-class people.

Who were the Latter-day Saint converts, then? Studies on the social backgrounds of these British converts have identified them as chiefly working class. In the most comprehensive study to date, Phillip A. M. Taylor found that only about eleven per cent of emigrants to Zion during the years 1840–69 were middle class; the remainder were mostly working class. (P. Taylor, pp. 149–51.) Another recent study suggests that the LDS population had a slightly lower percentage of skilled workers (artisans) than did the Primitive Methodists, the sect most closely resembling the LDS Church. Whereas the Primitive Methodist congregation contained about 48 per cent artisans, the Mormons had only about 32 per cent from this group. (From a chapter by Malcolm R. Thorp in a forthcoming book.) These skilled workers, often the most prosperous group among the common people, were also the most numerous members of evangelical sects. It is significant that the Church tended to attract converts from a lower social status than the artisan group, thus making it unique amongst churches of the time. Here were the meek and lowly being gathered.

Turning to Preston Branch records, we do in fact find a social composition that resembles Taylor's findings. Although only 33 of the members' occupations can be identified from branch records, this limited sample (see Table 2.1) does indicate that only four had middle-class backgrounds: two shopkeepers, a shopkeeper's assistant and a doctor. Whilst there were a number of artisans in the branch, as well as two foremen and a policeman, the majority were semi-skilled textile workers, including general labourers. (K. Johnson.) (These figures also demonstrate the diversity of employment in a town that was dominated by cotton manufacturing.)

As to patterns of residence of these early converts, 42 per cent came from urban areas having populations of over fifty thousand in the 1851 census, and nearly 75 per cent were from towns with populations of over ten thousand. (P. Taylor, p. 149.) (Preston, with a population of 72,136 in 1851, obviously fits this pattern.) Whilst the largest concentration of saints was in the Midlands, the North-west (where Preston is located) was a close second. (Cotterill, pp. 119–24.)

The LDS population in Preston was further typical of the city's population in that the branch contained a large percentage of immigrants from the surrounding villages and countryside. In 1852, for example, of the 206 members whose birthplaces were listed in branch records, only 53, or 26 per cent, were born in the city. Of the 207 members whose age could be determined at baptism, there were 123 who were under 25, indicating a young and single branch membership. In addition, 56 per cent of the branch members were women. (K. Johnson, pp. 1–2) These figures parallel those of a similar study of the Manchester Branch (Harris) – all of which suggests that early LDS converts tended to be uprooted emigrants, probably attracted by the greater economic opportunities of the urban centres as opposed to the declining cottage-industry villages and the farms. Also, in cities like Preston, conventional religious practices were often abandoned or ignored, whereas they were more often enforced in rural society. This freedom of choice was undoubtedly an important part of the conversion experience.

The Church tended to do well in regions of large concentrations of Nonconformists. The first missionaries of 1837, for example, found success in the very area that J. F. C. Harrison has called the 'burned-over district' of England: the industrial frontier of Lancashire and the West Riding of Yorkshire. (J. Harrison, *Quest*, p. 102.) Again, 'proud Preston' fitted the mould, with its long-standing Nonconformist tradition that flourished among the lower classes. (Phillips, p. 46.)

Many of the earliest LDS converts in Preston came from the Rev. Fielding's church, which had earlier broken away from the Methodists. According to Heber C. Kimball, Fielding's congregation included a number of religious seekers who were praying for further truth when the missionaries found them. (H. Kimball, *Journal*, p. 38.) In addition, Elder Kimball baptized a number of Preston's Aitkenites, a millennial religious group founded in the 1830s by the popular revivalist, Robert Aitken. (*Ibid.*) We find, as well, that the missionaries converted a number of Primitive Methodists in the industrial villages surrounding Preston. Elder Kimball and company enjoyed further successes in the nearby villages of the lower Pennines (Clitheroe, Waddington, Chatburn, Downham and Walkerfold) where revivalist religions had made many converts earlier. This entire area was populated by poor Methodists, Baptists and Congregationalists, for the local economy had depended upon hand-loom weaving, which as we have seen was in serious trouble by the late 1830s.

Although no data exist for previous religious affiliations of members of the Preston Branch, we do have figures for the early Church. In the most comprehensive study of the religious backgrounds of early converts, it was found that most of the converts (see Table 2.2) came from major religious denominations, such as the Church of England, various Methodist groups, Baptists, Congregationalists and Presbyterians. Of the converts studied, almost 70 per cent came from these 'mainline' denominations whilst only a small percentage came from 'splinter groups' that had broken away from the major churches. (Thorp, 'Religious Backgrounds'.)

Even so, the Church did attract many former 'splinter group' members, largely because such congregations initially welcomed the Latter-day Saints as just more evangelists from America. But when it became apparent that the Mormon missionaries meant to convert people to an entirely new church, chapel doors were closed to their preaching. They then adopted the methods used by most other groups, such as street preaching and open-air meetings. It was after this change in proselytizing methods that the Church began to attract a cross-section of working-class converts from the

Table 2.2, Last prior religious affiliation of LDS converts

	Total	%
Church of England	58	20.7
Methodist	70	25.0
Primitive Methodists	31	1.1
Baptists	31	11.1
Independents	17	6.1
Presbyterians	13	4.6
'Splinter groups' and other minor sects	36	12.9
Teetotallers	2	0.1
Catholics	2	0.1
Infidels	3	1.1
Religiously inclined but not specifically affiliated	41	14.6
Not religiously inclined	4	1.4
Total	280	100

leading denominations, and former 'splinter-group' members became a smaller percentage of the total number of converts.

A significant minority (about 15 per cent) of the LDS converts came from the ranks of those who were religiously inclined but not affiliated with any particular denomination. Many of these people (who formed the majority of the Victorian working class) preferred to exercise their faith unrestricted by a religious creed or minister, often tending to believe that organized religion was a middle-class interest that had no practicality in their own everyday lives. As a result of this attitude, no institutional church was ever very successful in winning over great masses of working people, not even the Latter-day Saints. (Inglis, pp. 1–2 and *passim*.)

In part, however, the masses' alienation from organized religion was the result of changes in the churches themselves. Even the Methodists, who had had great success amongst the common people in the days of Wesley, had by this time gained 'middle-class respectability' and were no longer actively proselytizing the working classes. Jabez Bunting, the most important Methodist leader of his day, admitted that the social conservativism of his church was a barrier to the 'poor people' and said that 'the main cause of their estrangement' from Methodism was their fondness for 'radicalism, infidelity, and socialism', rather than organized religion. Bunting was only partly correct in his analysis of Methodist failure, however. Also contributing to the working-class disillusionment were some of the policies he himself had been responsible for implementing, such as authoritarian ministerial control, limiting opportunities for lay participation in the church, and the elimination of popular evangelical activities such as camp meetings. As the same sort of alienation was also occurring amongst the Baptists, Presbyterians and Congregationalists, it seems to have been a fairly general pattern in the 1830s and 1840s, and the Latter-day Saints' success is no doubt partly due to this feeling of religious dissatisfaction amongst the common people. (Gilbert, p. 162.)

Another important characteristic of early LDS converts is that many of them had been religious 'seekers' before their conversion to the Church – 'seekers' being individuals who drifted from one church to another in search of religious truth. Of the 280 converts studied, 104 were identified as seekers. (Thorp, 'Religious Backgrounds', p. 54.) Some of them had been members of six or more religious organizations before becoming Latter-day Saints.

Daniel Williams was one such seeker. Born in 1801 in the parish of Penally, Pembrokeshire, South Wales, Daniel was only four years old when his father died, leaving the family destitute. Because of this, he said, 'we were taught to work for our bread when young'. When he was still a boy, his mother taught him to read from the Bible, and he often wondered 'how I could please God and get deliverance from sin, which at that early period of my life, had become a great burden on my mind'. Though he tried, young Daniel found no relief from this anxiety by reading the religious books and pamphlets of the time. When he was about twelve, he started to attend an Anglican Sunday School, which he continued to do for about two years, at which time the Congregationalists and Wesleyans began to preach in his neighbourhood. Daniel attended their meetings regularly, but concluded that neither of these denominations conformed to the New Testament in its baptismal practices. Soon afterwards, at the age of sixteen, he joined the Baptists. For many years he remained a Baptist, gained respect within the church, and was occasionally invited to preach.

In his early thirties, however, Daniel became disillusioned with the 'disunion' among the sectarian religions, and left the Baptist fold. He then joined a group of '10–15 others' at Tenby who were seeking for truth, but concluded after some time that they had become 'a sect of talkers'. About this time Daniel removed with his family to Ebbw Vale, where he was employed in the iron works. He then rejoined the Baptists, but remained spiritually unfulfilled. 'I could no longer be bound by their systems', he said.

It was while at Ebbw Vale that Daniel Williams read a copy of Elder Orson Pratt's tract, *Remarkable Visions*. Though he believed it to be true, he was too poor to travel to England to investigate the new religion, and then in 1846 his wife died, leaving him with two children to care for. Before long, however, his brother William joined the LDS Church, and this prompted Daniel to renew his investigation of the Mormons. He said the 'simplicity of their devotions gave me reason to believe that they were sincere'. After comparing the saints' teachings with those in the Bible, he concluded that the gospel they taught was 'perfectly scriptural', and he was baptized in March 1847. (Daniel Williams.)

The experience of Henry Savage is another example of the religious quest of 'seekers' before their conversion to the Church. His story is particularly revealing because of the depth of his frustration in the search for truth. When he was a boy, Henry attended Methodist classes with his mother. After serving in the navy, however, his religious perspective had changed so much that he no longer felt comfortable with the Methodists. 'I would hear them get up and testify to the pardoning love of God and how they knew their sins were forgiven, but I never could get excited to testify as they did...So I decided there was something wrong somewhere', he said. Henry thus resolved to search out the answers to his spiritual dilemma, but after investigating the doctrines of the Baptists, Calvinists, Spiritual Israelites, Trivinites, Millerites, *and* 'other sects and parties', he found he was still dissatisfied, and resolved to remain an 'infidel' and join no church at all. He read Thomas Paine's *Age of Reason*, the works of Voltaire, and 'many other "cure-alls" of the day', but to no avail. In this state of despair, Henry at last heard two LDS missionaries preaching and, after reading the Book of Mormon 'night and day', he offered himself for baptism. (J. Jones.)

Not all the early converts had been conscientious 'seekers', however. In some cases, the crises of death, serious illness or accident would bring questions to which an individual sought spiritual answers. Young James Wilson, for example, was employed as a 'tub-boy' in a Scottish coal mine. In 1844 he suffered a serious accident and lost the use of his leg, although he refused to have it amputated. About the same time his brother Thomas, who had been investigating the LDS Church, died. In the state of despondency caused by these two tragedies in his life, James heard the gospel preached. He said the missionary elder

> came to my bedside and sat down on an old chest while he opened to me the scriptures. He seemed to have learned the Bible by heart. He preached to me Faith, Repentance, Baptism, and the laying on of hands for the gift of the Holy Ghost – also the gifts of the ministration of Angels.

James was not baptized immediately, for he continued to be spiritually troubled. Also, his father opposed his leaving the Presbyterian church. But several years later, following his recuperation, he came into the Church. (J. Wilson.)

Accounts of British saints also contain anti-clerical statements that indicate more frustration with the ministers of the day than with their doctrine. Samuel Wagstaff, for instance, joined the Methodists after a spiritual crisis in his life, but became disenchanted by 'their continual call for money' which led him to believe that 'money was all they preached for'. He then joined the Congregationalists, but was similarly disappointed when their minister abandoned them for a larger congregation in Manchester, leaving the flock without a shepherd. Shortly afterwards, he moved to Southill and attended the Congregationalist meetings there, until the minister asked for more money. Wagstaff said the minister raised the pew rents and then told the poorer members of the congregation that if they could not pay, they would have to bring a stool and sit in the aisle. (Wagstaff.) John Spiers stated that he left the Church of England because of the 'character of her ministers [rather] than her doctrines', and Thomas Wilson wrote that he left the Methodists because he was disgusted at the 'Star Chamber proceedings' used against one of the members. (Whitney, *Utah*, 4: 396; T. Wilson.) Though this is not evidence that the early Victorian clergymen were morally or spiritually degenerate (in fact, there is evidence to the contrary), accusations of clerical insensitivity are not entirely unfounded. (Norman, pp. 123–66.)

But social and spiritual conditions were not the only factors that helped prepare Britain to receive the restored gospel. Although the

British system of government had long been known for its stability and its tradition of comparative liberty for the people, the conditions of true religious freedom were fairly new. To be sure, the Toleration Act had been passed in 1689, giving Protestant Nonconformists the right to worship, but in practice Nonconformists continued to be second-class citizens without the legal right to participate in politics, either nationally or locally. Furthermore, Nonconformist ministers were legally subject to governmental harassment as long as the Five-Mile and Conventicle Acts remained on the statute books. These acts, archaic remnants of Puritan times, limited the right of Nonconformist ministers to preach, and forbade non-Anglicans to assemble together for religious purposes. Although these laws had been generally ignored in the eighteenth century, as late as 1811 the arch-Conservative Home Secretary, Lord Sidmouth, had threatened to begin enforcing them again. Fortunately a successful campaign was mounted against that action, resulting in the repeal of the Five-Mile and Conventicle Acts in 1812. In practical terms this meant that only after 1812 could LDS missionaries (or any others) preach openly without legal interference. The next milestone of religious freedom was the repeal of the laws that barred non-Anglicans, including Catholics, from participating in politics. Once this was done, Britain had attained religious freedom in practice as well as theory. Thus, by the 1830s, as long as missionaries had obtained a licence to preach, and as long as meeting-places were properly licensed to hold services, there was no legal obstacle to preaching the gospel in Britain.

Important as were these changes in the law, even more important was the development of an attitude of religious toleration amongst the people. This was somewhat longer in coming, however. As one historian has observed, the political emancipation of non-Anglicans had, by the 1830s, allowed the number and political influence of those who supported toleration to increase, whilst those who opposed it had correspondingly lost influence. Thus, though the 1830s and 1840s saw no outstanding development in the *practice* of toleration, still many Christians had come to see it as an important ethical teaching and one of the marks of true religion. Even so, religious toleration, like other attitudes of mind, cannot be created by legislation, and in many places the changes came very slowly. (Henriques, pp. 260–8.)

Moreover, while the climate for toleration was changing for the better, there was still a different problem: that of sectarian rivalry, which often led to both verbal and physical excesses. Perhaps there was some exaggeration in Hammond's famous statement that 'There was more religious strife in Manchester or Bradford in the [1840s] than in the Roman Empire under the rule of Augustus', but the conflict over religious principles was a recognized feature of the age. Even though many religious groups had wide differences amongst themselves, they nearly always banded together against Roman Catholicism, as well as against Mormonism. (Phillips, pp. 1–3 and *passim*.)

This sectarian rivalry was a problem from the outset of the British Mission. Heber C. Kimball frequently alluded to 'opposition', especially from Methodist ministers. As he later recalled:

> During this state of things, our enemies were not idle but heaped abuse upon us with an unsparing hand, and issued torrents of lies after us, which, however, I am thankful to say, did not sweep us away. (H. Kimball, *Journal*, p. 33.)

One of the first public denunciations of the Church came in the form of a pamphlet by Richard Livesey, an Englishman by birth, and a Methodist preacher who had spent years in America prior to his return to England in the late 1830s. Livesey had evidently been engaged in anti-Mormon campaigns in America, for he brought with him a stock of arguments gleaned from various books and pamphlets that he had collected while in the United States. At Preston in 1838, he published a pamphlet entitled 'An Exposure of Mormonism, Being a Statement of Facts Relating to the Self-Styled "Latter-Day Saints", and the Origin of the Book of Mormon'. Here he repeated many of the stories found in E. D. Howe, as well as in letters from Kirtland which supposedly discredited Joseph Smith. (Livesey.) There was nothing new in Livesey's literature, most of which simply borrowed from arguments that Elder Kimball had undoubtedly already heard.

In spite of opposition, however, the gospel spread in Britain, and the growing attitude of toleration often assisted missionary work. On one occasion when Elders Kimball and Hyde were preaching in Preston, for example, a minister stepped forward and opposed them on the issue of infant baptism. He obviously hoped to thwart the missionaries' attempt to get their message across, but the assembled crowd interceded, demanding the minister's silence so that they could hear the elders. (H. Kimball, *Journal*, p. 22.) Such public demands for fair play occurred with increasing frequency at street meetings.

This is not to say that the early missionaries always had an easy task, any more than do modern ones. Missionary journals contain accounts of 'hooting' at street meetings, as well as of episodes where the crowd was friendly. The elders were often accepted, even cheered, just as they were also sometimes pelted with rotten eggs, vegetables, and even stones. In August 1837, for instance, Elder Willard Richards reported having stones and turnips thrown at him by an angry mob. (British Mission History, 20 Aug 1837.) Occasionally violence was more serious, as when crowds would press round missionaries as a prelude to shoving or fighting. One such instance from Church history was the interruption of a baptismal service at Lugwardine, Herefordshire, in June 1840. On that occasion, apostle Wilford Woodruff faced concerted opposition when attempting to conduct the service at the River Lug. He wrote:

> Looking for a suitable place for Baptizing, a man by the name of Pitt Came to us filled with the Devil & wrath at the head of a mob & commanded us not to Baptize in that river & threatened us much if we did so. Elder Richards Preached to Mr Pitt & warned him to repent & be Baptized or he could not be saved. But the Devil raged to such a degree in this man & his company we thought it wisdom to omit it on this occasion. We did so & retired & went our way, with this wicked man & the rest of the mob following us shouting, hooting, & yelling as though a part of hell at least had broke loose. The Saints were strengthened seeing that they were not of the world but the world hated them & we also went our way rejoicing that we were counted worthy to partake of thes[e] things. (Woodruff, journal, 19 Jun 1840.)

In assessing the Mormon experience in Britain, it must be remembered that such petty harassment was not confined to the saints but that most groups practising itinerant preaching, such as the Primitive Methodists, the Bible Christians, and others, had similar encounters with angry mobs bent on either mischievous entertainment or serious opposition. (Billington, p. 268.) In rural areas where the social powers of the Anglican vicar and the local squire continued to be influential, there tended to be more intolerant behaviour, and there were episodes in such areas where the local magistrates would not afford protection to the missionaries, but there were also many instances where elders went about without purse or scrip and were either well received or at least treated with indifference. Serious persecution was the exception, not the rule.

What was most significant about the early mission to Britain was the popular interest that accompanied missionary labours. In all the apostles' accounts of their missions both in 1837 and in 1840–1, there were reports of large numbers of people being receptive to the gospel message. Elder Heber C. Kimball stated that the people in the vicinity of Preston were similar to those encountered by the apostle Paul at Lydda, who 'gladly received the word'. He said that he would perform baptisms 'six or seven times a day' and that his invitations to preach were so numerous that he had to decline many opportunities. (H. Kimball, *Journal*, pp. 43–5.)

On one occasion, after attempting to excuse himself due to a busy schedule and fatigue, Elder Kimball finally agreed to preach at a Baptist church in a village north of Preston. He recorded that the congregation was overjoyed to hear both him and Elder Hyde preach on the resurrection and the first principles of the gospel, that tears ran down many faces, and that the attentive audience often applauded their message. Next morning, as the two elders were preparing to leave, they were greeted with a new request to preach, and were informed that many of the local shops had been closed to allow more people to attend. (*Ibid.* pp. 34–5.) On 7 September 1837, Elders Kimball and Hyde wrote to Isaac Russell that 'The people of this country want simple things. The majority of them are illiterate, and know but little about the bible and the more simple things you can teach them the better.' (Kimball and Hyde.) In addition, many other missionaries commented on the openness of the common people to the restored gospel.

John Bennion, who joined the Church in 1841, recorded his first encounter with the Church, when he went to hear Elders John Taylor and Joseph Fielding preach at the Aitkenite chapel in Liverpool. He wrote about the controversy that followed the meeting:

> There was quite a stir amongst the people as to whether these things were so or not; a few believed and obeyed, some got angry and kicked against it, while others gave heed to the priest saying, keep away from it for it is a dangerous delusion.

At first Bennion was one of those who rejected the message, 'fearing that I might get caught in the snare'. But one evening some time later, he met Elder Domville, who had previously been his class leader in the Aitkenite Church and was now a Mormon missionary. Elder Domville began to show Bennion how the gospel had been taught by the ancient apostles according to the scriptures. Brother Bennion later said Elder Domville's arguments were 'too plain and scriptural' for him to reject, and he resolved to investigate further. The more he learned about the new religion the more he was convinced that it came of God and not of man, and soon afterwards he was baptized. (Carter, *13*: 408–10.)

John Needham, a young draper, first heard the restored gospel preached at an open-air meeting in Preston in 1837. While walking down the street he heard an Aitkenite minister challenge Elder Orson Hyde. At the time, John was searching for a church that would answer his spiritual questions, and Elder Hyde's testimony made an impression on him. He began attending all the LDS street meetings he could. At Ledgwick in Preston, John Needham was present at an open-air meeting of about nine saints and forty investigators: 'Elder Hyde addressed the meeting and Elder [Joseph] Fielding generally testified of the truth of the things which were advanced. They preached in Ledgwick for some time and I continued to attend.' John soon became convinced that the message the elders preached was true, but he was too bashful to offer himself for baptism. Finally, after several months of investigation, he came forward and was baptized on 2 April 1838. When his employer learned of his conversion, John was immediately sacked. In addition, his family was distressed by his baptism, and attempted to prise him away from his new religion. Such actions were typical of the social pressures that faced new converts. (Needham, p. 6.)

In a letter written in September 1840, Elders Willard Richards and Brigham Young compared their missionary labours in England to similar efforts in the United States:

> We find the people of this land much more ready to receive the gospel, than those in America, so far as they do receive it, for they have not that speculative intelligence, or prejudice, or prepossession, or false learning, call it what you please, which they have there [in America]. Consequently we have not to labor with a people month after month to break down their old notions, for their priests have taught them but little, & much of that is so foolish as to be detected at a

Table 2.3. Reasons stated for LDS conversions

Reasons	Times listed
Primitive simplicity	36
Plainness of doctrines	9
Spiritual manifestations	24
Concept of authority (prophets, apostles, priesthood, etc.)	14
Book of Mormon	12
Message of 'A Voice of Warning'	10
Difference from other religions	6
Millennial teachings	6
Other reasons	23
Baptism by immersion	4
First vision	4
Divine revelation	1
Love of members	2
Plan of salvation	2
Impressed with missionaries	10

glance. Viewing the subject in this light we find ignorance a blessing, for the more ignorant of false notions the more readily they sense truth. (Walker.)

This sort of interest, coupled with intensive missionary work, resulted in the conversion of 600 people in 1837. And by the end of 1841, when most of the Quorum of the Twelve ended their mission, 6,729 new members had been baptized. (R. Evans, p. 244.) In fact, the LDS Church was the fastest-growing religious group in Britain in the 1840s, its early successes often being compared to John Wesley's triumphs in the eighteenth century.

It has been said that, amongst other things, it was the Church's emphasis on prophecy, millennialism, progress, apostolic authority, religious ordinances and universal salvation that made it so attractive to the common people. (Allen and Alexander, p. 21; P. Taylor, pp. 2, 38; Allen and Thorp, pp. 516–21.) Whilst these teachings undoubtedly influenced conversions, they do not all agree with the reasons stated by the converts themselves. Table 2.3 is based on a compilation of conversion accounts from literary sources. (Thorp, 'Religious Backgrounds', pp. 62–3.) It lists the factors that converts considered influential in their conversions.

Evidently converts considered the restoration of biblical truth the most attractive teaching of the new religion. The terms 'plainness of doctrines' and 'primitive simplicity' meant essentially the same thing – that LDS teachings conformed to their own image of pristine Christianity. With the emphasis that some historians have placed on the millennial concept in Mormon doctrine, it is interesting to note that few converts mentioned it as influencing their conversion. It is also significant that no convert in the group made mention of LDS communitarian ideals in their accounts, nor did emigration to America and the building of Zion have much influence on actual conversion (although these were frequently mentioned in personal records *after* the convert's baptism).

The Church's appeal to the common people, then, according to statements made by the converts themselves, had more to do with spiritual matters than with temporal ones. The converts from the British Isles became Latter-day Saints because they were looking for the gospel of Jesus Christ, and because they recognized it when they found it.

3

The Gospel Restored to England

James R. Moss

Liverpool harbour was a busy place on 19 July 1837. Over twenty ships arrived that day from such distant ports as Rio de Janeiro, Calcutta and Constantinople, with even more entering the harbour to begin loading for departure. Amongst this international assortment of ships, passengers and cargo the packet *Garrick* also docked at Liverpool, beating its rival ship *South America* by only a few lengths to win a $10,000 wager on which would make the fastest crossing from New York.

On board the *Garrick*, Elder Heber C. Kimball had his first sight of Liverpool, and recorded:

> I went to the side of the vessel and poured out my soul in praise and thanksgiving to God for the prosperous voyage, and for all the mercies which he had vouchsafed to me, and...the Spirit of the Lord rested upon me in a powerful manner; my soul was filled with love and gratitude, and was humbled within me, while I covenanted to dedicate myself to God, and to love and serve Him with all my heart...
>
> My feelings at that time were peculiar, particularly when I realized the object, importance, and extent of my mission, and the work to which I had been appointed and in which I was shortly to be engaged. (H. Kimball, *Journal*, pp. 14–15.)

Elder Kimball's companion, Elder Orson Hyde, also felt the spiritual impact of their arrival at Liverpool. Writing to his wife he reported:

> When we came in sight of Liverpool, the Spirit of God rested down upon us to a very great degree, and also when we landed... Pray for us that we may ever keep humble at the feet of our master, that righteousness and truth may be our motto, grace our support, and eternal glory our reward. (*MA*, p. 551.)

British Isles. Places prominent in Latter-day Saint history

The two apostles and their fellow missionaries – Willard Richards, Joseph Fielding, John Goodson, Isaac Russell and John Snider – went ashore and found lodgings. Elder Kimball wrote:

> The time we were in Liverpool was spent in council and in calling on the Lord for direction, so that we might be led to places where we should be most useful in proclaiming the gospel and in establishing and spreading His kingdom. (H. Kimball, *Journal*, p. 17.)

Three days later, 'feeling led by the spirit of the Lord to go to Preston', they took a coach north to begin their work.

Upon their arrival in Preston, the missionaries found themselves in the midst of a parliamentary election called by the young Queen Victoria upon her accession to the throne earlier that year. Elder Kimball reported that 'the streets presented a very busy scene; indeed I never witnessed anything like it before in my life'. (*Ibid.*) The elders unloaded their trunks from the coach and sent Elder Goodson to find lodging for six of them, whilst Elder Fielding went to find his brother James, the Nonconformist minister whom they had come to meet.

While awaiting the return of their brethren, the remaining missionaries caught sight of one particular election banner

> ...which was just [unrolled] before us the moment the coach reached its destination, [bearing] the following motto: 'TRUTH WILL PREVAIL', which was painted in large, gilt letters. It being so very seasonable and the sentiment being so appropriate to us in our situation, we were involuntarily led to exclaim, 'Amen! So let it be.' (*Ibid.*)

So powerful was the impression upon the elders that they took this slogan as the motto for their own work in Britain.

John Goodson soon found lodgings for most of the missionaries in a boarding house at the corner of St Wilfred and Fox streets in Preston, whilst Joseph Fielding found his brother James and decided to stay with him for the time being. On Saturday evening, the 22nd of July, the Rev. James Fielding invited the missionaries to visit him, having been previously introduced to their basic beliefs through letters written to him from Joseph and his sisters Mercy and Mary in Canada. Elders Kimball, Hyde and Goodson thus joined Joseph Fielding at his brother's house and conversed far into the night, with the elders giving James Fielding 'a short account of the object of our mission and the great work which the Lord had

The missionaries took lodgings at this corner home on St Wilfred Street in Preston, 1837. (*Courtesy of LDS Visual Resources Library.*)

commenced'. (*Ibid.*) At the end of the evening, James invited all the missionaries to attend his chapel services the following day.

Sunday morning, the 23rd of July, accordingly found the seven elders in the Vauxhall Chapel in Preston. Joseph Fielding later wrote:

> As my brother had previously read to his congregation a letter which we had sent from Canada, they were much interested. It appeared that brother James had raised their expectations very high by said letters. They were many of them sincere and willing to know the truth. (Fielding, p. 17.)

Elder Kimball further recorded that they 'went to hear Mister Fielding preaching, praying to the Lord to open the way for us to preach. The Lord moved on his heart to open his doors for us to preach without asking him for it.' (H. Kimball, manuscript journal, p. 14.) The prayers of Elder Kimball and his companions were answered when, at the conclusion of his morning sermon, the Rev. James Fielding introduced the missionaries and then announced

Vauxhall Chapel, Preston, where the Latter-day Saint Elders preached to the congregation of the Rev. James Fielding.

that they would occupy the pulpit for the afternoon service. It was no coincidence that on the same day a continent away, the Prophet Joseph Smith received a revelation for the Quorum of the Twelve Apostles, in which the Lord promised: 'Wherefore, whithersoever they shall send you, go ye, and I will be with you; and in whatsoever place ye shall proclaim my name an effectual door shall be opened unto you, that they may receive my word.' (D&C 112:19.) For Elders Kimball and Hyde, the prophesied blessing was granted the same day it was uttered.

On Sunday afternoon the two apostles spoke to a packed house in the Vauxhall Chapel. Elder Kimball wrote:

> It being noised abroad that some elders from America were going to preach, a large concourse of people assembled to hear us. I called their attention to the first principles of the gospel, and told them something of the nature of the work which the Lord had commenced on the earth; after which brother Hyde bore testimony, which was received by many, with whom I afterwards conversed. (*MS*, 17 Sep 1864.)

Later that day, Joseph Fielding reported: 'The pulpit was offered for the evening; Brother Goodson preached and I bore my testimony after him. The people were deeply impressed.' (Fielding, p. 18.)

The following day, the missionaries held a special prayer service to petition the Lord to give them the use of the Vauxhall Chapel and access to the Rev. James Fielding's congregation so that the people might be converted to the truth. Elder Russell served as spokesman for the group, praying:

> O Lord, we pray thee that this people to whom thy servants are now ministering may believe so as to receive and obey the glorious principles which thou hast revealed to us in the last days, that we also may have the use of the chapel so long as we need it...and the glory and honor be unto thee through Jesus Christ, Amen. (H. Kimball, manuscript journal, pp. 5–6.)

On Wednesday evening, Fielding again opened his chapel to the missionaries, at which time Elders Hyde and Richards spoke.

Following the Wednesday service, many of James Fielding's congregation accepted the invitation extended by Elders Hyde and Richards to be baptized by proper authority. At that, Fielding, apparently realizing that he was losing his congregation, closed the doors of his chapel to the missionaries. He eventually became a bitter enemy of the Church.

In an effort to appease his followers' desire to receive the ordinance of baptism, James Fielding arranged for a Mr Giles, a Baptist minister in Preston, to baptize all of his followers who desired it, but only one accepted. James Fielding's summary of this experience – 'Kimball bored the holes, Goodson drove the nails, and Hyde clinched them' – revealed both his reluctant admiration for the power of the missionaries' testimonies and his final break with their work. (H. Kimball, *Journal*, p. 19.)

For the remainder of the week, the elders talked to members of Fielding's congregation in their homes, and set the date for their baptism on the following Sunday, the 30th of July. The baptisms were to be performed in the River Ribble, which flowed through the southern part of Preston.

Early Sunday morning, Elder Kimball was awakened by Isaac Russell, who asked him for a priesthood blessing to cast out evil spirits that had been troubling him in the night, 'for he was so afflicted with evil spirits that he could not live long unless he should obtain relief'. (*Ibid.*) Elders Kimball and Hyde therefore arose and, laying their hands upon Isaac Russell's head, rebuked the evil spirits and commanded them to leave. What followed was one of the most vivid visions of evil spirits ever given to mankind. Elder Kimball reported:

...I was struck with great force by some invisible power and fell senseless on the floor as if I had been shot, and the first thing that I recollected was, that I was supported by Brothers Hyde and Russell, who were beseeching a throne of grace in my behalf. They then laid me on the bed, but my agony was so great that I could not endure, and I was obliged to get out, and fell on my knees and began to pray. I then sat on the bed and could distinctly see the evil spirits, who foamed and gnashed their teeth upon us. We gazed upon them about an hour and a half, and I shall never forget the horror and malignity depicted on the countenances of these foul spirits, and any attempt to paint the scene which then presented itself, or portray the malice and enmity depicted in their countenances would be vain.

I perspired exceedingly, and my clothes were as wet as if I had been taken out of the river. I felt exquisite pain, and was in the greatest distress for some time. However, I learned by it the power of the adversary, his enmity against the servants of God, and got some understanding of the invisible world.' (*Ibid.* p. 20.)

For a long time, Elder Kimball was concerned that he had somehow brought this attack upon himself by some unworthy thought or action on his part. It was not until he returned to the United States and talked with the Prophet Joseph about it that he understood the real reason for the attack. In response to his questions, the Prophet replied:

No, Brother Heber, at that time you were nigh unto the Lord; there was only a veil between you and Him, but you could not see Him. When I heard of it, it gave me great joy, for I then knew that the work of God had taken root in that land. It was this that caused the devil to make a struggle to kill you... The nearer a person approaches the Lord, a greater power will be manifested by the adversary to prevent the accomplishment of His purposes. (Whitney, *Kimball*, pp. 131–2.)

Others who were present when the evil spirits attacked the missionaries also learned great lessons from the experience. Elder Joseph Fielding recorded in his journal:

Upon the whole we got considerable instruction from the maneuvers of the devil. The spirit of the devil produces confusion, disorder and misery; the spirit of God produces calmness, order and happiness. If we never before knew that there were evil spirits, we did now. (Fielding, p. 24.)

The River Ribble as it flows past Avenham Park, Preston, site of the earliest baptisms, 30 July 1837.

After recovering from this frightening experience, the missionaries left their lodgings and walked to the River Ribble. It being summer, and a Sunday, a good portion of the population had gathered on the Avenham Brows above the river to stroll in the sunshine. However, word had spread throughout the town that the new ministers from America were going to perform outdoor baptisms, and this drew additional spectators to the river. Elder Kimball estimated that about eight thousand persons watched the brief services, probably a fairly accurate figure considering the thousands who were regularly recorded as attending open-air baptisms conducted by the Baptists at this time.

Regarding the service, Elder Kimball wrote:

> The Lord delivered us from the wrath of our spiritual enemies and blessed us exceedingly that day, and I had pleasure (notwithstanding my weakness of body from the shock I had experienced) of baptizing nine individuals and hailing them brethren in the kingdom of God. (H. Kimball, *Journal*, p. 20.)

The first person baptized was George D. Watt, who had been so eager for the privilege that he raced another convert to the river and 'being quicker of foot than the [other], out-ran him, and came first into the water'. (*Ibid.* p. 21.) All nine of those baptized on 30 July 1837 were members of the Rev. James Fielding's congregation.

Following the baptismal service on Sunday morning, the elders preached in Preston's market-place to a large crowd of people. They were opposed by one of the local ministers, but that seemed only to encourage the people to listen to the missionaries. More baptisms were performed the following day, as Joseph Fielding reported: 'On Monday, the 31st of July, I for the first time administered the ordinance of baptism to 7 or 8 men.' (Fielding, p. 19.) That same day the missionaries held a council and decided that 'Elders Richards and Goodson go on a mission to Bedford; Elders Russell and Snider to Alston, Cumberland; and Elders Hyde, Fielding and Kimball agreed to labor in Preston and the regions round about.' (*MS*, 24 Sep 1864.)

By Sunday the 6th of August, those baptized in Preston numbered nearly fifty. That evening, Elder Kimball assembled missionaries and members in the home of Ann Dawson, one of the first converts in Preston, and organized the Preston Branch of the Church, the first in Britain and later to become the oldest continuously functioning unit of the LDS Church in the world. With the organization of a branch, the converts could now be confirmed members of the Church. Elder Kimball reported:

> ...we fully explained to them the nature of that ordinance about to be performed. We then laid our hands upon between forty and fifty for the gift of the Holy Ghost, and confirmed them members of the Church of Jesus Christ of Latter-day Saints. While attending to this ordinance the Spirit of the Lord rested down upon us in a powerful manner, which caused us to rejoice exceedingly. Thus the work of the Lord spread and prevailed. (H. Kimball, *Journal*, p. 23.)

The work in Preston continued to progress. Feeling the need for written support of their testimonies, the missionaries published a tract entitled, 'A Timely Warning to the People of England'. The message was a call to repentance, concluding:

> Therefore, go forth, little tract, and tell the people of England, and all people into whose hands you may fall, that the Lord has spoken from the Heavens – that he hath sent forth his servants to them, preaching repentance, and baptizing for the remission of sins, to prepare them for the coming of the Son of Man, which is drawing near.

The same message was sounded by the elders with increasing frequency as the people of Preston and vicinity flocked to hear them preach. Elder Kimball reported:

> Calls from all quarters to come and preach were constantly sounding in our ears, and we labored night and day to satisfy the people, who manifested such a desire for the truth as I never saw before. We had to speak in small and very crowded houses, and to large assemblies in the open air. Consequently our lungs were often very sore, and our bodies worn down with fatigue. Sometimes I was guilty of breaking the priestly rules – I pulled off my coat and rolled up my sleeves and went at my duty with my whole soul, like a man reaping and binding wheat, which caused the hireling priests to be very much surprised. (R. Evans, p. 44.)

Elder Hyde wrote to Willard Richards in Bedford with encouraging news of the growth in Preston:

> Our time has been [spent] altogether in preaching and baptizing [so] that we have had scarcely time to sleep; and our labors have not in the least abated, but we are preaching and baptizing daily... We are so thronged whenever we preach, that some faint and have to be carried outdoors. Our prospects are better here than they ever have been before. (Hyde, 12 Oct 1837.)

As the Preston branch grew in numbers, it became necessary to find a larger meeting-hall than the parlour in Ann Dawson's boarding house where they had organized the branch. In September they hired the use of a hall that was known as 'the Cockpit' due to its earlier use for cock-fights. (See p. 119.) By 1832, however, the hall became the site of the Temperance movement in Britain, when seven men took a pledge of total abstinence from alcohol. Temperance societies soon developed in many parts of Britain, and the missionaries were later able to use them as an effective means of introducing the gospel. Elder Kimball later wrote:

> It was often said by temperance men who joined the Church that that movement was a preparatory work or forerunner to the introduction of the Gospel; in most every place we went where there was a Temperance hall, we could get it to preach in, many believing that we made men temperate faster than they did; for as soon as any obeyed the Gospel they abandoned their excesses in drinking; and none of us drank any kind of spirits, porter nor small beer, nor even wine, neither did we drink tea, coffee or chocolate. (*MS*, 1 Oct 1864.)

By 8 October 1837, the Preston branch had grown so large that it was divided into five separate branches. At the same meeting, thirteen more members were confirmed and six teachers and one deacon were ordained to assist the elders in caring for the needs of approximately 140 members in the Preston area. Elder Fielding reported: 'All was conducted in perfect order and unity. The Teachers rejoiced, and spoke as being thankful and as being determined to be faithful. May the Lord bless them.' (Fielding, p. 38.)

Such growth did not go unnoticed by the clergymen in Preston, and opposition soon appeared. On the 7th of October, Elder Fielding wrote in his journal:

> We are spending this day in fasting and prayer that we may obtain more influence over the powers of darkness. They are all exerted to darken our minds and to hinder the work and the whole armor of god is in requisition. There is not a society in Preston or about it, as we are informed, but what is opposing us and complaining of our influence in their Churches. (*Ibid.* p. 37.)

The following month, Elder Kimball wrote to his wife:

> There is a prospect of some persecution in this place, though we have two police constables very friendly to us, one of whom has been baptized, and we are taking every measure in our power to go on safely. The Methodists and members of the Revd James Fielding have become like demons or like the lionness robbed of her whelps, being set on by their priests, they have undertaken to break up our meetings. Last evening they made an effort but we sent for the police. They came forth, knocked one man down and seized another but he pleaded so hard they concluded to let him go, followed another to his lodging but he had fled. (H. Kimball, letter to Vilate Kimball, 12 Nov 1837.)

The elders' response was to redouble their efforts, and the work continued to progress in spite of the opposition. As the weather worsened and winter approached, requests for baptism often required the missionaries to perform their outdoor ordinances in very difficult conditions. Elder Kimball reported:

> I have had to go into the water to administer the ordinance of baptism six or seven times in a day, and frequently after having come out of the water and changed my clothes, I have had to return again before I reached my home; this, too, when the weather was extremely cold, the ice being from twelve to fourteen inches thick, which continued so about twelve weeks, during which time I think there were but ten days in which we were not in the water. (H. Kimball, *Journal*, p. 43.)

As Christmas Day approached, the brethren decided to celebrate the holiday by holding a mission conference in the Cockpit. Five people were baptized early that morning and at ten o'clock the members met for the first conference of the Church in Britain. Following the opening prayer, more than a hundred little children were blessed. Elder Fielding reported, 'as the place we met in is round, and the bottom of bare earth, it reminded us of the account of Christ blessing the children'. (Fielding, p. 48.) Several brethren were ordained to offices in the Aaronic Priesthood and several new converts were confirmed. Branches of the Church organized earlier in the Preston area were further organized with local leaders. And the Word of Wisdom was publicly preached for the first time. Reflecting on the significance of this conference for the Church in Britain, Elder Kimball wrote:

> The spirit of the Lord was with us during our interview, and truly the hearts of the Elders were rejoiced beyond measure, when we contemplated the glorious work which had begun, and had to exclaim, 'It is the Lord's doings, and it is marvelous in our eyes; and blessed be the name of the Lord.' I felt greatly humbled before the Lord, who had crowned our labors with such signal success, and had prospered us far beyond my most sanguine expectations. (H. Kimball, manuscript journal, p. 30.)

The missionaries' first effort to proselytize beyond Preston began the day following the first baptisms in that city. The brethren met in council on Monday evening and 'continued in fasting and prayer, praise and thanksgiving until two o'clock in the morning'. (Whitney, *Kimball*, p. 137.) At that meeting, Elder Fielding reported, they 'set apart Bro. Goodson and Richards to go to Bedford. The Lord was present with us. In the morning they took their journey, and on the same day, Bro. Russell and Snider left us to go 150 miles north. Elder Kimball, Elder Hyde and myself were now left in Preston.' (Fielding, p. 19.)

The destination of Elders Russell and Snider was the town of Alston, near the Scottish border, a beautiful little market town set on a hill. Elders Russell and Snider contacted relations and friends in Alston, and within a month had baptized enough converts to organize a branch there. But when the work met with strong opposition almost immediately, Elder Snider unfortunately lost much of his enthusiasm for missionary work and became increasingly homesick. Within a month of his arrival he left Elder Russell in Alston and returned to Preston, where he stayed for a few weeks and then sailed back to America.

Elder Russell remained in Alston and struggled to hold the little branch together. In October he wrote to his wife of his lonely mission:

I have never suffered so much in the way of persecution before as I have done here, but you need not let this trouble you for though I have suffered some personal violence yet not a hair of my head will be suffered to fall to the ground and my labors have not been in vain. Our number is indeed small, amounting to about twenty-three baptized persons, but great numbers are believing and [those] who have obeyed are firm to a man and very intelligent and willing to stand by me in life or death. They have to endure a good deal of reproach for the truth's sake but they count it all joy to suffer for the name of Jesus. (Russell, 23 Oct 1837.)

Elder Russell spent most of the following five months working in Alston, returning to Preston in November to confer with the other missionaries there, and again in December to attend the mission conference held on Christmas Day. His work in Alston became increasingly subject to persecution and attack by local clergy. In writing to his wife of the support from local members against these attacks, he reported:

They stood by me truthfully in a late contest I have had with the priests before the public, to see fair play and protect me from harm for indeed the priests here are wolves of the first quality and do not scruple to say publicly that they [would] be glad to take away my life if they had an opportunity since their wickedness has been exposed. (*Ibid.*)

Though the Alston branch was small and Elder Russell himself would later, through his own apostasy, negate much of the good he did there, in 1837–8 it was a valuable outpost for the developing Church in Britain, and Isaac Russell laboured faithfully to protect it. Elder Kimball's frustration over the disaffection of John Snider was evident in his report of Snider's departure: 'Bro. Snider became discouraged, could not preach and became like a drone. The day will come when he will repent of it, for not being more diligent in the cause of Christ.' (H. Kimball, manuscript journal, p. 34.) In contrast, Elder Kimball reported very favourably on Elder Russell's work in Alston:

...we were favored with the company of Elder Russell, who had returned from Cumberland. He met with considerable opposition from his own kindred, as well as from ministers of the different denominations, who sought every opportunity to destroy his influence. Notwithstanding the great opposition, he was instrumental in bringing upwards of sixty souls into the kingdom of God, and left them rejoicing in the truth. (Whitney, *Kimball*, p. 192.)

The work of Elders Richards and Goodson in Bedford in many ways mirrored that of Russell and Snider in Alston. Their initial contacts when they arrived in Bedford on the 2nd of August were relations of the missionaries, in this case the Rev. Timothy Matthews, a brother-in-law to Joseph Fielding. After settling in at the Swan Inn in Bedford that Sunday morning, the two missionaries visited Timothy Matthews and were invited to attend his church services that same afternoon, which they did. Upon his further invitation, they preached in his chapel that evening, the first LDS sermons delivered in the south of England.

Timothy Matthews had been curate of Colmworth and Bolnhurst, and from 1821 until his death in 1845 was preacher at the Primitive Episcopal Church of Christ Church, Bedford. He was a colourful preacher who occasionally would call his congregation together by blowing a trumpet or bugle in the streets of Bedford. When Elders Goodson and Richards first contacted him, he 'expressed great joy at their arrival, and manifested his sincerity by walking arm in arm with the elders through the streets of Bedford, calling on the members of his church, and inviting them to attend the lecture of the elders, at his chapel vestry that evening'. (*TS*, 15 Aug 1842, p. 881.)

As had been the case with his brother-in-law the Rev. James Fielding in Preston, the Rev. Timothy Matthews at first opened his chapel to the missionaries but later closed it when he himself refused to accept the full message of the restoration. Initially the response was positive, however.

> In the evening, his church assembled in the vestry, and elders Goodson and Richards continued to lecture and testify of the work of God, on that and the three following evenings in the same place, with the entire approbation of Mr Matthews, who at the close of the lectures publicly bore testimony to the truths advanced, and called upon his people to know why they did not come forward for baptism. (*Ibid.*)

The result was that after a week of preaching in Matthews's chapel and in private houses at Bedford, the elders baptized five members of his congregation. Thereupon Matthews barred the missionaries from further preaching in this chapel, 'under the pretence that some of the proprietors of the chapel might not be pleased with the elders occupying the vestry', but he continued to attend the meetings they held in private homes.

The Rev. Timothy Matthews initially expressed a desire to be baptized by Elders Goodson and Richards. As Joseph Saville, a member of his congregation, requested to be baptized along with Matthews, the 15th of August was set for their baptism.

> At the hour appointed, Mr Saville met the elders at the place previously designated by Mr Matthews; but as he did not make his appearance according to promise, after waiting for him an hour, Mr Saville was baptized, [following which] the elders repaired to Mr Matthews to learn the cause of his not fulfilling his engagement, and were informed by Mr Matthews' family that he had gone out in the country to preach. (*Ibid.*)

In writing about this incident, Elder Kimball identified the cause of Matthews's disaffection from the Church:

> In the interval, however, Brother Goodson, contrary to my counsel and positive instructions, and without advising with anyone, read to Mr Matthews the vision seen by President Joseph Smith and Sidney Rigdon, which caused him to stumble, and darkness pervaded his mind, so much so, that at the time specified he did not make his appearance, but went and baptized himself in the river Ouse; and from that time he began to preach baptism for the remission of sins. (Whitney, *Kimball*, p. 148.)

Prior to leaving the United States, Elder Kimball had been instructed by President Joseph Smith to preach only the first principles of the gospel, and not to teach the deeper doctrines in what came to be Section 76 of the Doctrine and Covenants. Elder Kimball had faithfully passed this direction along to Elders Goodson and Richards, but Elder Goodson apparently felt that since Timothy Matthews was a practising minister he would be capable of accepting the principles contained in the vision. The resulting reversal of Matthews's feelings showed clearly that he was not, however, and he soon became an enemy of the Church, following the missionaries from town to town and preaching against them even while he adopted many of their basic teachings and practices as his own.

A week later, John Goodson left Bedford for London, but he apparently did not reach the city or else stayed only a short time visiting friends and relations. He soon returned to Bedford but left again, this time for Preston, on the 12th of September, and within another month sailed for America with John Snider.

Elder Willard Richards stayed on in Bedford for the next five months, labouring on his own as had Elder Russell in Alston.

Feeling the need for spiritual strength in his lonely ministry, he devoted many days to fasting. His work met with increasing opposition, usually initiated by the Rev. Timothy Matthews. Elder Richards reported that on the 18th of August he had 'quite a commotion on our way home by scoffers', and on the 20th of August added: 'I began to address the company collected but was soon interrupted and on our return I was freely pelted with garnish, etc., by the multitude'. (W. Richards, 18, 20 Aug 1837.)

The opposition only increased Elder Richards's courage. He wrote:

> Having been moved by the spirit for a week to attack Satan in his stronghold, I this day preached repentance and baptism to the congregation at St Paul's church as they came out of the door at 1:00 p.m. (*Ibid.* 1 Oct 1837.)

Elder Richards soon expanded his proselytizing efforts to areas outside Bedford. In a letter of 12 October 1837 from Elder Kimball, he was counselled:

> The harvest is ripe and souls are perishing for the word of life. It seems hard for the elders to be idle and settle down in a small branch of the Church when there is such a large world of people. May God give you energy to go forth in his name and cry aloud and we say unto you to go forth to the country without purse or scrip as God has commanded and if you should leave the branch two or three weeks they will take no harm and the Lord will bless you in so doing. (H. Kimball, letter to W. Richards, 12 Oct 1837.)

Elder Richards responded to this counsel by preaching in villages and towns such as Gamlingay, Potton, Little Croxton, Morden and Bassingbourn, as well as St Albans, Kempston and Baldock. As usual, his successes were met with opposition from the established clergy and others, but he continued his work undeterred. When he finally left Bedford in March 1838, there were two branches of the Church there.

Although the growth of the Church in towns such as Alston and Bedford was important to the missionaries' work in Britain in 1837, it was relatively insignificant in comparison to the greater growth of the Church in the Preston area. Elders Kimball, Hyde and Fielding remained in Preston, where they spent much of their time proselytizing and caring for the growing branches they had organized. But they also felt it important to leave Preston at times to take the gospel to outlying villages in the Ribble valley.

One of the most important conversions of this period took place in the village of Eccleston, some ten miles south of Preston. Elder Kimball had left Preston to visit the village of Wrightington and stopped along the way at the home of Amos Fielding, who was to accompany him in his proselytizing. Brother Fielding informed Elder Kimball that a family by the name of Moon in the village of Eccleston had requested a visit in order to discuss the principles of the gospel. Elder Kimball wrote:

> Accordingly, Brother Fielding and I paid them a visit that evening. We were very kindly received by the family, and had considerable conversation on the object of my mission to that country, and the great work of the last days; they listened with attention to my statements but at the same time they appeared to be prejudiced against them, rather than otherwise. We remained in conversation until a late hour, and then returned. On our way home, Brother Fielding observed that he thought our visit had been in vain, as the family seemed to have considerable prejudice. I answered, and said, Brother Fielding, be not faithless, but believing, we shall yet see great effects from this visit, for I know there are some of the family that have received the testimony and will shortly manifest the same. (H. Kimball, manuscript journal, p. 50.)

Elder Kimball and Brother Fielding continued on their journey to Wrightington and remained there a few days proselytizing. On their way back to Preston, Elder Kimball felt impelled to visit the Moon family again. When he knocked on the door, he was greeted by Mrs Moon, who exclaimed, 'Come in, come in! You are welcome here. I and the lasses have just been calling on the Lord, and praying that he would send you this way.' (*Ibid.* p. 51.)

On 6 December 1837, Elder Kimball baptized Hannah and Mathias Moon, with four of their daughters. He returned more than once to Eccleston, and eventually baptized the remainder of the family, a total of thirteen. Before he left for America in 1838, Elder Kimball had expanded his work with the Moon family, their relatives and close friends, to baptize over thirty people in Eccleston, six of whom were ordained elders and served as missionaries in the Preston area. One of that number was John Moon, son of Hannah and Mathias, who would lead the first company of saints across the ocean to Zion in 1840, and another, Francis, would write a letter to the saints in Britain after his arrival in Nauvoo, confirming that he had met the Prophet Joseph and that the work was indeed of God.

Another village south-west of Preston figures prominently in this period of Heber C. Kimball's mission: Longton, just over five miles from Preston, near the confluence of the Douglas and Ribble rivers. Immediately following the Christmas Day conference of 1837, Elders Kimball and Hyde visited Longton. Elder Hyde had previously preached there with John Goodson before Elder Goodson returned to the States, but no one had yet been baptized. Elder Kimball reported:

> The people asked Brother Hyde why he did not 'bring Kimball down, to hit the rock a crack with his big sledge and let the water flow out.' I preached from Hebrews 6th chapter, 1st verse... I preached a plain and simple discourse, and according to my calling I taught them to repent and be baptized, that they might be saved, and if they did not they would be damned. Elder Hyde bore testimony. After meeting I baptized ten, and in the morning after, several more. It being very cold weather – the streams all frozen over – we had to repair to the sea to administer the ordinance. (Whitney, *Kimball*, p. 177.)

Elders Kimball and Hyde returned to Longton and baptized additional converts during the following three months, eventually organizing a branch of the Church there.

Proselytizing in the villages upstream from Preston actually began with the 4th of August baptism of Jennetta Richards in Preston. Elder Kimball confirmed her immediately following her baptism in the River Ribble, the first confirmation performed in Britain. Jennetta, the daughter of the Rev. John Richards of Walkerfold, was in Preston visiting Thomas Walmesley who, along with his wife, had been among the first converts baptized on the 30th of July. After her baptism, Jennetta grew anxious about her relationship with her father and wondered how she could tell him of her conversion to the Church. As she prepared to return to Walkerfold the next day, she wept for fear of rejection by her family. Elder Kimball said to her:

> 'Sister, be of good cheer, for the Lord will soften the heart of thy father, that I will yet have the privilege of preaching in his chapel, and it shall result in a great opening to preach the gospel in that region.' I exhorted her to pray and be humble. She requested me to pray for her, and gave me some encouragement to expect that her father would open his chapel for me to preach in. I then hastened to my brethren, told them of the circumstances and the result of my visit with the young lady, and called upon them to unite with me in prayer that the Lord would soften the heart of her father, that he might be induced to open his chapel for us to preach in. (Whitney, *Kimball*, p. 138.)

Willard, Jennetta, and little Heber John Richards, March 1845, Nauvoo.

George Darlington Watt, born 12 May 1812, Manchester, Lancashire. The first to be baptized in the British Isles. (*Courtesy of Ronald G. Watt.*)

Elder Kimball's prayers were answered the following week when he received a letter from the Rev. John Richards:

Sir: You are expected to be here next Saturday. You are given out to preach in the forenoon, afternoon, and evening. Although we be strangers to one another, yet, I hope we are not strangers to our blessed Redeemer, else I would not have given out for you to preach. Our chapel is but little and the congregation but few – yet if one soul be converted, it is of more value than the whole world. I remain in haste, John Richards. (H. Kimball, manuscript journal, p. 22.)

Elder Kimball arrived in Walkerfold on the 12th of August and spent the night with the Richards family, conversing about the gospel until a late hour. The next morning he went with Mr Richards to his chapel, where he preached three times that day as scheduled. He reported:

Nearly the whole congregation were melted down into tears. After I had concluded the services of the day, Mr Richards gave out another appointment for me to preach on Monday evening, which I attended to. I likewise, by request of the congregation, preached on Wednesday evening. (*Ibid.* pp. 22–3.)

At this point John Richards recognized what Fielding in Preston had recognized earlier: that when the gospel in its fullness is preached by authorized servants of the Lord, those who are pure in heart will respond and seek baptism. On Thursday, Elder Kimball baptized six members of Richards's congregation, with more to follow on succeeding days. The Rev. John Richards then closed the doors of his chapel to Elder Kimball, but reopened them the following Sunday for the afternoon and evening services. Elder Kimball later recorded:

I baptized most of Mr Richards' members, and he afterwards told me I had ruined his flock. I pitied the old gentleman, but I had a duty to perform which outweighed all other considerations. I shall ever remember with gratitude his generous hospitality. (*MS*, 24 Sep 1864.)

Although the Rev. John Richards thereafter forbade Elder Kimball's preaching in his chapel, he remained a friend of the Church, unlike other clergymen such as Fielding and Timothy Matthews. One reason for this was the close association members of his family had with the Church. His son, an attorney in Preston, helped the missionaries obtain preaching licences as well as permission to use the Cockpit for religious services. More importantly, his daughter Jennetta later married Willard Richards and for ever united Richards's family with the LDS Church.

The circumstances surrounding the courtship and marriage of Willard and Jennetta Richards are unique. Jennetta was baptized and confirmed by Elder Kimball before she had even met Willard, yet the first time Elder Kimball wrote to Willard following her conversion, he told Elder Richards, 'Willard, I baptized your wife today'. The potential courtship was kept in abeyance while Elder Richards continued his proselytizing work in the town of Bedford where he had gone the week of Jennetta's baptism, but upon his return to Preston in March of the following year, Elder Richards found Heber still convinced of the union and encouraging him to get acquainted with Jennetta. The following month, Willard wrote the following in his journal:

While walking in Thornley plucked a snowdrop from through the hedge, and carried it to James Mercer's; hung it up in his kitchen. Soon after Janetta [*sic*]

Richards came in the room, and I walked with her and William Parker to Ribchester to attend meeting with brothers Hyde and Kimball at Brother Clark's. While walking with them...I said Richards was a good name, I never wanted to change it, 'do you?' said I to Janetta. 'No, I do not,' was her reply and I think she never will. (W. Richards, 22 Mar 1838.)

Several months of intermittent courtship followed, interrupted by the requirements of Willard's missionary work. They were married on 24 September 1838. Elder Richards wrote in his journal that day:

Most truly do I praise my Heavenly Father for his great kindness in providing me a partner according to his promise. I received her from the Lord and hold her at his disposal. I pray my Heavenly Father he will bless us forever, amen. (*Ibid*, 24 Sep 1838.)

The branch at Walkerfold was soon followed by another at the ancient city of Ribchester, site of a Roman fort and location of a Christian church from the thirteenth century. Elder Kimball reported a visit to Ribchester on the 25th of September, and on the 27th of October Elder Fielding recorded a two-week visit to the towns around Preston, noting that he spoke 'first at Ribchester, but had not much liberty'. Elder Kimball returned to Ribchester to strengthen the branch there and found increased opposition that eventually turned to persecution:

I was instrumental in building up a branch in Ribchester. A mob of Catholics had combined, that when I went to baptize any persons they would pelt me with stones. I made arrangements with each of the candidates to go singly to the place of baptism, and about the time the last one got there I started quickly, got to the place and baptized them all. As I was baptizing the last one the mob came up and were disappointed in their vengeance, for I came out of the water, and they did not know how many I had baptized. (Whitney, *Kimball*, p. 168.)

The most spiritual experiences of Elder Kimball's Ribble valley ministry occurred in the two small villages of Chatburn and Downham, lying just south of the River Ribble on the northern side of Pendle Hill. He had been near these places during his visits to Walkerfold, and later determined to visit them, whereupon he got an interesting response from some of the other missionaries:

Having mentioned my determination of going to Chatburn to several of my brethren, they endeavored to dissuade me from going, informing me that there could be no prospect of success whatever, as several ministers of different denominations had endeavored in vain to raise churches in these places. This did not discourage me in the least; I went in the name of Jesus Christ. My testimony was accompanied by the Spirit of the Lord and was received with joy, and these people who were represented as being so hard and obdurate, were melted down into tenderness and love, and the effect seemed to be general. (*MS*, 1 Oct 1864.)

The people of Chatburn welcomed Elder Kimball by obtaining the use of the tithe-barn in the village and providing a large barrel in the centre upon which he could stand to preach. He spoke on the first principles of the gospel, the need for redemption, and the coming resurrection. At the conclusion of his sermon he announced that he stood ready to perform the ordinance of baptism for any who desired it and were willing to accept the covenant offered through faith and repentance. He later wrote:

When I concluded I felt someone pulling at my coat, exclaiming, 'Maister, Maister.' I turned round and asked what was wanted. Mrs Elizabeth Partington said 'Please sir, will you baptize me?' 'And me?' 'And me?' exclaimed more than a dozen voices. Accordingly I went down into the water and baptized twenty-five. I was engaged in the duty, and confirming them and conversing with the people until after midnight. (Whitney, *Kimball*, p. 171.)

Elder Kimball went the following day to Downham where he baptized between twenty-five and thirty, then returned the next day to Chatburn. The interest he generated in these two villages now began to be general. He recorded:

The congregation was so numerous that I had to preach in the open air, and took my stand on a stone wall, and afterwards baptized several. These villages seemed to be affected from one end to the other; parents called their children together, spoke to them on the subjects which I had preached about, and warned them against swearing, and all other evil practices, and instructed them in their duty. (*Ibid*.)

Elder Fielding accompanied Elder Kimball on this first visit to Chatburn and Downham, assisting in preaching and baptizing and organizing branches not only at these two villages but also at Clitheroe and Waddington. Elder Fielding also testified of the remarkable spiritual outpouring that attended this visit:

There is a wonderful work in Downham and Chatburn, two small villages. It appears as though the whole of the inhabitants were turning to the Lord from 10 to 90 years old. It is truly affecting to see them. While I was praying one day previous to baptizing 17, the little girls kneeled around me; some leaned against my back and some against my arm. They are full of love for us and each other. (Fielding, p. 57.)

Subsequent visits to Chatburn and Downham produced similar experiences for both the missionaries and the members of the Church. Upon their return to Chatburn, Elder Kimball reported,

> Having been observed drawing nigh to the town, the news ran from house to house, and immediately on our arrival, the noise of their looms was hushed, the people flocked to the doors to welcome us, and see us pass. The youth of the place ran to meet us, and took hold of our mantles and then of each others hands; several having hold of hands went before us singing the songs of Zion, while their parents gazed upon the scene with delight, and poured out their blessings upon our heads, and praised the God in heaven, for sending us to unfold the principles of truth, the plan of salvation to them. (H. Kimball, manuscript journal, p. 49.)

Elder Kimball's experiences in Chatburn and Downham were the counterpoint to his terrifying experience with evil spirits at the beginning of his mission, and the capstone of his spiritual triumph. When he and Elder Fielding took their final farewells there before returning to the States, it was one of the most touching moments in the history of the Church. Elder Fielding recorded:

> It was very affecting to witness our parting with them. The streets were almost lined with [people], weeping and looking after us. Brother K. left his blessing on them and the whole place, walking with his hat off. They all followed us with their eyes as far as they could see us, many of those even that had not been baptized. (Fielding, pp. 57–8; see also pp. 3–4 herein.)

The little villages of the Ribble valley provided fertile ground for the seed of the restored gospel in Britain, and the spiritual experiences that accompanied the missionaries there formed a strong foundation for the growth of the Church in that area.

The expansion of the Church in Alston, Bedford and the Ribble valley was a source of great strength to the Church in Preston, but it was countered by the growing opposition of the local clergy and the press. The first source of strong opposition was the clergy, as already mentioned – specifically James Fielding in Preston, Timothy Matthews in Bedford, and others who lost members of their congregations to the LDS missionaries. One of these others was the Rev. Robert Aitken, a close friend of Timothy Matthews who had established congregations in Liverpool, London, Preston, Burslem and other towns. As the Church began to grow in Preston, Aitken

...commenced his attack on the principles of righteousness...and while furiously pounding his pulpit with the Book of Mormon, and warning his people to beware of the Latter Day Saints and their doctrines, saying that they and their record came from hell, called upon his people to use all their efforts to put down the work of God, or stop the progress of the Latter Day Saints; and if it could not be put down without, prayed that God would smite the leaders. (*TS*, 15 Aug 1842, p. 882.)

Aitken had initially been visited by the missionaries and acknowledged the correctness of their preaching on such doctrines as baptism, but later rejected any further discussions with them when he lost part of his congregation in Preston. Following Aitken's first attack on the Church, Elder Kimball reported:

The next Sunday Elder Hyde and myself went to our meeting room, read the thirteenth chapter of first Corinthians, and strongly urged upon the people the grace of charity which is so highly spoke of in that chapter, and made some remarks on the proceedings of the Revd Robert Aitken, who had abused us and the Book of Mormon so very much. In return for his railing we exhorted the Saints to pray that the Lord would soften his heart and open his eyes that he might see that it was hard to 'kick against the pricks'. This discourse had a very good effect, and that week we had the pleasure of baptizing fifty into the kingdom of Jesus, a large number of whom were members of Mr. Aitken's church. (Whitney, *Kimball*, pp. 150–1.)

Another minister who attacked the Church in Preston was William Giles, the Baptist minister to whom James Fielding turned to baptize his followers in a vain attempt to halt the growth of the Church. Shortly after the first mission conference of the Church on Christmas Day 1837, Giles prepared and delivered a series of three lectures, in which he attacked and ridiculed the Church. Joseph Fielding wrote:

A man named Giles is lecturing against us, the Book of Mormon, etc. He treats all with great contempt and ridicule, and often makes his hearers laugh. He has given it out that he wishes us to hear him, but we have washed our feet against him because he rejected our testimony. (Fielding, pp. 50–1.)

Preston newspapers diligently reported Giles's lectures and are thus the first British press reports of the growth of the LDS Church. The *Preston Chronicle* reported, on 13 January 1838:

On Thursday evening the Reverend W. Giles delivered an able and interesting lecture on the claims of the Book of Mormon to divine authority. The object of the lecture, which was the first of a series, was to expose the alleged absurdities contained in the book bearing the above appellation, pretending to be a new revelation. The Reverend gentleman was listened to throughout a long lecture with intense interest and profound attention, and unquestionably gave great satisfaction to the large and respectable audience which attended. Mr. G. will resume the subject next Thursday evening. (*Preston Chronicle*, 13 Jan 1838.)

The *Preston Pilot* and the *Preston Observer* printed almost identical reports, following Giles's discourses with interest.

The Giles lectures fanned the fires of opposition to the Church in Preston more than anything the missionaries had previously encountered. Elder Kimball noted the increased activity, but also felt the elders' publicized offers to debate on the subject considerably strengthened the Church's position. Both members and missionaries tried to respond to the obviously biased press reports, but whenever they did their letters were either returned out of hand or rejected in print, with comments from the editors that they 'did not wish to get involved' in religious controversy. Yet the press continued to report on Church growth from a negative and increasingly ridiculing stance, such as the following article entitled 'Religious Fanaticism':

The American 'Saints' who profess to have discovered in the New World, a 'new' revelation, and who have made this town the principal scene of their labours, have, singular to say, succeeded in making a great number of converts in the town and neighbourhood. Their disciples, however, comprise only very ignorant persons, as the glaring absurdity of the 'new revelation' on which their faith is founded, has caused it to be repudiated by those who are capable of judging for themselves. (*Preston Chronicle*, 17 Mar 1838.)

These early press reports make it clear that the early converts to the Church in the Preston area had to have great faith in order to embrace the truth and continue their course in the Church. Baptism often meant social ostracism, possible loss of employment, and public ridicule. But as is often the case, the attacks on the Church by the clergy and press also opened many doors to the missionaries when the fair-minded people in the north of England sought to decide for themselves. Joseph Fielding indicated his awareness of this benefit from opposition when he wrote:

Three different priests of the sects were lecturing against us last sabbath week, but according to the decree, it has turned against themselves and for us. One named Dent, of the Church of England, held up the Book of Mormon to his congregation as an object of scorn and laughter. Another named Worrell of the

Methodists, did the same, calling us impostors, etc., yet they never spoke to us. They judge us by hearsay. Will this do at the bar of God? But the foolishness of God is wiser than men and the weakness of God is stronger than men. (Fielding, p. 54.)

As Elder Fielding observed, the work of the Lord continued to progress in spite of, or even because of, the attacks on the Church by the clergy and the press. Elder Kimball reported that during the first months of 1838,

...great numbers were initiated into the Kingdom of Heaven; those who were sick were healed; those who were diseased flocked to us daily; and truly their faith was great, such as I hardly ever witnessed before, consequently many were healed of their infirmities. We were continually employed day and night, some nights hardly closing our eye-lids. The task was almost more than we could endure; but realizing the circumstances of this people, their love of the truth, their humility and unfeigned charity, caused us to use all diligence and make good use of every moment, for truly our bowels yearned over them.

The work kept spreading; the prospect of usefulness grew brighter, and the field opened larger and larger; while the cries of 'Come, and administer the words of life unto us,' were more and more frequently sounding in our ears. I do not remember during the last six months I was in England of retiring to my bed earlier than midnight, which was also the case with Brothers Hyde and Fielding. (Whitney, *Kimball*, p. 190.)

Those 'last six months' drew to a close all too soon, and on 14 February 1838 Orson Hyde wrote to Willard Richards in Bedford:

The time is drawing near for us to begin to think about going home; and to take some measures in relation to it. Our advice to you is that you go around and see your brethren and put them in order as well as you can, ordaining such officers among them as their circumstances may require... You have now about one month to regulate your matters and prepare for home... 'The South America' will sail...on the first day of April next, and we want to be in readiness to enter on board her. (Hyde, 14 Feb 1838.)

Elder Hyde's announcement of their impending departure had come only after much discussion amongst the brethren. Though they felt a great need to continue proselytizing in England and wanted to expand the work into other areas of the British Isles, Elders Kimball and Hyde were needed at home, both to strengthen the Church in the United States and to help their families overcome the effects of being uprooted from Ohio to Missouri in their absence. Elders Goodson and Snider having already returned home in 1837, only the two apostles, Elder Richards, and the native Englishmen Fielding and Russell were left in Britain.

Elder Hyde's letter to Willard Richards also raised the possibility, however, that Elder Richards might not have to return to America with the two apostles:

> This letter is written to you on the supposition that you wish to go home to America with us. But it may be that your eye has caught a glimpse of your '*better part*' and [you] may wish to remain awhile. If so you are at liberty to stay but if not you are as one of us to fare as we fare, etc. (*Ibid.*)

This obvious reference to the possible marriage of Elder Richards and Jennetta Richards foreshadowed Willard's decision to remain in England and serve with Joseph Fielding in the mission presidency. But he still had to conclude his work in Bedford in order to return to Preston and assume new responsibilities there upon the departure of the apostles.

Elders Kimball, Hyde and Fielding spent February of 1838 visiting the branches they had established in the towns surrounding Preston. Elder Fielding reported good progress in his part of this work:

> Feb. 14, Wednesday. On Monday returned to Preston from Waddington, having been off 18 days and baptized 17. Had more liberty and power than ever before.... I feel much encouraged in the work; it is going on well in general. (Fielding, pp. 53–4.)

The two apostles made similar reports as they set in order the branches they had established.

Willard Richards joined his brethren in Preston on the 7th of March and spent the remainder of the month with them visiting branches and confirming his decision to remain in England following the apostles' departure. Much of their time was also spent in planning for a final mission conference to be held in Preston, at which time the entire Church in Britain would be organized to strengthen the members in the months and years ahead when they would be without apostolic leadership in their own land.

On Sunday, 8 April 1838, the members of the Church in Britain met in a mission conference at 9 a.m. in the Cockpit. About 700 members were present, representing between fifteen hundred and two thousand who had been baptized in England since the arrival of the missionaries less than a year before. As Elder Kimball surveyed the people during the opening hymn, he

> ...contemplated the congregation then assembled, which had been brought into the kingdom, through our instrumentality in such a short time, [and] was truly grateful to my heavenly Father, and my soul did magnify his holy name, while my aspirations ascended to heaven, that all those who had embraced the gospel might, through endurance of faith unto the end, share in the glories of the eternal world, and sit down with Abraham, Isaac and Jacob in the kingdom of our Father. (H. Kimball, manuscript journal, p. 37.)

The business of the conference was to set in order the Church in Britain. To that end, several brethren were ordained to offices in the Aaronic and Melchizedek priesthoods, and given responsibilities in connection with the branches then organized. Following these ordinances, Elder Kimball reported:

> We then laid hands upon forty individuals who had previously been baptized, for the gift of the Holy Ghost; after which about one hundred children were presented to us to receive a blessing, and the same day we baptized twenty individuals for the remission of sins, and then proceeded to administer the sacrament to this numerous assembly; we then gave some general instructions to the whole church, respecting their duty to God and to one another, which were listened to with great attention, and were treasured up in the hearts of most who were present. (*Ibid.* p. 38.)

A major act of the conference was the release of Elders Kimball and Hyde as presiding officers of the Church in Britain, and the establishment of a new mission presidency to supervise the Church in future. Elder Joseph Fielding was called as mission president, with Willard Richards as his first counsellor, and William Clayton as his second counsellor. (Whitney, *Kimball*, p. 192.) Elder Fielding's report of this calling revealed his earnest desire to fulfil it with honour:

> Of the five who have been laboring, I myself, certainly am the least, and yet strange as it may appear, they have ordained me Presiding High Priest, with Elder Willard Richards...and Elder William Clayton in company with me as Counselors. This work seems far too great for me; my heart is ready to sink at the Thought, and nothing but a full belief that it is the Will of God could ever have induced me to take it upon me, but I know that my Strength is in the Lord, and I intend to be faithful, if I die under it; but little did I think that such a thing would have fallen upon me in this way. (Fielding, p. 60.)

The conference lasted eight hours, with the business and counsel from the presiding brethren occupying the entire time. Elder Kimball reported that they

...proceeded to give instructions to the official members, reminding them of their several duties, and callings, and the responsibilities which rested upon them, pressed upon them the necessity of being humble and faithful in the discharge of their duties, so that by patience, by meekness, and by love unfeigned, they might commend themselves to God and to the church of Jesus Christ. (H. Kimball, manuscript journal, p. 37.)

Following a short break, the meeting reconvened at 7 p.m. to hear Elders Kimball and Hyde deliver their farewell addresses to the saints in Britain. Elder Kimball reported:

Brothers Hyde and myself spoke to them concerning our labors in that land, the success of the ministry, and the kindness we had experienced at their hands, and told them we expected before long to see them again, after we had visited the Church and our families in America... I could not restrain my feelings, and they found vent in a flood of tears. It would have been almost an impossibility for us to have left this affectionate people, if we had not had the most implicit confidence in the brethren who had been appointed to preside over them in our absence; but knowing that they had the confidence of the Church, we felt that affairs would be conducted in righteousness. (Whitney, *Kimball*, p. 193.)

Following their farewell to the saints, the two apostles conducted their final leadership meeting with the new mission presidency and about eighty priesthood leaders and members. At that time, several important blessings were also pronounced upon the heads of certain members. Sister Ann Dawson was one of these, receiving a special blessing for having allowed the missionaries to use her home for lodging as well as the earliest meeting-place for the Church in Preston. Two other sisters – Hannah Greenwood and Jennetta Richards – received patriarchal blessings from Elders Kimball and Hyde, in anticipation of their marriages later that year to Elders Joseph Fielding and Willard Richards. The apostles then instructed the Church leadership on the need for order, unity and discipline to prevent apostasy. Towards the end of the meeting (soon after midnight), a most touching exchange of love took place between the new and retiring mission presidents. Elder Fielding wrote:

After prayer, as I was now considered as the head or representative of the Church here... I rose and on my own behalf, and on behalf of the Church, and on behalf of my native land, returned thanks to Elder Kimball and Hyde for their kindness and faithfulness to me; for their faithfulness and diligence in building up the Church, regulating and instructing them in the truth, for they had labored almost night and day to build them up, etc., and for coming from their homes and families to plant the standard of truth which had been so long fallen, in this my native land. For these things I felt unspeakably thankful, and pray that they might safely and pleasantly cross the great waters, and find their families in peace.

Brother Kimball then said that as he and Bro. Hyde had now resigned their office as to the Church here they felt now to stand as representatives of the Church in America, and proposed that they should give me and my two brethren Richards and Clayton the hand of fellowship in token of union or oneness between the trio. Brother Kimball then took my hand and, according to what was in his heart, pronounced a blessing on me and the Church, then of Bro. Richards and then of Bro. Clayton, and Bro. Hyde followed him in the same manner. It was a delightful yet an affecting time. (Fielding, pp. 62–3.)

Thus the leadership was transferred from Elders Kimball and Hyde to Elders Fielding, Richards and Clayton, from the American missionaries to the native British elders, from the land that had served as the host society for the restoration of the gospel in this dispensation to the land that would serve as the host society for its great international expansion in the years to come. In the act of transferring priesthood power from the first American missionary to a native Englishman, the Lord established both a pattern for future mission leadership and a recognition that the strength of the Church lay not in nationality but in personal righteousness.

The following day, Monday 9 April 1838, Elders Kimball and Hyde left Preston for Liverpool to await passage on a ship bound for New York. Elder Kimball's reflections on the parting showed once again the great love he had for the British saints:

Notwithstanding the variegated scenery of the country, which in England is very beautiful, my mind reverted back to the time when I first arrived in that country; and the peculiar feelings of mind when I traveled from Liverpool to Preston some months before. Then I was a stranger in a strange land, and had nothing to rely upon but the kindness and mercy of that God who had sent me there. While I mused on these things my soul was humbled within me, and I had to exclaim, 'surely this is the Lord's doings and marvelous in my eyes,' for then I had hundreds of brethren, to whom I was united in bonds the most endearing and sacred, and who loved me as their own souls, and whose prayers would be continually offered up for my welfare and prosperity. (H. Kimball, manuscript journal, p. 41.)

Upon their arrival in Liverpool, the brethren found their departure would be delayed due to revised shipping schedules, and so took lodgings to await the sailing of the *Garrick* on the 20th of April. In the intervening days, word of their delay reached Church members in Preston, and Elders Fielding and Richards were able to travel to Liverpool to receive further training and instruction. They were also able to report to Elders Kimball and Hyde the feelings and actions of the membership following the apostles' departure, and to plan to counteract any problems that might arise in future.

One such problem was a report from the mission leadership confirming a belief that Brother Thomas Webster, a prominent member of the Preston Branch, would seek to usurp the leadership of the branch after the departure of the apostles. To forestall such action, Elders Kimball and Hyde wrote the following letter, which Elders Fielding and Richards took back to Preston with them:

> Dear Brothers and Sisters in Preston: It seemeth good unto us and also unto the Holy Spirit to write you a few words which cause pain in our hearts, and will also pain you when they are fulfilled before you; yet you shall have joy in the end. Brother Webster will not abide in the Spirit of the Lord, but will reject the truth, and become the enemy of the people of God, and expose the mysteries which have been committed to him, that a righteous judgement may be executed upon him, unless he speedily repent. When this sorrowful prediction shall be fulfilled, this letter shall be read to the Church, and it shall prove a solemn warning to all to beware. Farewell in the Lord. (Whitney, *Kimball*, p. 197.)

Upon their return to Preston with this letter, Elders Fielding and Richards showed it to William Clayton and another member and then dated and sealed it for any unfortunate but necessary future use. That use became required when Brother Webster later challenged the leadership of the Church in Britain and had to be excommunicated. At the time of this difficulty for the Church, the letter written by the two apostles was opened and read, resulting in the loss of Brother Webster's influence within the Church, the reaffirmation of the leadership of the proper mission presidency, and a renewed appreciation for the prophetic insight of Elders Kimball and Hyde.

As the sailing date for their departure grew closer, Elder Kimball's love for the saints impelled him to write one last farewell letter, specifically addressed to the members in Chatburn and Downham who had so openly and completely accepted the gospel and were even then being severely persecuted for that acceptance. The letter provided a fitting climax to this first apostolic mission in Britain, and also provided a framework within which the British members could live the principles of the gospel until the return of the Quorum of the Twelve in 1840:

Beloved Brethren: Having given all diligence to make known unto you the common salvation of our Lord Jesus Christ, which ye have so joyfully received from my lips, I feel now [moved] to write to you a few words for your consolation, and the confirming of that hope which is possessed by you, that ye may be steadfast and immovable, always abounding in the work of the Lord, and it may be made manifest unto all men that our labors have not been in vain.

Be kind and affectionate one towards another, manifesting your faith by your works – doing as well as saying. If there is any among you destitute of daily food, feed him; if any one be naked, clothe him; if any be cast down, raise him up; if any among you are sick, send for the Elders, or Priests, that they may come and pray for you, and lay their hands upon you, and the prayer of faith shall heal the sick; therefore, brethren, let your faith be centered in God, for He is able to do all things, to forgive sins and heal the sick, for you know this, that God has said these signs shall follow them that believe.

Now, brethren, I exhort you in the name of my Master, to contend for that faith which was once delivered to the Saints; for the same faith will produce the same effects; for God has not changed, neither has His word changed; heaven and earth shall pass away, but there shall not one jot or tittle of His word fail; all shall be fulfilled; whether it be by His own voice or the voice of His servants, it is all the same; therefore, brethren, do not live by bread alone, but by every word that proceedeth forth from the mouth of God.

Dear brethren and sisters, be patient, be humble, be prayerful, visit your secret places. Pray in your families morning and evening, ye who are heads of families, and neglect not the assembling of yourselves together; but speak often one to another concerning the things of the kingdom, and diligently follow after every good thing, remembering that the diligent hand maketh rich. Let these things be and abound with you, and ye shall be neither barren nor unfruitful in the knowledge of God. Let your eyes be single, and your bodies shall be filled with light.

Now, to you, brethren, who have been ordained to watch over the flock, I would say, stand in your places and magnify the offices which ye have received of the Lord Jesus, to feed His sheep. Feed the lambs; watch over the flock in all things; be not partial to any one; remember these things, and the blessing of God shall attend in all things.

Dear Brethren and Sisters, I give you the gratitude of my heart for the kindness which you have bestowed upon me and my brethren; for when I was hungry, ye fed me; when I was naked, ye clothed me; when I was destitute, ye gave me money; when I was a stranger, ye took me in and lodged me; and, as ye have done these things to me and my brethren in our necessities; for I am not forgetful of those things and I do ever remember you in my prayers, praying my heavenly Father to sustain you, enable you to walk worthy of the holy vocation unto which ye have been called, unto the end. Amen.

Finally, brethren and sisters, farewell. Pray for me and my brethren; and may God of all grace sanctify you wholly, and bring you into my Father's kingdom. Adieu. This from your beloved brother in Christ, Heber C. Kimball. (Whitney, *Kimball*, pp. 195–7.)

As Elders Kimball and Hyde sailed out of Liverpool harbour on 20 April 1838, they left behind not only blessed memories of sacred experiences, but also the beginnings of the restored Church of Jesus Christ in the British Isles. The little stone that Daniel had prophesied had begun to roll forth to fill the earth, as the kingdom of God had begun to expand. Within the single year that the apostles and their companions had laboured in England, the seeds of gospel truths had been planted in the hearts of the people, the foundations of Zion had been laid, and the work of the Lord had begun to go forth in great power. While there would yet be many 'hard places' ahead and much persecution by those who did not understand, The Church of Jesus Christ of Latter-day Saints had come to Britain, and the assurance was already felt that, eventually, truth would prevail.

4

The Call of the Apostles to the British Isles

V. Ben Bloxham

On 8 July 1838, at Far West, Missouri, USA, the word of the Lord came to the Prophet Joseph Smith:

> Verily, thus saith the Lord: Let a conference be held immediately; let the Twelve be organized; and let men be appointed to supply the place of those who are fallen... *And next spring let them depart to go over the great waters, and there promulgate my gospel, the fulness thereof, and bear record of my name... Let them take leave of my saints in the city of Far West, on the twenty-sixth day of April next* [*1839*], *on the building-spot of my house, saith the Lord.* [my italics] (D&C 118:1, 4, 5.)

This revelation, which was one of seven that came to the Prophet Joseph during his seven months in Far West, was a divine commission from the Lord Jesus Christ to his apostles, commanding them to take the gospel to Britain. And considering the detail in which this revelation was given – including the very date and place of the apostles' departure – this was apparently a mission not only of crucial importance but also unlike any Christian proselytizing experience since New Testament times.

With the arrival of President Joseph Smith on 5 March 1838, Far West became the headquarters of the Church until the spring of 1839 – when the saints, threatened with the 'Extermination Order' of Governor Boggs, were finally driven from the state. The Prophet, along with other Church leaders, was betrayed into the hands of his enemies on 31 October 1838 by Col. George M. Hinkle, and illegally imprisoned for six months in the gaol at Liberty, Missouri. In April 1839 his guards permitted Joseph to escape, having realized that there was no legal case against him, and he

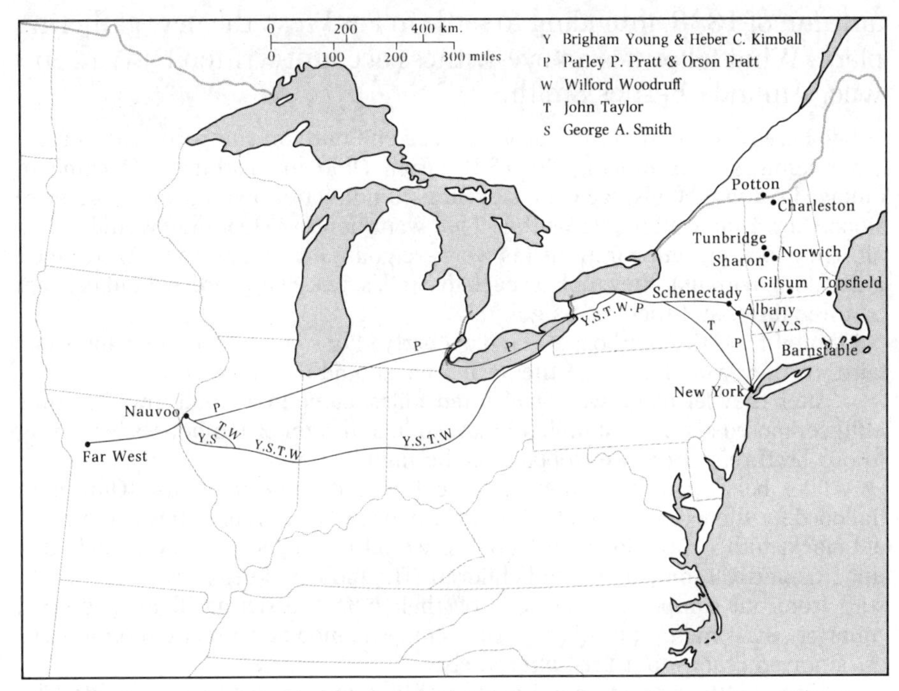

Journeys of the Apostles from Far West, Missouri, to New York City, USA

immediately headed for Missouri's eastern border, the Mississippi River.

After crossing the Mississippi eastward into Illinois, Joseph made his way to the town of Quincy, where his fellow-prisoners, having been released earlier, had sought refuge. (At the time of Joseph's betrayal, Far West had a population of about 2,000 inhabitants, whilst altogether there were about 12,000 LDS men, women and children in Missouri who sought asylum in Illinois during the hard winter of 1838–9.) To appreciate the intense hatred the Missouri mobs had for the saints and the resultant persecution to which they were subjected, one example of the horror of the situation will be sufficient.

Amongst those who attempted to gather to Zion in Missouri at this time was Brother Warren Smith, who had previously moved with his family to Kirtland, Ohio, where he had assisted in the building of the temple there. As persecution became intolerable in Kirtland, he joined the general exodus of saints to Missouri in the autumn of 1838, intending to settle in Far West, the new gathering place. What follows is an eye-witness account written by Warren's wife, Amanda Barnes Smith.

I do hereby certify that my husband, Warren Smith, in company with several other families, was moving [in 1838] from Ohio to Missouri. We came to Caldwell county. Whilst we were traveling, minding our own business, we were stopped by a mob; they told us that if we went another step, they would kill us all. They took our guns from us (as we were going into a new country, we took guns along with us); they took us back five miles, placed a guard around us, kept us three days, and then let us go.

I thought – Is this our boasted land of liberty? For some said we must deny our faith, or they would kill us; others said, we should die at any rate.

...After they let us go we traveled ten miles, came to a small town [Haun's Mill] composed of one grist mill, one saw mill, and eight or ten houses belonging to our brethren; there we stopped for the night.

A little before sunset a mob of three hundred came upon us. [Our] men hallooed for the women and children to run for the woods; and they ran into an old blacksmith's shop, for they feared, if we all ran together, they would rush upon us and kill the women and children. The mob fired before we had time to start from our camp. Our men took off their hats and swung them, and cried 'quarter' [i.e., 'mercy'] until they were shot. The mob paid no attention to their cries nor entreaties, but fired alternately.

I took my little girls, my boy I could not find, and started for the woods. The mob encircled us on all sides but the brook. I ran down the bank, across the mill-pond on a plank, up the hill into the bushes. The bullets whistled around me all the way like hail, and cut down the bushes on all sides of us. One girl was wounded by my side, and fell over a log, and her clothes hung across the log; and they shot at them, expecting they were hitting her; and our people afterwards cut out of that log twenty bullets.

I sat down and witnessed the dreadful scene. When they had done firing, they began to howl, and one would have thought that all the infernals had come from the lower regions. They plundered the principal part of our goods, took our horses and wagons, and ran off howling like demons.

I came down to view the awful sight. Oh horrible! My husband, and one son ten years old, lay lifeless upon the ground, and one son seven years old, wounded very badly. The ground was covered with the dead. These little boys crept under the bellows in the shop; one little boy of ten years had three wounds in him; he lived five weeks and died; he was not mine.

Realize for a moment the scene! It was sunset; nothing but horror and distress; the dogs filled with rage, howling over their dead masters; the cattle caught the scent of the innocent blood, and bellowed; a dozen helpless widows, thirty or forty fatherless children, crying and moaning for the loss of their fathers and husbands; the groans of the wounded and dying were enough to have melted the heart of anything but a Missouri mob. (Joseph Smith, *HC 3*: 323–5.)

Meanwhile, the time had arrived for the apostles to take their departure for England as instructed by the Lord. The brethren had to decide, now that they were free from their oppressors and in safe country, whether to depart for their mission from Illinois and forget about Far West, or risk their lives by returning to a temple site that was now in the hands of their enemies. After all, they had been driven out, and what was left for them in Far West? The faithful members had all been removed; why not just leave from Illinois? Why give the Missouri mobs one more chance to make good their boast that they would murder any Mormon who returned to the temple site?

Although the apostles did not know it, President Joseph Smith had escaped from the Liberty gaol; but as he had not yet arrived in Illinois, they could not get his counsel on the matter. Wilford Woodruff, who had been called to the apostleship along with John E. Page, John Taylor and Willard Richards (in the same revelation that gave instructions for the mission to Britain) but had not yet been ordained, wrote that

> having determined to carry out the requirements of the revelation, on the 18th of April 1839, I took into my wagon Brigham Young and Orson Pratt; Father Cutler took into his wagon John Taylor and George A. Smith [the latter having also been called to the apostleship but not yet ordained], and we started for Far West. On the way we met John E. Page, who was going with his family to Quincy, Illinois. His wagon had turned over, and when we met him he was trying to gather up with his hands a barrel of soft soap. We helped him with his wagon. He then drove into the valley below, left his wagon, and accompanied us on our way. On the night of the 25th of April we arrived at Far West, and spent the night at the home of Morris Phelps. He had been taken a prisoner by the mob, and was still in prison.
>
> On the morning of the 26th of April, 1839, notwithstanding the threats of our enemies that the revelation which was to be fulfilled this day should not be fulfilled; notwithstanding ten thousand of the Saints had been driven out of the state by the edict of the governor; and notwithstanding the Prophet Joseph and his brother Hyrum Smith, with other leading men, were in the hands of our enemies in chains and in prison, we moved on to the Temple grounds in the city of Far West, held a council, and fulfilled the revelation and commandment given to us.
>
> ...There were present of the Twelve Apostles: Brigham Young, Heber C. Kimball, Orson Pratt, John E. Page, and John Taylor; they proceeded to ordain Wilford Woodruff and George A. Smith to the apostleship. (M. Cowley, p. 101.)

Four other apostles not present on this occasion were Orson Hyde, Parley P. Pratt, William Smith and Willard Richards. Orson Hyde and William Smith were both in suspension because of unfaithfulness; Parley Pratt was lying in a gaol at Richmond, Missouri; and Willard Richards was in England and had not yet been ordained. Altogether this accounts for eleven apostles; there was one vacancy (due to the martyrdom of David W. Patten) which was not filled until just before the Quorum returned from England in 1841.

The seven available apostles were back in Quincy, Illinois, by 2 May 1839, ready to settle their families and the Church in a new location so that they could proceed on their way to Britain. They had to move their families to Nauvoo, provide shelter for them, and help the Church itself get situated in the new gathering-place before they could continue with their mission to Britain. Still, within three months of their 'taking leave' in Far West, they were on their way – but not without considerable sacrifice. Poverty and the pressure of time meant that their families would have to be content to subsist on the barest of essentials. The Prophet Joseph assured them, however, that their wives and children would be looked after.

Aside from providing housing, the apostles' greatest problem was coping with a sickness known as 'the ague', a malarial type of infectious disease. It must have seemed to them that if the Missourians didn't get them, the mosquitoes would. This moved President Joseph Smith to take action, as described by Heber C. Kimball:

> July 22nd [1839], the Prophet arose from his bed of sickness, when the power of God rested upon him, and he went forth administering to the sick. He commenced with the sick in his own house, then visited those who were camping in tents in his own door-yard, commanding the sick in the name of the Lord Jesus Christ to arise from their beds and be whole; when they were healed according to his words. He then went from house to house, and from tent to tent, upon the bank of the river, healing the sick by the power of Israel's God, as he went among them.

In spite of these miraculous healings, the obstinate sickness returned intermittently throughout the summer. In fact, five of the apostles were plagued with it right up to the day they arrived in New York City.

The Apostles left Nauvoo (then known as Commerce) in August and September 1839 to commence their mission to the British Isles. Nauvoo had become the headquarters of the Church in May 1839.

Nine apostles participated in the mission to Great Britain: Brigham Young, Heber C. Kimball, Orson Hyde, Parley P. Pratt, Orson Pratt, John Taylor, Wilford Woodruff, George A. Smith and Willard Richards. (The two who did not go, William Smith and John E. Page, eventually fell away from the Church. The twelfth place in the Quorum was vacant at the time.) Elder Richards was already in England, having gone there with Elder Kimball in 1837, and Elder Orson Hyde remained temporarily in Nauvoo.

Not all seven of the apostles who left for England at this time departed from Nauvoo together; rather, as their circumstances permitted they left in pairs or in small groups. The pathetic departure of Elders Young and Kimball was described by the latter as follows:

September 14th, President Young left his home at Montrose [across the river from Nauvoo] to start on the mission to England. He was so sick that he was unable to go to the Mississippi, a distance of thirty rods, without assistance. After he had crossed the river he rode behind Israel Barlow on his horse to my house, where he continued sick until the 18th. He left his wife sick with a babe only three weeks old, and all his other [five] children were sick and unable to wait upon each other. Not one soul of them was able to go to the well for a pail of water, and they were without a second suit to their backs, for the mob in Missouri had taken nearly all he had.

On the 17th, Sister Mary Ann Young [his wife] got a boy to carry her up in his wagon to my house, that she might nurse and comfort Brother Brigham to the hour of starting.

September 18th. Charles Hubbard sent his boy with a wagon and span of horses to my house; our trunks were put into the wagon by some brethren; I went to my bed and shook hands with my wife who was then shaking with a chill, having two children lying sick by her side; I embraced her and my children, and bade them farewell. My only well child was little Heber P. [not yet five years old], and it was with difficulty he could carry a couple of quarts of water at a time, to assist in quenching their thirst.

It was with difficulty that we got into the wagon, and started down the hill about ten rods; it appeared to me as though my very inmost parts would melt within me at leaving my family in such a condition, as it were almost in the arms of death. I felt as though I could not endure it. I asked the teamster to stop, and said to Brother Brigham, 'This is pretty tough, isn't it; let's rise up and give them a cheer.' We arose, and swinging our hats three times over our heads, shouted: 'Hurrah, hurrah for Israel.' Vilate [Heber's wife], hearing the noise, arose from her bed and came to the door. She had a smile on her face. Vilate and Mary Ann Young cried out to us: 'Goodbye, God bless you.' We returned the compliment, and then told the driver to go ahead. After this I felt a spirit of joy and gratitude, having had the satisfaction of seeing my wife standing upon her feet, instead of leaving her in bed, knowing well that I should not see them again for two or three years. (Whitney, *Kimball*, pp. 265–6.)

Although John Taylor was not a victim of the ague when he and Wilford Woodruff left Montrose, his parting was none the less painful. He wrote:

The thought of the hardships they [his wife and three small children] had just endured, the uncertainty of their solitary room – the prevalence of disease, the poverty of the brethren, their insecurity from mobs, together with the uncertainty of what might take place during my absence, produced feelings of no ordinary character. (Roberts, *Taylor*, pp. 67–8.)

And Elder Woodruff described his departure thus:

Early upon the morning of the 8th of August, I arose from my bed of sickness, laid my hands upon the head of my sick wife, Phoebe, and blessed her. I then departed from the embrace of my companion, and left her almost without food or the necessaries of life. She suffered my departure with the fortitude that becomes a saint, realizing the responsibilities of her companion. (M. Cowley, p. 109.)

Elder George A. Smith, the last of the apostles to leave Nauvoo, left under equally discouraging circumstances, described by the Prophet Joseph Smith as follows:

[They] upset their wagon on the bank of the river, before they got out of sight of Commerce. Elders Smith and Turley were so weak they could not get up, and Brother Hedlock had to lift them in again. Soon after, some gentlemen met them and asked who had been robbing the burying-ground – so miserable was their appearance through sickness. (Joseph Smith, *HC* 4:10.)

In almost unjust contrast to these tragic scenes is Elder Parley Pratt's account of his own cheerful departure:

On the 29th of August, 1839, I took leave of my friends in Nauvoo and started for a foreign land. I was accompanied by my wife and three children (having obtained my son Parley from his nurse, Mrs Allen), and Elders Orson Pratt [Parley's brother and fellow apostle] and Hiram Clark. We journeyed in our own private carriage, drawn by two horses....

On all sides, as we turned our eyes, we beheld a boundless field of grass and flowers, with here and there a small grove of timber; the landscape was level or diversified with gentle swells; the surface smooth as a garden; the soil extremely rich; and, although there was not a road marked by art, yet our carriage rolled as smoothly and easily as if it had been on a railway. (P. Pratt, pp. 294–6.)

The apostles of the Lord were now on their separate ways to a common destination: England. The first leg of the journey, from Nauvoo to New York City, would have covered more than a thousand miles – from the Mississippi River to the eastern sea-coast of North America – even if they had kept to a fairly straight course, but most of them, like the Pratt brothers, followed a more winding route that allowed them to stop at the homes of saints along the way, visit members of their own families whom they had not seen for years, and strengthen the branches of the Church in the places they visited. For the most part, the journey was made 'without purse or scrip', meaning that they took very little money and few provisions, trusting in God to look after such details for them.

Elders Young and Kimball, who travelled together for most of the way, discovered upon reaching Kirtland, Ohio, that they had apparently been assisted by an unseen benefactor who had been replenishing Elder Young's supply of money from time to time. Elder Kimball described it thus:

Elders Brigham Young, Heber C. Kimball, John Taylor, and George A. Smith visited Kirtland on their way to New York City in the autumn of 1839. Some of the Apostles preached in the Kirtland Temple in an attempt to revitalize the testimonies of the saints. (*Photo courtesy of Keith W. Perkins.*)

Brother Brigham had one York shilling left, and on looking over our expenses we found that we had paid out over $87.00 out of $13.50 we had at Pleasant Garden [Indiana], which is all the money we had to pay our passages with. We had traveled over 400 miles by stage, for which we paid from 8 to 10 cents a mile, and had eaten three meals a day, for each of which we were charged fifty cents, also fifty cents for our lodgings. Brother Brigham often suspected that I had a purse of money which I had not acquainted him with, but this was not so; the money could only have been put in his trunk by some heavenly messenger, who thus administered to our necessities daily as he knew we needed. (Whitney, *Kimball*, p. 273.)

On the 26th of November these two apostles took passage, as the Pratt brothers had done earlier, on a steamboat that would take them down Lake Erie to Buffalo, New York; and while they were on board a violent storm arose. During the storm, according to the Prophet Joseph Smith, Elder Brigham Young

> went on deck, prayed to the Father in the name of Jesus, when he felt to command the wind and the waves to cease, and permit them to proceed on their journey in safety. The winds abated, and he gave glory, honor, and praise to the God who rules all things. (Joseph Smith, *HC* 4:23.)

Elder George A. Smith continued to suffer severely from the ague, becoming so emaciated from the disease that he was mistaken for an old man while he was staying at an inn at Stockbridge, Massachusetts, with Elder Young. Two other guests in the inn were heard to say:

> 'Do you know that old gentleman who came in on the stage?' the first one asked, referring to George A., then twenty-two.
>
> 'No,' his companion replied. 'Do you know the young man who waits on him?' Brigham was thirty-eight. (Pusey, p. 39.)

When Elders Young and Smith at last arrived in New York City, on 31 January 1840, they found the Pratt brothers and Elder Kimball already there, whilst Elders Taylor and Woodruff were already in England. The apostles' journeys and time in New York City are summarized in Tables 4.1 and 4.2.

When the apostles arrived in Britain, they realized how successful Elder Kimball's first mission had been. They saw that the gospel appealed to the British people, especially the humble, and they knew that the Lord had directed the missionaries to particular places where he had prepared people to receive them. They knew, too, that Satan was there to stir up opposition, and that they would encounter many obstacles. But most of all they knew that the harvest was great and the labourers few.

Next to the restoration of the gospel itself, that first apostolic mission outside North America had been as important to the success of the Church as any experience of the nineteenth century, for in the nine months Elder Kimball and his companions spent in Britain, more than a thousand new members had been baptized, providing a source of strength for the struggling young Church as well as a solid base to build upon in future.

Table 4.1

	Left Nauvoo	Arrived NYC	Days en route
Brigham Young	18 Sep 1839	31 Jan 1840	136
Heber C. Kimball	18 Sep 1839	17 Jan 1840	122
Parley P. Pratt	29 Aug 1839	24 Oct 1839	57
Orson Pratt	29 Aug 1839	13 Nov 1839	77
John Taylor	8 Aug 1839	13 Dec 1839	128
Wilford Woodruff	8 Aug 1839	8 Oct 1839	62
George A. Smith	21 Sep 1839	31 Jan 1840	133

Table 4.2

	Days in NYC	Date sailed	Ship
Brigham Young	37	9 Mar 1840	*Patrick Henry*
Heber C. Kimball	52	9 Mar 1840	*Patrick Henry*
Parley P. Pratt	137	9 Mar 1840	*Patrick Henry*
Orson Pratt	117	9 Mar 1840	*Patrick Henry*
John Taylor	6	19 Dec 1839	*Oxford*
Wilford Woodruff	72	19 Dec 1839	*Oxford*
George A. Smith	37	9 Mar 1840	*Patrick Henry*

During the period between the two apostolic missions, the Church in Britain was under the direction of Joseph Fielding as president, and Willard Richards and William Clayton as first and second counsellors, respectively. It was a time when the presidency not only laboured hard to retain their members and leaders, but also made valiant efforts to continue the growth that had started before Elders Kimball and Hyde returned to the States. Perhaps their most difficult task was to cope with rebellion and disaffection amongst Church members, but a growing tide of persecution also had to be dealt with, as the clergy of other churches felt the loss of their members, and as families became divided. Furthermore, in 1838, at the time of their call, none of the presidency themselves had been members of the Church for more than two years, and so they were required to strengthen one another as well.

President Joseph Fielding was under no illusion that his would be an easy task after Elders Kimball and Hyde had gone. He estimated that there were about a thousand members in twenty branches of the Church when he was appointed president in Britain. (Fielding, p. 19.) Two years later, at a conference in Preston on 15 April 1840, the membership of the Church in Britain was reported as 1,686. (Joseph Smith, *HC* 4:120.) In his journal, President Fielding wrote: 'No doubt we shall have a sifting. There are many in the Church who will not stand, but purity is better than numbers.' (Fielding, p. 20.) With characteristic realism, he also wrote about the effects of persecution:

The Gospel Net gathers some good and some bad; the bad must be cast away. There is chaff among the wheat, but storms arise and will arise and blow away the chaff. Every wind has its use; it both strengthens the good and blows off the bad. (*Ibid.* pp. 25–6.)

One event that soon became a problem to President Fielding was the apostasy of Thomas Webster in Preston. Within a few months of the apostles' departure in 1838, he became dissatisfied with Church leaders and brought suit against them, making accusations that were later proved false.

Webster then held a meeting with six of his followers, during which he administered the sacrament to them even though one had been excommunicated from the Church. This led to his own excommunication. After that, Webster lectured in the Leeming Street Baptist chapel, at the invitation of the Rev. William Giles, 'to expose the mysteries of Mormonism'. Although Webster was unsuccessful in drawing many of the saints away after him, mission leaders had been aware of that danger. (See p. 101.)

The first Church member to die in England created another difficult situation in Preston. Sister Alice Hodgson of Everton Gardens, Preston, was the wife of Miles Hodgson and the daughter of Ann Dawson, the latter two having been among the first nine persons baptized into the Church in England. Before her death, Alice had suffered a long illness. At the request of the family, President Willard Richards administered to her, after which it was her wish to be left in the hands of the Lord, and hence her family dismissed the doctor. When she died, on 2 September 1838, the family accepted her death as the will of the Lord, but the enemies of the Church seized the opportunity to arraign both Elder Richards and Ann Dawson before the mayor's court in Preston, accusing them of 'killing and slaying' Alice with a 'black stick'. President Fielding was present at the hearing and described it as follows:

We have just come from the town hall [Thursday 3 Oct 1838], where we have been to hear Bro. Richards and Sister Ann Dawson, our old housekeeper, answer to a charge of having aided in killing Alice, her daughter, because we took her out of the hands of the doctor, but our enemies were disappointed. This was an attempt to condemn Bro. Richards. This was suffering purely for righteousness' sake. (*Ibid.* p. 38.)

A third difficult situation in the Preston Branch involved President Richards's wife, Jennetta. Jennetta was the daughter of the Rev. John Richards of Walkerfold, and the details of her conversion and baptism have already been related (see pp. 88–91). On the day she was baptized (4 August 1837), Elder Heber C. Kimball had prophesied to Willard Richards that she would become his wife. (Whitney, *Kimball*, pp. 138, 143.) Just over a year later, on 22 September 1838, they were married in the Registry Office at Preston, with Joseph Fielding and his wife Hannah as witnesses.

Elder Richards had been called to the apostleship on 8 July 1838, a month before Jennetta's baptism, but as he was not ordained until Brigham Young and others of the Twelve arrived in England in April 1840, Jennetta unknowingly married an unordained apostle. The Preston Branch did not know of his apostolic calling, either, and the Prophet Joseph later recorded some of the difficulties Elder Richards experienced in Preston:

From the time that Elder Willard Richards was called to the apostleship, in July 1838, the devil seemed to take a great dislike to him, and strove to stir up the minds of many against him. Elder Richards was afflicted with sickness, and several times was brought to the borders of the grave, and many were tempted to believe that he was under transgression, or he would not be thus afflicted. (Joseph Smith, *HC* 3: 276.)

Unfortunately Elder Richards's problems were compounded when he married Jennetta. Although she was deeply committed to the gospel, she apparently had the misfortune of being both well educated and well dressed, which would have set her apart from a group that had been deprived of such advantages, as most of the members in Preston had. She thus became the object of unfair criticism, and the Prophet Joseph's history has this to say about her:

Some were tried and tempted because Elder Richards took to himself a wife; they thought he should have given himself wholly to the ministry, and followed Paul's advice to the letter. Some were tried because his wife wore a veil, and others because she carried a muff to keep herself warm when she walked out in cold weather; and even the President of the Church there [Joseph Fielding] thought she had better done without it; she had nothing ever purchased by the Church; and to gratify their feelings, wore the poorest clothes she had, and they were too good, so hard was it to buffet the storm of feeling that arose from such foolish causes. Sister Richards was very sick for some time, and some were dissatisfied because her husband did not neglect her entirely and go out preaching; and others, that she did not go to meeting when she was not able to go so far.

From such little things arose a spirit of jealousy, tattling, evil speaking, surmising, covetousness, and rebellion, until the Church but too generally harbored more or less of those unpleasant feelings: and [one] evening [9 March 1839] Elder Halsal came out openly in council against Elder Richards, and preferred some heavy charges, none of which he was able to substantiate. Most of the Elders in Preston were against Elder Richards for a season, except James Whitehead, who proved himself true in the hour of trial.

...Sister Richards bore all these trials and persecutions with patience. Elder Richards knew the cause of these unpleasantries, his call [to the apostleship] having been made known to him by revelation; but he told no one of it. (*Ibid.* pp. 276–7.)

Thus, whilst Elder Richards had been spared the persecution and disease that his fellow apostles had endured in America, he was nevertheless tempered by similar trials in England. Though his wife bore him a son, the child died in infancy; as in New Testament times, no one was tried more than the apostles.

A more serious problem that President Fielding had to deal with was the apostasy of Isaac Russell. Unlike Thomas Webster, Brother Russell did take many people with him when he left the Church. One of Elder Parley P. Pratt's Canadian converts, Russell had accompanied Elders Kimball and Hyde to England in 1837, and had been instrumental in establishing branches of the Church at Alston and Brampton.

Isaac Russell had been born in Alston, Cumberland, on 13 April 1807, the last of thirteen children born to William and Isabella Peart Russell. The Russells had emigrated to Canada in 1818 and had settled near Toronto, where they were living when the LDS missionaries found them. Elder Heber C. Kimball later described Isaac Russell's work in Alston as follows:

He met with considerable opposition from his own kindred, as well as from ministers of the different denominations, who sought every opportunity to destroy his influence. Notwithstanding the great opposition, he was instrumental in bringing upwards of sixty souls into the kingdom of God, and left them rejoicing in the truth, under the watch-care of Elder Jacob Peart [his cousin]. (Whitney, *Kimball*, p. 192.)

Upon his return to Kirtland with Elders Kimball and Hyde, Russell removed to Far West, Missouri, when the rest of the saints did. Soon afterwards, however, he lost his faith and became an enemy to the Church, styling himself a prophet. Unfortunately he succeeded in drawing away a following of about thirty people, including his own relations and some fellow Canadian converts. Encouraged by this modest following, Russell next attempted to recruit his English converts to his cause.

Elder Heber C. Kimball, knowing of Russell's apostasy, became concerned about the branches in Cumberland where Russell had laboured. He wrote to President Fielding, asking him to 'go and strengthen them in the name of the Lord, for I think that Russell is leading them astray'. (*Ibid.* p. 246.) President Fielding sent Willard Richards to Alston, and it was fortunate he did, for Russell had in fact sent a letter to his converts there, telling them that the Church in America had gone astray and that he alone remained faithful. President Fielding summarized Elder Richards's experience in Alston as follows:

> It was well indeed that Bro. Richards went over [to Alston]; they were going astray sure enough...Bro. Richards took a copy, or an extract from Bro. Kimball's letter...[and] they were soon convinced of the truth of the matter. (Fielding, p. 37.)

President Joseph Fielding had known Isaac Russell in Canada, before either of them had joined the Church. Like Russell he was an Englishman by birth, having been born 26 March 1797 at Honeydon, Bedfordshire, the fourth son of ten children born to John and Rachel Ibbotson Fielding. Joseph, however, was the first of the Fielding children to be born in Bedfordshire, the first three having been born in Halifax, Yorkshire, before the family had moved to Honeydon. Joseph and two of his sisters, Mary and Mercy, later emigrated to Canada. After joining the Church and returning to England as a missionary, Elder Fielding was set apart as president of the British Mission in April 1838. During his presidency he worked out of Preston, and while there, he was married to Hannah Greenwood, on 11 June 1838. Two children were born to them in Preston, before they emigrated to Nauvoo in October 1841.

President Fielding's two counsellors, Willard Richards and

William Clayton, were able men who, like President Fielding, devoted their full time to the work of the Church. Elder Richards's service and faithfulness were so complete that he was ordained to the apostleship while still in England. Elder Clayton laboured for most of his mission in Manchester, where he built up the Manchester Branch to about 240 members. Having left the British Church in the hands of these three leaders for two years, Elder Heber C. Kimball now returned, with others of the Twelve, for a second apostolic mission in Britain.

On 14 April 1840, the Quorum of the Twelve Apostles assembled in Elder Willard Richards's room at 21 Pole Street in Preston. It was the first time that such a meeting had been held anywhere outside the United States. Brigham Young, as senior apostle, was called to the chair; John Taylor was appointed secretary. After opening with prayer, the brethren ordained Willard Richards to the apostleship, set him apart as a member of the Quorum of the Twelve, and then sustained Brigham Young as 'standing president' of the Quorum. (Woodruff, journal, 28 Apr 1840.)

Those present at the historic meeting were Brigham Young, Heber C. Kimball, Parley P. Pratt, Orson Pratt, John Taylor, Wilford Woodruff, George A. Smith and Willard Richards. (Elder Orson Hyde, having been reinstated to the Quorum, left Nauvoo the day following this meeting in Preston, and would join his brethren in England later.)

The first conference conducted by the Quorum of the Twelve in Britain was held in Preston's Temperance Hall ('the Cockpit') on 15 April 1840. This hall seated about 800 people, and was located near Stoneygate at the bottom of St John's Place and Greystock's Yard, between St John's church and the market-place. It had been built about 1800 by the 12th Earl of Derby as an arena for cock-fighting (hence its nickname) although it had been closed for cock-fighting in 1830 and was thereafter used for more worthy functions. In 1832 it was licensed as a meeting-place for the Preston Temperance Society, with the Earl of Derby forfeiting all rent on their behalf. (Hewitson, p. 226.)

At the 15th of April conference, it was reported that the Church in Britain included 34 branches, 1,677 members, 34 Melchizedek priesthood-holders, and 100 Aaronic priesthood-holders. The branches were in six counties in England (Bedfordshire, Cheshire,

Cumberland, Herefordshire, Lancashire and Staffordshire) and in two counties in Scotland (Lanarkshire and Renfrewshire). Further business of the conference included: the appointment of Elder Hiram Clark as a counsellor to President Joseph Fielding of the British Mission (replacing Elder Willard Richards, who was now an apostle); the establishment of a Church periodical (the *Millennial Star*); and a discussion of the importance of ordaining a patriarch in Britain.

The next day, the 16th of April, the Twelve again met in council and, among other matters of Church business, appointed Parley P. Pratt editor of the *Millennial Star*; assigned Brigham Young, Heber C. Kimball and Parley P. Pratt to obtain a British copyright for the publication of the Doctrine and Covenants and the Book of Mormon; and approved the name of Peter Melling to be ordained patriarch. Peter Melling was thus the first man outside the United States to be ordained a patriarch in this dispensation. He was a native of Preston, and was at that time 53 years of age. Elder Brigham Young ordained him to his new office on 17 April 1840. (E. Watson, p. 72.)

In a letter to Church headquarters in Nauvoo, Heber C. Kimball reported these meetings and stated:

> There have been about eight or nine hundred persons baptized since [Elders Kimball and Hyde] left. The gospel is spreading, the devils are roaring. As nigh as I can learn, the priests are howling, the tares are binding up, the wheat is gathering, nations are trembling, and kingdoms tottering; 'men's hearts failing them for fear, and for looking for those things that are coming on the earth.' The poor among men are rejoicing in the Lord, and the meek do increase their joy. The hearts of the wicked do wax worse and worse, deceiving and being deceived. (Joseph Smith, *HC* 4:115.)

Following these historic meetings, the Twelve separated to their various places of labour, according to the inspiration of the Lord: Brigham Young, Willard Richards and Wilford Woodruff to Herefordshire; Heber C. Kimball to the branches he had established two years before near Preston; Parley P. Pratt to Manchester; Orson Pratt to Scotland; John Taylor to Liverpool; and George A. Smith to the Staffordshire Potteries. (R. Evans, p. 128.)

5

The Apostolic Foundations, 1840–1841

V. Ben Bloxham

Elder John Taylor was probably the first Latter-day Saint to write to England about the restoration of the gospel. He did so at the request of Joseph Fielding who, like himself, was an Englishman by birth, having emigrated to Upper Canada and accepted the gospel there through the efforts of Elder Parley P. Pratt. (Roberts, *Taylor*, p. 46.)

Now, after an absence of several years, Elder Taylor stood on familiar ground in Liverpool. He had lived there twice in his 31 years, first when his father was a collector of excise there (1814–19) and again when he himself spent one year (1822) apprenticed to a cooper.

Elder Taylor, with his companions, Wilford Woodruff and Theodore Turley (an elder who had been called to serve a mission in Britain and who had travelled with the two apostles), arrived at Liverpool on 11 January 1840. Two days later they went by rail to Preston to meet Elder Taylor's old friend, Joseph Fielding, who was serving as president of the British Mission. Elder Woodruff later recorded that 'we truly rejoiced to have an interview with President Fielding'. (Woodruff, journal, 16 Jan 1840.)

On Friday the 17th of January a council was held at the home of Elder Willard Richards, where it was decided that Elder Taylor and President Fielding should go to Liverpool to open that city for the preaching of the gospel, while Elders Woodruff, Turley and Hiram Clark were to go to the Staffordshire Potteries area, and once there, enquire of the Lord as to opening the work in Bir-

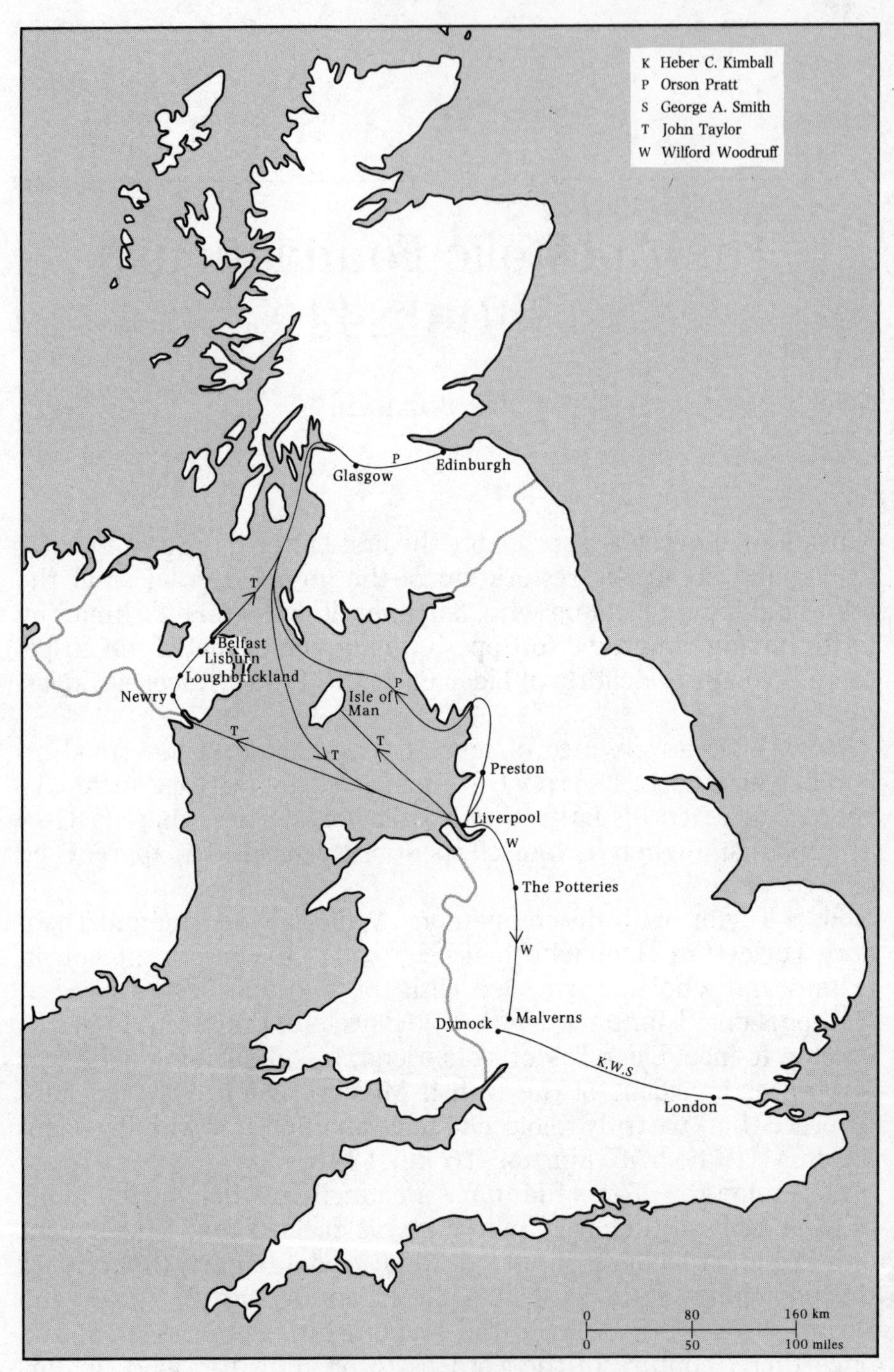

Journeys of the Apostles in the British Isles, 1840–1

mingham. Elder Richards was to proceed as the spirit directed him.

Elder Woodruff and his companions were the first to depart, taking a train to Manchester on the 18th of January. Elders Taylor and Fielding set out for Liverpool soon after, and had a day that was filled with unusual experiences. President Fielding wrote:

> On the 22[nd of January 1840] Elder Taylor and I left Preston to go to Liverpool; stopped at Tarleton that night. Brother T[aylor] preached in the eve[ning] at Bro. Wm. Blackhurst's to a house full of attentive hearers, [and] some persecutors. We sat a while after the meeting with Bro. B[lackhurst] and family. Bro. T[aylor] spoke in tongues. We returned to Deacon Rawcliff's (LDS) to sleep; we felt well. Bro. T[aylor] prophesied, first in tongues and then by interpretation, [and then gave] a blessing [to] me; something like this: 'Bro. Fielding, thou has been faithful in thy office and the Lord has seen thy diligence and hath blessed thee, and He will bless thee more and more. He shall pour His spirit upon thee in a manner that thou has not thought of, nor has it entered into thy heart. Thou shalt lift up thy voice to multitudes in the East and in the West, in the North and in the South, and thou shalt bring many to Zion' – and much more in the same strain, which caused me to rejoice even unto tears and I feel to praise the name of the Lord. (Fielding, p. 50.)

Arriving in Liverpool the next day, Elder Taylor paid a visit to his brother-in-law, George Cannon, where he was invited to spend the night, while Elder Fielding lodged at a tavern. This was the unheralded beginning of the work in Liverpool. It began, as it often has, with an acquaintance, a friend, a referral. In this case it was a brother-in-law, reinforced by a letter of introduction from Mr Cannon's sister, Leonora Taylor.

On their first Sunday in Liverpool (26 January 1840), Elders Taylor and Fielding attended services at an Aitkenite chapel on Hope Street, where the Rev. Timothy R. Matthews was pastor. Mr Matthews was married to President Fielding's sister Ann, and was one of the men to whom John Taylor had originally written from Canada at Joseph Fielding's request. He had therefore been introduced to the restored gospel during the first mission to England, when Willard Richards and John Goodson had laboured in Bedford in the summer of 1837. For a while it appeared that both Timothy and Ann would join the Church, as he opened his chapel in Bedford to them and even announced his own imminent baptism to his congregation. At the last minute, however, his heart was changed, and thereafter the Rev. Timothy Matthews became an active enemy of the Church, although he adopted some LDS practices in his own congregation, such as baptism by immersion. (R. Evans, pp. 39–40, 97; see also pp. 84–5 herein.)

Knowing all this, the two elders went to the Aitkenite chapel, not with any illusions of converting Mr Matthews, but because, as Elder Fielding said:

Here were some honest souls who had been baptized by Mr Matthews, in the sincerity of their heart[s]. I felt to love them and to sing with them as Saints, believing many of them would be [Saints], and would tell us at some time how they felt at seeing us. (Fielding, p. 51.)

The Rev. Timothy Matthews was not at the meeting, but a sincere and spirited young assistant preached on the deplorable state of the church, its lack of spirituality and its tendency towards worldliness, and prayed for the gifts of the spirit and for the millennial reign. This was just the opening that Elder Taylor was praying for. When he arose and asked for the privilege of addressing the congregation, he was courteously denied permission (so as not to displease their pastor), but was invited to meet eighteen of their leading men in the vestry. Elders Taylor and Fielding therefore retired to the vestry with the others, and Elder Taylor addressed them as follows:

Gentlemen, friends and brethren: I have listened with deep interest to the things that I have heard this morning. I have observed with peculiar emotions the deep anxiety, the fervent prayer and the strong solicitude manifested by you in relation to obtaining the Holy Ghost. I have been pleased with the correct views you entertain in regard to the situation of the world. We believe in those things as you do. We hear that you believe in baptism and the laying on of hands, so also do we. Brethren and friends, we are the humble followers of Jesus Christ and are from America. I lately arrived in this place, and have come five thousand miles without purse or scrip, and I testify to you, my brethren, that the Lord has revealed Himself from heaven and put us in possession of these things you are so anxiously looking for and praying that you may receive. ('Glory be to God', was shouted by many present, and great emotion manifested.)

That thing has taken place which is spoken of by John in the Revelation, where he says: 'I saw another angel fly in the midst of heaven, having the everlasting gospel to preach unto them that dwell upon the earth, and to every nation and kindred and tongue and people, saying with a loud voice, Fear God and give glory to him, for the hour of his judgment is come.' Brethren, we the servants of God are come to this place to warn the inhabitants of their approaching danger, and to call upon them to repent and be baptized in the name of Jesus Christ, and they shall receive the gift of the Holy Ghost.

I feel an anxious desire to deliver this testimony. I feel the word of the Lord like fire in my bones and am desirous to have an opportunity of proclaiming to you those blessings that you are looking for, that you may rejoice with us in those glorious things which God has revealed for the salvation of the world in the last days. (Roberts, *Taylor*, pp. 77–8.)

His listeners were divided in their reaction to Elder Taylor's impassioned address, some weeping for joy, others accusing him and his companion of being 'Mormons'. To this, the apostle replied, 'No, we belong to the Church of Jesus Christ of Latter-day Saints, called by our enemies the "Mormon Church".' (*Ibid.* p. 78.) His detractors then 'said their pastor, Mr Matthews, said he had examined their book [the Book of Mormon], etc., [and] was satisfied that it was of the devil'. (Fielding, p. 51.)

That evening they returned to the Aitkenite congregation on Hope Street, bearing in mind Elder Taylor's prophecy that 'there are many who will become Saints among them, but they, like others, are sadly under the influence of priests'. (Roberts, *Taylor*, p. 79.) Elder Fielding described their experience as follows:

In the evening we went again to Mr Aitkin's meeting; sat in the same place as in the morn[ing]. A Mr Story preached. At the end of the meeting, sinners were invited into the vestry; but while this was going on, one of the leaders came to us and invited us home to his house. At this, his friends looked troubled, but we went with him. His name is Mitchell. We soon entered into conversation; we saw him to be an honest man. We talked with him and his wife till midnight; [we] slept there. He was well satisfied; this was just what we [had] hoped for, that the Lord [would] open the heart of one or two to converse with us. (Fielding, pp. 51–2.)

The Mitchells were baptized soon afterwards, being two of the first ten converts to the Church in Liverpool.

The next Sunday, the 2nd of February, the two elders had booked a large hall on Preston Street that had a seating capacity of over four hundred. Here Elder Taylor gave the first LDS public discourse in Liverpool to a crowd of about 300, taking his text from Jude 3: 'It was needful for me to...exhort you that ye should earnestly contend for the faith which was once delivered unto the saints.' He then gave credit to the Protestant reformers, beginning with Martin Luther, for laying essential groundwork for the restoration of the gospel of Jesus Christ in the last days, and proceeded to announce that restoration to the congregation. (Roberts, *Taylor*,

p. 79.) In a letter to President Joseph Smith, Elder Taylor reported the following:

Our being in town soon got rumored about and I suppose about 300 attended our first meeting; in preaching, the power of God rested upon the people, and on my asking them if it was not good news they shouted 'yes' – while many wept under the influence of the spirit; after preaching, ten persons came forward to be baptized, some of which felt convinced as soon as they saw us that we were men of God, and others had dreamed about us. Thus we see that the power was of God and not of man and to Him be the Glory. (*TS 2*:13, p. 401.)

In a letter to his wife soon afterwards, Elder Taylor further reported their progress:

As regards the situation of things here, they are still progressing: I told you about our coming to Liverpool; the first time I preached, ten came forward, [and] we have been baptizing since; last week we baptized nine: we are to baptize tomorrow; how many I know not. The little stone is rolling forth; one of the brethren dreamed he saw two men come to Liverpool, they cast a net into the sea and pulled it out full of fishes, he was surprised to see them pick the small fish out first and then the large; well, if we get all the fish I shall be satisfied. (*TS 1*:7, p. 110.)

Thus the work in Liverpool had begun. The new converts, according to Elder Fielding, were thoughtful for the welfare of the missionaries and took care to see to their needs. He wrote:

We want for nothing temporal. Sister Arrington in particular has been [generous], always even when most others were cast down, almost like the disciples at the time our Lord was betrayed, she still stood by us, believed our words, gave us money in time of need and fed us liberally at all times. Her sister, Mary Dixon, is of the same stamp. (Fielding, p. 68.)

During this time Elders Taylor and Fielding stayed at the home of George Cannon, who was also soon numbered amongst their converts, as was his wife. Brother Cannon read the Book of Mormon twice before his Baptism, concluding that 'no wicked man could write such a book as this; and no good man would write it, unless it were true and he were commanded of God to do so'. (Fielding, p. 54; R. Evans, p. 101.)

Elder Taylor continued to preach in the Preston Street hall every Sunday until the last day of March, when he moved to a hall on Renshaw Street that was closer to the town centre. (Fielding, pp. 64, 68.) Within a few days, however, his work was interrupted by the arrival of the rest of the Twelve, who came into Liverpool on 6 April 1840. Elder Taylor went to Preston to meet his brethren, Elders Brigham Young, Heber C. Kimball, Parley and Orson Pratt, and George A. Smith. (Elder Reuben Hedlock had accompanied them from New York on the *Patrick Henry*.) (Fielding, p. 70.) At the conclusion of the Preston conference, it was decided that Elder Taylor should return to Liverpool and continue his labours there. (Roberts, *Taylor*, p. 83; Joseph Smith, *HC* 4:120; R. Evans, p. 128.)

Thus from the 20th of April to the 26th of May, Elder Taylor continued to preach in Liverpool. During this time he conferred the Aaronic and Melchizedek priesthood upon some brethren he had chosen to assist him in his labours. These men were particularly helpful in advertising his lectures at the Renshaw Street hall. On the 26th of May Elder Taylor travelled to Manchester to assist Brigham Young and Parley P. Pratt in the selection of hymns for a hymn-book to be published in Britain; he remained there four days, then returned to Liverpool with Elders Young and Kimball. All three preached in Liverpool the next day, Sunday the 31st of May, and on the 3rd of June Elders Young and Taylor visited printers.

On the 27th of July, Elder Taylor took the gospel to Ireland and Scotland, where he remained for about a fortnight. Before his departure, however, he hired the Music Hall in Liverpool for twelve months for the purpose of giving public lectures on the doctrines and history of the Church. These lectures also included the main events of religious history, from the fall of Adam to the atonement of Christ, then through the apostasy to the restoration. Elder Taylor also addressed such topics as the essential authority of the priesthood; the ordinances necessary to salvation; the visitations of God and angels in the last days; the Book of Mormon; the gathering of Israel; and the final redemption of the earth.

These lectures were well attended, and the subjects he addressed soon became topics for popular religious discussions. (Roberts, *Taylor*, p. 88.) In a letter to the Prophet Joseph, Elder Taylor reported:

> We have the largest Hall in this place, and men of respectability and influence begin to look at [the gospel]; it has for some time been almost exclusively confined to the lowest grade of society, particularly in the manufactory districts,

but I think the time is not far distant when the trumpet will sound loudly through all parts of this land and all classes will hear it. (*TS 2*, 13:402.)

The Music Hall on Bold Street, Liverpool, made of plain brick with a portico, is one of the few buildings from this period of Church history that is still standing today.

Elder Taylor laboured diligently to enlighten the local clergy about the restoration, but none were interested, although in some cases he did make a favourable impression. For example, one aged Methodist minister, upon being told about the restoration and rejecting it, asked whether Elder Taylor intended calling upon all the ministers in Liverpool. He replied that he did, and furthermore, he intended asking them for permission to preach in their chapels. Upon hearing this the old gentleman said he doubted very much that any Methodist ministers would permit him to preach from their pulpits, and suggested that

he would probably have to do as the venerable founder of Methodism had done – go into the highways and the fields.

'But when Paul, the despised Christian, went into the synagogues of the Jews, bigoted and fallen as they were,' replied the Elder, 'they said to him and his companions, "Brethren, if ye have a word of exhortation for the people, say on."'

'That is what I say,' answered the Methodist, 'say on.'

'Yes,' replied Elder Taylor, 'but this is not in your synagogue, sir.'

To this gentle hint he could only say that he thought the trustees would not consent to it. In parting, he shook the Elder by the hand and wished him God-speed. (Roberts, *Taylor*, pp. 80–1.)

Elder Taylor thus summarized his attempts to win the clergy to the restored Church:

We called upon many of the leading ministers of different denominations, and delivered our testimony to them; some received us kindly, some otherwise, but none would let us have their chapels to hold forth in; they were so good in general, and so pure, that they had no room for the gospel; they were too holy to be righteous, too good to be pure, and had too much religion to enter into the kingdom of heaven. (*TS 2*, 13:401.)

Feeling satisfied that the work in Liverpool was progressing well, and since the local elders were actively engaged in building up the Church there, Elder Taylor decided that the time had come to take the gospel to the Isle of Man, to the people called Manx. He therefore left for Douglas on 16 September 1840, accompanied by Elder Hiram Clark and Brother William Mitchell. (Roberts, *Taylor*, p. 89.)

On about the 18th of September Elder Clark and Brother Mitchell went to Ramsey, a small town some fifteen miles north of Douglas. Elder Taylor went part of the way with them, when they stopped at a secluded spot to pray.

The burden of that prayer was that an effectual door might be opened to them in that island for the proclamation of the gospel; that gainsayers might be put to shame, and that the word might be confirmed by signs following the believers. After prayer they each sought a stone and placed it at the foot of a tree, on which Elder Taylor carved their names and the date of their being there. He also ordained Brother Mitchell a Deacon; and at the request of Elder Clark he also laid hands upon his head that he might have the gift of tongues and the interpretation thereof; and afterwards Elder Clark blessed Elder Taylor. For some time they spoke in tongues, sang, prophesied, and finally separated to their respective fields of labor, each to thrust in his sickle and reap. (Roberts, *Taylor*, pp. 90–1.)

Returning to Douglas, Elder Taylor arranged to stay in the home of a Jewish family, Solomon and Ann Pitchforth. He also made arrangements to use the Wellington Rooms for a series of public lectures. His lectures there were favourably received, and as a result some of the local clergy accused him of teaching false doctrine. In particular, a Rev. Thomas Hamilton challenged Elder Taylor to a public debate, a challenge that Elder Taylor accepted. The outcome was disastrous to Hamilton, but Elder Taylor was not impressed, 'as he was a very ignorant man'. (*Ibid.* p. 93.) In a letter to President Joseph Smith, dated 3 February 1841, Elder Taylor explained how he responded to his critics in Douglas:

I held a discussion with one man, a preacher, which had a tendency to enlighten the eyes of the public. Another wrote in the papers, and I answered him; another published pamphlets, and I answered them; another delivered lectures and I answered them; and finally [I] challenged any of them to meet me before the public and prove the Book of Mormon and my doctrine false if they could, but this they were afraid to do and gave up the contest. I see, sir, more clearly every day the impossibility of overturning the principles of truth by any of the foolish dogmas or lame reasoning of this present generation, and how should they? for God has revealed it, and His arm supports it. (*TS* 2, 13:401–2.)

Of his labours outside Douglas, Elder Taylor reported:

I went to a country place on the Island and sat down in the chimney corner, and talked to a few neighbors who came in, and baptized eight and confirmed them the same night, before I left them, nor would they wait until morning. (*Ibid.* p. 402.)

It is possible that the 'country place' he referred to was the farm-house of Charles Cowley near the village of Kirk German, where he baptized at least two couples – Charles and Ann Cowley, and John and Catherine Quayle – in October 1840. According to Charles's account, he had 'been seeking and praying for correct information concerning the Will of God' for many years when:

One night, Ann Killip Cowley [Charles's wife] dreamed that an American minister was preaching the gospel and singing the song 'Come to the Supper'. When morning came, she could still remember this song, and all the next day she'd find herself humming the tune.

Not long after that, they read in the newspaper about a 'minister' from America who was in Douglas...preaching a strange gospel. John Quayle, a brother-in-law of Ann's and a cousin to Charles, went to Douglas to hear this 'minister' preach. The 'minister', as they called him, was Elder John Taylor, who later became President of the Church...Quayle was so impressed with his teachings that he brought him back to the home of Charles Cowley...

[That evening] Elder Taylor opened [a cottage meeting at the Cowley home] with the song 'Come to the Supper', the same tune Ann Cowley had heard in her dream. She sang along with him, although her only guide was the memory of her dream. After the meeting, Elder Taylor answered many questions and they became convinced that he taught the gospel of Jesus Christ, restored with all its gifts and blessings...Both couples were baptized the following day and confirmed members of the church that evening, after which they held another meeting, where they all bore their testimonies – Ann in tongues while Brother Taylor interpreted it. (C. Cowley.)

In summarizing his mission to the Isle of Man, Elder Taylor wrote:

I would just remark that the truth came off victorious in the Isle of Man, and although I may say with Paul that 'I have fought with beasts at Ephesus', yet I feel thankful to my Heavenly Father that I have escaped unhurt. The standard of eternal truth is planted there, many are rejoicing in the liberty of the gospel of Jesus Christ...and many more are believing and on the eve of coming forth...There have been seventy baptized in all; thus in spite of all the combined powers of earth and hell, the 'Truth will prevail'. (*MS 1*: 53.)

By Christmas Day 1840 there were about forty members in Douglas, when a branch was organized there, and by February 1841 the branch had grown to seventy. Amongst the faithful Manx families represented in the Church today are the Cowleys,

Wilford Woodruff, who laboured in the Staffordshire Potteries, the Herefordshire area, and London

Cannons, Callisters and Quayles. Elder Taylor returned to Liverpool in December 1840, where he continued to labour until the end of his mission.

While Elder Taylor had been labouring in Liverpool and the Isle of Man, Elder Wilford Woodruff, with Theodore Turley and Hiram Clark, had gone to the Staffordshire Potteries area. They had left Preston by train on 18 January 1840, and after spending a few days in Manchester with William Clayton and the saints there, arrived in Burslem on the 21st of January. Here, according to Elder Woodruff, they:

> found a church of Latter-day Saints in these potteries of about 60 members, under the care of Elder Alfred Cordon, a potter by trade, who labored 6 days in a week for his daily bread, and preached 5 evenings in a week, and 3 times on the Sabbath. (*TS 2*, 3:314.)

The next day they visited the town of Hanley and, because of its location in the centre of the Potteries area, chose it as their headquarters. That day Elder Woodruff met the Benbow family for the first time.

William Benbow was a grocer in Hanley, and lived at Hanley market-place with his wife Ann and their six children. Elder Woodruff recorded that they 'sup'd at Brother William Benbow's', and though 'Brother Benbow was not at home...we were much pleased with his Lady, Sister Ann Benbow. She was strong in [the] faith and manifested much interest at our arrival [in] England from America'. (Woodruff, journal, 22 Jan 1840.) The Benbows had been baptized less than three weeks before Elder Woodruff met them, and were the first of the Benbows to join the Church. (Cordon, 4 Jan 1840.)

In the next forty days in the Potteries area, forty converts were added to the Church and many more were showing interest. It seemed to Elder Woodruff that he was going to enjoy a fruitful harvest there and he fully expected to remain there for some time, preaching every night of the week and two or three times on Sundays. He sent Elder Turley on to Birmingham, it being his birthplace and the home of many of his relations.

On Sunday the 1st of March, Elder Woodruff preached twice to large congregations in the Hanley City Hall, and administered the sacrament to the saints. He met them again that evening, and:

while singing the first hymn the spirit of the Lord rested upon me and the voice of God said to me, 'This is the last meeting that you will hold with this people for many days.' I was astonished at this, as I had many appointments out in that district. When I arose to speak to the people, I told them that it was the last meeting I should hold with them for many days. They were as much astonished as I was. At the close of the meeting four persons came forward for baptism; we went down into the water and baptized them. (M. Cowley, p. 116.)

The next day Elder Turley returned from Birmingham, and Elder Woodruff later wrote:

Elder Turley returned to the Potteries from Birmingham, wishing me to go there to erect the standard, as it was his native place, and he thought I should do better there than himself; he had preached a few times in public this side of Birmingham, but not in Birmingham. (British Mission History, 11 Mar 1840.)

Not knowing whether he should in fact go to Birmingham, or stay in the Potteries area, or whether there was yet another place where he should labour, the apostle went in secret to the Lord. 'The answer I received', he said, 'was that I should go to the south; for the Lord had a great work for me to perform there, as many souls were waiting for His word.' (*Ibid.*)

Elder Woodruff had spent thirteen nights in the home of William and Ann Benbow during the past forty-five days, and therefore would probably have become acquainted with William's connections in Herefordshire. In fact, after the Lord instructed Elder Woodruff to go 'south', the apostle said he

conversed with brother William Benbow upon this subject, who had lived in Herefordshire and had friends still residing there, and much wished me to visit that region of country, and generously proffered to accompany me to his brother's house and pay my fare, which I readily accepted. (*TS 2*, 9:327.)

Thus on Tuesday 3 March 1840, Wilford Woodruff set out for Herefordshire with William Benbow and his eight-year-old son. They travelled the last fourteen miles on foot, and arrived at the home of John Benbow in the evening of the 4th of March. Elder Woodruff described this momentous occasion as follows:

I found Mr Benbow to be a wealthy farmer, cultivating three hundred acres of land, occupying a good mansion, and having plenty of means. His wife, Jane, had no children. I presented myself to him as a missionary from America, an elder of the Church of Jesus Christ of Latter-day Saints, who had been sent to him by the commandment of God as a messenger of salvation, to preach the gospel of

John Benbow occupied this house from 1832 to 1840. Wilford Woodruff gave the first gospel sermon in the South-west of England here on 5 March 1840. (*Courtesy of W. Dee Halverson.*)

life to him and to his household and the inhabitants of the land. He and his wife received me with glad hearts and thanksgiving...[and] after receiving refreshments we sat down together, and conversed until two o'clock in the morning. Mr Benbow and his wife rejoiced greatly at the glad tidings which I brought to them. (M. Cowley, pp. 116–17.)

Elder Woodruff's statement that John Benbow was 'a wealthy farmer' was a fairly accurate assessment of his social status. Though he had, through his own industry, arrived at a position of 'occupying a good mansion, and having plenty of means', he was not independently wealthy, nor was he of the gentry. He styled himself a yeoman, as did his friend Thomas Kington, whom Elder Woodruff was soon to meet.

Regarding his first few days at the Benbow farm, the apostle wrote:

Mr John Benbow kindly entertained me for the night, during which time I spent several hours in laying before him an account of the origin, rise, and progress of the Church of Jesus Christ of Latter-day Saints, and like good old Cornelius the Spirit of God was upon him, and he received my testimony with all his heart. (*TS 2*:9, p. 327.)

Not only did the Benbows rejoice in the news of the gospel, but Elder Woodruff also

rejoiced greatly at the news that Mr Benbow gave me, that there was a company of men and women – over six hundred in number – who had broken off from the Wesleyan Methodists, and taken the name of United Brethren...

[Benbow also said that the Brethren had been] searching for light and truth, but had gone as far as they could, and were continually calling upon the Lord to open the way before them, and send them light and knowledge that they might know the true way to be saved.

When I heard these things, I could clearly see why the Lord had commanded me, while in the town of Hanley, to leave that place of labor and go to the south, for in Herefordshire there was a great harvest-field for gathering many Saints into the Kingdom of God. (Woodruff, *Leaves*, p. 79.)

The next day, 5 March 1840, Elder Woodruff told Mr Benbow he would like to preach the gospel to the people, and the latter offered 'a large hall in his mansion' and then advertised Elder Woodruff's lecture for that evening. 'As the time drew nigh', the apostle wrote, 'many of the neighbors came in, and I preached my first gospel sermon [in Herefordshire] in the house.' (*Ibid.*)

He preached again the next night in the same place, and afterwards baptized six people, including John and Jane Benbow, and four preachers of the United Brethren. (Woodruff, baptismal record.)

The next Sunday, Elder Woodruff preached at Froome's Hill in the morning, at Stanley Hill in the afternoon, and at the Benbow home in the evening. Whilst he was working hard to preach to as many as a thousand people during the day, the rector of the local parish had 'only fifteen' persons in attendance at his service. That evening, as Elder Woodruff arose to speak to a packed house,

A man entered the door and informed me that he was a constable, and had been sent by the rector of the parish with a warrant to arrest me.

I asked him, 'For what crime?'

I told him that I, as well as the rector, had a licence for preaching the gospel to the people, and that if he would take a chair I would wait upon him after [the] meeting.

> He took my chair and sat beside me.
>
> I preached the first principles of the everlasting gospel for an hour and a quarter. The power of God rested upon me, the Spirit filled the house, and the people were convinced.
>
> At the close of the meeting I opened a door for baptism, and seven offered themselves. Among the number were four preachers and the constable.
>
> The latter arose and said, 'Mr Woodruff, I would like to be baptized.'
>
> I told him I would like to baptize him. I went down to the pool [on the Benbow farm] and baptized the seven. (Woodruff, *Leaves*, p. 80.)

Afterwards, the constable told Elder Woodruff that he had gone to the rector and 'told him if he wanted Mr Woodruff taken up for preaching the gospel, he must go himself and serve the writ, for he had heard him preach the only true gospel sermon he had ever listened to in his life'. (*Ibid.*)

The rector next sent two of his clerks 'as spies' to one of Elder Woodruff's lectures, but they also believed and were baptized. After that, according to Elder Woodruff, 'the rector became alarmed and did not dare to send anybody else'. (*Ibid.* p. 81.)

On the 9th of March Elder Woodruff baptized twelve more members of the Benbow family, as well as five of Jane Benbow's cousins by the name of Homes. Shortly thereafter, William Benbow took his leave, with his young son (who had also been baptized), to return to Hanley. Their parting was a sorrowful one, for within the month, William and his family would be emigrating to Nauvoo. Elder Woodruff said, 'He left with a bowed head. It was a dark day to us both. The waves of sorrow rolled on our souls.' (*TS* 2, 9: 328.) But William Benbow left Herefordshire having seen a latter-day apostle baptize 32 people in five days, many of whom were his own relations.

On the 15th of March Elder Woodruff requested an interview with the leader of the United Brethren, Mr Thomas Kington. This was granted, and Mr Kington listened to Elder Woodruff as he 'laid the whole work of the fulness of the gospel before him'. (Woodruff, journal, 17 Mar 1840.) He was 'an humble man of God', the apostle observed, and 'heard my sayings and testimony with candor... We parted with good feelings and he made it a matter of prayer.' (*TS* 2, 9: 328.)

Four days later, on 21 March 1840, Thomas Kington and his wife were baptized, with two others. Elder Woodruff wrote in his

Wilford Woodruff baptized sixty-five members of the United Brethren in this pool, including John and Jane Benbow and Thomas and Hannah Kington, March 1840. (*Courtesy of W. Dee Halverson.*)

journal: 'Glory Hallaluyah [*sic*], the work of God rolls on.' (Woodruff, journal, 21 Mar 1840.) Within eighteen days of his arrival in Herefordshire, Elder Woodruff had baptized the two most influential members of the United Brethren, John Benbow and Thomas Kington, as well as fifteen of their preachers.

With the conversion of Benbow and Kington, Elder Woodruff was able, with their help, to bring all but one of the United Brethren into the Church, as well as many others who were not officially members of the group. Of the fifty preachers listed on the United Brethren's Preachers' Plan for March 1840, Wilford Woodruff himself baptized forty. In the time he spent in Herefordshire, he baptized 301 people. (Woodruff, baptismal record.)

The conversion of all the United Brethren preachers introduced Elder Woodruff to a remarkable plan for preaching the restored gospel. From Benbow and Kington he learned of their Preachers' Plan, a printed schedule of their meetings for the next three months for all their congregations throughout Herefordshire,

UNITED BRETHREN PREACHERS' PLAN
OF THE FROOMS HILL CIRCUIT, 1840

BEST OF ALL, GOD IS WITH US.

But the Lord said unto me, Say not, I am a child: for thou shalt go to all I shall send thee, and whatsoever I command thee thou shalt speak.

Be not afraid of their faces: for I am with thee to deliver thee.—JEREMIAH i. 7, 8.

LORD'S DAY PLAN

PLACES AND TIME		APRIL			MAY					JUNE				JULY
		12	19	26	3	10	17	24	31	7	14	21	28	5
Frooms Hill	10	3 s	9	20	38	‡ P	1 C	11	18	6	5	4	30	16
Hill	2	3	9	20	38 P	‡ C	1	11	18	6	6	7	36	5
M Stanley Hill	10 and 6	1 P	3 C	5	9	20	34	23	38	33	11	6	4	7
Ridgeway Cross	10	10	24 P	12 C	3 S	38	13 P	1 T	28	22	14	19	6	2
M Greenyeal	2	10	31	12 P	3 C	38	20	1	28	13	14	19	6	2
M Moorend Cross	6	8	13	26	12	3 S	28	26	33	17	21	15	19	14
Coldwall	10	15 P	8 C	21	24	12	3 S	20	32	28	33	2	38	1
M Pale House	2	15	8	21	31 P	12 C	3	20	32	28	33	2	38	1
M Ledbury	2 and 6	16 P	15 C	8	26	21	9	3 S	25	2	22	17	23	24–31
M Malvern Hill	6	19	16	15	28	8 P	21 C	12	3 S	38	1	28	18	17
Keysend Street	10	18	21 P	1 C	15	16	8	2	12	3 S	32	38	28	6
M Wind Point	2	18	21 P	1 C	15	16	8	2	12	3	32	38	28	6
M Woferwood	2	4	10	19	27	26	16 P	33 C	19	20	12	10	34	15
M Hope Rough	2	7	14	10	30–36P	5 C	24	16	34	26	29–35		37	27
Rough Leasowe	2	22	4	33	14 P	18 C	33	27	1	16	20	12	‡	3
Dunns Close	6	22 P	7 C	33	14	18	33	27	1	16	20	12	‡	3 S
M Ashfield	10	6	22 P	4 C	19	10	14	15	21	‡	3 S	16	20	12
Crowcutt	2	6	22 P	7 C	19	10	14	15	21	‡	3	16	20	12
Old Starridge	10	28 P	1 C	6	22	4	19	18	10	14	27	21	16	20
M Birchwood	2	28	1 P	6 C	22	7	19	18	10	14	27	21	16	20
M Alfrick	2	12	15	28	33 P	6 C	22	19	26	17	7	14	1	33
M Shucknell Hill	10	17	2	29 P	1 C	23	4	24	8	35	30	32	3 S	36
M Lugwardine	6	17	2	35 P	1 C	23	00	31	8	29	38	32	8	36
M Marden	10	23	34	30	2	35 P	6 C	7	30	24	8	34	36	37
M Stokes Lane	10 and 6	30–36	23	34	6	37	2 P	6 C	4	1	24–31	4	8	37
M Ashperton	6	2	30	23	34	17	32 P	37 C	6	7	9	1	24	8
Mission	2	2	36	23	34	17	32	37	6	4	9	1	31	8

Gloucestershire and Worcestershire. He also learned of their plans for advancing preachers from 'trial' to 'full' preacher status, for adding new men and women to serve trial periods, and for dismissing unworthy or unqualified preachers, as well as the process of adding and dropping meeting-places, and licensing persons and places for preaching. Elder Woodruff was so impressed with this organization that he simply adopted it practically intact, for use by the Latter-day Saints. After converting all the United Brethren preachers, most of the names on their March 1840 Preachers' Plan could even remain unchanged, as the same people were sent to preach LDS doctrine thereafter. A copy of the United Brethren's Preachers' Plan for March 1840 is reproduced on these two pages, having been re-set from the original in the Historical Department of the Church.

WEEK DAY PLAN

PLACES AND NIGHTS		APRIL 12	20	27	MAY 4	11	18	25	JUNE 1	8	15	22	29	JU. 6
Frooms Hill	M.	1P		1T		1L		1		1		1		1
Ledbury	T.	1P		1T		1		1		1		1		1
Lugwardine	W.	1P		1T		1		1L		1		1		1
Marden	Th.	1P		1T		1		1		1L		1		1
Shucknell	F.	1P		1T		1		1		1		1L		1
Ashfield	M.		1P		1T		1L				1		1	
Crowcutt	T.				1L				1				1	
Tenbridge	T.		1				1				1			
Dunnsclose	W.				1T				1				1	
Birchwood	W.		1P				1				1			
Colwall	Th.		1P		1T		1		1L		1		1	
Malvern Hill	F.		1P		1T		1		1		1		1L	
Stanley Hill	M.	PM		PM		PM		PM		PM		PM		PM
Hope Rough	T.	PM		PM		PM		PM		PM		PM		PM
Green Yeal	W.	PM		PM		PM		PM		PM		PM		PM
Old Starridge	Th.	PM		PM		PM		PM		PM		PM		PM
Moorend Cross	F.	PM		PM		PM		PM		PM		PM		PM

COMMITTEE—J. Benbow, J. James, J. Hill, J. Parry, T. Clark, J. Morgan, A. Perkins, P. Holt, T. Jenkins, W. Possons.—To meet at the Hill, or wheresoever the Elders may appoint, the First Wednesday in each Month.

QUARTER DAY June 21st, at KEYSEND STREET, to commence at 9 o'clock, M.

REFERENCES—Stanley Hill, L. Lovefeast, P. Publish, T. Tickets, C. Collection, S. Sacrament, M. Preachers to meet the Classes.

Every Preacher who loves the Lord and souls, will be punctual to attend his or her appointments, or get them supplied by one that do love the Lord.

1 J. Gailey
2 C. Price
3 T. Clark
4 J. James
5 M. Rowberry
6 J. Parry
7 J. Morgan
8 J. Pullin
9 J. Hill
10 A. Perkins
11 W. Jenkins
12 P. Holt
13 M. Possons
14 S. Badham
15 T. Jones
16 W. Possons
17 E. Lambert
18 J. Burns
19 J. Meeks
20 M. Jenkins
21 M. Halard
22 M. Powell
23 G. Davies
24 J. Gailey
25 M. Preece
26 T. Jenkins
27 M. Badham
28 J. Lucy
29 A. Graves
30 P. Green
31 M. Wall
32 H. Pullin
33 E. Phillips
34 S. Tomkins
35 J. Green

ON TRIAL.

36 J. Powell
37 T. H.
38 W. W.
39 ‡

But of course Elder Woodruff's success in Herefordshire did not come without opposition. Within a month of his arrival at the Benbow farm, serious problems developed between John Benbow and Mrs Ann Freeman, the owner of the property on which his farm was situated. As John's tenure on the farm was a freehold, which entitled him to a life-long lease, Mrs Freeman probably could not have evicted him. But as she also owned the advowson of the local parish (the right to select the rector of the parish), she was evidently approached by the local minister, as his patron, to do something about the religious activity at John Benbow's Hill Farm. The Anglican ministers in the area even sent a petition to the Archbishop of Canterbury requesting Parliament to ban the Mormons from British soil. (Woodruff, journal, 29 Mar 1840.) Nothing, however, came of the petition, except a reprimand to the petitioners.

Still, it appears that Mrs Freeman created a situation sufficiently difficult to cause John Benbow to leave Hill Farm by his own choice. On the 30th of March Elder Woodruff mentioned for the first time that Benbow was having trouble with his landlady, and just eleven days later Benbow had already sold his freehold tenure and farming equipment, and had vacated the farm. Within six months, on 8 September 1840, John and Jane Benbow and fifty of their fellow saints emigrated to America, with Brother Benbow paying the passage for forty of them.

Before Elder Woodruff left Herefordshire on the 10th of April to meet the newly arrived brethren of the Twelve in Preston, he continued to preach and baptize almost every day. On a 30th of March visit to the Baptist church in Ledbury, Elder Woodruff found the minister there especially friendly. He wrote:

> I had not been in town an hour before many flocked around me to see me and give me the hand of fellowship, though strangers unto me. The Baptist minister [the Rev. G. H. Roper-Curzon] opened his chapel for me to preach in, and he went into the pulpit with me and opened the meeting by reading the 35th chapter of Isaiah and praying mightily for me; I then arose and preached to a large and attentive audience and when I closed thirteen offered themselves for baptism, notwithstanding it was the first meeting we had held in the town. (*TS 2*, 9:329.)

He was told that he 'had preached to the largest congregation that ever met in the chapel. The Minister was believing and bid me God-speed.' (Woodruff, journal, 30 Mar 1840.)

During the next ten days, Elder Woodruff laboured in Gloucestershire and Worcestershire for the first time. While there he baptized 71 people and walked 62 miles. He also saw, for the first time, the only chapel owned by the United Brethren, the Gadfield Elm Chapel in Eldersfield, Worcestershire.

In these ten days, Elder Woodruff suffered more persecution than he had yet seen in England. At The Leigh in Gloucestershire, for instance, he went to Brother Daniel Browett's home to baptize ten people, but because a mob of about a hundred gathered to prevent the baptisms, the owner of the pool withdrew his permission for its use. As Elder Woodruff spent the next hour trying to find a suitable place to baptize, the mob mocked him, calling 'You American,

Gadfield Elm Chapel, built by the United Brethren in 1836. Given to the LDS Church by John Benbow and Thomas Kington, 1840. Brigham Young, Wilford Woodruff and Willard Richards preached here. (*Courtesy of W. Dee Halverson.*)

where are you going to wash your sheep?' Eventually the owner of the pool relented, and Elder Woodruff proceeded with the baptisms, but not without the mob jeering 'with the tongue of slander, and throwing a dog into the pool where I was baptizing'. (*Ibid.* 5 Apr 1840.)

Shortly afterwards, he received a letter from Elder John Taylor, informing him that five more of the Twelve had arrived in England and had called a conference in Preston for the 15th of April, which he was asked to attend. He therefore returned to the Hill Farm to make preparations for his journey to Preston, but discovered that 'Brother John Benbow had sold his possessions and entirely left the Hill farm and taken up his abode for a season at Froomes Hill'. (*Ibid.* 10 Apr 1840.) When he found Brother Benbow, the latter gave him £2 to assist him on his way.

After his conference with the Quorum (see pp. 119–20), Elder Woodruff returned to Herefordshire, this time in company with

Elders Brigham Young and Willard Richards. Summarizing his earlier experience there, Elder Woodruff wrote:

When I left Herefordshire, I had labored one month and five days, had baptized more than forty preachers, and about 120 members, making 160 in all, and [had] more than 30 established places of preaching, licensed according to law, which opened a wide field for the spread of the work in that country. I was absent from this field ten days, during which time I sat in conference and council with the Twelve, and church in general, on the 14th, 15th, and 16th of April, it being the first council and general conference we had ever held in a foreign nation. (*TS* 2, 9:330.)

Elder Young spent about a month in Herefordshire, working sometimes on his own and sometimes in company with Elder Woodruff. Elder Richards spent about two months in the area, 24 April to 23 June 1840, working most of the time with Thomas Kington, preaching and baptizing. The three apostles were together on the 18th of May for a feast with the saints who had been United Brethren, where Elder Richards 'remarked that he did not believe there had ever been such a company of Saints prepared in so short a time and bid fairer for the kingdom of Heaven than the company now before us...'. (Woodruff, journal, 18 May 1840.) After dinner the three apostles anointed and blessed Mary Pitt, the sister-in-law of Thomas Kington and sister to William Pitt (who would later become the director of the Pitt Brass Band of Nauvoo and Salt Lake City). She had been an invalid for eleven years, not being able to walk without crutches. After the blessing she was completely healed and, the next day, walked through the town of Dymock to the amazement of the people, 'but the wicked did not feel to give God the glory'. (*Ibid.*)

Two days later the three apostles held what has been called the 'Beacon Conference' on top of Herefordshire Beacon. Elder Woodruff had been there three times before, but it was the first time for Elders Young and Richards. Elder Woodruff wrote:

We walked to Wind Point and Elders Young, Richards and myself walked on to the top of the part of Malvern Hills called Herefordshire Beacon. Here we united in prayer and held a council and unitedly felt that it was the will of God that Elder Young should go immediately to Manchester to assist in publishing a collection of hymns...and also to immediately print and finish 3000 copies of the Book of Mormon...We walked from the hill into the valley and took the parting hand with Elder Young, who started for Manchester. We, Elder Richards and myself, tarried and preached at Wind Point. (*Ibid.* 20 May 1840.)

John Benbow, prominent member of the United Brethren. He and Thomas Kington financed the publication of the first British edition of the Book of Mormon and the hymn-book in 1840. (*Courtesy of W. Dee Halverson.*)

The two particular benefactors who made possible the publication of the Book of Mormon and the hymn-book in England were John Benbow and Thomas Kington. Benbow donated more than £200 and Kington £100, sums that would be comparable to about £10,000 ($15,000) in today's money.

There is a noteworthy parallel between Herefordshire Beacon and the Hill Cumorah, and between John Benbow/Thomas Kington and Martin Harris. Herefordshire Beacon, like Cumorah, was made sacred by the divine work of three apostles of the Lord, and thus deserves to be remembered in the history of the saints. And John Benbow and Thomas Kington, like Martin Harris, gave their worldly means as well as their talents to the support of the Church. Once having put their hands to the plough, Benbow and Kington never looked back. When their work was finished in Utah, they died in full fellowship, within two months of each other, in 1874. Their wives, Jane Homes Benbow and Hannah Pitt Kington, also deserve to be remembered. Both had money before they married, and Sister Benbow's money was at least part of what her husband gave towards the publishing of the Book of Mormon in England. Sister Kington's house in Dymock, which was hers before her marriage, was often used by the apostles and missionaries as a home and meeting-place. Both women were loyal to the Church and supportive of their husbands. Both were barren and left no posterity. And both died before reaching the Salt Lake Valley, Jane at Winter Quarters and Hannah at Nauvoo. To converts such as these we owe the very survival of the restored Church.

During their last month in Herefordshire, Elders Woodruff and Richards, with the help of Thomas Kington, continued to preach and baptize, but they also turned their attention to organizing the saints to carry on the work of the Church after the apostles' departure. Elder Richards and Brother Kington, working together, baptized between fifty and sixty people during this time. Elder Woodruff baptized 145.

On Sunday, 14 June 1840, the saints met in the Gadfield Elm chapel, where they organized twelve branches of the Church, with twenty-six officers. Also organized was the 'Bran Green and Gadfield Elm Conference', with Thomas Kington as conference president. On the next Sunday, the 21st of June, a similar conference was held at Stanley Hill, near Hill Farm. There the 'Froomes Hill Conference' was organized, thus bringing to an end the United Brethren, for that society existed thereafter only as a part of the restored Church. (*Ibid.* 14 and 21 Jun 1840.)

Three months earlier, on 6 April 1840, when the main body of the Twelve had at last arrived in Liverpool, Brigham Young's first official act had been to shout 'Hosanna!' three times in gratitude for his safe arrival in England. He and his companions, Elders Heber C. Kimball, Parley P. Pratt, Orson Pratt and George A. Smith, along with Reuben Hedlock, then found lodgings at 8 Union Street, not far from the docks, in the same house where Elder Kimball had lodged in 1837.

Upon their arrival in Liverpool, Elders Heber C. Kimball and George A. Smith took a walk through the city. They came upon a large market-place, and Elder Smith (who was only twenty-two at the time) wrote in his journal that he had never seen anything like it:

There were fruits and vegetables of great variety and beauty from all climates. Brother Kimball said he would buy me anything I desired. I chose a large onion,

Brigham Young. 'We went out and bought tall, black hats for 13s. 6d.'

which cost one penny. I ate it with a craving appetite and shed many tears over it. (Jarvis, p. 69.)

Each of the apostles then purchased a tall black hat, as they were in vogue at the time.

When all the missionaries were settled in their lodgings, according to Elder Young, they 'held a meeting, partook of the sacrament, and returned thanks to God for his protection and care exercised over us while on the waters, and asking that our way might be opened before us to accomplish our missions successfully'. (E. Watson, p. 69.) Their immediate destination was Preston, but before leaving Liverpool they searched out Elder John Taylor to inform him of their arrival and invite him to a conference the following week at Preston. On the 8th of April they took the train to Preston, where the saints welcomed them with enthusiasm and rejoicing.

Upon learning of their arrival, Willard Richards went immediately to Preston to greet his friends, whom he had not seen for three years. He found Brigham Young so emaciated from the effects of ague, sea travel and lack of food that Willard did not recognize him – and they were first cousins! Still, undaunted by any physical infirmity, Elder Young scheduled a public meeting for the following Sunday, the 12th of April, in 'the Cockpit'. A large congregation attended, and the apostles bore witness of the divine work in which they were engaged.

Two days later, when all the brethren of the Twelve had arrived in Preston, they held a historic meeting – 'being the first council held by a majority of the Quorum of the Twelve in a foreign nation'. (E. Watson, p. 70; see also p. 119 herein.)

During the 376 days that Brigham Young and his fellow apostles were to spend in Britain, much work had to be done, and no one understood that better than President Young. It was he who had responsibility for the entire British Mission, both missionaries and members. But he was eminently qualified for the task. Although he was to spend some time in the six areas of Manchester, Liverpool, Herefordshire, Preston, the Potteries and London, it was in Manchester and Liverpool that Elder Young laboured most. Manchester served as the headquarters of the Church throughout this period, and it was from there that President Young directed the British Mission. Regarding his own duties, he wrote:

> I was much confined to the office [in Manchester] for several months, proof-reading the Hymn Book, conducting and issuing the *Millennial Star*, Hymn Book and Book of Mormon, giving counsel to the Elders throughout the European Mission, preaching, baptizing and confirming. (E. Watson, p. 79.)

Indeed, President Young travelled extensively in all the areas where missionaries laboured, baptized many people himself, and preached about every three days. In addition, he personally directed the publication of the hymn-book, indexed and published the Book of Mormon, and supervised the emigration of the saints from Liverpool.

The doctrine of gathering did not become an official practice of the Church in Britain until Elder Young and his fellow apostles had arrived. The gathering from places outside North America was delayed because of the continual persecution of the saints in America, which made it impossible for the Church to provide a safe and permanent place for gathering until after 1847. Even so, Nauvoo became the first gathering place for the British saints. During Brigham Young's presidency in the British Mission, six companies of saints emigrated to America, with President Young personally supervising and organizing each one.

The first company of saints to embark for America under the direction of the Church was headed by John Moon and consisted of 41 passengers, including several of the Moon family. All were from the Preston area. This company sailed on the *Britannia*, which left Liverpool on the 6th of June and arrived at New York on 20 July 1840.

The next group to leave was led by Theodore Turley, and included John Benbow and about fifty others from the Herefordshire area. They sailed from Liverpool on the *North America* on 8 September 1840, with about 200 saints on board. The last ship to leave with emigrant saints in 1840 was the *Isaac Newton*. She set sail on the 15th of October with fifty Scottish converts, the first ship to carry saints to New Orleans.

Elder Hiram Clark was leader of the fourth company, which left Liverpool on 7 February 1841 on the *Sheffield* with 235 saints. Nine days later Daniel Browett took a group of 109 saints on board the *Echo*, leaving Liverpool on the 16th of February. The *Uleste* sailed on the 17th of March with 54 saints under the direction of Thomas Smith and William Moss, and the last ship to leave with Latter-day Saints during this period was the *Rochester*, which embarked on 21 April 1841. She carried, amongst the 130 saints aboard, seven apostles, returning from their mission to Britain.

Altogether more than 800 converts and returning missionaries sailed out of Liverpool for America during the period of the apostolic mission. Others may have gone on their own rather than in one of the six organized companies, as did William Benbow, who sailed from Liverpool on the very day that Brigham Young and his fellow apostles arrived there. But in the case of William Benbow and a Moss family before him, it was an independent undertaking, as the Church did not have a programme for assisting saints to emigrate at that time – such a programme was one of the achievements of the apostolic mission of 1840–1.

President Young's first view of the English countryside came when he spent a month in the Malvern Hills area of Herefordshire, which he described as 'the most beautiful range of hills in England, being among the highest and affording the most splendid prospect of the surrounding country for 30 miles'. (E. Watson, p. 73.) Here he was not only able to preach the gospel and baptize, but the setting itself, with its sparse population and rolling hills, allowed him time to relax, to think and plan, and to recover his health. It was no accident that he chose to work alone during much of the time he spent in the Malvern Hills. Herefordshire needed Brigham Young, but perhaps he also needed Herefordshire.

During his time there, President Young preached in the Gadfield Elm chapel, which was then the only Latter-day Saint chapel in the world. (It had become such upon the conversion of most of the United Brethren, who had built it.) This little church had a seating capacity of 100, and when Brigham Young was in the pulpit, there wasn't even standing room for the crowd that would attend. The Gadfield Elm chapel, built of native stone in the quiet countryside of Worcestershire, stands today with its walls intact and a few beams across the roof, like a lonely gravestone in a forgotten cemetery. It is the last surviving memorial to the United Brethren, that group of people whom the Lord raised up in the shadows of the Malvern Hills. It served the people who built it, and the Latter-day Saints who inherited it, and then was sold to assist the poorer saints to gather to Zion. Skeletal as it now is, the Gadfield Elm chapel stands as a reminder of one of the greatest missionary experiences of all time.

President Young arrived in Manchester, following his ministry with Elder Woodruff in Herefordshire, on 21 May 1840. Besides directing the entire British Mission from his office there, he also set in order the Church in Manchester. Regarding this, he wrote that he had

> organized the Priesthood in Manchester to meet every Sabbath morning, and distribute themselves throughout the different parts of the city to preach in the streets. In this way they occupied about forty preaching stations, at each one of which the congregation were notified of our regular meetings in the Carpenter's Hall. This so annoyed the sectaries, particularly the Methodists, that they made complaints to the mayor, who issued an order to have all street preachers arrested. I went to the Priesthood meeting in the morning and felt impressed to tell the brethren to go home. The police, who had been instructed to arrest all street preachers that morning, took up about twenty, who all proved to be Methodists. When the magistrate learned they were not 'Mormons', they were dismissed. (E. Watson, pp. 82–3.)

Once in Manchester, Elder Young hired Carpenter's Hall, and was the first of the apostles to preach there. Of the 137 places of worship in Manchester in 1844, only 39 were Church of England, which indicates that Manchester was largely Nonconformist. Carpenter's Hall itself was associated with Nonconformity, due to its being the 'Sunday resort of the Chartists'. (Faucher, p. 25.) This hall was used by the Church for three of its four general conferences during the mission of the apostles, the one exception being the first conference, which was held in Preston.

The first Manchester conference (6 July 1840) was attended by all the apostles in Britain except Orson Pratt, who remained in Edinburgh. Reports were given at this conference of 41 branches, 2,513 members, 56 elders, 126 priests, 61 teachers and 13 deacons. This represented an increase, in the course of three months, of 842 members, with corresponding increases in the respective priesthood offices. At this conference, twenty elders, besides the apostles, volunteered to devote themselves full time to the ministry. (E. Watson, p. 78.)

At the second Manchester conference on the 6th of October, an even greater increase in membership was reported: baptisms for the quarter numbered 1,113, bringing total Church membership in Britain to 3,626. In response to an appeal for labourers in the vineyard, 42 brethren volunteered, and a fund was established to offer assistance to needy missionaries. (*Ibid.* p. 80.)

The apostles held one last general conference in Manchester on 16 April 1841, just two weeks before their departure for America. At this historic event all nine of the apostles were present for the first time, Elder Orson Hyde having at last arrived in Britain. (He would labour in Britain only three months, however, before continuing on his way to Jerusalem to dedicate the land for the return of the Jews.) At the time of this conference total membership stood at 5,814, an increase of 2,188 for that quarter. (*Ibid.* p. 95.) When the statistics of this last conference are compared with those of the first conference in Preston in April 1840, the increases were as follows: 4,143 new members, 102 elders, 251 priests, 131 teachers and 60 deacons. In addition, two patriarchs had been ordained since the first conference.

During the early part of the apostolic mission, Elder Heber C. Kimball had been assigned to tour the branches he had established in Preston and the Ribble Valley during his first mission. His tour was a complete one, and personally rewarding to Elder Kimball. He reported:

At this time I can truly say that I have never felt more to rejoice than I have done in my late visits to the churches. The Saints, in general, as they have been baptized into one body, are partakers of one spirit, whether they be Jew or Gentile, bond or free...It is evident our labor is not in vain in the Lord. (Whitney, *Kimball*, p. 284.)

At the July 1840 Manchester conference, however, Elder Kimball was one of those assigned to take the gospel to London. As Elder Woodruff explained:

From this conference we designed to go forth and open other new places, and while numbers of our brethren went into new places in different parts of Europe, Elders Kimball, G. A. Smith, and myself concluded to visit London. (*TS* 2, 9: 330.)

Accordingly, these three apostles met about a month later in Dymock, Gloucestershire, at the home of Thomas Kington, spent a week in that area, and then set out for London. They were driven as far as Cheltenham by Elder Daniel Browett, then travelled by coach to Farringdon, Berkshire, where they took 'the cars' (the train) to Paddington. (Woodruff, journal, 12–17 Aug 1840.) From there they went by horse-drawn bus four miles to London Bridge, where they arrived at 4 p.m. on the 18th of August.

The three apostles now found themselves in the world's largest city, and Elder Woodruff wrote:

I am now in the great city of London, the largest, most noted and populous commercial city in the world, containing a population of about one million, five hundred thousand people. I am in company with Elders H. C. Kimball and G. A. Smith. We are the first Elders of the Church of Latter-day Saints that have ever walked the streets of London.

O London, as I walk thy streets and behold the mass of human beings passing through thee, and view thy mighty palaces, thy splendid mansions, the costly merchandize wherewith thou art adorned, even as the capital of great Babylon, I am ready to ask myself, 'What am I and my brethren here for?' And as the Spirit answers, 'To warn thee of thine abominations and to exhort thee to repent of thy wickedness and prepare for the day of thy visitation, thy mourning, thy calamity, and thy woe', I am ready to cry out, 'Lord who is sufficient for these things?'

O mighty God of Jacob, clothe us with thy power. Let the power of the Priesthood rest upon us and the Spirit of our ministry and mission, and enable us to warn the inhabitants of this city in such a manner that our garments will be clean of their blood and that we may seek out the honest in heart and the meek from among men and have many souls as seals of our ministry. (*Ibid.* 18 Aug 1840.)

Their destination was the home of Mrs Mary Ann Allgood, the sister-in-law of Theodore Turley, who had suggested that they call on her. The Allgoods lived at 19 King Street in Southwark. To get there the three apostles crossed London Bridge on foot, then went along Borough High Street for a quarter-mile until they came to King Street (now Newcomen Street). Down King Street about a hundred yards, on the north side of the street, was the Allgood home.

Elder Woodruff wrote that Mrs Allgood 'treated us with kindness, gave us some refreshment and then directed us to a publick house', the King's Arms. (*Ibid.*) Evidently she actually accompanied them to the King's Arms to see that they had lodging there, 'until she could find them accommodations with a family'. (Joseph Smith, *HC* 4: 180; S. Kimball, p. 72.) She continued to be hospitable to the missionaries throughout their stay in London.

King Street, as it was then called, ran from Borough High Street to Long Lane, the main road leading to Bermondsey. Before 1760 it had been a cul-de-sac called the 'Axe and Bottle Yard', but in that year the south gate of London Bridge was taken down (along with all the other buildings on the bridge) and sold at auction. Also sold was a fine old sculpture of the royal arms that had hung above the gate since the reign of King George II. A stonemason bought this sculpture and incorporated it into a public house when the Axe and Bottle Yard was extended to connect with Long Lane. Thus the pub became known as the King's Arms and the new thoroughfare as King Street. The street name remained for more than two hundred years until, in 1879, the Post Office requested a general renaming of London streets. As there were too many other 'King' Streets, the name was changed to 'Newcomen', for the Newcomen Charity was located there.

The King's Arms that stands on Newcomen Street today was built some fifty years after the brethren were in London, but when the new building was erected in 1890 the original royal arms from the old London Bridge were retained. The apostles stayed at the King's Arms for two nights, the 18th and 19th of August.

The three brethren soon discovered that they were in one of the more colourful London suburbs. Borough High Street was the main thoroughfare from London to Canterbury, and therefore one of the principal routes to the Channel and the Continent. Moreover, it had long been the neighbourhood of London's theatres (including Shakespeare's Globe Theatre in the seventeenth century), and was therefore the Soho/Shaftesbury Avenue district of its time. Consequently the King's Arms was a busy place. Elder Woodruff wrote:

There is so much passing of drays and horses and singing and [hallooing] at all hours of the night in the streets that it [was] with difficulty that I could sleep at night. (*Ibid.* 19 Aug 1840.)

And Elder George A. Smith added:

The cries of pedlars, the noise of thousands of wagons, coaches and gigs, with the night songs of streetwalkers, served to keep [us] country men awake, till overcome by the labors of the day, we finally sank into forgetfulness. (Pusey, pp. 41–2.)

Finding the noise unbearable at the King's Arms, the elders moved further down King Street, to Mrs Hannah Loft's Coffee Rooms (58 King Street), where they lodged for the next four nights.

Their last place of lodging in Southwark before moving into Central London was at Mr Robert Merrifield's, 15 Gloucester Row, Grange Road. It was through the kind efforts of Mrs Allgood that this accommodation was found, and the three apostles stayed there for just over two weeks, from the 24th of August to the 8th of September. (Kimball Family.) Mr Merrifield was a shopkeeper, and apparently had a few rooms to let above his shop. Elder Smith said that they 'occupied a second floor: Elders Kimball and Woodruff the front room and Elder Smith the back room'. (Jarvis, p. 73.) The twenty-two days they spent in Southwark went unrewarded in terms of conversions. Drawing on his previous experience, Elder Kimball suggested that they go 'to see the Teetotal Society... to see if they will let us [use their] Hall. We have received great kindness from them in Preston.'

They thus attended a Teetotal meeting on the 27th of August at the Temperance Hall on St George's Road near Elephant and Castle, where Elders Woodruff and Smith addressed the Temperance Committee. They arranged to use the hall at the earliest available date, which was the 7th of September. In the meantime they would continue to search for opportunities to preach the gospel.

They had already come in contact with the celebrated Rev.

Robert Aitken, who had a thriving congregation in Zion's Chapel on Waterloo Road in Southwark. This was the same Aitken that had adamantly opposed the missionaries in Preston and in Liverpool, but who unwittingly had also provided the elders with their first converts in each place. The elders were impressed with his oratory and his perceptions of the evils of the world, 'but notwithstanding Mr Aitken has some sublime truths,' Elder Woodruff wrote, 'yet he is building a great house without any foundation, by rejecting the first principles of the Gospel'. (Woodruff, journal, 23 Aug 1840.)

By the 28th of August they were determined to break through the barriers of darkness. Elder Woodruff recorded:

> We all started out in the morning, to go through the City of London to see if we could find any man that had the Spirit of God and after wandering several miles through the City, not knowing whitherto we went, we came to an Ephraimite walking in the street. We stepped up to him and spoke to him, though it was the first time we had ever seen him. Br Kimball asked him if he was a preacher. He said he was. He seemed to have a good spirit. His name was Manning. He had been to America, and was a native of Gloucestershire. [He] had come to London for the purpose of going to South Australia. But he was now in trouble. He had just buried his one child and another lay at the point of death. Br Kimball told him his child should live. He gave us some information where we could preach, etc. (*Ibid.* 28 Aug 1840.)

Later that day, the elders stopped at Mr Manning's lodgings and learned that his child had indeed recovered, and the next day, perhaps in response to Mr Manning's 'information', they went to Smithfield Market, 'for the purpose of preaching at 10 a.m.', but were told by the police that the Lord Mayor had prohibited street meetings in that area. At that,

> a Mr Connor stepped up and said, 'I will show you a place outside of his jurisdiction', and guided them to 'Tabernacle Square', where they found an assembly of about 400 people listening to a preacher who was standing on a chair. When he got through another preacher arose to speak.
>
> Elder Kimball stated to the first clergyman, 'There is a man present from America who would like to preach'; which was granted; when Elder George A. Smith delivered a discourse of about twenty minutes, on the first principles of the Gospel, taking for his text, Mark 16:16; after which Elder Kimball asked the preacher to give out another appointment at the same place for the American Elder to preach; when he jumped up and said, 'I have just learned that the gentleman who has addressed you is a Latter-day Saint; I know them – they are a very bad people; they have split up many churches, and have done a great deal

of hurt.' He spoke all manner of evil, and gave the Latter-day Saints a very bad character, and commanded the people not to hear the Elders, 'as we have got the Gospel, and can save the people, without infidelity, socialism, or Latter-day Saints'.

Elder Kimball asked the privilege of standing on the chair to give out an appointment himself. The preacher said, 'You shall not do it; you have no right to preach here'; jerked the chair away from him, and ran away with it. Several of the crowd said, 'You have as much right to preach here as he has, and give out your appointment'; whereupon Elder Kimball gave out an appointment for 3 o'clock p.m.; at which time a large congregation was gathered.

After opening the meeting by singing and prayer, Elder Woodruff spoke about thirty minutes, from Gal. 1:8, 9, upon the first principles of the Gospel. Elder Kimball followed upon the same subjects. The people gave good attention, and seemed much interested in what they had heard. The inhabitants who lived around the square opened their windows to four [storeys] high; the most of them were crowded with anxious listeners, which is an uncommon occurrence. (Joseph Smith, *HC* 4:183–4.)

Mr Connor invited the elders to his home at 52 Ironmonger Row, which was adjacent to the parish church of St Luke's, not far from Tabernacle Square. Whilst Woodruff and Smith taught the gospel to the Connor family and others, Elder Kimball felt compelled to return to Tabernacle Square, where he found a large assembly of people still discussing what they had heard from the American missionaries earlier in the day. That same day, Mr Connor requested baptism.

The next day, 31 August 1840, Elder Kimball baptized Henry Connor in a public pool called 'Peerless Pool' that was 200 yards from his house. This was the first baptism and beginning of the Church in London. Although the apostles could not have known, at the very time they were having such a struggle to open the work in London there were two eight-year-old boys living there who would eventually become fellow members of the Quorum of the Twelve Apostles: George Teasdale and Charles W. Penrose.

Their first indoor preaching was done on the 6th of September at a Methodist school at 137 Bowl Court in nearby Shoreditch. All three of the apostles preached there on that occasion, but when they returned the next time they were met with such opposition that they abandoned their plans. The next day was the 7th of September, the date for which they had reserved the Temperance Hall on St George's Road. The meeting was disappointing, however. Elders Kimball and Woodruff spoke to a small audience of about thirty persons, none of whom was moved to action. Later that day Elders Kimball and Smith met the Rev. Robert Aitken, who acknowledged their doctrine to be true and treated them kindly, but neither was he moved to action.

Without any promising prospects in Southwark and with opportunities opening up on the other side of the river, especially in the St Luke's parish area, the elders moved on the 9th of September to lodgings at 40 Ironmonger Row, across the street from their only convert, Henry Connor. This became the lodging-place of the London missionaries for the next two and a half years.

After spending one night in their new lodgings, Elder Woodruff left London to attend conferences that had been planned in Herefordshire. His parting journal entry read:

On September 9th I paid my bills, called upon friends in company with Brothers Kimball and Smith, and on the day following I parted from the brethren and friends in London to return to Herefordshire. We had spent twenty-three days in the great Babylon of modern times and had found it harder to establish the Church there than in any other place we had ever been. We had baptized one man, and ordained him a Priest; six others had given in their names to be baptized on the following Sunday; and at this time there was some little prospect of the Reverend Robert Aitken receiving the work. I therefore left London, feeling that our mission and labors had not been altogether in vain. (M. Cowley, p. 126.)

Elder Woodruff attended the Bran Green and Gadfield Elm Conference on the 14th of September, and the next week presided at the Froom's Hill Conference. At these conferences totals of 1,007 members and 40 branches were reported in Herefordshire, where seven months earlier Elder Woodruff had begun proselytizing for the first time. Meanwhile, Elder Kimball, reflecting on the progress of the work in London, wrote:

Brother Woodruff has been gone two weeks, and we [had] baptized only one here in the city before he left. He felt almost discouraged and said he never saw such a hard case before... every door closed against us and every heart. We have traveled from day to day from one part of the city to the other, to find someone that would receive our testimony. It seemed all in vain for some time, but at last we found one Cornelius that was ready to receive our testimony as soon as he heard it. On Sunday, the morning after I was taken with Cholera I went forward and baptized four. I thought it would do me good to go into a cold bath. Last night I went into the water and baptized four more. Some more are going on Sunday. The ice is broken in London, and the gospel has got such a hold that the devil cannot root it out. (Jarvis, pp. 73–4.)

Elders Kimball and Smith remained in London until the 29th of September, when they left to attend the approaching conference in Manchester, after which Elder Smith returned to London on the 10th of October. The next week, Elder Woodruff joined him at the Connor home at 52 Ironmonger Row. The lodgings they had taken, across the street at 40 Ironmonger Row, were in a house owned by Peter and Elizabeth Morgan. Elder Woodruff described their circumstances as follows:

> We have to pay vary [*sic*] high for every thing here in the City of London: lodgings, board, and sittings and everything else. With the greatest prudence we cannot get along much short of a pound a week, each person, and what few saints there are at present in this city are vary poor and not able to assist us at present. But I trust in the Lord to soon open a door in this city whareby [*sic*] the cause of God can roll forth. But it certainly is the darkest prospect all things considered of any place I have been in since I have been in the vineyard. But the Lord is with us and we are not discouraged. (Woodruff, journal, 17 Oct 1840.)

The next evening, which was Sunday, Elders Woodruff and Smith had visitors from the unseen world: first the forces of evil came, then angels. Elder Woodruff described these remarkable experiences as follows:

> We retired to rest in good season and I felt well in my mind and slept until 12 at night. I awoke and meditated upon the things of God until near 3 o'clock and while forming a determination to warn the people of London and overcome the powers of darkness by the assistance of God, a person appeared unto me which I considered was the Prince of Darkness, or the Devil. He made war with me and attempted to take my life. He caught me by the throat and choaked [*sic*] me nearly to death. He wounded me in my forehead. I also wounded him in a number of places in the head. As he was about to overcome me, I prayed to the Father in the name of Jesus for help. I then had power over him and he left me, though much wounded.
>
> [Then] three personages dressed in white came to me and prayed with me and I was immediately healed and [they] delivered me from all my troubles. (*Ibid*. 18 Oct 1840.)

Elder George A. Smith was also involved in this singular experience:

> It seemed as if there were legions of spirits there. They sought our destruction...These powers of darkness fell upon us to destroy our lives, and both [of us] would have been killed, apparently, had not three holy messengers come into the room with light. They were dressed in temple clothing. They laid their hands

upon our heads and we were delivered, and that power was broken so far as we were concerned. (*DN 38*:389–90.)

Four days later Elders Woodruff and Smith hired a hall for three months from Mr Jacob Barrett. Called Barrett's Academy, it was at 57 King Square, on the corner of Goswell Road and President Street. They then had 500 handbills printed to advertise their meetings. That evening they attended a meeting of the Wesleyan Methodist Church in John Wesley's City Road Chapel, near Tabernacle Square. Elder Woodruff recorded:

It was considered one of the greatest missionary meetings ever held in the City of London. The chair was occupied by the Lord Mayor of the City of London. He was a noble looking man...The object of this meeting was for the Wesleyan Methodists to send out foreign missionaries and to make collections enough to clear themselves of a debt of £50,000. The most splendid talents of Europe were gathered together on this occasion. Ministers of the Church of Scotland, of England, and of the Wesleyans were present in large numbers. (Woodruff, journal, 22 Oct 1840.)

Though the sermons were impressive and the surroundings fine, Elder Woodruff lamented:

But in the midst of all this scenery, who can imagine my feelings? None but those placed in like circumstances. Though I had a mission and a message to the inhabitants of London and stood in their midst ready to deliver it as soon as God opened my way, yet I was as little known to them as Jonah was to the citizens of Niniva [Nineveh] while in the whale's belly and I clearly saw and realized that notwithstanding this great display of talent, power and policy, to send missionaries to the heathen, they as much need an humble messenger of God to teach them the first principles of the Gospel of Jesus Christ as Niniva did a prophet, to cry repentance unto them. (*Ibid.*)

For the two days following this Wesleyan meeting, Elders Woodruff and Smith were occupied 'in circulating and posting up' their handbills, advertising their meetings at Barrett's Academy. Lectures were scheduled for Tuesday and Thursday evenings and twice on Sundays. (*Ibid.* 24 Oct 1940.) They began their meetings on Sunday the 25th of October, and about fifty people attended the first one. Although the elders held their meetings in Barrett's Academy faithfully as advertised, people were slow to respond.

Elder George A. Smith was assigned to return to the Staffordshire Potteries on the 10th of November. He had laboured in that area before coming to London, and had written, at that time:

For the last twenty days I have been so busy with preaching, counseling, baptizing, confirming and teaching the people, that I have not had time to journalize any, and have seldom gone to bed before two o'clock in the morning as people were constantly in my room inquiring about the work of the Lord. (Jarvis, p. 71.)

His account of his London experience was something of a contrast:

From the time I began laboring in London to the present, I used every exertion consistent with my health and strength to plant the Gospel Standard; every visit I made or call or association, was one of continued effort to bear my testimony, to teach, to warn the people and thereby fulfill my calling; and I believe that I can truly testify before the Lord that my garments are clean of the blood of the inhabitants of the British metropolis. (Jarvis, p. 76.)

Except for a few saints, Elder Woodruff was now on his own in London. Though he continued to labour diligently, he did not perform a baptism in London until the 29th of November, over two months after he had first arrived there. The contrast between London and Herefordshire weighed heavily on his mind.

On the 30th of November, he was joined by fellow apostles Brigham Young and Heber C. Kimball. This was President Young's first visit to London, and in the eleven days he spent there he seemed eager to see and do everything he could. After preaching several times at Barrett's Academy, Elder Young left London on the 10th of December.

On the 16th, Elders Kimball and Woodruff baptized four persons, including their landlord and his wife. Four days later they were invited to preach by the Rev. James Albion, minister of an independent church called Ebenezer Chapel on Commercial Road. Elder Woodruff had met him several times before this, and had so impressed the minister that he had announced to his congregation that he was a Latter-day Saint, and that they should not consider him their minister any longer. He also announced that Elder Woodruff would preach to them the next Sunday, the 27th of December. A month later, James Albion was baptized by Elder Woodruff. He and Dr William Copeland, who was baptized on the 12th of January by Elder Kimball, were the two most influential converts the apostles had in London.

The brethren did occasionally take time to enjoy some of the offerings of the city. Elder Woodruff related one such incident in a rather light-hearted vein:

Elder Kimball called upon me and I took a walk with him and Doctor Copeland and his wife over Blackfriars Bridge and on our return home in the midst of a crowd, we lost Br Kimball and Sister Copeland, and in looking them up, I lost Dr Copeland, and Br Kimball [lost] Sister Copeland, so that there [were] no two of us...[that were] together. But after being separated a while, we all four providentially met at Covent Garden, and saw the wonderful performance of Shakespeare's [Midsummer] Night's Dream...etc., and returned home. (Woodruff, journal, 23 Dec 1840.)

In addition, Elders Kimball and Woodruff both sat for their portraits while in London. The artist was Mr Filippo Pistrucci of 40 Charlotte Street, Fitzroy Square.

At last a London Conference was organized, on 14 February 1841, as the missionary labours in the metropolis drew to a close. The minutes of the conference, as taken down by Elder Woodruff, show branches of the Church at Bedford, Ipswich, Woolwich and London, with a total of 106 members. Lorenzo Snow was called to serve as president of the London Conference. Elder Woodruff's minutes concluded with the following remarks:

This was the day which we had desired long to see; for we had labored exceedingly hard to establish a Church in London, and at times it seemed as though we would have to give it up; but by holding on to the work of our Divine Master and claiming the promises of God, we were now to leave an established London conference with a prosperous Church planted in the metropolis, under the care of our beloved brother, Lorenzo Snow. (M. Cowley, pp. 136–7.)

Regarding the Church in London, President Snow said:

I believe sincerely and strongly that a great work will eventually be accomplished in this vast city, but I can scarcely expect it will be done hurriedly...I baptized seven yesterday, making nine that I have baptized in London since Elders Woodruff and Kimball left, and making eleven that have received the gospel in this city since conference. (Romney, pp. 54–5.)

By August 1841 Church membership in London had grown to more than two hundred.

During the time that the elders were struggling to establish the Church in London, Elder Parley P. Pratt was pursuing his mission duties in Manchester – duties that were different from those of most of his fellow apostles. He had charge of publishing the gospel through word and song more than preaching, although he did a considerable amount of that, as well. About his work during this time, he wrote:

THE

LATTER-DAY SAINTS

MILLENNIAL STAR.

EDITED BY PARLEY P. PRATT.

No. 1. Vol. I. MAY, 1840. Price 6d.

PROSPECTUS.

The long night of darkness is now far spent—the truth revived in its primitive simplicity and purity, like the day-star of the horizon, lights up the dawn of that effulgent morn when the knowledge of God will cover the earth as the waters cover the sea. It has pleased the Almighty to send forth an Holy Angel, to restore the fulness of the gospel with all its attendant blessings, to bring together his wandering sheep into one fold, to restore to them "the faith which was once delivered to the saints," and to send his servants in these last days, with a special message to all the nations of the earth, in order to prepare all who will hearken for the Second Advent of Messiah, which is now near at hand.

By this means, the Church of Jesus Christ of Latter-day Saints (being first organized in 1830) has spread throughout many parts of America and Europe; and has caused many tens of thousands to rejoice above measure, while they are enabled to walk in the light of truth.

And feeling very desirous that others should be made partakers of the same blessings, by being made acquainted with the same truths, they have thought proper to order the publication of a Periodical devoted entirely to the great work of the spread of truth, sincerely praying that man may be led to carefully examine the subject, and to discern between truth and error, and act accordingly.

The Millennial Star will stand aloof from the common political and commercial news of the day. Its columns will be devoted to the spread of the fulness of the gospel—the restoration of the ancient principles of Christianity—the gathering of Israel—the rolling forth of the kingdom of God among the nations—the signs of the times—the fulfilment of prophecy—recording the judgments of God as they befall the nations, whether signs in the heavens or in the earth "blood, fire, or vapour of smoke"—in short, whatever is shown forth indicative of the coming of the "Son of Man," and the ushering in of his universal reign on the earth. It will also contain letters from our numerous elders who are abroad, preaching the word both in America and Europe, containing news of their success in ministering the blessings of the glorious gospel.

As an Ancient Record has lately been discovered in America, unfolding the history of that continent and its inhabitants, as far back as its first peopling after the flood, and containing much historical, prophetical, and doctrinal knowledge, which is of the utmost importance to the present age, we shall give such extracts from time to time as will be most interesting to the lovers of truth.

From this source we shall be able to pour a flood of light upon the world on subjects before concealed—upon the history of a nation whose remnants have long since dwindled to insignificance in midnight darkness, and whose former greatness was lost in oblivion, or only known by the remains of cities, palaces, temples, aqueducts, monuments, towers, fortifications, unintelligible inscriptions, sepulchres, and bones.

The slumber of ages has now been broken. The dark curtain of the past has been rolled up. The veil of obscurity has been removed, as it regards the world

Elder Parley P. Pratt served as first editor of the *Millennial Star*, 1840–2. Included on the wrapper of the initial issue was 'The Morning Breaks', which Elder Pratt wrote especially for the premier number. Those lyrics, put to music by George Careless, have since become one of the most popular hymns in the Church.

While engaged in editing and publishing the *Star*, I also preached the gospel continually to vast congregations in and about Manchester, and the spirit of joy, faith and gladness was greatly increased, and the number of the Saints was multiplied. I also assisted my brethren in selecting, compiling, and publishing a hymn-book. In this work was contained nearly fifty of my original hymns and songs, composed expressly for the book. (P. Pratt, p. 265.)

One of these hymns was 'The Morning Breaks', which was first published in the premier issue of the *Millennial Star*:

The morning breaks, the shadows flee;
  Lo! Zion's standard is unfurled!
The dawning of a brighter day
  Majestic rises on the world...

Angels from heaven, and truth from earth
  Have met, and both have record borne;
Thus Zion's light is bursting forth,
  To bring her ransomed children home.

(*Ibid.*; see also *Hymns*, no. 1.)

The first British edition of the Book of Mormon, in which Elder Pratt was so heavily involved, came from the printer in Liverpool on 21 January 1841, in a printing of 5,000 copies. Two copies of this edition, bound in morocco leather and imprinted in gold, were presented to Queen Victoria and Prince Albert. The Queen's copy is now in the Royal Library at Windsor, whilst the Prince Consort's copy was evidently sold with the rest of his personal library, following his death in 1861.

Elder Parley P. Pratt stayed on as president of the British Mission after the other apostles left in 1841. During his eighteen-month presidency some 1,200 saints emigrated to America, and the Church continued to flourish. At the end of his tenure, in October 1842, President Pratt wrote:

Some hundreds had emigrated from this conference, and still it numbered near one thousand, five hundred members, all of whom had been gathered in about two years, and that from an obscure beginning in a small basement in Oldham Road, [Manchester]. (P. Pratt, pp. 278–9.)

This reflection of Elder Pratt's, upon his departure from England, was much like that of President Brigham Young as he stood on board the *Rochester*, with the others of the Twelve, after their glorious 376-day mission in Britain. His final journal entry, as they looked back on the land where the harvest had been so great, read:

> It was with a heart full of thanksgiving and gratitude to God, my heavenly Father, that I reflected upon His dealings with me and my brethren of the Twelve during the past year of my life, which was spent in England. It truly seemed a miracle to look upon the contrast between our landing and departing from Liverpool. We landed in the spring of 1840, as strangers in a strange land and penniless, but through the mercy of God we have gained many friends, established churches in almost every noted town and city in the kingdom of Great Britain, baptized between seven and eight thousand, printed 5,000 Books of Mormon, 3,000 Hymn Books, 2,500 volumes of the *Millennial Star*, and 50,000 tracts, and emigrated to Zion 1,000 souls, established a permanent shipping agency, which will be a great blessing to the Saints, and have left sown in the hearts of many thousands the seeds of eternal truth, which will bring forth fruit to the honor and glory of God, and yet we have lacked nothing to eat, drink or wear: in all these things I acknowledge the hand of God. (E. Watson, pp. 96–7.)

Brigham Young seemed to express the feelings of all the apostles and missionaries who laboured in Britain when he said, 'I find fathers and mothers, sisters and brothers, wherever I go'. (*Ibid*. p. 86.)

Building the Kingdom

THE SUBJECT of these chapters is the waxing and waning of conversion and emigration. From our modern point of view, the Church's emigration policy may seem confusing, but in this case parable is more illuminating than policy. In the parable of the olive trees, the Lord takes the young and tender branches and plants them in the nethermost parts of the vineyard 'according to his will and pleasure'. (Jacob 5: 8–14.) When the servant questions his master's logic, the Lord of the vineyard says 'Counsel me not'. (*Ibid.* v. 22.) Ultimately these branches are grafted back into the mother tree.

In Church history the early converts, the young and tender branches, were transplanted to strengthen the Church at its centre. New generations then sent missionaries back to their ancestral lands, to revitalize the 'mother tree'. Every young missionary who has been called to labour in lands where his own forebears accepted the gospel knows the joy and thanksgiving that fill his days. Two years there is but his tithe of his life.

Church members throughout the world are heirs of those early emigrants from the British Isles. And saints in Britain today are aware of those who, 'according to his will and pleasure', stayed and carried the Church through some lean periods. Whilst we do not always understand how the parable guides our lives, we do understand the labouring in the vineyard: building the kingdom is central to our membership. These chapters are about missionary work, without which, according to President Spencer W. Kimball, the Church would 'wither and die on the vine'.

6

The British Gathering to Zion

RICHARD L. JENSEN

THE CONCEPT of the gathering shaped the course of Church history in Britain for more than a century. For decades missionaries declared it in the same breath that announced the dispensation of the fullness of times. It aroused enthusiasm and controversy, swelled congregations, and then depleted them. The emigration of approximately 65,000 saints from the British Isles provided great strength to the establishment of the Church in Nauvoo, and later in Salt Lake City and the American West. Until the practice of gathering was modified, the Church in the British Isles had little sense of permanence, for hearts were set on a home across the ocean.

The gathering of Israel, one of the great themes of biblical prophecy, took on new meaning for the Church as early as September 1830. In a revelation received at Fayette, New York, Joseph Smith and others learned of their responsibility to bring together the Lord's 'elect' at one location in America, preparatory to the second coming of Christ. (D&C 29:1–11.) After that, the Church's role in the gathering began to unfold rather quickly. Soon the saints in New York and Pennsylvania were counselled by revelation to gather in Ohio, where headquarters were temporarily established in the realization that the saints would eventually move to another central location. (D&C 37; 28:9; 62:21–2.) Then the centre for gathering was designated in Missouri, where many of the saints settled in the 1830s. (D&C 57:1–5.)

Although the Church's earliest proselytizing efforts were confined to the United States and Canada, revelations foretelling a world-wide gathering came as early as March 1831, when the

Lord revealed that in the last days his saints would gather at a New Jerusalem in the western hemisphere, just as the Jews would gather at the Jerusalem in the Holy Land. (D&C 45: 24–5, 64–71.) Then in April 1836 Moses appeared to Joseph Smith and Oliver Cowdery in the Kirtland Temple, restoring the keys of the gathering of Israel – a visitation that re-emphasized the Church's responsibility for a gathering of world-wide scope. (D&C 110: 11.)

But achieving the fulfilment of these scriptural promises was to be a slow and demanding process. The expulsion of the saints from Missouri in 1838–9 was the climax of many hardships they experienced in connection with the gathering, and it led some to question for a time whether they should still attempt to settle together.

The Prophet Joseph Smith, finally freed from imprisonment in Missouri in the spring of 1839, moved quickly to reaffirm the importance of the gathering and to designate a new location – and Commerce (later Nauvoo), Illinois, became the rallying point for the saints. Soon the time would be ripe for the gathering to reach across the sea. In fact, Brigham Young and other members of the Quorum of Twelve Apostles scarcely had time to settle their families at Nauvoo before they left for their previously appointed mission to the British Isles. There the Church had been growing for nearly three years, and an important part of the apostles' mission in Great Britain would be to initiate LDS emigration to Nauvoo.

The United States and the British colonies in North America had always held some appeal for potential emigrants. Beginning soon after 1800, a dramatic increase in population, coupled with abrupt changes in employment conditions in the British Isles, brought economic uncertainty to large numbers of people. Despite Britain's rapid industrial development and economic growth, thousands of families were now unable to sustain themselves adequately. Thus by the 1830s emigration to North America seemed more than ever before to hold the promise of a better life. That decade saw the beginning of a large and sustained increase in the number emigrating from the British Isles to America, the total exceeding 20,000 as early as 1834.

The depression that racked Britain in 1837–42 has been called 'the grimmest period in the history of the nineteenth century'.

(J. Harrison, *Early Victorians*, p. 12.) And it was followed by other difficulties that made America seem more attractive still. The Irish potato famine brought emigration to an all-time high in the later 1840s and early 1850s, and from then until the First World War more than 100,000 individuals left the British Isles for the United States each year, except for periods in which America experienced serious economic problems.

Obviously these factors that led so many of their countrymen to emigrate also influenced LDS converts in the British Isles. But Joseph Smith instructed the first overseas missionaries not to preach the gathering until the Church was well established, and until the Spirit directed them to introduce the topic. (Joseph Smith, *HC 2*: 492.) Accordingly, Heber C. Kimball and his companions did not preach the principle of gathering in their 1837 mission to Britain. But in April 1840, soon after arriving in England, Brigham Young and the other apostles determined that the time was at hand. They agreed to begin by quietly encouraging the saints to emigrate; for the time being they would avoid making any public announcement, which would very likely arouse controversy.

Now converts began to catch the vision of their own role in fulfilling ancient prophecy and following modern revelation. They began to feel the urgency of preparing for Christ's second coming – and theological reasons then combined with economic and social motives for the gathering, to bring about a significant, continuous religious migration.

And so the gathering of Israel out of Great Britain began. Nauvoo had barely been established when the first organized company of forty-one British saints set out for it in June 1840. They were like Joshua's advance scouts, one of them thought, crossing the Atlantic Ocean rather than the River Jordan into the promised land. Before the group's departure from Liverpool on the packet-ship *Britannia*, Elders Brigham Young and Heber C. Kimball came aboard, appointed officers, stretched a curtain across a ship's cabin for privacy, and gave the entire group an apostolic blessing. The company consisted of one large extended family, four other families, and two additional individuals. Forerunners of multitudes, they sailed down the Mersey on the 6th of June, and safely reached New York on the 17th of July, having contended with only routine problems: strong headwinds and seasickness. (Moon.) Some reached Nauvoo soon afterwards, others not until the following spring.

The report of Francis Moon, one of the emigrants from the *Britannia*, was the first strong encouragement published by the Church for the British saints to emigrate. (*MS 1*: 252–5.) Brother Moon found Nauvoo a promising new settlement, relatively undeveloped but full of opportunity. He wrote of fertile soil, of owning cows that grazed free of expense, of the price of potatoes and beef. He also told of his acquaintance with Joseph Smith, whom he found to be truly a prophet, and from whom he had learned precious new principles. Joseph Smith had begun to introduce teachings about vicarious work for the dead in August 1840, at about the time the first British immigrants reached Nauvoo. Brother Moon appealed to his fellow British saints to come and help bring great things to pass, among which would be the building of 'the house of the Lord', a temple.

In these early years, the admonitions to emigrate to Zion set a pattern followed for several decades. Important points were repeated countless times in various ways, such as the following.

(1) The Lord's people were always commanded to gather together, and the Lord was now again calling saints, through a living prophet, to emigrate.

(2) The saints could accomplish more to build the Lord's kingdom on the earth through combined efforts as a gathered people.

(3) The saints were commanded to gather out of 'Babylon', the sinful world, that they might not partake of her sins. By separating themselves from the world, they sought to live a life more pleasing to God, and to become sanctified.

(4) Prior to the second coming of Christ, wars and natural disasters would plague the nations, and there would be true safety only in Zion. These events were near at hand.

(5) Latter-day Saints – particularly the poor – would have greater economic opportunities and better chances to achieve their individual potential in Zion than in Europe.

However, words of caution were also given repeatedly, beginning with Brother Moon's report. Those who emigrated with unrealistic expectations of the material and spiritual conditions in Zion risked disillusionment. They must realize that the inhabitants of Zion were still mortals with their own struggles to face, and that many of the economic opportunities would materialize only through effort. Emigrants whose motives were largely selfish might well join the ranks of apostates and detractors. The First Presidency helped establish the religious tone of the emigration effort in an 1841 epistle, in which they concluded:

> Let those who can, freely make a sacrifice of their time, their talents, and their property, for the prosperity of the kingdom; and for the love they have to the cause of truth, bid adieu to their homes and pleasant places of abode, and unite with us in the great work of the last days, and share in the tribulation, that they may ultimately share in the glory and triumph. (*MS 1*: 273.)

Within a year nearly a thousand followed the lead of the *Britannia*'s advance company. Before he and others of the Twelve left the British Isles on 21 April 1841, Elder Brigham Young supervised the chartering of several ships for LDS emigrants, and he and his fellow apostles organized the departing companies. (Later mission leaders would follow this pattern of centralized direction established by Elder Young.) Most of the emigrant saints sailed from Liverpool, which was one reason why the British Mission office was located in that city between 1842 and 1933, as assisting with emigration was one of the most important functions of the mission presidency and staff. This involved contracting for ships, ticketing, provisioning, berthing, helping emigrants find lodging before sailing, and a host of other details – work that could be so demanding at times of peak emigration that the health of the mission staff was sometimes endangered.

Early plans called for a concentration of the British saints at the new settlement of Warren, adjacent to Warsaw, Illinois. (*MS 2*: 147.) However, the Church was unable to obtain conditions that were as favourable as they had anticipated, so Nauvoo itself became the primary gathering place. Life in a newly settled town like Nauvoo required adjustments for British immigrants, even if the people were hospitable. Mary Ann Weston Davis, a new convert from Gloucestershire and recently widowed, married widower Peter Maughan, father of five young children. During the cold winter of 1841–2 they lived in the home of Elder Orson Hyde of the Quorum of Twelve Apostles, who was away on a mission. Using a chest for a table, she found that without a cupboard much of her fine English chinaware was gradually broken, but 'we were all well and could eat our mush with my silver tea spoons till they were broke'. Laying her feather beds on the floor in the absence of bedsteads, Sister Maughan found that one of them froze to the floor and could not be moved until spring. By that time Elder Hyde had returned and needed his own home, so the Maughans camped outside on their own plot of land until they were able to have a house built. These were just the beginnings of a challenging, pioneering life for the Maughans. (Maughan.)

Nauvoo needed manufacturing enterprises if it were to become the self-sufficient city Joseph Smith envisaged. Moreover, many of the British saints would be unable to gain employment in the trades for which they had been trained unless industries were established at Nauvoo. Hence calls went out for British LDS capitalists to emigrate and establish such industries. (*MS 1*:255; 268–9; 269–73.) Members of the Quorum of the Twelve also suggested that the saints could foster international trade, thus providing increased opportunity for emigration whilst strengthening Nauvoo's economy. British saints, they suggested, might ship goods to Nauvoo, and in turn the Nauvoo saints could charter ships in America to carry both emigrants and goods from Europe, presumably with profits from the sale of the goods.

Although suggestions for trade and industry were often made, these needs of the saints were not yet effectively met. In England, Reuben Hedlock suggested that a joint-stock company could help supply what was wanted. (*MS* 4:204; 5:157–8, 171–7.) The idea was developed in more detail and presented as an official proposal at an April 1845 conference of priesthood brethren from throughout the British Isles, at which Wilford Woodruff presided. Detailed articles of incorporation for the company were drawn up at a marathon sixteen-hour committee meeting during the conference, then thoroughly examined, discussed, amended and approved by all those in attendance. The stated goals of the company were to establish manufacturing enterprises in America (presumably Nauvoo and vicinity) by exporting machinery, and to import foodstuffs from America for the consumption of stockholders and for sale to others. The company planned to enlist many shareholders by selling shares at an extremely low price and by eventually returning company profits to the shareholders, although all profits for the first five years would be reinvested in the company in order to expand its business. (*MS* 5:171–7.) The company was intended to facilitate emigration, with the saints utilizing the same ships that would carry the company's goods and machinery to America.

Optimism prevailed in the wake of the conference. Elder Woodruff seemed proud to report in his journal that the conference had transacted 'more business than ever was transacted before in one conference of the Latter Day Saints in the British Dominions'. He felt that the founding of the company was 'laying the foundation for much good'. (Kenney, 2:535, entry for 9 Apr 1845.)

Complications soon arose, however. In order to conform to a new law regarding registration of joint-stock companies, the articles of incorporation had to be extensively rewritten. A solicitor was retained at considerable cost, and the complicated process of registration delayed the start of business for more than a year. Meanwhile, in America, the saints were forced to leave Nauvoo, and plans were made to move west. Thus it seemed that the best route to the new Church headquarters would be by way of California, either by sailing through the Straits of Magellan or by crossing the isthmus of Panama. In view of this, the British and American Commercial Joint Stock Company, as it was now named, expanded its plans. Its new deed of settlement, the major document required for registration, stated that the company's main goals were 'to trade as merchants usually do between the United Kingdom of Great Britain and Ireland and all parts of North and South America by importing and exporting and buying and selling articles of merchandise, trade and commerce and for such purposes to purchase and hold a charter or hire ships and vessels and to manufacture the raw materials and produce of the said countries and to establish therein manufactories of any kind'. (Registration papers.) The deed was finally completed just days before Elder Woodruff departed for America on 23 January 1845 to gather his scattered family. Although he apparently did not take a leading part in the effort to establish the company, he agreed to serve as one of its sixteen directors, purchased ten shares of stock, and must have approved the direction the company was taking, as he signed the deed of settlement.

Continual encouragement was given to the British saints to subscribe for shares in the company, and missionaries preached support of the Joint Stock Company as well as the gospel. Tentative plans were made to charter a ship with a company of emigrants for Winter Quarters. But the plan never came to fruition. The company's funds were mismanaged. Unfortunate 'loans' to Reuben Hedlock consumed much of the available capital – more than £500. Brigham Young and the Twelve, hearing reports at Winter Quarters that the Joint Stock Company and Church affairs in the British Isles were awry, sent Elders Orson Hyde, John Taylor and Parley P. Pratt to Britain to bring things under control. They reached Liverpool on 3 October 1846, and under their direction the company was dissolved and its remaining assets distributed to the stockholders. Fortunately only sixteen persons held twenty or more shares, and as all the stockholders had agreed beforehand that they would not receive any return on their investment for the first five years, they were perhaps better able to cope with their losses. In any case, the failure of the Joint Stock Company was not so damaging as it might have been had the mismanagement been allowed to continue.

From the standpoint of public relations and maintaining morale, mission leaders made some wise decisions following the demise of the company. They quickly pursued another alternative which, though it ultimately had no direct effect on the emigration of the saints, still helped to maintain an urgent focus on emigration: they prepared a petition to Queen Victoria, requesting that the British government assist poor Latter-day Saints to emigrate to Vancouver Island or to the portion of the Oregon Territory that Britain had secured by treaty with the United States in June 1846. This petition suggested that the government provide not only the means to ship the poor to North America, but also either employment or provisions that would help them subsist until they could raise adequate crops. Accompanying the document was the outline of a plan for awarding the emigrants land grants in the area to be settled. Reportedly bearing the signatures of nearly 13,000 individuals, the petition was received by the Prime Minister, Lord John Russell, on behalf of the Queen, and copies were sent to all Members of Parliament. (*MS 8*: 142; *9*: 64.)

This was not an unusual request, coming at a time when the Irish potato famine and other economic difficulties brought many such calls for government assistance. However, in response to similar suggestions, the British Colonial Office had recently decided against allotting any funds to emigrants to North America, opting instead to provide only information to prospective emigrants and limited emergency aid to settlers. It was feared that opening the floodgates for emigration of the poor would not only drain government coffers but also deposit large numbers of people in British North America who would be unable to make a living on their own. Thus, although the British saints' petition brought an interested response from one Member of Parliament (John Bowring), it evidently never became the subject of any significant parliamentary discussion. (*MS 9*: 74–5, 169.)

Like the leaders of the British Mission, Church authorities at Winter Quarters also expressed the hope that Vancouver Island could be a gathering place for the saints from the British Isles, especially since the Church in North America was again without a permanent headquarters. (*MS 9*:98, 104.) Thus, even while its chances for success faded, the petition to the Queen encouraged the poorer British saints to maintain the hope that somehow they might obtain financial assistance for emigration. Meanwhile, Church members were instructed to prepare for emigration at short notice but to await word before making final arrangements. (*MS 9*:171–2.) In the event that the British government should decide to give financial assistance to the saints before Brigham Young and his party of pioneers could establish new headquarters for the Church, the British saints would gather at Vancouver. (*MS 9*:243–4.)

During this period of expectant waiting for definite word about the future headquarters of the Church, the saints in Britain turned their energies to sharing the gospel with their neighbours and relations, and the Latter-day Saint message spread quickly during this period, bringing the British Mission's greatest numerical growth of the century in the years 1847–51.

In February 1848, after word was received that the pioneers had established a settlement in the valley of the Great Salt Lake, mission leaders began to encourage the saints to emigrate to Council Bluffs, Iowa, by way of New Orleans, and to continue onward to the new Church headquarters as soon as they could arrange the necessary overland transportation. (*MS 10*: 40–1.) The Quorum of the Twelve admonished all who could be called saints to gather, and

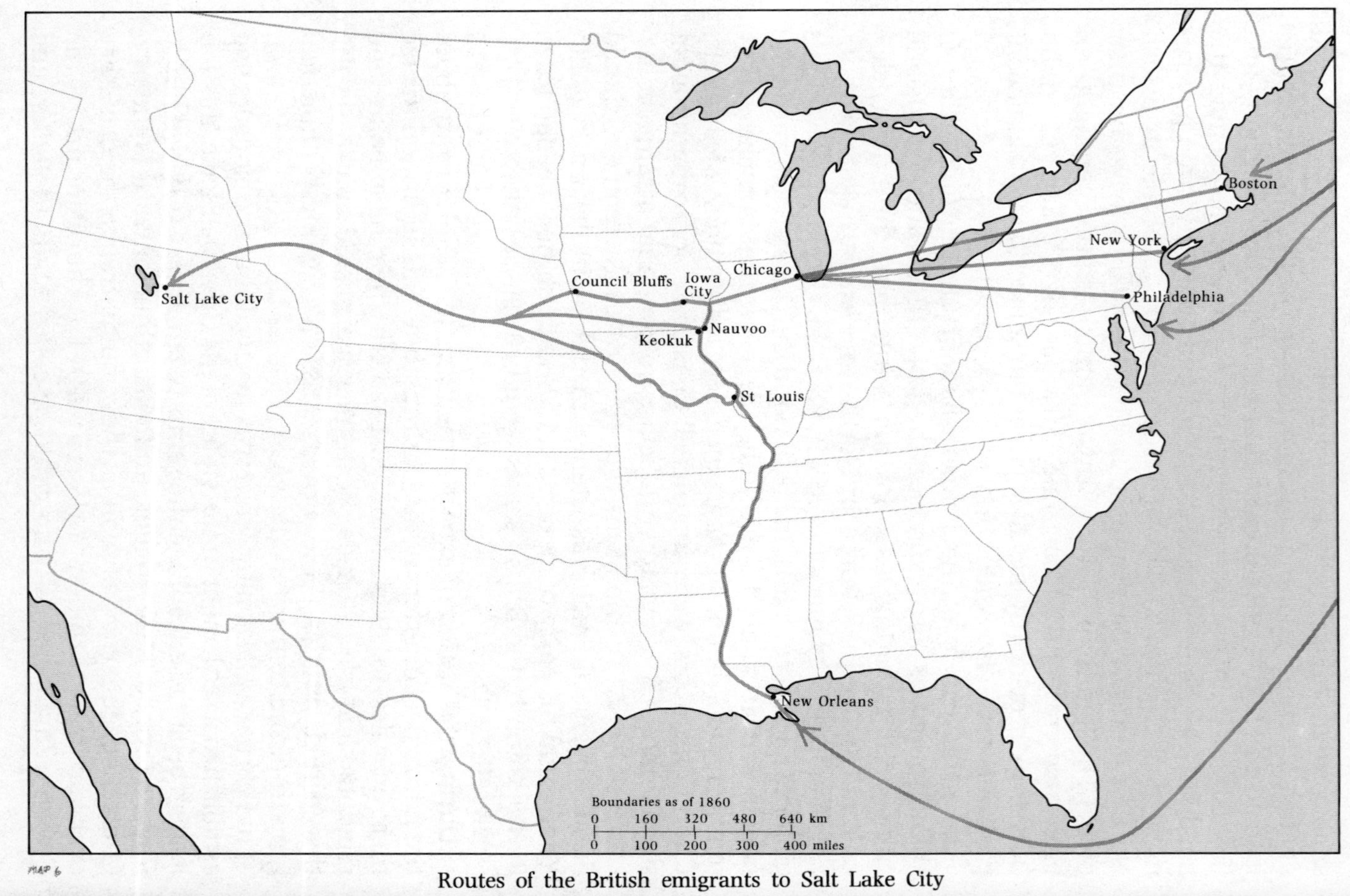

Routes of the British emigrants to Salt Lake City

to bring seeds, implements and educational materials, as well as models and descriptions for the construction of machinery. Moreover, anticipating the construction of another temple, they called for emigrants to contribute a wide variety of items 'to beautify, to adorn, to embellish, to delight, and to cast a fragrance over the House of the Lord'. (*MS 10*: 81–8.) The more wealthy members were to help the poor emigrate, and the suggestion was made that their assistance might be in the form of loans, to be repaid as promptly as possible. As at Nauvoo, the Twelve also called for 'those who have the intelligence and the means' to establish factories at Salt Lake City in which the poor could be employed. (*Ibid.* p. 86.) British Mission leaders further counselled Church members to prepare to emigrate 'in good earnest, not with unwise precipitancy, but with a full and deliberate purpose of heart to bring it to pass'. (*MS 10*: 89.)

To preside over the British Mission and supervise emigration, Elder Orson Pratt of the Quorum of the Twelve Apostles was sent to Britain in 1848. He helped to organize and refine emigration procedures, requiring a more orderly flow of emigrants through Liverpool and clarifying some of the preparations necessary for the voyage. (*MS 10*: 241–7.)

By now Church members had long benefited from the British Mission's management of the emigration enterprise. They purchased tickets from their own LDS passage brokers, and were shepherded by assigned leaders through the processes of final arrangements, thus avoiding the pitfalls of deception, cheating and outright robbery to which many emigrants were subjected. President Orson Pratt further offered to sell Latter-day Saints a variety of provisions to supplement the rather sparse fare that shipowners were then required by law to provide. Occasionally LDS emigrants who conducted this business outside the established Church channel would encounter problems, and the publication of their woes undoubtedly reinforced their leaders' counsel to use Church-sponsored arrangements. Lucius Scovil, sent by President Pratt to serve as LDS emigration agent at New Orleans in late 1848, reported that a company of 'sharks' there had 'bamboozled' some companies of immigrant saints, causing them unnecessary delays before taking the steamer up the Mississippi River to St Louis. (*MS 11*: 72.)

There were considerable challenges involved in helping the poorer saints to emigrate and become established in the Salt Lake Valley. President Orson Pratt estimated that wealthy British saints assisted nearly two hundred of their poorer brothers and sisters to emigrate in the spring of 1849. (*MS 11*: 106.) Still, many of these same poor emigrants were simply left to their own devices after their companies reached Iowa and those who could afford to continue their journey had done so. This posed a particular problem at Kanesville, Iowa, where there were already many poor from among the Nauvoo refugees. (*MS 11*: 263.)

In fact, the systematic assistance of these poorer saints was not effectively begun until the Church had been able to establish itself more firmly in the Salt Lake Valley. It was not until late July 1849 that profitable trade with California-bound 'gold-rushers' and the promise of more abundant crops put President Brigham Young in a position to encourage immigration to the valley. At that time, in Church councils, plans began to mature for community-based financial aid to the poor who wished to emigrate. (Young, letters to Orson Pratt, 24 Jul 1849, and to Wilford Woodruff, 25 Jul 1849.)

Thus the Perpetual Emigration Fund (PEF) was begun in September 1849, in fulfilment of a solemn covenant made in the Nauvoo Temple shortly before the exodus, that 'to the extent of our property and influence, we never would cease our exertions, until all the Saints who desire, should be removed to a place of safety'. (Bullock; PEF Co. minutes.) Donations were to provide the basis for a revolving fund, which would be invested in oxen purchased in the American mid-west. LDS refugees in Iowa would hopefully provide their own inexpensive wagons and the bare essentials in provisions and supplies, and once the oxen had transported these evacuees from their temporary locations to the Rocky Mountains, the oxen would be sold in Utah. The proceeds, accompanied by repayment for transportation by those who were aided, would then be used to buy more oxen.

In the autumn of 1849 donations of $5,600 [£1,120] from the saints in the Salt Lake Valley were taken to Iowa to initiate the operation of this fund. (Clark, *Messages*, *2*: 31–6; Young, letter to Thomas L. Kane, 20 Oct 1849.) Donations from the British Isles and from Iowa, as well as from the Salt Lake Valley, were considered essential to the operation of the PEF, and PEF assistance to Europe was to begin as soon as possible after the removal of the Nauvoo refugees. (Clark, *Messages*, 2:35; 47–8; 60.) Franklin D. Richards, then president of the British Mission, declared that the fund would operate 'so long as there shall be a poor Saint upon the face of the earth unable to gather to Zion', and called upon all those who wished for Zion to be firmly established – 'yes, all who wish for deliverance from the plagues of Babylon, and eternal life in the Kingdom and glory of God' – to donate. (*MS 12*:136.)

President Richards further directed that an agent be appointed in each branch of the mission to receive and account for PEF donations, and that he forward these funds and records to a conference (district) treasurer, who would in turn send them to the Liverpool office quarterly or as otherwise required. A record of the donations would be 'preserved in the archives of the church, until the day when men shall be judged according to the deeds done in the body, out of the books which will be opened'. (*Ibid.* pp. 136–7.)

First priority in the use of PEF funds was given to transporting Nauvoo refugees who had not yet completed the trek west. A major proportion of these were evacuated from the mid-west states by the end of 1852. Under Brigham Young's direction, British donations to the PEF were then used to assist the poor to emigrate from the British Isles, beginning in 1852. Early that year 250 British emigrants received PEF assistance. (*MS 14*:72.)

Beginning with the 1853–4 emigration season, the PEF's assistance to British emigrants began to accelerate. (Young, letters to Samuel W. Richards, 30 Sep and 29 Oct 1852, 29 Mar and 1 Jun 1853.) With the Church's energies and resources thus concentrated on emigration, the years 1853–6 saw a greater number of British saints sail for America than in any other four-year period in Church history. The fact that this peak of emigration coincided with the Crimean War illustrates both that the saints were particularly apt to emigrate during periods of international tension and war, and that Church leaders were generally able to make more resources available at such times. President Franklin D. Richards wrote in 1855:

I would say again in reference to the emigration of the Saints to the States, that the horrors of war, the prevalence of hunger, producing bread riots, and the general depression of trade all serve to render it as impossible to stop emigration as it would be to dam up the Hudson [River] with bulrushes. (F. D. Richards, letter to John Taylor, 2 Mar 1855.)

In addition to the PEF, the Church provided a service that helped many of its members prepare to emigrate. Church leaders administered individual savings accounts for emigration purposes, collected on a local level and transmitted to the mission office.

By this time the Church had more than a decade of experience in organizing emigrant groups, and in dealing with shipping firms and provision merchants. Mission leaders were thus able to offer relatively healthy and efficient arrangements for transporting the greatest possible number of people across the Atlantic at low cost. In fact, when concern about the undesirable conditions of emigration led to Parliamentary investigations of the business, the Church's emigration practices were scrutinized and praised. In 1854 Elder Samuel W. Richards, who had superintended LDS emigration in Britain for several years, was questioned at length by a select committee of the House of Commons regarding the way in which LDS emigration was conducted. After that interview, Monckton Mills M.P. (later Lord Houghton) reported that the committee

came to the conclusion that no ships under the provisions of the 'Passengers' Act' could be depended upon for comfort and security in the same degree as those under [Elder Richards's] administration. The ordinary emigrant is exposed to all the chances and misadventures of a heterogeneous, childish, mannerless crowd during the voyage, and to the merciless cupidity of land-sharks the moment he has touched the opposite shore. But the Mormon ship is a Family under strong and accepted discipline, with every provision for comfort, decorum, and internal peace. On his arrival in the New World the wanderer is received into a confraternity which speeds him onwards with as little hardship and anxiety as the circumstances permit, and he is passed on from friend to friend, till he reaches the promised home. (*Edinburgh Review*, Jan 1862, pp. 198–9.)

Thereafter word was circulated in the British press that members of the select committee felt Christian shipowners could learn much from the Latter-day Saints about 'how to send poor people decently, cheaply, and healthfully across the Atlantic'. (*MS 16*: 523.)

The parliamentary investigations led to a new Passengers' Act that took effect in October 1855, designed to improve conditions aboard emigrant ships. Though the Latter-day Saints had avoided many of the problems the act sought to correct, they still benefited from the changes it brought. Peas, beef, pork and potatoes were added to the standard ship's fare, which had earlier been dominated by biscuits and oatmeal; and more space was allotted on board for each passenger. Under these conditions, as President Franklin D. Richards reported to Brigham Young, many of the LDS emigrants were living better aboard ship than they had at home. (F. D. Richards, letter to Brigham Young, 25 Nov 1855.) (In fairness to LDS emigration agents, it should be noted that even before the 1855 Passengers' Act, they supplemented the legal requirement of rations with some of the items listed.)

Improvements in sailing vessels and routes also benefited the saints who sailed at this time. By the mid-1850s they were making the crossing on larger ships and were berthed on two decks rather than one. Furthermore, railway connections were by then available from ports in the north-eastern USA to Council Bluffs, Iowa. To avoid the risk of contagious disease often encountered on the Mississippi, the saints stopped sailing to New Orleans after 1855, going instead to New York, Boston or Philadelphia, and taking the railway from there. This shortened the sea voyage by an average of more than two weeks. (Sonne, p. 73.) And the saints made good use of their time aboard ship by sewing canvas tents and wagon covers for the overland journey to Salt Lake City. (Plans for one such tent are included in a letter from Franklin D. Richards to James Ferguson, 21 Mar 1856.)

In order to help as many members as possible emigrate as quickly and inexpensively as they could, Church leaders in the 1850s made several innovations in financing emigration and in transporting the saints. Some emigrants could afford to pay their own fares across the Atlantic and to buy the wagons, oxen, provisions and equipment necessary for the trek to the Salt Lake Valley. Those who did so were called 'independent' emigrants. During this period Church agents helped these people by selling them everything required for their 'outfit' for crossing the plains, and by incorporating them into the Church's organization of emigrant companies. Other emigrants paid their own fares across the Atlantic and then stayed for some time at the port of entry or another location, like St Louis, while they earned enough to 'outfit' themselves for the trip west. These were called 'States' emigrants, or 'ordinary' emigrants.

Another arrangement was what amounted to low-cost rental of Church-owned teams and wagons for the trip across the plains. Church agents estimated costs beforehand and charged emigrants an amount that would allow a small margin of safety, then refunded the excess that had been paid. In 1855 this low-cost method of emigration was placed under the jurisdiction of the PEF.

Finally, many emigrants received assistance from either the Church or the PEF to emigrate. If President Young learned of craftsmen who could fill needs in important enterprises, he might direct that they be sent to Utah by the PEF. If British immigrants in Utah requested Church leaders to help their relations in Britain to emigrate, the British Mission president might be authorized to furnish means for their transportation. Also, missionaries serving in Britain were occasionally asked to nominate worthy members of long standing for emigration assistance, and during most of the 1860s the PEF participated in the Church Trains system (see pp. 182–3). As a result, more than a third of all European LDS emigrants from 1852 to 1887 received some kind of PEF assistance to emigrate, either for the entire journey or for the overland portion.

Saints who were assisted by the PEF were generally expected to pay as much as possible towards their own emigration expenses. At times, pre-payment of part of the cost or a donation to the PEF would allow a person either to receive PEF assistance or to nominate someone else for assistance. This was particularly true in 1853–5, when a variety of options for partial payment or donations were put into effect. The aim was to help as many emigrate as possible, and to obtain from them the much-needed cash to cover the costs of the journey. The result, however, was that so many took advantage of these options that Church resources were quickly exhausted, leaving little prospect that the Church or the PEF could provide assistance in 1856.

Two features of the 1856 emigration made it unusual. First, Brigham Young and others in the Salt Lake Valley donated valuable property to the PEF, which was sold to British saints of substantial means. The most important such transaction was the sale of President Young's White House in Salt Lake City to Thomas Tennant, a well-to-do Yorkshire farmer. (F. D. Richards, letters to Brigham Young, 25 Nov 1855 and 4 Apr 1856; letters to Thomas Tennant,

28 Dec 1855 and 11 Jan 1856; account with Thomas Tennant, 23 May 1856; letter to Daniel Spencer, 27 May 1856.) The cash obtained in this way provided much of the means for assisted emigration that year.

The second feature was the use of handcarts, an idea President Young had advocated as early as 1851. An entire company of handcart emigrants required only one or two teams and wagons (to carry equipment and the sick) and the carts were much less expensive than wagons. Under normal circumstances, this was a good solution to the need for low-cost transportation. Church personnel had the expertise to put it into operation, and many emigrants were excited to have the possibility of making their way to Zion even if it meant taking fewer possessions and pulling a cart all the way. (Hafen and Hafen; D. Smith.)

Most of the handcart companies in 1856 had a successful experience. However, a series of unfortunate circumstances resulted in tragedy for the last two companies of the year, those led by Captains James G. Willie and Edward Martin. It was not clear how many emigrants could be assisted until arrangements were finalized for the sale of the donated Salt Lake City property, and that depended on the sale in the British Isles of the property of Brother Tennant and others. Final arrangements took so long that the last shiploads of emigrants had to leave later than planned. Furthermore, Orson Spencer, who was to serve as LDS immigration agent at St Louis, died, and his replacement, Elder Erastus Snow, was unable to make early emigration arrangements as expected. Other Church leaders east of the Missouri River did not have a clear understanding of their responsibilities. And lastly, the construction of some handcarts was not begun early enough to have the last of the emigrants provisioned in time for an early departure. (Young, letters from John Taylor, 10 Aug 1856 and 24 Feb 1857; letter from Erastus Snow, 17 Jan 1857; D. Spencer, May–Oct 1856; D. H. Smith.)

As a result of these complications, the last two handcart companies were not prepared to leave Florence, Nebraska, until the 4th of September. Anxious that the handcart emigrants reach Salt Lake City, Church authorities who met in council at Florence urged that all proceed onward. Men of more experience deferred to the authorities, rather than re-emphasizing their earlier counsel, which was that it was usually unsafe to pass through the mountains that late in the year. (D. Spencer, May–Oct 1856.)

Snow came early to the Wyoming mountains that year, resulting in the loss of many lives for the Martin and Willie companies. The saints in Utah mounted a heroic rescue effort that brought survivors safely to the valley. (Cornwall and Arrington.) President Brigham Young, who had taken a special interest in the handcart project, was dismayed at the tragic turn it had taken. He directed that in future no emigrants should leave the outfitting point so late, and he gave stern directions that Church councils must benefit from *all* the wisdom available to them.

President Young kept high hopes for the successful operation of the handcart programme in later seasons. He sent further instructions for construction of the best possible handcarts, and began to establish supply stations along the trail that would assist the emigrants as well as the transport of goods and the post. However, tensions between the Church and the United States government soon led to the 'Utah War' (1857–8), which brought an end to most of these activities. Though handcart companies continued until as late as 1860, they then gave way to the most effective campaign the Church had ever mounted for emigration purposes: the Church Trains system.

In 1860 the saints learned that they could successfully send teams and wagons east to the frontier outfitting point in the spring and bring back people and goods the same season. This avoided the need of making large purchases of teams and wagons in the midwest each year, and flour for emigrants could be hauled east to meet them. Cash from the British saints was still the key to paying transatlantic shipping costs and most railway fares, but by using its modest profits from the sale of tickets and provisions, the Church was able to assist missionaries and Church leaders who had served for many years in Britain to emigrate.

Little assistance across the ocean was offered by the PEF during these years, but any emigrant who was able to reach the frontier outfitting point was allowed to travel in the Church Trains (wagon trains) and signed an agreement to repay the PEF $40–60 (about £8–10) per adult and proportional charges for children of varying ages, plus the cost of any extra provisions. Church Trains went east for emigrants most years between 1860 and 1869, the only exceptions being 1865, when President Young chose to concentrate

Church resources on building canals and the Salt Lake Temple, and 1867, when the Church recovered from the expenses of the 1866 emigration season and waited for the U.S. transcontinental railway to come nearer the Salt Lake Valley.

Although the financial transactions of the Church Trains operation became the concern of the PEF, it was more a Church effort than a company enterprise. Bishops of Utah wards were assigned to provide a given number of teamsters, wagons, ox teams and equipment for the round trip and outfitting these teams became a community effort. Then as the Church Trains arrived back home bishops were assigned to help emigrants who had not made prior arrangements to find homes and employment throughout the territory. Typically, emigrants would remain only briefly encamped on Salt Lake City's public square before being escorted to their new location.

Meanwhile, in the eastern half of North America the American civil war raged from 1861–5. During those years (which were also peak years for the Church Trains system) the textile industry of Great Britain was severely curtailed for lack of cotton imports from the American South. This in turn made it difficult for some British saints to earn money for their emigration. At the same time, they realized that the war posed a serious threat to railway lines in the United States, and they were frequently reminded of the urgency of emigrating before conditions became even worse. Thus many who were highly motivated found ways to overcome obstacles during this period, resulting in heavy immigration with the Church Trains system.

The Charles H. J. West family was typical of British saints at this time. They had been attempting for nine years to save enough money to emigrate to Zion when they counselled with missionaries in 1862 about how better to reach their goal. The problem, as Brother West explained it, was 'that we had children faster than we could get means for our emigration'. The elders suggested that they use their savings to send two of their children to Utah that year. With mixed emotions they arranged for Brother and Sister King, a childless couple from their own branch of the Church, to take their daughters, aged six and ten, to Utah. The Kings promised they would care for the girls as if they were their own children, and even though the Wests had complete faith in their friends, they still experienced an indescribable anguish as they bade their daughters farewell. Brother King's wife and mother both died during the journey, but he was as good as his word and found a home for the West girls with a Bishop Mills in Provo, Utah. Hearing of their safe arrival, the remainder of the West family in England found their motivation to save greatly increased. Brother West wrote that the children in Zion were like a lodestone, drawing the family towards them with great attraction. The Wests were able to emigrate aboard the packet-ship *Amazon* in June 1863 and were reunited with the children later that year. (C. West.)

The average married LDS adult emigrating on the *Amazon* had been a member of the Church for more than ten years. Apparently families of varying economic status took equally long to save funds for the voyage, confirming the truism that family spending tends to keep pace with income. Single adults on the *Amazon* were generally able to emigrate three or four years sooner than married persons. (*Ensign*, Mar 1980, p. 18.)

Elijah Larkin, a Cambridge policeman, had been attempting for eleven years to raise funds for himself and his family to emigrate. With a sustained effort he raised the amount needed, but his wife would agree to emigrate one day and change her mind the next. Fortunately her last change of heart before departure time was in favour of emigrating. When a fellow policeman tried to dissuade him from leaving, Brother Larkin used the opportunity to sell the man a Book of Mormon, a copy of the Doctrine and Covenants, other literature, and a ticket to a farewell party sponsored by the Cambridge branch for its departing emigrants. (Larkin.) Aboard the ship *Amazon* the Larkin family joined nearly nine hundred other Latter-day Saints from England, Wales, Scotland and Ireland.

The *Amazon* was one of very few ships to embark from London (rather than Liverpool) with LDS emigrants. Perhaps this was one reason that the 'Uncommercial Traveller' himself, Charles Dickens, decided to investigate the situation personally. Dickens had earlier befriended a young Mormon boy, William H. Culmer, and had interviewed Billy's family at length about their circumstances and their plans to emigrate. Though none of them happened to be aboard the *Amazon* (despite Culmer's later statement that two of them were) they must have piqued Dickens's curiosity enough for him to decide to investigate further. (Culmer, pp. 144–56.)

Most of what the famous author had heard about the Mormons

was negative, except for what the Culmers had told him. He went on board half expecting an unpleasant experience but determined to be an unbiased observer. He was pleasantly surprised. In a fair and entertaining article published a fortnight later he described his experience in detail, changing names and otherwise obscuring identities but still capturing his perception of the spirit of the emigrant company. In only one respect was he relatively unsuccessful; he was unable to draw any of the passengers or British Mission president George Q. Cannon into any in-depth conversation about their religion. The saints' motto during the nineteenth century, learned at the expense of hard experience, was 'mind your own business', and Dickens failed to penetrate the guarded front they often presented to inquiring strangers whose intentions were not clear.

Dickens was most impressed by the orderliness, sobriety, sensibility and serenity of the Mormon emigrants. After describing their conditions he concluded:

> I went on board their ship to bear testimony against them if they deserved it, as I fully believed they would; to my great astonishment they did not deserve it; and my predispositions and tendencies must not affect me as an honest witness. I went over the *Amazon*'s side feeling it impossible to deny that, so far, some remarkable influence had produced a remarkable result, which better known influences have often missed. (Dickens, p. 444.)

With a characteristic touch of ironic humour Dickens wrote that had he not known the *Amazon*'s passengers were Mormons he might have called them, 'in their degree, the pick and flower of England'. (Dickens, p. 446; see also *Ensign*, Mar 1980, pp. 16–19.)

In 1867–9 LDS emigration from the British Isles underwent a revolutionary change – from sailing ships to steamers and from ox wagons to the railway. President Brigham Young had hoped for the time when rail connections would make the way easier for LDS travel and shipping, but it also promised mixed blessings. Replacing the Church wagon trains with railway trains would mean additional cash outlay for fares – cash that relatively few could afford. Also, there was certain to be an influx of outsiders into Utah, and the claim was being made that they would soon outnumber the saints, decrease the influence of the Church, and bring about major changes in the Utah way of life.

With the completion of the U.S. transcontinental railway in 1869, the year 1868 provided the saints' last opportunity to save cash for emigrants, while at the same time increasing the numbers of the Church members in Utah. Early reports gave British saints the impression that President Young wanted to see them all leave their native land that year and emigrate to Zion. Later word was more moderate, but the intention was nevertheless to move as many people as possible. And in fact, more Latter-day Saints left the British Isles in 1868 than in any single year thereafter.

Before the change to steamships and rail, emigrant companies were fortunate to reach Salt Lake City within five months of their departure from Liverpool. After the change the trip often took three weeks or less, and there were far fewer deaths en route. The Church shipped its passengers exclusively on steamships operated by the Guion Line for a quarter of a century. Because of the positive business relationship developed with the company, Church members were usually guaranteed the lowest fare available, and sometimes had a lower fare than any other emigrants. Some of the Guion ships were among the fastest to cross the North Atlantic, and the saints were generally happy with their service. When U.S. Secretary of State William Evarts issued a circular in 1879 that seemed to aim at discouraging LDS emigration from Europe, Guion was not intimidated but stood firmly by their long-time customers. William H. Guion, a partner in the firm, promptly interviewed Evarts himself and obtained clarifications that helped at least partially to dispel the cloud that had gathered over the entire Church emigration system. (Jensen, 'Steaming Through', p. 7.)

Shipping firms had long been aware that passengers often stretched the truth in order to save money on their fares, but in 1880 President John Taylor learned that the ages of a number of LDS children had been reported incorrectly some time previously. He therefore instructed British Mission president William Budge to pay the Guion company the balance of the amount the passengers should have paid. Guion passenger agent George Ramsden declined the payment, saying the company knew nothing about the matter, but President Budge insisted that President Taylor knew about it and the president's instructions had to be carried out. Mr Ramsden declared that this once more confirmed that the Latter–day Saints 'were the most honest people that he had ever done business with',

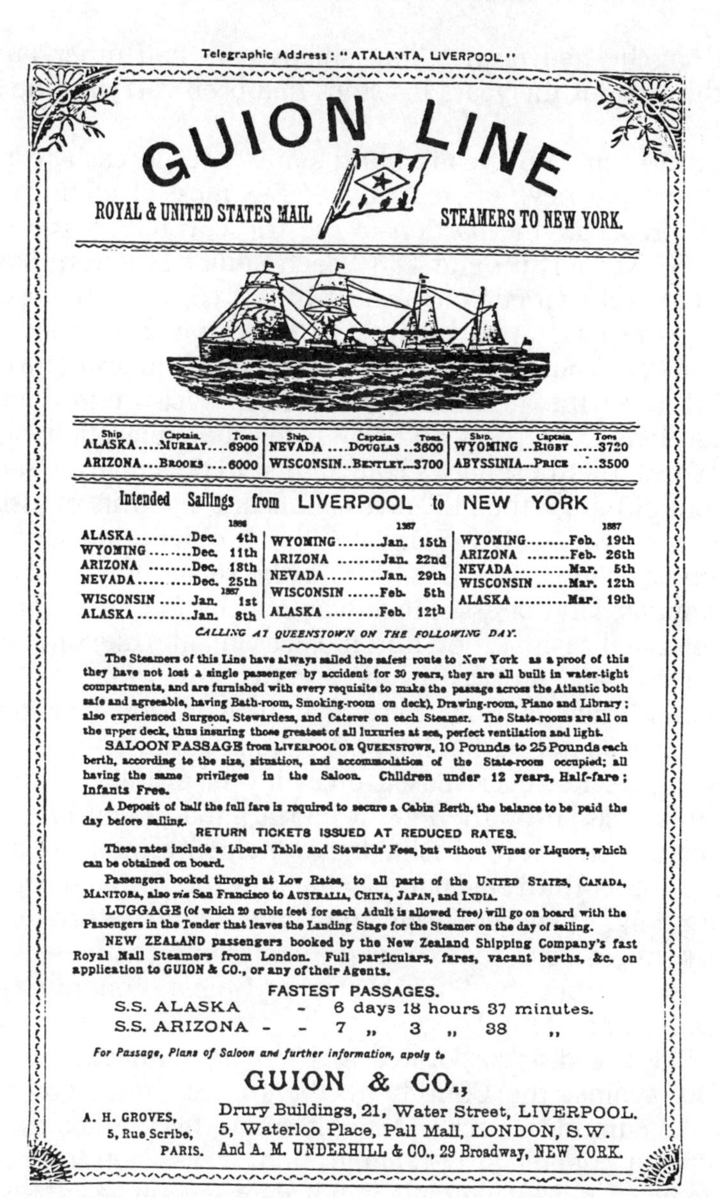

The Guion Line of steamships transported more Latter-day Saint emigrants across the Atlantic than any other carrier. (1886–87 advertisement.)

something he had been telling shipowners and other businessmen throughout the years his ships had been carrying the saints. (Budge.)

Beginning in 1869, emigrating saints needed cash to pay for their entire journey, whereas in 1861–8 most of them had been allowed credit for the portion of the trip covered by the Church Trains. Between 1869 and 1887 each adult's fare from Liverpool to Salt Lake City varied from about £11 to £16, with other expenses bringing the total to as high as £19. During this period special donations designated for certain categories of emigrants were distributed under the auspices of the PEF. A 'Welsh Fund' gathered contributions from Utah and Idaho for the emigration of saints from Wales. Ward primaries contributed to the emigration of children. But although the PEF gave significant amounts of assistance in the years 1869, 1871–5 and 1878–81, other financial aid from individuals eclipsed PEF help during the steam era. Probably the most popular kind of assistance was sent by friends and relatives who deposited cash at the Church offices in Salt Lake City and had a 'Church draft' sent to the prospective emigrants, along with notification that the funds were now available for their journey.

The PEF was not particularly effective in gaining repayment for its assistance, however. Based on study of a limited number of emigrants assisted by the PEF, it appears that about one-third of these paid their entire indebtedness, including interest; approximately another third paid part of what they owed; and the last third paid nothing. However, aside from any actual return of funds, the investment represented by the emigrants themselves was a good one, both for the Church and for Utah's economy. (Jensen, 'Financing', pp. 23–6.)

The PEF was disincorporated in 1887, in connection with proceedings against the Church by the United States government under the Edmunds–Tucker Act. Although this marked the end of a significant chapter in LDS emigration, it was not an important turning point, as PEF aid had dwindled for several years. Declining economic conditions in the American West were a more critical factor in reducing the number of saints who emigrated. Friends and relatives in America were less able to send money abroad, and British saints were less confident of their opportunities upon arriving in the United States.

Under these circumstances Church encouragement of emigration was modified. In June 1894 the First Presidency and the Quorum of the Twelve Apostles concluded that converts distant from Church headquarters 'should not be encouraged to emigrate until they are firmly grounded in the religion by labor and experience', and that those who were earning good wages and were in relatively favourable circumstances should 'not be encouraged to emigrate to this place, where labor is so scarce'. (A. Cannon, 21 Jun 1894.)

Economic improvement and a corresponding increase in emigration in 1900–10 corresponded with a moderate increase in positive statements about emigration, suggesting that only moderate changes had been made in Church policy. Meanwhile the building and purchase of chapels in Britain signalled a new emphasis on strengthening the Church far from headquarters. Yet the feeling persisted that Zion in America should eventually be home for faithful saints. The 1906 visit of President Joseph F. Smith to Europe, the first by a president of the Church, emphasized the lively interest he and other Church leaders took in the saints in the British Isles and in the growth of the Church there. Still, President Smith repeatedly expressed the hope that the listening saints would 'live to gather to Zion and rejoice on the mountains in the midst of the people of God and receive the fulness of the blessings of the gospel'. He counselled them not to be in a hurry to emigrate, but to study the gospel and prepare themselves mentally for the fact that life would hold challenges in Zion as well as in their native land. (*MS 68*:580, see also *68*:725.)

During the next few years, as anti-Mormon agitation in Britain focused particularly on emigration, the Church took several opportunities to clarify its position with regard to the gathering. It was charged that the Church was promoting emigration by providing land and other incentives, and that large numbers of young women were being recruited for immoral purposes. In response, the First Presidency and British Mission spokesmen did not disavow emigration, but indicated gentle changes in direction. They pointed out that it was the desire of the Church that members strengthen the Church locally and help maintain permanent branches by remaining in the British Isles for some time before emigrating. Church leaders did not urge emigration, but many families had relatives in America, or other personal reasons to emigrate. Thus the Church continued to facilitate their relocation by organizing emigrant groups in order to save them expense and trouble. The Church did not offer land to emigrants, and as for the 'white slave trade' involving young women, the charges were without foundation. (*MS 69*:120–3; *73*:136–9; *74*:2–3; *83*:600–1; Clark, *Messages*, 5:201.)

By 1912, European Mission president Rudger Clawson found it necessary to instruct emigrant companies to make themselves as inconspicuous as possible. Earlier groups had lustily sung LDS hymns at their departure, had held religious services aboard ship, and had frequently taken opportunities to share the gospel message with fellow passengers and ship's personnel. Now emigrating saints were instructed to forgo all such activities to avoid the danger of offending, even making sure not to leave any religious literature in view. (Clawson.) At the same time, emigration figures were eliminated from the compilation of mission statistics published annually in the *Millennial Star*.

Still, though they were instructed to maintain a low profile, the emigrants were not forgotten in Zion. Between the turn of the century and the First World War, a special system of communication was developed, involving the British Mission office, the Presiding Bishop's Office, and the Church transportation officer in Salt Lake City, in addition to the missionaries who shepherded the emigrants from England to Utah or other locations. The bishop at the family's intended destination was to be notified beforehand of their planned arrival; the British Mission transmitted information to Church headquarters regarding immigrating families' employment needs and qualifications; and a member of the Presiding Bishop's staff met each arriving train bearing an immigrant party, 'debriefed' the missionary responsible for the group, and sent a report to the First Presidency. (PBO: Immigration Papers.)

Church supervision and assistance during the journey was still needed and appreciated. Missionaries were often able to help obtain more comfortable accommodation on the railway carriages than officials initially offered the group. When the service aboard trains was troublesome, presumably the Church transportation agent could exert an influence on behalf of future companies. One of the most worrying features of the trip was the examination of in-

'New York City: scene in Castle Garden on the arrival of Mormon converts from Europe.' (From *Frank Leslie's Illustrated Newspaper*, 23 Nov 1878). Latter-day Saint immigrants between 1855 and 1890 landed at this processing centre and stayed here until their departure for the West.

dividuals by immigration officials. It was not unusual for small numbers of immigrants to be detained for hours, days or even weeks because of health problems or other difficulties. Some were even returned to their homeland. Although missionaries were instructed that they would be of no benefit in staying with such unfortunate individuals, and should proceed on their way with the rest of the group, still the missionary could often advise the immigrant on the most effective way to pass the immigration procedures, and he could later inform the person's friends or relations of the problem. (*Ibid.*)

The First World War and post-war economic conditions in Utah held Latter-day Saint emigration relatively low, although three of the inter-war years – 1920, 1921 and 1923 – saw more than 200 emigrants to North America. During this period the Church continued to cover expenses for emigrating British saints who had served as missionaries in their native land – a practice that had been carried out in various ways throughout much of the Church's history. (European Mission misc. papers; Teasdale.)

When emigration to Zion resumed after the Second World War, Church members discussed the topic openly and frequently. In 1947–51, emigrating families were listed in the 'personal' columns of the *Millennial Star*, along with births, deaths and marriages; and the prominent journalist Vivian Meik, a British convert, wrote glowingly in the June 1948 *Star* about his first year's experience as an immigrant in Zion. (*MS 110*: 162–3, 187.)

Europe's post-war economic growth made it more attractive for the saints to remain in the British Isles, but perhaps more importantly the Church moved to make blessings available to saints in Britain that previously had only been available in America and Canada. With the dedication of a temple at Newchapel, south of London, and the creation of stakes in the British Isles, the saints were counselled more firmly than before to remain where they were and build up Zion at home. President T. Bowring Woodbury, concerned that the British Mission was 'starved for leadership and constantly stripped of its strength through emigration', told the saints in 1959 that they had been placed in their homelands for the purpose of building the Lord's kingdom there, and that the dedication of the London temple had removed the last valid reason for emigrating. (*MS 121*: 4.) President Woodbury's counsel to Church members in general reemphasized the position of other postwar mission leaders. Still, like others throughout the history of the British Mission, in private counsel these leaders recognised the importance of varying individual and family needs. As a result, they continued to sustain decisions by a limited number of saints to emigrate. Local Church members who were aware of the general counsel to remain in the British Isles sometimes found this apparent discrepancy frustrating. On the other hand, the general encouragement to stay – tempered by compassion and understanding – was increasingly effective.

The British saints had come full circle. The first encouragement to emigrate had spoken of helping to build temples and of the blessings to be received therein, and for more than a century blessings uniquely available in America had drawn the saints there. Now the blessings of Zion were available in Britain. Still, the American connection remained an important factor in the lives of many British saints. A visit to Salt Lake City played an important role in the conversion of some, and visitors to General Conference brought renewed enthusiasm and strength home with them. Many of the saints had relations or friends in America, and a network of caring and communicating continued to reach across the sea in both directions. A few individuals and families continued to seek opportunities they felt they could find more readily in the United States, Canada, Australia or New Zealand, but some of these eventually returned to their homeland and assisted in strengthening the Church there.

Although the days of mass emigration to Zion are past, the contributions of the British LDS emigrants in Church history can hardly be overstated. The strength of the early Church was largely due to great numbers of dedicated British immigrants in Nauvoo and the Salt Lake Valley. With much of the British emigration coming relatively early, these saints were in a position to exert a particularly significant influence upon the Church in its most formative years. A brief review of some of the contributions made by individuals may suggest the more far-reaching role British immigrants have played in LDS history.

George Q. Cannon was one of the most influential Church leaders of the nineteenth century, having been called to the apostleship beginning in 1860, and thereafter serving as counsellor to Presidents Brigham Young, John Taylor, Wilford Woodruff and Lorenzo Snow. He was also the Utah Territory's delegate to the U.S. Congress, 1873–82.

John R. Winder was a counsellor in the Presiding Bishopric, 1887–1901, and counsellor in the First Presidency to President Joseph F. Smith. Charles W. Penrose was already an accomplished writer before he emigrated to America, where he wrote Church literature, frequently served as a Church spokesman, and was called to be an apostle in 1904, later serving as a counsellor to two Church presidents: Joseph F. Smith and Heber J. Grant. Charles W. Nibley, a prominent businessman in Utah, Idaho and the Pacific North-west, was Presiding Bishop of the Church in 1907–25, and then counsellor to President Heber J. Grant in 1925–31. George Teasdale, James E. Talmage and Charles A. Callis were all members of the Quorum of the Twelve Apostles, and John Longden served as assistant to the Quorum of Twelve, 1951–69.

Brigham H. Roberts, a member of the First Council of the Seventy, 1888–1933, was a theologian, assistant Church historian, author and politician. Author, compiler and scriptorian George Reynolds was a member of the First Council of the Seventy, 1890–1909, and Edward Stevenson, born a British subject in Gibraltar, was a member of the First Council of the Seventy in 1894–7. John Wells served as counsellor in the Presiding Bishopric, 1918–38.

Two British-born Church leaders whose emigration followed different patterns were President John Taylor, who had already settled in Canada before Parley P. Pratt brought the gospel message to his home, and Elder Derek Cuthbert of the First Quorum of the Seventy, who was the first general authority to be called while residing in Britain. (See photographs on pp. 200–202.)

After emigrating, Mary Fielding Smith helped establish organizations for donations to the Nauvoo Temple amongst the saints of Britain, and more importantly, she exerted a profound influence on her young son, Joseph F. Smith, who later became president of the Church.

The British connection was particularly important for the Primary Association of the Church. Matilda M. Barratt served as first counsellor to Sister Louie B. Felt in the first general Primary presidency of the Church, 1880–8. In addition, she made generous financial contributions to the Church beginning in the 1870s, which benefited emigration and education. May Anderson served on the Primary general board for fifty years, and was its second general president, 1925–39. She also helped establish kindergartens in Utah and conceived the idea that eventually led to the establishment of the Primary Children's Hospital in Salt Lake City. May Green Hinckley, an 1891 emigrant from Derbyshire, initiated what became the Gleaner Girl programme in the Young Women's Mutual Improvement Association, and was the Church's third general president of the Primary, 1940–3. (Madsen and Oman, pp. 35–110.)

Ruth May Fox was general president of the Young Women's MIA, 1929–37, Richard Ballantyne is credited as founder of the Sunday School, and the Church's genealogical programme has been influenced by immigrants like George Fudge, Frank Smith and David E. Gardner. Welsh-born Martha Hughes Cannon was an early Utah physician and the first woman in the United States to become a state senator. John T. Caine was a delegate to the U.S. Congress from the Utah Territory, 1883–93, and William Spry, Governor of Utah in 1909–17, was Commissioner of the USA General Land Office, 1921–9. James Sloan of County Tyrone, Ireland, was Nauvoo's first city recorder. William C. Staines, the Church's transportation agent at New York, 1869–81, was also Utah's territorial librarian.

British contributions to the arts in the Church have been considerable. William Pitt organized the Nauvoo Brass Band, which later played a prominent role in Utah music and theatre, and seven of the Salt Lake Tabernacle Choir's first eight directors were born in the British Isles. These were John Parry, born in Flintshire; James Smithies and Charles J. Thomas, from Lancashire; Robert Sands of Ireland; George Careless, from London; Ebenezer Beesley of Oxfordshire; and Evan Stevens, from South Wales. In addition, Thomas C. Griggs served the choir as an assistant conductor. Choir conductors Thomas and Careless had the benefit of excellent training in England before their emigration, and this was also true of Tabernacle organist Joseph J. Daynes, who had performed concerts in his native land as early as the age of six before emigrating to Utah a few years later.

Southampton native Joseph Ridges studied organ construction in England before emigrating to Australia to seek gold. Instead, he found the gospel there and eventually gathered with the saints in Salt Lake City, where he built the famous Salt Lake Tabernacle organ.

A host of hymns and songs, including ninety-four in the 1985 hymn-book, have either text or music written by British emigrants. Amongst these are 'High on the Mountain Top', with music by Ebenezer Beesley; 'Come, Come, Ye Saints', with text by William Clayton; 'We Thank Thee, O God, for a Prophet', with text by William Fowler; 'Gently Raise the Sacred Strain', with music by Thomas C. Griggs; 'Oh, Say, What Is Truth?', with text by John Jaques; 'Far, Far Away on Judea's Plains', text and music by John M. Macfarlane; 'Joseph Smith's First Prayer', with text by George Manwaring and music by Adam Craik Smyth; 'Israel, Israel, God Is Calling', with text by Richard Smyth; and 'For the Strength of the Hills', with music by Evan Stevens. Many Latter-day Saint hymns and songs were first published in the British Mission's *Millennial Star*.

William W. Major, a self-trained artist from Bristol, emigrated to Nauvoo and was later the first LDS artist to paint in Utah. Other artists from the British Isles included Sarah Ann Burbage Long, early Utah portrait painter; and John Tullidge, Reuben Kirkham, Alfred Lambourne and H. L. A. Culmer, landscape painters. Charles R. Savage, a native of Southampton, was a prominent photographer in early Utah.

Significant contributions in literature were made by authors Edward Tullidge, T. B. H. Stenhouse and Emma Marr Petersen, and by George Bickerstaff of Bookcraft Publishers. John Lyon, a poet from Ayrshire, donated the proceeds from his volume of poetry, *The Harp of Zion*, to the Perpetual Emigrating Fund Company. In Utah, Brother Lyon was a drama critic and assistant territorial librarian. Newspaper editors included John Taylor of *Times and Seasons* and the *Nauvoo Neighbor*, George Q. Cannon of the *Salt Lake Herald*, Charles W. Penrose of the *Deseret News*, Edward L. Sloan of the *Salt Lake Herald* and James Ferguson of *The Mountaineer*.

Latter-day Saint society was also strengthened by the British connection in business and industry. Miles Romney, an English architect, was foreman of construction on the Nauvoo Temple, and a prominent builder in Utah. Initial attempts to manufacture sugar and iron in Utah were largely unsuccessful, but helped bring skilled workers to the territory, and British saints whose investments made these pioneering efforts possible included Thomas Tennant, Joseph Russell and John W. Coward. John Sharp, a Scottish coal miner, became superintendent of the quarry for the Salt Lake Temple, superintendent of the Utah Central Railway, and director of the Union Pacific Railroad. The Castleton brothers, 1863 emigrants on the ship *Amazon*, became prominent merchants in Salt Lake City, as did William Jennings. Henry Dinwoodey established a successful furniture factory; and David Eccles founded one of the major banking firms in the Intermountain West. Charles W. Nibley was successful in the lumber and sugar industries.

The graph on the following page shows the number of saints who emigrated from the British Mission to North America by decades. (Piercy, pp. 14–17; British Mission shipping lists; Euro-

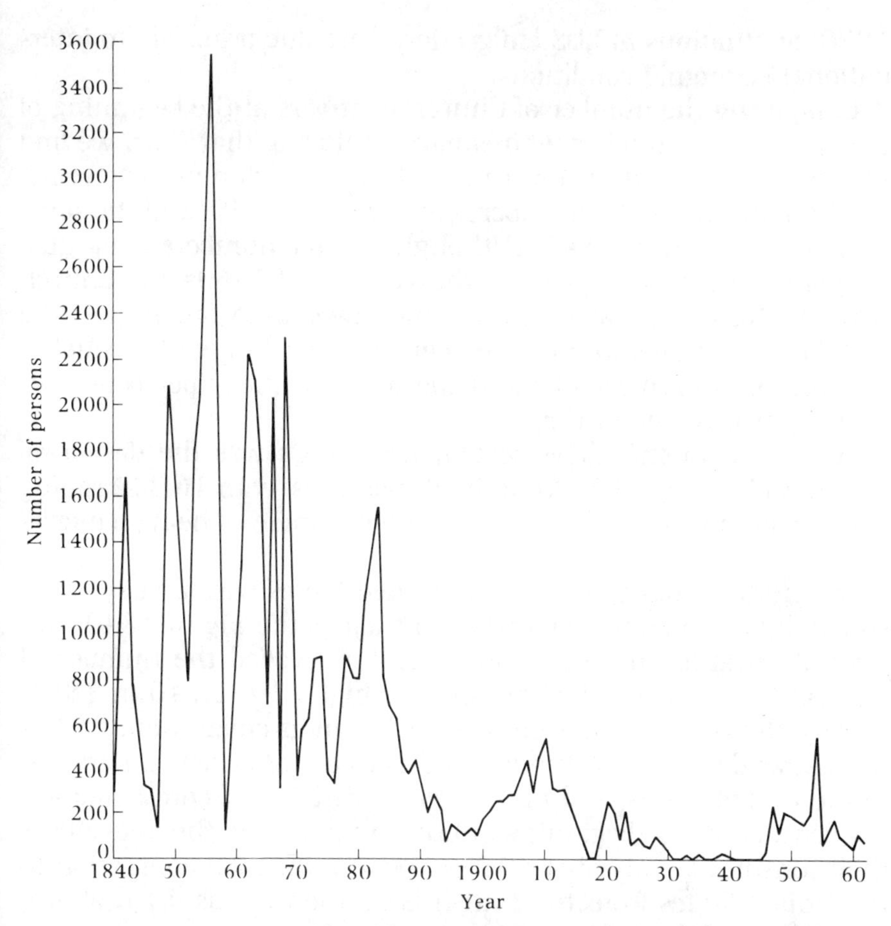

Emigration of British Latter-day Saints to the USA

pean Mission statistics; *MS*; PBO, reports, 1907–55; PBO, record of members, 1956–62; Jenson, 'Church Emigration'.) Apparently no systematic recording of emigration figures has been done since 1962. Appendix A (page 442) shows mission membership each year. As can be seen in the graph, one of the most striking features of the LDS emigration was its wide variation from year to year. From the 1840s to the 1860s this was due largely to the priority given to emigration in the use of Church resources. The Utah War of 1857–8 caused an abrupt decline in emigration, but the U.S. civil war had no apparent dampening effect and may actually have increased the urgency with which saints sought to emigrate. After

1870, fluctuations in LDS emigration were due primarily to international economic conditions.

Comparing the number of Church members at the beginning of a year with the number who emigrated during that year, we find that there was rapid turnover in the British Mission in early years. About a quarter of the members emigrated in 1840, and the same proportion again in 1841. Although greater numbers emigrated during each of several years in the 1850s and 1860s, the Church was relatively large at that time and fewer than one-fifth of the members emigrated in any one year. But in 1883, with a smaller number of Church members in the mission, thirty per cent emigrated – nearly one in three.

As shown in the above graph, the 1850s was the decade of heaviest LDS emigration from the British Isles, with 16,342 sailing from Liverpool. The 1860s was another decade of heavy emigration, involving 14,967 British saints.

Emigration from Britain to the United States was already widespread by the time the saints began their gathering in 1840. Not long afterwards, the Irish potato famine swelled the number of emigrants, which reached an all-time high of 272,740 in 1851. During the three highest decades of Mormon emigration, 1840–69, Latter-day Saints comprised 1·2 per cent of British emigration to the United States, and in one year, 1862, they represented 4·6 per cent. From the beginning of LDS emigration to the mid-1950s they constituted only about 0·2 per cent of the total emigration to the United States from the British Isles. (Sources as listed above, plus *Historical Statistics*, pp. 56–7.)

7

Church Growth in England, 1841–1914

Richard O. Cowan

The English saints must have felt something of a let-down when most of the apostles returned to America on 20 April 1841 following their glorious year-long mission in Britain. Still, they had Elder Parley P. Pratt, an apostle and one of the most popular missionary-leaders in the history of the Church, to preside over the British Mission – and for the rest of the nineteenth century and into the twentieth, most of his successors as mission president were also apostles. (See Appendix B.) This was evidence of the importance the general authorities prophetically attached to the work in Britain, for the very life-blood of the young Church was in its present and future British converts, and there were many challenges ahead.

The work begun by the apostles continued to flourish after the depature of the Twelve until the middle of the nineteenth century. During that time the number of Latter-day Saints in Britain increased more than fivefold:

1841	5,814	1846	10,894
1842	7,514	1847	12,139
1843	7,975	1848	17,902
1844	7,797	1849	26,012
1845	9,032	1850	30,747

During these same years the saints in America were experiencing a series of difficult events. In 1844 the Prophet Joseph Smith and his brother Hyrum were martyred at Carthage gaol in

General Authorities born in the British Isles (Arranged in alphabetical order)

Charles A. Callis 1865–1947
Quorum of the Twelve Apostles, born 4 May 1865, Dublin

George Q. Cannon 1827–1901
First Counsellor in the First Presidency, born 11 Jan 1827, Liverpool

Derek A. Cuthbert 1926–
First Quorum of the Seventy, born 5 Oct 1926, Nottingham

John Longden 1898–1969
Assistant to the Council of the Twelve Apostles, born 4 Nov 1898, Oldham

Charles W. Nibley 1849–1925
Second Counsellor in the First Presidency, born 5 Feb 1849, Hunterfield, Midlothian

Charles W. Penrose 1832–1925
First Counsellor in the First Presidency, born 4 Feb 1832, London

George Reynolds 1842–1909
First Council of the Seventy, born 1 Jan 1842, Marylebone, London

Brigham H. Roberts 1857–1933
First Council of the Seventy, born 13 Mar 1857, Warrington

James E. Talmage 1862–1933
Quorum of the Twelve Apostles, born 21 Sep 1862, Hungerford, Berks

John Taylor 1808–1887
President of the Church, born 1 Nov 1808, Milnthorp, Westmorland

George Teasdale 1831–1907
Quorum of the Twelve Apostles, born 8 Dec 1831, London

John Wells 1864–1941
Second Counsellor to Presiding Bishop, born 16 Sep 1864, Carlton, Notts

John R. Winder 1821–1910. First Counsellor in the First Presidency, born 11 Dec 1821, Biddenham, Kent

Illinois. Two years later the exodus from Nauvoo began and the saints started on their epic trek west across the plains. In 1847 President Brigham Young declared 'This is the right place' as the first band of pioneers entered the Salt Lake Valley, and they immediately began their vital task of subsisting in a wilderness, as they struggled to make the desert 'blossom as the rose'. (Isaiah 35:1.) By 1850 there were an estimated 11,380 Church members in Utah (most of them still living in rough-hewn log houses) with an additional 15,531 saints either at the Missouri River settlements, scattered across the plains, or at other locations in North America. At the same time there were 30,747 members in the British Mission. Thus there were actually *more* members of the Church in Britain in 1850 than there were in North America. (Clark, thesis, p. 68.)

The spiritual strength of the apostles' personal leadership was a major impetus to the British Mission's growth during the 1840s and in succeeding decades. In its early years the mission was headed by such notable men as Elders Orson Hyde, Franklin D. Richards and Orson Pratt. Elder George Q. Cannon returned to his native land as mission president in 1862, as would the other British-born apostles George Teasdale (in 1887), Charles W. Penrose (in 1906), and James E. Talmage (in 1924). The men who served as British Mission presidents also included in their ranks seven future presidents of the Church: Brigham Young, John Taylor, Wilford Woodruff, Joseph F. Smith, Heber J. Grant, George Albert Smith and David O. McKay.

Perhaps the greatest strengths provided for the English saints by these leaders came from the nature and power of their apostolic office. By revelation they had been designated as 'special witnesses of the name of Christ in all the world' authorized 'to build up the church, and regulate all the affairs of the same in all nations', and 'holding the keys, to open the door by the proclamation of the gospel of Jesus Christ'. (D&C 107:23, 33, 35.)

Growth slowed between 1842 and 1845 when mission presidents were not members of the Twelve, but the rate of growth began increasing again in 1845 when Elder Wilford Woodruff returned to preside. Growth accelerated to unprecedented levels after 1847 when the pioneers successfully established their settlement in the Salt Lake Valley and calls went out for the saints abroad to come and help build up Zion in the tops of the mountains. This growth, however, also set the stage for some problems which surfaced particularly when the apostles were not present.

Such a problem arose with the 'Joint Stock Company', which was organized in 1845 to promote emigration and related ventures. (See pp. 170–2.) When the company's funds were mismanaged, Brigham Young sent Elders Parley P. Pratt, Orson Hyde and John Taylor to England, and they disbanded the Joint Stock Company in the autumn of 1846. As these three apostles sailed for America early the next year, they hoped that they had left the mission stronger. Their experience with this problem confirmed the need to provide strong leadership for the rapidly growing British Mission, not only for its own sake but because it was soon to become the base from which the Church would expand into other European countries.

From the beginning, headquarters for the British Mission were located in England. In 1842 (the year after most of the Twelve left for home) the mission office was moved from Manchester to Liverpool, where it remained for many years. At that time the mission president was responsible only for the Church's work in Great Britain, as there were no other missions in Europe until France was opened in 1849; then Scandinavia (initially Denmark), Italy and Switzerland in 1850; and Germany in 1852. From the outset, these and later European missions were under the jurisdiction of the British Mission president.

Elder Franklin D. Richards, who served in 1850–2, was the first to have the title 'President of the European Mission'. Thereafter those who held that position exercised general jurisdiction over mission presidents on the Continent, and at the same time presided personally over the work in Great Britain – a dual responsibility that continued until 1929 when these two functions were separated. (Jenson, *Encyclopedic History*, pp. 237–8.) The double responsibility carried by these mission presidents may be one reason why almost all of them were apostles. Even though they had to devote some of their time to visiting missions on the Continent, the presence of a resident general authority in England had a powerful influence for good upon the English saints.

The internal organization of the Church in England followed the pattern already established in mission fields in North America. When there were enough converts to form a congregation, a branch was organized. The very name 'branch' reflects the way in which the Church initially grew: members in one locale would carry the gospel message to friends and relatives in adjoining areas; hence the resulting new congregation could logically be regarded as a 'branch' of the parent unit. There were nearly 100 branches in England at the time of the Twelve's departure in 1841, and with the rapid growth during the 1840s the number of these units increased steadily.

Again, as had been done in North America, a number of contiguous branches would meet together for periodic conferences. These larger groups would then become formal administrative units with defined boundaries and were originally *called* 'conferences' (until the name was changed to 'districts' in the 1920s to avoid confusion). The first of these units was formed in 1840, and by the mid-1850s there were thirty-two. (*Ibid*. p. 94.)

As the number of conferences grew, the British Mission created a yet larger unit which was unique to this area. The conferences were grouped into 'pastorates', over which the 'most efficient elders were chosen to preside'. (*Ibid*.) But rapid Church growth created more than a need for larger ecclesiastical units. There was also a keen demand for LDS literature.

Three-fifths of the English saints in 1850 had been baptized within the past three years, creating a situation much like the one the Church faces in South America today. These new converts had to be instructed in the basic doctrines and procedures of the Church. President Orson Pratt recognized that the English saints were 'scattered from one end of the land to the other, and unless there is a united exertion on the part of the officers of the Church, there cannot be maintained that union necessary to the enjoyment of the blessings of the Kingdom of God, and the further advancement of the work in this country'. (British Mission History, 5 Oct 1850.) Providing adequate literature would be a key means of achieving this goal.

'While members have been added by thousands,' President Franklin D. Richards said, 'the Church itself lack[s] that diligent faithful instruction in daily duty which the laws and ordinances of the Church contemplate.' He believed that the rapid increase in membership was 'glorious' but that it was 'a far nobler and wiser act to govern well than to make conquest'. (*Ibid.* 15 Dec 1851.) Once again, Church publications would be an important means of providing the necessary instruction. President Richards therefore lamented that the printed word had not circulated more widely: 'The Book of Mormon and Doctrine and Covenants are not so highly appreciated by the Saints generally as they would be if the Saints were more familiar with their contents... In them is definitely pointed out the order of the Church, and the duties of the several offices thereof... It is quite inexcusable for the Saints to remain ignorant of their precious contents'. (*Ibid.* 5 Oct 1850.)

There were several reasons why the required literature should be published in England rather than Utah. In their comparatively rustic circumstances, the saints in the Salt Lake Valley had only a small hand-operated press on which they were publishing their newspaper and a few other items. Furthermore there was a severe shortage of paper, and the expense of shipping it to Utah raised its cost to about six times the price of paper in the eastern United States. (The members were urged to donate rags which could be made into paper, but this did not begin until the mid-1850s.) Great Britain, on the other hand, was one of the great industrial nations of the world; the facilities for publishing were readily at hand, and since more than half the Church's members were in Great Britain in the early 1850s, it made good sense that most Church publishing should be done there in order to avoid expensive shipping charges. Thus the Church's publishing activities became one of the major responsibilities of the British Mission president.

Publishing new editions of the Book of Mormon, Doctrine and Covenants, and hymn-book became important projects. (Even in later decades when more adequate presses were available at Church headquarters in America, the printing plates prepared in England were often sent to Utah to be used in publishing scriptures and hymn-books there.) In addition to these larger works, the British Mission over the years published hundreds of thousands of magazines, tracts and pamphlets. All these had to be reviewed and approved by the mission president and his assistants. Elder George Reynolds, a young British convert, captured the feelings of those called to perform this important but sometimes routine work in the mission office:

> The work in this office is very much like any other kind of work, one day's labor very much resembles that of its fellows. It is like laying up adobes. There is a great sameness. It lacks the interest of going round visiting the Saints, proclaiming the gospel, visiting fresh scenes and forming the acquaintance of new faces. (Van Orden, p. 41.)

Among all the publications issued from the Liverpool office, probably the most significant was a pamphlet that eventually became one of the four standard works of the Church – the Pearl of Great Price.

Late in 1850, Franklin D. Richards succeeded his fellow apostle Orson Pratt as president of the British Mission. President Richards was not entirely new to this office. He had first come to Britain as a missionary in 1846 and had been appointed to preside over the Scottish Conference. He next became a counsellor to the mission president, Orson Spencer, and because of President Spencer's poor health, the 26-year-old Elder Richards had been obliged to assume major responsibility for affairs in the president's office. Following his release in 1848, Franklin returned to America and gathered with the saints, who by then were settling in the Salt Lake Valley. On 12 February 1849 he was one of four men added to The Quorum of the Twelve Apostles.

By autumn of that year Elder Richards was back in Great Britain. During much of 1850 he again served as acting mission president – this time officially, however – in the absence of President Pratt.

Franklin D. Richards served four times as President of the British Mission, 1847; 1851–2; 1854–6; 1867–8.

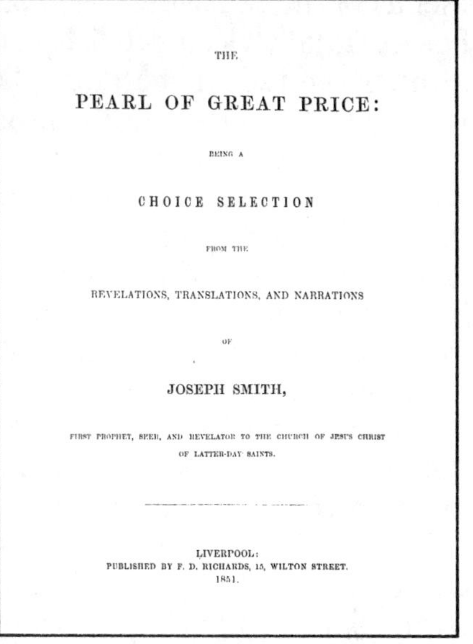

THE

PEARL OF GREAT PRICE:

BEING A

CHOICE SELECTION

FROM THE

REVELATIONS, TRANSLATIONS, AND NARRATIONS

OF

JOSEPH SMITH,

FIRST PROPHET, SEER, AND REVELATOR TO THE CHURCH OF JESUS CHRIST OF LATTER-DAY SAINTS.

LIVERPOOL:
PUBLISHED BY F. D. RICHARDS, 15, WILTON STREET.
1851.

First edition of the Pearl of Great Price, compiled and published by Franklin D. Richards, Liverpool, 1851.

Thus President Richards was well prepared when he took up the reins of leadership. The publishing of Church literature would be one of his major responsibilities. 'By the help of God I undertook the mighty task', President Richards confided in his journal, 'and soon realized the inspirations of the Holy Ghost with me.' (*PGP Symposium*, p. 5.)

President Richards soon turned his attention to collecting materials that would provide valuable instruction for the saints but were not readily available. He collected items that shed light on gospel principles as well as on ecclesiastical procedures, and published his compilation at Liverpool in 1851, a paper-bound pamphlet that sold for just one shilling. He selected his title from the Master's parable of the merchant who sold his entire collection of gems in order to acquire one superior 'pearl of great price'. (See Matthew 13:45–6.)

In his preface, Elder Richards explained that 'the following compilation has been induced by the repeated solicitations of several friends of the publisher'. He pointed out that most of his material had originally been published in the very early days of the restoration, and so had become relatively unavailable 'except to a few who have treasured up the productions of the Church with great care from the beginning'. He acknowledged that his compilation was not intended to be 'a pioneer of faith among unbelievers' but that he felt sure, on the other hand, that 'true believers in the divine mission of the Prophet Joseph Smith, will appreciate this little collection of precious truths as a *Pearl of Great Price* that will increase their ability to maintain and to defend the holy faith by becoming possessors of it'. (F. Richards, PGP, preface.)

On 15 July 1851 the *Millennial Star* announced that President Richards's pamphlet would soon be available. It 'will be a source of much instruction and edification to many thousands of Saints who will by an acquaintance with its precious contents be more abundantly qualified to set forth and defend the principle of our holy faith before all men. *The Pearl of Great Price* will recommend itself to all who appreciate the revelations of truth as hidden treasures of everlasting life.' (*MS 13*:216.)

The first addition of the Pearl of Great Price included a variety of significant materials. Extracts from a prophecy of Enoch (now Moses 6:43–7:69) showed how Adam was taught the gospel of Jesus Christ and how Enoch saw latter-day events including the glorious city of Zion. The account of an interview between Moses and God (now Moses 1) is a preface to Moses' writing in the book of Genesis but was not known until revealed to Joseph Smith in 1830. Translations from the book of Abraham provide insights into our pre-earthly existence, the purpose and creation of this world, and events of Abraham's own life. The Prophet's 'translation' or inspired revision of Matthew 24 (now Joseph Smith—Matthew) clarifies the Saviour's prophecies of his second coming. A key to understanding the Revelation of John (now D&C 77) also sheds light on prophecies of latter-day events. The prophecy on war (D&C 87) had never before been published. Given in 1832, it predicted future wars – including the American civil war that would break out in 1861, exactly a decade following the publication of this prophecy in England. In the revelation, Great Britain is mentioned as the nation to which the southern States would turn for aid. Extracts from Joseph Smith's own history (now Joseph Smith

—History) and verses from two revelations in the Doctrine and Covenants (sections 20 and 107) provide insights into the restoration, doctrine and practice of the Church, and thirteen brief statements (later known as the Articles of Faith) summarize the Church's basic teachings. To conclude his compilation, President Richards chose the poem 'Truth' by British convert John Jaques. Written at Stratford-upon-Avon, Brother Jaques's poem had been published about a year earlier in the *Millennial Star* (*MS 12*: 240), and is today the text for the hymn 'Oh Say, What Is Truth?' Obviously this literature contributed greatly to new converts' understanding of the gospel and the Church.

Perhaps President Richards and his associates did not fully realize the significance of what had been done. He did not refer to the publication of this future canonized scripture in his journal, nor does the *Star*'s enumeration of his accomplishments as mission president mention it. (*MS 14*: 168.) Nevertheless the members of the Church immediately recognized President Richards's work as a major contribution to their literature, and as early as 1857 President Brigham Young included the Pearl of Great Price amongst the few key books he placed in the foundation stone of the Salt Lake Temple, then under construction. (JH, 13 Aug 1857.)

The next edition of the Pearl of Great Price was prepared in Utah under the personal direction of Elder Orson Pratt. This second edition included all the material now in the book of Moses as well as a revelation on celestial marriage (now D&C 132). Once again paper-bound, it sold for fifty cents in the USA. It was this edition that was officially adopted as one of the Church's standard works at the fiftieth half-yearly conference on 10 October 1880. There the assembled saints first sustained President John Taylor and his counsellors and then unanimously voted to accept the recent editions of the Doctrine and Covenants and the Pearl of Great Price 'as from God and binding upon us as a people and as a Church'. (*CR*, Oct 1880.)

But this was only the beginning of the British Mission's contributions to the literature of the Church. After George D. Watt, the first British convert to the Church, emigrated to America in 1842, he was assigned to learn 'phonography', an early type of shorthand. From 1851 to 1869 he recorded many of the sermons of President Brigham Young and other Church leaders – work he did largely without pay. In 1853 the First Presidency wrote to the 'Saints abroad': 'Elder Watt now proposes to publish a *Journal* of these Reports in England, for the benefit of the Saints at large, and to obtain means to enable him to sustain his highly useful position of Reporter. You will perceive at once that this will be a work of mutual benefit', the Presidency concluded, 'and we cheerfully and warmly request your cooperation in the purchase and sale of the above named *Journal*.' (*JD 1*: v.)

Thus *The Journal of Discourses* began 1 November 1853 at Liverpool as a sixteen-page twice-monthly periodical. In 1855, after twenty-four issues had appeared, they were compiled into the first volume. In his preface Watt expressed confidence that 'these Sermons will prove a source of light, information, and joy', and that they 'will be most valuable, as a gauge of doctrine, a rule of restitute, and a square to life, furnishing at the same time an extensive repository of historical information'. (*Ibid*. p. vii.) This same pattern was repeated for the twenty-six volumes which appeared up to 1886, making a total of 9,774 pages of enlightening discourses. (P. Richards, pp. 1–2.) During the next century this valuable collection would be a frequently cited doctrinal resource and would pass through several additional printings.

Alongside these two extraordinary contributions to the corpus of Church literature, the British Mission kept up publication of the *Millennial Star*. In fact, the mission president almost always served as the *Star*'s editor, and since most of these men were apostles, their editorials and articles were often important sources of doctrinal understanding for the British saints. The *Millennial Star*'s influence was not limited to Britain, however. It increasingly circulated to many other parts of the world, including America, as the Church did not begin publishing literature in Utah until later in the nineteenth century. Thus, since many important announcements, doctrinal treatises, and new hymns were first published in the *Star*, it remains today a major source of historical information for the whole of the Church in the nineteenth century, not just for the Church in the British Isles.

During the first five years of its existence, the *Millennial Star* was issued monthly, but beginning in mid-1845 it was published twice-monthly, In the mid-1840s there were about 1,500 subscribers, but by 1852 the number had reached 22,000. Then, under the leadership of President Franklin D. Richards, the *Star* became a weekly, and the price per issue was reduced from threepence to one penny.

During this period mission headquarters and the *Millennial Star* editorial offices had undergone several moves from one rented building to another. Then in 1855 the Church took a lease on an office at 42 Islington Street, Liverpool, and the British Mission remained quartered there for the next half-century '"Forty-two Islington" became a familiar household phrase kindly known to tens of thousands of Latter-day Saints the world over'. (*MS 82*: 747–8.)

Until 1861 the *Star* and other mission publications were printed at a variety of commercial printers in Liverpool. In that year, however, President Brigham Young directed George Q. Cannon, the recently arrived mission president, to purchase the Church's own printing press. From this time onward the *Star* was issued from the Islington Street address, and in the coming decades a number of compositors, pressman and others skilled in various phases of the printing trade were called on missions to assist the staff in the Church's Liverpool publishing office.

Reflecting on the *Star*'s contributions, Elder Richard L. Evans, a future general authority who served as associate editor of the *Millennial Star* in the 1920s, wrote: 'Each week of every year the Latter-day Saints' *Millennial Star* goes forth in British lands as an expounder of doctrine, as a teacher of lofty precepts, a bearer of timely news, a minister of comfort and cheer, a messenger of good will, and as a herald of salvation'. (R. Evans, p. 149.)

As far-reaching as these publications were, the Pearl of Great Price, *The Journal of Discourses*, and the *Millennial Star* were not the British Mission's only contributions to Church literature. From the beginning, the publication of missionary tracts and pamphlets represented a major share of the work done by the mission office staff. President Orson Spencer, for example, made a lasting contribution to Latter-day Saint literature when he published a series of fifteen letters he had written to a Baptist minister on various gospel topics. The English saints used these tracts to share the gospel with their neighbours, and the *Millenial Star* published the following report of such efforts in the town of Crewe in 1848.

I must speak the praise of Sisters T. and W. Every Sunday Morning they practice delivering Elder Spencer's most valuable letters to the Citizens. They leave them on a principle of exchange, leaving a number, and calling for the one they left the previous Sunday. They take the streets by rotation, and frequently call at two hundred houses in one forenoon, and attend the regular meetings besides. Now what credit do such women not deserve? They are frequently abused; but they ever defend the principles, and go like bold soldiers. (S. Spencer, pp. 48–9.)

Another correspondent from Tottington reported to President Spencer that 'many hundreds of houses in this vicinity are now supplied with your valuable letters... Some of our good brothers and sisters go around, each in their district, and change the tracts every Sunday. In some cases they raise the devil, in others they are attended with good results.' Because of these efforts a growing number of 'friends' attended branch meetings. 'The Church of England minister in this village', the correspondent was pleased to note, 'lately preached a sermon from your 12th letter, on the Millennium.' (*Ibid.* p. 49.)

During the 1850s Liverpool emerged as the leading book supply depot for LDS literature. From here publications were shipped to other parts of Britain, to the Continent, and eventually to South Africa, India, Australia, the Pacific islands and even to North America. As this was a time when Church leaders wanted to centralize the production and distribution of mission-oriented literature and to discourage the output of independent pamphleteers, there came to be an even closer association between mission administrators and publishing. The Liverpool office began printing larger quantities of only a few authorized missionary tracts and pamphlets, which not only reduced cost but also ensured that the literature would be of a higher printed quality and would consistently represent the accepted teachings of the Church.

The business of Church publishing was not without its drawbacks, however. During the 1850s a rather involved system for distributing Church literature emerged. Book agencies were organized in each conference, and large quantities of literature were sent out on credit. Soon, collecting the money owed on books became an increasingly burdensome task for the central office and during the later 1850s, money received as tithes sometimes had to be diverted to pay debts owed to outside printers. (Whittaker, pp. 45–9.)

The Church in England soon began to experience patterns of growth and decline. In the 1840s conditions had been ripe for the introduction of the restored gospel into England. Great Britain was the centre of a vast world-wide empire – extending from Canada in the west to India in the east, and to Australia and New Zealand in the southern hemisphere. Even the earth's longitudes were measured from the Royal Observatory at Greenwich, and England sat astride the line dividing east from west. Outlying areas of her empire provided raw materials for her factories as well as markets for the products of her industry, and her major cities of London, Birmingham, Manchester, Leeds and Liverpool had more than doubled in population during the preceding forty years.

On a specified Sunday in March 1851 a religious census was conducted throughout England and Wales. This census reported that the lowest level of religious observance was found in metropolitan areas, where church building had lagged far behind population growth. It also confirmed that new religions, such as the Latter-day Saints, typically took root first among the working classes in the cities, and that Nonconformists were more common in these metropolitan areas whilst the established Church of England dominated the rural countryside. (Cotterill, pp. 114–19.)

In 1851 (the year of this religious census) LDS Church membership in Britain peaked at 32,894 – a level that would not be seen again until the booming growth of the 1960s, over a century later. The census further revealed that 7,500 people attended LDS Sunday morning services, 11,100 attended afternoon services, and 16,500 evening services at 222 separate meeting-places. Of these, sixty per cent were either in London or one of the industrial areas of northern and central England. The largest single congregation, some 1,200, attended the evening service at Birmingham, located in the heart of the industrial Midlands. (*Ibid.* pp. 119–24.)

However, the very forces that had paved the way for the Church's growth in England now opened the door to its decline. The bulk of the converts had come from the working class, attracted to the gospel at least partly by the vision of a better life in 'The Valley', and these people now responded by the thousand to the

Table 1. *Conversion and emigration, 1840–1910*

Years	Converts	Emigrated
1840–50	42,316	6,832
1851–60	37,215	12,972
1861–70	14,977	10,094
1871–80	6,345	6,886
1881–90	5,457	7,758
1891–1900	3,991	1,512
1901–10	8,062	3,615

invitation to 'gather to Zion'. In fact, during the two decades between 1870 and 1890 the number emigrating from England to Utah actually exceeded the number coming into the Church through baptism. (R. Evans, pp. 244–5.) (See Table 1.)

Hence during the first half-century of its existence in Great Britain, the Church served partly as an agency for recruiting builders for the Zion in America. As converts came in one door, a similar number of emigrants went out another. Had there been no gathering, the Church in Britain would likely have continued to grow rather than beginning to decline, and by 1890 there could well have been more than 47,000 saints in Britain rather than only the 2,770 who actually were there. Furthermore, those who did not emigrate were sometimes frustrated and disillusioned because they had not been able to join the gathering, and some of these would drop out of activity in the Church.

In effect, the two years between the departure of Elder Heber C. Kimball and his associates in 1838 and the arrival of the nine apostles in 1840 had been a time of sifting. In the face of persecution and other difficulties, the weaker members dropped away whilst the stronger ones remained. This same process continued, perhaps with more intensity, during the 1850s. Great stress was placed on keeping the commandments and on being a faithful and active member of the Church – an emphasis that received strong affirmation from the brethren in America as a spirit of 'reformation' and spiritual re-awakening swept through the Church in Utah. On 30 October 1856 President Brigham Young wrote to Elder Orson Pratt (then the British Mission president) instructing him that this reform movement should also commence in the British Isles. 'The Saints are dead, and do not drink at the living fountain,' he said; 'the fire of the Almighty is not in them.' Mission leaders were instructed to 'trim off the dead branches, so that the tree may thrive, grow, and expand'. (Peterson, p. 141.) A comparison of membership, conversion and emigration figures suggests that many either dropped away and were lost or were formally excommunicated during that decade.

Members who wished to remain in the Church were expected to renew their covenants in earnest – and to show that earnestness by being re-baptized. Adherence to the law of tithing, the Word of Wisdom, and other gospel principles was prerequisite to re-baptism. The prime articulator of these reform principles was Elder Ezra T. Benson, a counsellor in the mission presidency. He went about the mission 'like a two-edged sword', one missionary recalled, 'cutting on all sides everything that is impure'. (*Ibid.* pp. 145–6.)

The impact of this reform in England was, in fact, more one of pruning than of reforming. Many did not see the need to be re-baptized and declined the ordinance. Even some branch presidents refused to reform, and so were released. 'When the branches are all trimmed and set in order,' Elder Pratt sadly reported in May 1857, 'the Saints in these lands will not number more than about one half as many as...in 1850.' (*Ibid.* p. 149.)

Instances of a decline in faithfulness were not limited to the local members or to those in low positions, either. In 1860 when Elders Amasa Lyman and Charles C. Rich arrived to preside jointly over the British Mission, they found some lamentable conditions that they reported to President Brigham Young. During the previous two years sizeable amounts of the precious and scarce tithing funds had been diverted to support some missionaries in 'fine circumstances'. President Young promptly replied that tithes should henceforth not be used to support missionaries. (Arrington, *Rich*, p. 231.)

Elders Lyman and Rich also reported that many missionaries who had been called to act as 'pastor' (a supervisory office of considerable responsibility) 'attach so much ease and dignity to the position, that their usefulness is measurably destroyed or swallowed up in creature comforts'. (Peterson, p. 149.) Apparently this problem had begun developing at least three years earlier.

In 1857 the *Millennial Star* had instructed:

It is the duty of a Pastor to set an example of diligence to all the officers over whom he presides… A Pastor should not only visit the Conferences under his charge as often as circumstances will admit, but he should make it convenient to visit the several Branches as often as possible; he should diligently inquire concerning the condition and welfare of each Branch, strengthen the Saints, and set in order the things which are wanting.

He should not merely tell others what to do, but 'should be an example in doing, as well as in counselling to do'. He should be willing to preach in official meetings and in the streets, and occasionally to perform the duties of teachers and deacons. 'If he consider himself highly honoured and favoured of the Lord,' the instructions concluded, 'let him manifest it by becoming the servant of all, and a pattern for all.' (*MS 19*: 504–5.)

While Elder Joseph F. Smith was presiding as a pastor in Leeds, he felt it necessary to rebuke a local elder publicly, saying: 'I wish those who are in the habit of drinking liquor [would] keep off the stand on the Sabbath, when their breath smells.' Before the day was over, he received a note from one offended member, who returned his elder's licence. 'I have burnt up my hymn-book and all other works that I have', it read, 'and will burn the Book of Mormon as soon as I find it.' Elder Smith lamented such a lack of faith: 'Oh! when will men learn that in rejecting their own salvation, they themselves alone are the sufferers?' He expected the saints and especially the local leaders within his jurisdiction to set a proper example by strictly living the standards of the Church. 'If we wish the people to do right, then we, who minister unto them must do right ourselves, then they will follow us and the example we set before them.' (Joseph Fielding Smith, pp. 200–1.)

Within a few years the decline in membership would cause the office of pastor to be dropped. The number of conference units in the British Mission peaked at thirty-three in 1855 and then began a gradual decline as many of these units were consolidated. This process accelerated during the late 1860s, the total number dropping from twenty-nine to fourteen between 1867 and 1871. With the number of conferences cut in half, the need for pastorates diminished, so these unique units were dissolved.

During these decades, events abroad began to have a greater influence upon the Church in Britain. Such crises as the Crimean

War (1845–6) and the Franco-Prussian War (1870–1) tended to occupy the attention of the English people. Also, a separate series of events had a powerful impact on the Church in America and hence also on the English saints. For instance, the practice of plural marriage was announced publicly for the first time in 1852, and this provided new fuel for the continual anti-Mormon attacks. The handcart tragedy in 1855 dampened the enthusiasm for emigration and thus also cooled the more general interest in the Church. Then, when the United States government sent a hostile army to Utah in 1857, President Brigham Young directed the saints in outlying colonies to congregate into the more central area for protection, and he called all missionaries to return home. In the following year no missionaries at all were sent anywhere in the world, and only eighteen were sent out in 1859. (*DN*, *Church News*, 22 Feb 1964, p. 13.) Conditions in the British Mission deteriorated yet further in the aftermath of this 'Utah War'. Even *The Times* applauded USA President Buchanan for sending troops 'to rid the world of the "blight" of Mormonism'. (Arrington, *Rich*, p. 230.)

Still, the saints in England saw the hand of God in some of these international events. They recognized the outbreak of the American civil war in 1861, for example, as the literal fulfilment of Joseph Smith's prophecy published in the Pearl of Great Price ten years earlier. They realized that this was the prophesied 'beginning' of 'the time...that war will be poured out upon all nations' (D&C 87:1, 2). 'The nations of Europe cannot escape from it,' the *Millennial Star* declared. 'But the Lord has provided a place of refuge for those who will accept it.' Hence this was one more reason for emigrating to the Zion in America. (*MS 23*:299–300.)

With civil war in America, the number of missionaries coming from Utah was again cut. Whilst forty-eight had arrived in England in 1860, only six came the following year. This led to the calling of many more local missionaries, one of whom was Elder George Reynolds, a young convert from London and a future general authority. (Van Orden, pp. 8–9.)

For the next decade the number of missionaries coming to Great Britain remained relatively low. When Elder Joseph F. Smith arrived to preside over the mission in 1874, he sadly noted that there were only twelve elders to cover all of England. These missionaries, however, were not the twenty-year-old single elders we know in the twentieth century. They were generally young *married* men who made a substantial sacrifice as they left their wives and small children to proclaim the gospel message abroad.

When President Young had instructed that tithing funds no longer be used for the elders' support, he indicated that local members could provide food and lodging if they were willing and able. For the most part, the missionaries travelled 'without purse or scrip', depending for their necessities on the kindness of those they met.

For example, following a conference at Nottingham, one missionary, Elder A. B. Taylor, decided to return on foot to his field of labour in the Leeds Conference. He planned to preach in villages along the way wherever he could gain a hearing, stating his intention of 'keeping clear away from the Branches of the Saints and of trying the hospitality and Christian spirit of the "gentiles"'. He met with an 'almost universal indifference'. In one village, however, he did have some success:

> I saw in a village a crowd of men. I spoke to them, and asked them, if they did not think we could have a good meeting there. They seemed to be agreeable to the proposition; so I went and asked the people in their houses to come and listen to me. The people turned out better on this occasion, over one hundred being present. I preached to them for three-quarters of an hour; and before I had finished a dog fight took place in close proximity to our meeting, which did not draw away more than one-half of my congregation. I thought I was doing pretty well, for when an Englishman in Yorkshire would rather stay and hear a man preach than see a dogfight, it is a good sign. I did not mention the name of 'Mormon' to the people until I had nearly concluded my remarks. I told them that the Gospel had been restored in this day, the kingdom of God set up again, and that men were called of God to administer in the ordinances of the Gospel 'as was Aaron'; and then I finally brought in the name of Joseph Smith and mentioned the Book of Mormon. I offered them some tracts, when several stepped up and accepted them. (*MS* 36:266.)

Whilst the missionaries often had to take the brunt of the opposition directed against the Church, the local members were by no means immune. Sometimes persecution was aimed at branches or other groups of saints, but most often it hit individuals or families quite directly. Hostile landlords would sometimes order converts out of their homes. Some employers withdrew work from Mormons unless they would renounce their faith. And, perhaps most difficult of all, many families disowned their own members when they accepted the gospel. Such pressures were most intense in rural areas, where the poorer saints had fewer options in employment or lodging and where the clergy of the established church had more pervasive influence.

As has been mentioned, the discouraging conditions faced by both missionaries and members increased their yearning for better circumstances in Zion. And this yearning, intensified by persecution, became the theme for several new hymns written by British converts. Three of these, 'O Ye Mountains High', 'Beautiful Zion for Me', and 'We Thank Thee, O God, for a Prophet' soon became well-known Mormon favourites. Though they came to be loved by saints around the world, they were written and first sung in England.

In 1854 Charles W. Penrose, a 22-year-old English convert, had been serving as a missionary for a prolonged period. He wrote:

> I was walking on a dusty road in Essex. My toes were blistered and my heels too. I had been promised that if I would stay in the mission field another year I should be released. That was the cry every year: 'Brother Penrose, if you will stay and labor another year, we will see that you are released to go to Zion.' But it kept up for over ten years. Of course I had read about Zion and heard about the streets of Salt Lake City, with the clear streams of water on each side of the street, with shade trees, and so on. I could see it in my mind's eye and set it to a tune – the Scotch ditty, 'O Minnie, O Minnie, Come o'er the Lea'.

Later that day, at a cottage meeting in Mundon he sang 'O Ye Mountains High' for the first time. (J. Cornwall, p. 160.)

Elder Penrose did not realize his desire of going to Zion until 1861. Then, only three years later, he was called to return to Britain to serve as editor of the *Millennial Star*. In 1867 when Brigham Young, Jr, was released as president of the British Mission, Elder Penrose hoped to return home with him. He was told, however, that he was needed where he was and would have to stay longer. Once again he yearned for his mountain home:

> 'Oh, Brigham, Brigham, Brigham, beautiful Zion for me. I wish I were going with you.' Then he said, 'Brigham, do you know the song "Beautiful Isle of the Sea"?'
>
> Brother Young said, 'Yes.'
>
> 'Well,' said brother Penrose, 'I will write you a hymn, "Beautiful Zion for Me".' (*Ibid*. p. 13.)

The third and best-known hymn, 'We thank Thee, O God, for a Prophet', was written by another convert, William Fowler, at about this same time. Although his parents were from Sheffield, he was born in Australia while his father was there on military assignment. By the time William was nine the family was back in Sheffield, but within a few years he was left an orphan. At about the age of eighteen, he began thinking seriously about religion. He attended Methodist services but did not feel satisfied. Then a friend took him to hear the Mormon elders at the Hall of Science on Rockingham Street. He was baptized in 1849.

Two years later he was ordained a priest and commenced service as a missionary. He worked hard and endured much reviling for the sake of the gospel. Later he took work as a grinder and polisher of cutlery, but lost this job because he had joined the Church. Elder Joseph F. Smith, who laboured in Sheffield during the early 1860s, recalled how one day Brother Fowler brought in his new hymn and requested that the choir learn it: 'We thank thee, O God, for a prophet to guide us in these latter days.' (*Ibid*. pp. 210–11.) Thus Brother Fowler expressed his assurance that 'deliverance is nigh', that 'the wicked who fight against Zion / Will surely be smitten at last', and that

> ...on to eternal perfection
> The honest and faithful will go,
> While they who reject this glad message
> Shall never such happiness know. (*Hymns*, 19.)

This hymn, first sung by the saints of the Sheffield Branch, has come to represent, perhaps more than any other, the faith of Latter-day Saints the world around.

Although the opposition that led these brethren to express their faith in hymns was fairly universal in the lives of the English saints at this time, there were certain periods when the persecution became more intense and even violent. These times of greater persecution were often directly related to similar upsurges in America. The announcement of plural marriage was apparently what led to the outbreak of anti-Mormon demonstrations in Birmingham, a city where the Church had enjoyed particular success. The saints had, in fact, purchased or taken leases on several chapels formerly used by other denominations in that city. Then, in 1857, the Rev. Brindley, a revivalist preacher, began agitating against the Church.

For several weeks Sunday and weekday meetings were interrupted:

> Unruly mobs...howling and whistling during the singing of hymns, and groaning with unwonted fervour during prayers, have even pelted the members of the congregation with stones and mud on their way homewards. On the afternoon of Sunday last, a man named Thomas Horsley, on leaving Allison-street chapel, was seized by a crowd of people, who tore his coat in pieces, and treated him in such a manner that he had to place himself under the protection of a policeman. He got into a cab, hoping thereby to escape, but the mob followed him as far as Islington-row, hooting at him, and pelting both him and the cabman with stones. On Thursday night, a man named Roe, one of the deacons of Thorpe-street chapel, was beaten with sticks and otherwise roughly handled by a crowd which had assembled in the neighbourhood, where, we may remark, hundreds have nightly gathered for several weeks, with the view of disturbing the Mormon meetings. (*MS 19*: 532.)

One Sunday evening the Rev. Brindley was preaching almost across the street from one of the Latter-day Saint chapels. Following his meeting, a crowd of 1,500 to 2,000 persons gathered.

> A rush was at once made to the chapel, where President Aubrey was preaching at the time. The aisles and unoccupied seats were speedily filled, and then a running fire of comment on the sermon was commenced, and carried on by the intruders for some five or ten minutes. Much of the language would have disgraced the lowest pothouse, and at last Aubrey abruptly closed his discourse, pronounced the benediction and dismissed his flock. It was with great difficulty that they forced their way through the crowd in the chapel yard and the street. The women were hustled, insulted, and bespattered with mud; the men had their hats knocked off and were pushed about from side to side; and hootings, oaths, tin-kettle harmonies, etc., lent completeness to a scene such as is not often witnessed in Birmingham on a Sunday evening. The police were sent for, and quiet was partially restored. However, as soon as the constables had gone away, the door of the chapel was burst open, the crowd rushed in, the front windows were smashed, and the mob conducted themselves as they liked for nearly half an hour. (*Ibid.*)

Only the appearance of some policemen prevented the mob from burning the building. The following morning they once again broke into the chapel, ransacked the cupboard, 'and a large number of music and school books were torn up in pieces and strewn about the yard'. That evening a newspaper reporter visited the chapel to see what damage had been done. 'While he was inside, a shower of stones came rattling through the smashed windows.'

After the *Birmingham Journal* had given an account of these events, it declared:

A repetition of these disgraceful scenes must not be permitted... In this country the Mormons are observers of the law; they seem to live as decently moral lives as their neighbours of the same class; they do go through the forms of worship, which may be more than many of their assailants can say; And the law of the land must give them the protection which it accords to all 'religions', pretend or genuine. There must be no more religious bonfires in Birmingham. (*Ibid.*)

At least one Birmingham minister seemed to agree with the *Journal*'s opinion. The Rev. Dr Miller, in whose parish some of the worst anti-Mormon excesses had occurred, told his followers that violence was not the proper means of resolving the situation. 'Arguments and differences should be concluded by prayer, reason, moral and spiritual persuasion, not force and tumult.' (Cotterill, p. 329.)

'Birmingham has a character for being as liberal and free a town as any,' another local paper stated, 'but there [are] still in it men who substitute clamour for argument, and 'rowdyism' for reason...Whatever we may think of the Church of Jesus Christ of Latter-Day Saints, and however much we may prefer the Saints of former days, we cannot but respect earnest propagandism on the part of those who believe they have important truths to communicate.' (*MS 19*: 345–6.)

These comments from Birmingham seemed to herald a moderating of the press's view of Mormonism that became more marked in the 1860s. The 1851 religious census had shown Britain how the Latter-day Saints were meeting the needs of people in many cities throughout England, whilst the Mormon pioneers' success in establishing their city in the Rocky Mountains further demonstrated the saints' abilities, and the press, particularly the more liberal papers, increasingly reported the English saints' accomplishments. Whereas in the past the press had portrayed the typical Mormon convert as unschooled, hardly literate, of society's lower orders – the country yokel or the unskilled labourer, the willing dupe for the sharp practices of itinerant Mormon missionaries – yet the achievements of the saints in establishing their mission in

Britain, as well as in the settlement of the American wilderness, could not be entirely overlooked. (Cotterill, pp. 263–4.)

Not all the Church's problems were caused by outsiders, however. Occasionally apostate Mormons presented difficulties. During the summer of 1857 Mr W. S. Parrott returned from Utah to his native town of Bath. Addressing a crowd of some two thousand, he urged his audience to 'put down and stamp out' Mormonism in that city. Some of those present duly proceeded to vandalize the local Mormon chapel, breaking twenty windows and threatening to set fire to the building. The police then offered protection to the saints who, in appreciation, declared that this action was 'religious liberty personified'. (*MS 19*: 532.)

Fortunately other Mormon converts returned to their native land with the object of building the kingdom. In 1867 George D. Watt, the first to be baptized by the original missionaries in 1837, returned to England on a special short-term mission. At a conference held on the 21st of April in the Temperance Hall on Grosvenor Street in Manchester, he was invited to join the leaders on the stand and to speak. He took advantage of this opportunity to give 'an interesting account of affairs in Utah...contrasting the comfort, peace, and prosperity prevailing there with the misery, poverty, and many evils prevailing in [England]'. He specifically refuted 'the evil reports in circulation concerning President Young'. As he left for home a short time later, he shared his powerful testimony by letter with his yet sceptical countrymen:

> Since thirty years ago I have had the privilege of traveling among strangers by land and by sea to bear my humble testimony of the things which I know. I have also been greatly blessed with the privilege of dwelling with the Saints [and I have seen] marvelous displays of the power of God in behalf of His people... For thirty years I have watched the growth of this church and kingdom, and I do know that it has been delivered from destruction and overthrow by the power of the Almighty... This is my testimony, and by it I warn all who shall read it that God did call upon Joseph Smith, Jr., and did give unto him power to lay the foundation of His church...[and] did call upon His servant Brigham Young, a master builder, to build upon the foundation which Joseph the Prophet has laid according to the revelations and commandments which have been given of the Lord through him. (Stringham and Flack, pp. 78–81.)

When the United States Congress passed the Edmunds–Tucker Act in 1882 (making plural marriage illegal in the USA), new impetus was given to the 'raid' or anti-Mormon crusade in Utah. This resulted in a corresponding increase in attacks on the missionaries and members of the Church in England. Elder David H. Morris recorded the following in his journal during 1887:

We went into Portobello Rd. and began to sing,... and before Bro. Schofield had spoken more than half an hour the crowd began to crowd around us and before we knew it we each had a crowd around six or eight deep and until eleven o'clock we had it pretty hot. Every point they brought up we answered it so that every intelligent person that stood around us could see that we cut our enemies all to pieces, however there were a few of the same ones who used their influences to get the rough element to make a noise which they did and when we left a large crowd followed us throwing horse manure and other things at us. But with all this I felt better coming away under these circumstances than I did going to hold a meeting for if anything makes me feel tired it is the thought of holding an outdoor meeting. (Morris, p. 161.)

On another occasion Elder Morris wrote, 'the powers of Hell were combined against us'. When one of the missionaries began speaking, 'a lot of men with banjos started up and sang some comic songs and everything seemed as though our meeting would be a failure, but there were some men who wanted the truth and the Devil knew it and tried to foil us'. (*Ibid*. p. 19.) And in October he recorded:

Most of the shops had in their windows large placards 18 × 24 inches headed 'Mormon Devils', or 'Latter-day Devils'. All this combined raised such a feeling against us that a mob of some five hundred broke open the doors and filled every room, breaking some of the windows [and] throwing out into the street tracts... etc., cutting the window curtains, tearing down the iron fence and brick wall upon which it stood in front of the house, and scattering the material in the house. I am very anxious to hear the particulars. From what Nephi said, Bro. Ballard was the only Utah Elder present, and finding it useless to talk with the mob, he had to hide in Sister Young's for safety. (*Ibid*. p. 72.)

Such attacks were directed not only against local missionaries and saints. Elder Morris recalled an occasion when the mission president, Elder George Teasdale, a member of The Quorum of the Twelve Apostles and a native of England, was addressing a meeting in a large hall. He had spoken about half an hour 'when the disturbance became so great he had to quit and stopped preaching'. (*Ibid*. p. 33.) Reflecting on such experiences, Elder Morris believed they would probably help the missionaries more than they would hinder: 'It seems as though the devil is going to help us to spread the Gospel, for the people who took no interest in our tracts before are very likely to [now,] after reading the tracts against us.' (*Ibid.* p. 66.)

As a matter of fact, the anti-polygamy campaign in America benefited England in at least one instance. In December 1886 when Brigham H. Roberts, a newspaper editor and future general authority, was about to be put on trial for having more than one wife, Church leaders decided he should depart immediately for England. There he could make a valuable contribution as associate editor of the *Millennial Star*. At British Mission headquarters in Liverpool, he spent most of his days working on the *Star*, whilst his evenings were occupied with missionary preaching meetings and his weekends taken up with conferences in various parts of the country.

Elder Roberts was very much impressed with London on his first visit there, and wrote home: 'I am desperately in love with London, and if I were a man of the world I would live here.' He conceded, however, that it was extremely difficult to preach the gospel in Hyde Park. Nevertheless, a missionary associate later described Roberts as the nemesis of other preachers in Hyde Park. 'They were forced to drive him from the place...because their followers deserted them whenever "that Mormon" began to speak.' (T. Madsen, pp. 161–7.)

While Elder Roberts was in England, William Jarman, an ex-Mormon, was giving a series of inflammatory lectures against Mormonism throughout the country. 'I hereby challenge all the Mormon missionaries from Utah to meet me upon a public platform', Jarman would say, 'to discuss the doctrines and practices of the so-called "latter-day Saints" in Utah, or refute my statements, if they can, or dare. I defy them to do so!' (*MS 19*: 750.) He gloated that this challenge was always met by silence. At length mission president George Teasdale appointed Elder Roberts to respond. He agreed to debate if there would be an impartial moderator in charge. After some delay, the debate took place in London. Jarman told the audience how he had been in Utah and had been forced to flee for his life, having to hide in a tree from the lions and tigers of the Rocky Mountains. When he denounced Roberts as a 'Mormon thug' and a 'Latter-day Devil' who had been sent by the Church to murder him, the moderator warned him against violating the conditions of the debate. Jarman was incoherent as he made his concluding statements.

For the next few months Elder Roberts gave a series of public lectures of his own on the Book of Mormon as a witness for Christ and on similar topics, and supplied articles to the press to counter the impact of the thousands of leaflets distributed by Jarman. In the spring of 1888 the two had another face-to-face confrontation at Sheffield. When the pro-Jarman mob rushed at Elder Roberts following an outdoor meeting, a policeman bodily threw the Mormon out of harm's way, warning him, 'Thou'll get thy nut crack if thou don't mind.'

At another meeting in a nearby hall, Jarman's supporters hid short bars of iron in the sleeves of their coats, intending to maul the elders at the end of the meeting. Though the mob thirsted for blood, the police successfully escorted the Mormons to safety. Even though the press published the fact that Jarman had recently escaped from a mental asylum, the masses boisterously continued to support him. Elder Roberts hoped that at least the thinking people would weigh the arguments of both sides and then reach an intelligent decision. (T. Madsen, pp. 167–77.) In like spirit, a writer in the *Millennial Star* declared: 'We feel assured that good will result from these proceedings ultimately as Mr Jarman's statements are so transparent [that] thoughtful people are convinced of their untruth and are led to inquire after the facts.' (*MS 19*:751.)

In 1890 President Wilford Woodruff announced that no further plural marriages would be authorized. In America this brought a period of relative goodwill towards the saints, but in England persecution continued, though not at the level of the 1880s. Elder Joseph Fielding Smith, serving in Britain as a young missionary at about the turn of the century, experienced this continuing opposition. He recorded: 'I went into a butcher shop one day, offered a man some literature, and he grabbed a butcher's knife and said, "I'll kill you." I knew he wouldn't and I didn't get frightened and I didn't run, but in his heart was that feeling of opposition and hate. I knew in England he wouldn't kill me. If he had been in the United States, I don't know what he would have done.' (McConkie, p. 26.)

A new fire of anti-Mormon agitation was sparked in America with the election of Elder Reed Smoot to the United States Senate.

The opening decade of the twentieth century, known as the 'progressive era' in the States, brought with it a reform-minded climate, and a number of magazines published lengthy series of articles attacking the Mormons and alleging perpetuation of plural marriage in defiance of the law. Once again these events had an impact across the Atlantic. In England, the anti-Mormon crusade reached its height in 1911, when people like the Rev. Daniel H. C. Bartlett, an Anglican vicar, led an anti-Mormon rally in Liverpool; and Hans Peter Freece, the son of a Mormon polygamist and a former member of the Church, described how well-dressed Mormon elders flattered thousands of English girls into joining the harems in Utah; and the indefatigable Winifred Graham wrote several novels in which the beautiful but naive heroine was rescued just in time from the crafty Mormon missionaries. To boost circulation, English papers vied to publish the most lurid exposés of Mormon polygamy, and even *The Times* simply accepted as fact the reports that polygamy still flourished in Utah. (See Thorp, 'Mormon Peril' and 'Winifred Graham'.)

Hence physical violence was directed once again at the missionaries and English saints. British Mission president Rudger Clawson reported 'scenes of violence and mobocracy' at Birkenhead, Bootle, Heywood, Sunderland, Seaton, Hirst, Nuneaton, Birmingham, Bristol, London, Ipswich and Norwich. One elder was tarred and feathered, another hit in the face with a brick, another had a handful of lime thrown in his face causing temporary blindness, another bled profusely from the scalp when hit with a potato studded with broken glass, and the elders were generally 'hustled about and handled roughly'. (Thorp, 'Mormon Peril', p. 69.) President Litchfield of the Newcastle Conference reported that 'we cannot walk along the street without being molested'. On various occasions 'stones, horse manure, and other objectionable missiles were thrown' at the missionaries. (*Ibid.* p. 86.) Following a series of disturbances in south London, the owner of Stockwell Institute, which the Mormons had rented for their meetings, asked them to leave.

As a result of numerous complaints the Home Secretary, Winston Churchill, made the following report: 'Inquiry has from time to time been made into allegations which have reached the Home Office, but no ground for action has been found. I am informed that polygamy is now forbidden by the rules of the Mormon Church as well as the laws of the United States.' The Home Office sent questionnaires to the police in the major cities where the Mormons were active, but found no evidence that the elders were preaching plural marriage. The head constable of Liverpool remarked: 'Personally I cannot see that the promise of only a share of a husband, however attractive he might be, is bait likely to catch a modern girl.' (*Ibid*. p. 82.)

Although attacks against the saints continued through the closing years of the nineteenth century and into the opening years of the twentieth, there were, at the same time, signs that a new day of growing acceptance was dawning for the Church in England. For example, Dr James E. Talmage, who would become an apostle two decades later, was well received when he was invited to speak about the Great Salt Lake in the 1891 meeting of the Royal Microscopical Society in London. 'I regard the occurrences of this night as very significant,' he wrote in his journal. 'Not because I have gained recognition in so august a society, but because a representative of the Latter-day Saints' Church – one of the despised Mormons – has been so received.' (Talmage, pp. 99–100.)

As time permitted, Dr Talmage also met missionaries and spoke at various Church meetings. When he visited his boyhood homes in Hungerford and Ramsbury, he was shunned by his relations. However, the town hall was filled to capacity when he was invited to speak on 'Utah and the Mormons'. There he dispelled misconceptions about the saints and their religion so successfully that afterwards several of his relations insisted that he stay in their homes on future visits.

One of the greatest obstacles the missionaries faced was the stubborn prejudice the English people held toward the Mormons, 'based on the lurid falsehoods regarding their moral practices that were circulated and believed at every level of society'. In 1898, therefore, the First Presidency approved the request from British Mission leaders that a series of lectures on Mormonism be given by one 'whose credentials would be instantly recognized and respected by the British public'. That person was Dr James E. Talmage, then president of the University of Utah. He was an experienced and effective lecturer and was a member of 'a number of high-level British scientific societies'. This gave him the desired stature in the eyes of the British press and public, and arrangements were made for him to give eight stereopticon lectures in leading cities throughout Britain. Proprietors of the halls warned that audiences would be slim during the summer: darkness would not fall until about 9.15 p.m., besides which the weather was hot and most people left the cities for a holiday in the country or at the seashore. Even the theatres of London closed during this season. Nevertheless, mission leaders went ahead with their plans, and some of the elders contributed funds from their own pockets to purchase the stereopticon equipment.

When Dr Talmage disembarked from his ship at Newcastle upon Tyne, he found the city 'liberally sprinkled' with 'flaming' saffron posters and handbills announcing his lecture that night. Several hundred interested people packed the hall and other hundreds had to be turned away. This same experience was repeated on successive nights in other cities, Elder Talmage and his assistants having to meet a tight schedule in order to keep their appointments. (*Ibid.* pp. 145–7.)

The impact of the lectures in correcting false impressions far exceeded the dearest hopes of British Mission leaders. In many locations the very newspapers that had formerly published bitter attacks against the Church now praised Dr Talmage's presentations. *The Independent* of Barnsley praised his 'eloquent and graphic' descriptions of the Mormons' fight to conquer the western desert. The *Bradford Observer* noted that a large audience gave 'close attention' to his two-hour lecture. Dr Talmage 'did not preach Mormonism, but he praised the Mormons in many an eloquent sentence', the *Glasgow Evening Times* reported. Audiences were very responsive, even cheering references to Brigham Young's leading the people to overcome formidable hardships in establishing their civilization in the Rocky Mountains. (*Ibid.* pp. 147–8.)

A group of 'rabid anti-Mormons' unwittingly helped to promote Dr Talmage's final lecture at Wigan, near Liverpool. Mistaking him for the Rev. T. DeWitt Talmage of Brooklyn, whose book attacking the Mormons was well known, they printed additional handbills of their own. Their leaders stood in the public market-place for over a week urging 'all the passers-by to attend the lecture and hear the truth regarding Mormonism'. As a result, the hall was filled over an hour before the lecture began, despite a downpour of rain. (*Ibid.* p. 149; *MS 60*: 505.)

In 1904 when Elder Heber J. Grant arrived in England to preside over the European Mission, one of his first tasks was to secure a headquarters building. His wife Emily had lived in Islington Street, Liverpool as a girl when her father, Daniel H. Wells, had presided over the mission. During the intervening years, however, the neighbourhood had deteriorated to the point that it was almost a slum. Eventually they located a comfortable two-storey red brick mansion at 10 Holly Road. Its large drawing-room served as a chapel for the Liverpool branch, and there was room for the mission office and living quarters. (Gibbons, *Grant*, p. 137.) This commodious structure, which the mission bought rather than taking a lease, was a tangible symbol of the Church's stability and stature in England at the dawn of the new century.

President Grant made many friends for the Church in England, just as he had done in America among the business leaders with whom he had frequent contact. Concerning his impact in Britain, a biographer wrote:

> The Saints all over the mission were inspired by his impressive personality, the zeal and fervency of his words and the power and penetration of his testimony. Wherever he went, he added to the dignity of the cause which he represented. Friends and foes alike held him in esteem and respect for his sincerity, his manly defense of his people and his religion. (B. Hinckley, p. 109.)

At this time there were a number of young people from Utah studying music in England and President Grant frequently took them with him to conferences, where the quality of their music added to the spirit of the meetings he conducted. 'He dignified and popularized the Church. Wherever he went, people came out to listen to him.' (*Ibid.*)

Nevertheless, anti-Mormon feeling still showed itself from time to time. When a new missionary, Elder Hugh B. Brown, arrived from Canada in November 1904, he was assigned to labour in Cambridge. Before he left for his assigned area, however, the conference president informed him that there had been threats upon the lives of the next Mormon missionaries who set foot in that city. 'As you are the missionary that is going to set foot in that city,' the president continued, 'I thought you might be interested.' When the

Liverpool's 42 Islington Street served as the headquarters for the British Mission and *Millennial Star* office beginning in 1855 and continuing until 1904.

elders arrived in Cambridge, they discovered that word of their coming had preceded them. Posters proclaimed: 'Beware of the vile deceivers; the Mormons are returning. Drive them out.' Despite these unsettling conditions, the young missionary was left to begin his work in Cambridge on his own. Elder Brown overcame his fears and spent all day Friday and Saturday going from door to door, attempting to distribute religious tracts and interest people in gospel conversations. Having no apparent success, he returned to his lodgings very discouraged:

> As I was sitting in that room alone on Saturday evening, I heard a knock on the door. The landlady answered and I heard a man's voice say, 'Is there an Elder Brown lives here?' I of course thought it was the advance guard of the mob and I was terribly agitated. The landlady said, 'Yes, come in,' and he came into my room. He was holding a tract in his hand and as he looked at me, a raw cowboy-type of lad, he asked, 'Are *you* Elder Brown?' I could understand his amazement at finding so young and apparently incapable a man representing the Church, but when I told him I was, he said, 'Did you leave this tract at my door this afternoon?' My name was on it and I couldn't deny it, so I said, 'Yes.'
>
> He said, 'Elder Brown, last Sunday a group of us in the Church of England left the church because we could not agree with our minister. He was not teaching what we believed to be the Gospel.' And then he said, 'Will you come by tomorrow night and be our pastor?' He told me of having prayed through the week that before the next Saturday, the Lord would send them a new pastor. 'There are seventeen of us in all, and we believe the Lord has sent you to us.' (Campbell and Poll, pp. 30–1.)

The young and inexperienced missionary spent a sleepless night. On Sunday he went for a walk among the beautiful old buildings of Cambridge University, feeling quite insecure and alone. At the appointed hour, he went with much trepidation to the house where the group waited. As he entered the room, 'they stood, out of respect for the new pastor, and that scared me', Elder Brown recalled. In a kneeling prayer, he poured out his heart to God: 'These people are seeking for the truth. We have the truth, but I am not able to give it to them without Thy help. Wilt Thou take over and speak to these people through the Holy Spirit and let them know the message of truth?' He spoke for forty-five minutes, or rather, he later testified, the Lord spoke through him. At the end of the service, the people closed around him 'with outstretched hands, many of them with tears in their eyes, and said, "This is the Gospel we have been asking for. This is the message we wanted our minister to give us, but he would not."' (*Ibid*. pp. 31–3.)

Elder Brown encountered no overt opposition. In fact, another minister even offered the use of his hall, and by the autumn of

1905 a small branch with seventeen members was functioning at Cambridge.

Later, when transferred to Ipswich, Elder Brown felt quite encouraged by the conditions he found there, and he wrote:

Although we are not permitted to hold street meetings, our hall is so situated that by raising the windows the public can hear our hymns, and often we have a large audience on the street who can hear every word uttered by the speaker... One by one they are venturing inside, and our attendance is constantly increasing as well as our membership. 'Truth shall prevail.' (*Ibid.* p. 34.)

Still later in Elder Brown's mission, a preacher in another conference wrote to President Grant demanding that 'the best man in the mission be assigned to meet him on the platform'. The president wrote to Elder Brown: 'You are the man who should go and meet this man and represent the Church.' Elder Brown welcomed the challenge. In the debate, the minister spoke first, and then the young missionary 'occupied almost an hour in teaching the first principles of the Gospel and the Restoration'. At the conclusion of the meeting the minister conceded: 'I have been opposing you Mormons right along, but I want you to know that what I have heard tonight has convinced me that I am wrong and you are right. I want to join the Church.' (*Ibid.* p. 36.)

A spiritual highlight in Elder Brown's mission was a conference in Bradford, 'the first modern British-wide assembly of Elders'. He described these proceedings as 'the best and most spirited meeting I have ever attended. President Grant spoke with great power... Most every elder wept with joy. Some whose testimonies had been weak declared "Now I know." Many even of the most energetic Elders were heard to say that they had received a great awakening touch.' (Arrington, *Presidents*, p. 239.) Just before closing the meeting, President Grant paused and said: 'Brethren, there [is] sitting in this audience someone who will someday be a member of Council of the Twelve and I predict this in the name of Jesus Christ.' (Campbell and Poll, p. 37.)

A long-to-be-remembered event in the lives of the English saints was the 1906 visit of President Joseph F. Smith, the first president of the Church ever to visit Europe while serving as prophet. President Smith arrived in London on Sunday the 26th of August, and the same day addressed the saints in two conference meetings at Finsbury Town Hall. He bore powerful testimony of the saving

Joseph F. Smith, first President of the Church to visit the British Isles, 1906.

mission of Jesus Christ, and of the latter-day restoration of the gospel through his own uncle, the Prophet Joseph Smith. He also cautioned his listeners to 'study the Gospel and do not be in a hurry; but when you go to Zion do not expect that you are going there just to lie in a bed of roses'. He warned them that they would face the same kinds of challenges there as in England. (*MS 68*: 580.)

In yet another session, President Smith along with the mission president, who was Elder Heber J. Grant, instructed the missionaries. One of them was Elder Hugh B. Brown, who many years later recalled:

I have never...before or since felt the feeling that came over me as I sat and listened to those two men speak. I was young and untrained, but somehow I knew in my heart that what they said was true. I thought at that time how wonderful it would be if by righteous living I could come to a point where I would be in companionship with such men, little knowing what lay ahead for me. It was the highlight of my mission. (Campbell and Poll, p. 37.)

During the following week President Smith visited other parts of England and Scotland. On Sunday the 2nd of September he again addressed large conference meetings, this time in Exchange Hall at Blackburn near Liverpool. 'It is God who is directing this work', he testified, 'and it is my business to seek His mind and will and be susceptible to the inspiration of His holy Spirit...that I might understand when He speaks.' (*MS 68*: 675.) But President Smith's powerful spiritual influence was not limited to the hundreds who heard him in person, for during the next two months the *Millennial Star* published complete transcripts of his sermons given in London and Liverpool.

The English members who heard their living prophet speak could now look back on a significant Latter-day Saint heritage in their own country. They and their spiritual forebears had endured much for the gospel. Nevertheless, out of those decades of adversity had come thousands of stalwart saints, several beloved hymns, and publications of enduring importance – including one of the Church's standard scriptural works. Now, in the opening years of the new century, English saints could look forward to even further progress. However, the glorious destiny of the Lord's kingdom in England would not be realized quickly. The English saints would have to endure two world wars as well as the difficult intervening years before they would begin to witness the fulfilment of their hopes.

8

The Welsh and the Gospel

RONALD D. DENNIS

TO IDENTIFY the first native-born Welshman to receive the gospel in this dispensation presents a difficult and probably impossible task. The sparse and patchy records kept in the early days of the Welsh Church simply do not give that information. There are, however, several early converts who had inescapably Welsh surnames, such as Frederick G. Williams, converted in November 1830; Joshua Lewis, who was baptized by the missionaries sent to the Lamanites of Missouri in the winter of 1830–1; Selah J. Griffin, ordained an elder in June 1831; and Hiram Griffith, ordained a teacher in October 1831. There is no indication that any of these individuals had been born outside the United States, but their names are a strong indication of ancestral roots in Wales.

When Wilford Woodruff experienced his amazing success in Herefordshire in 1840, he was labouring only about twenty miles from the border of Wales. Amongst his converts were John Davis, William Evans, Samuel Jones, William Williams, John Powell, John Parry and James Morgan. Given the 'Welshness' of these names and the geographical proximity to Wales, at least some of these converts probably had relations across the border in Wales. Certainly they would have been inclined to take the gospel to their kin soon after converting to Mormonism themselves.

James Morgan, for example, had family members in the little castle town of Skenfrith, located just over the border in Monmouthshire. Morgan was baptized on 18 May 1840 in Dymock, and on the same day was ordained a priest and baptized three people himself. It is not difficult to imagine him a short time later, perhaps

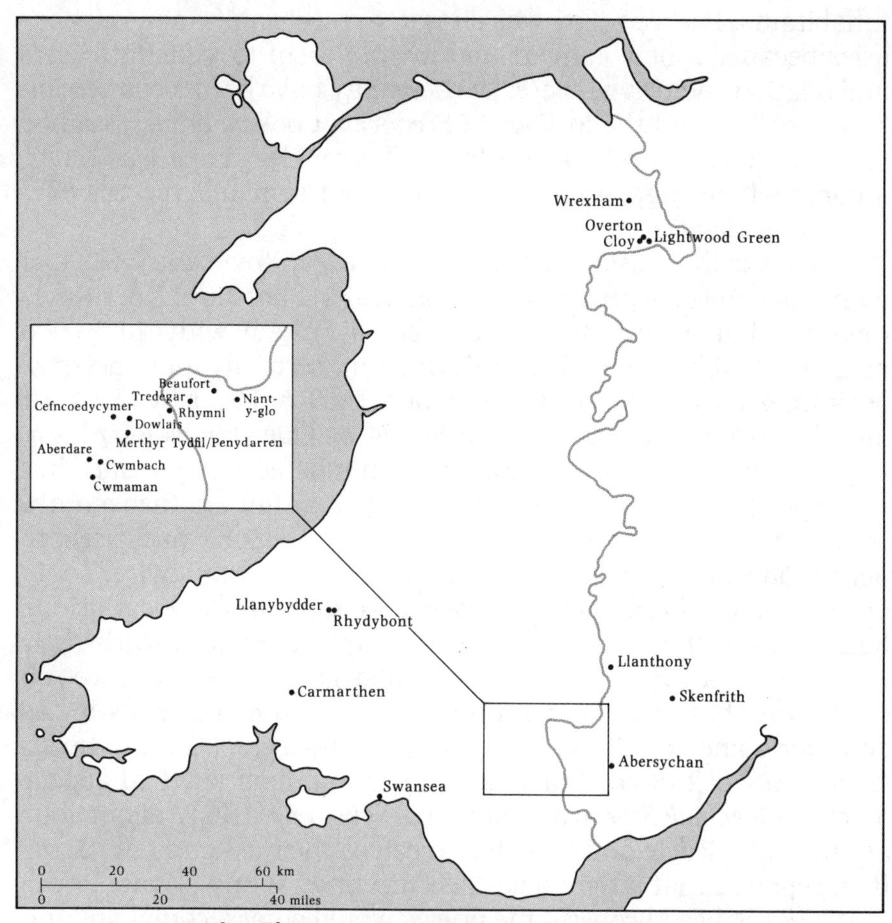

Wales. Places prominent in Latter-Day Saint history.
(Map shows the nineteenth-century boundary for Wales.)

in June or July, exhorting his family to follow his example and that of his sister Margaret, whose baptism preceded his by five weeks.

The first missionary to preach in Wales could well have been James Morgan or any of several others in similar circumstances. The first official Church missionary to Wales, however, was Elder Henry Royle, who was called at a conference in Manchester on 6 October 1840 to 'go to Cly [*sic*], in Flintshire'. (*MS 1*: 168.) 'Cly' is no doubt 'Cloy', located about two miles from Overton. Cloy was hardly more than a string of farmhouses situated on the outskirts of Overton. And Overton itself consisted of fewer than two thousand inhabitants. Perhaps Cloy was chosen to receive Mormon missionaries because a new convert had invited them to visit his friends and relations who lived there. Or there may have been a connection between Cloy and the in-laws of Frederick Cook, a priest assigned to accompany Elder Royle. (Sister Cook's maiden name was Davis, a name which suggests roots in Wales, but available records offer no further detail.)

Whatever the reason for the choice of area, Royle and Cook met with immediate success upon their arrival in Flintshire. Elder Royle reported that by the 30th of October a branch with thirty-two members had been established in Overton, certainly an impressive beginning for just three weeks' work. (*MS 1*: 192.) By the next month Royle and Cook had been joined by Elder James Burnham, who reported that the converts then numbered fifty-six and that the opposition was increasing. (*MS 1*: 212.) After another month, Burnham wrote that the number in that 'region' had risen to nearly one hundred and that he had been 'stoned' twice, 'only once receiving harm'. He also said that some of the local priests had followed the missionaries around and tried to disturb their meetings. 'They call us robbers and infidels, declaring that we rob other churches. If the opposition continues to increase, as it has done for some time past, we shall perhaps loose [*sic*] our heads soon.' (*MS 1*: 238–9.) Burnham's third and final letter to appear in the *Millennial Star* was dated 10 February 1841, about four months after Royle and Cook had received their assignment. Burnham reported that if they held their meetings at any private house that had not been licensed, the priests would enter a complaint and have the home owner fined. He also wrote, 'I have organized two branches of the church, consisting of about 150 members.' (*MS 1*: 284.)

One hundred and fifty converts in four months was a rather dramatic opening for such a small area. Hence the opposition is less surprising when one imagines the priests seeing their own congregations so quickly diminished. After Elder Burnham's third letter, the *Millennial Star* is silent as to further developments in Overton, except for the 6 April 1841 conference report of 170 members. (*MS 1*: 302.) At this time the Overton Branch became part of the Liverpool Conference, and its statistics were no longer reported separately.

During this early period of Church growth in Wales, an Elder James Burgess was in Overton for a short time and wrote about the local reaction to Mormonism in his journal.

At night we went to a preaching and a very rough meeting. We had some men come and [they] tied the door and smoked some sulphur through the keyhole and when we came out they followed us and rung old cans and hinges after us. But we were not afraid of them. (Burgess, 8 Jan 1841.)

About a year later, Elder Charles Smith, a convert from Ellesmere, was in Lightwood Green, about a mile from Overton, and in his journal on 27 January 1842 he recorded the fracas which had taken place that evening during a meeting held at the home of Brother William Cross. While Elder Smith was speaking, a handful of townspeople sneered at what he was saying. When Cross's son-in-law 'collared one of them to put him out of doors [the] rest began striking the brethren', but the saints succeeded in clearing the room. Those expelled were soon joined by others carrying large sticks, with which they began to beat the door. Smith wrote that the whole house seemed to be besieged. Stones were thrown through the windows, and one of the sisters received a 'dreadful gash on the side of the nose'. Finally Cross's son-in-law fired a gun to disperse the mob. They retreated but threatened revenge. (Charles Smith, 27 Jan 1842.)

The Overton saints are rather a mystery in Welsh Church history, as no existing records make further mention of them. Even Dan Jones, upon his arrival in the area as a missionary in 1845, gave no indication that there were any members of the Church in the North Wales Conference. However, one possible explanation as to what may have become of them is given by Elder Charles Smith in his brief but informative journal: 'I went...to meet with the brethren and sisters [in the Overton area], the greatest part of them being about to start for America.' (*Ibid.*) Thus it appears that many of the Overton converts were quick to follow the counsel of Church leaders and emigrated about a year after their conversion. This would explain why, nearly three years later, Elder Robert Martin reported that there were but seventy-five members scattered throughout North Wales. (*MS* 5:74.) Their names, however, remain unknown because of the incomplete records of that period.

At the time when these missionaries were having such success in North Wales, those proselytizing in the borderlands of South Wales had yet to establish a Welsh branch. Elder James Palmer, who was baptized on 13 April 1840, a convert from the United Brethren, recorded in his journal some of his early proselytizing visits to South Wales. One entry (that appears to be for some date in November 1840) reads, 'I preached at Skenfrith. Was opposed by a Roman Catholic.' A short time later he wrote that he and Elder Martin Littlewood 'visited Skenfrith again...We were opposed again by the same Roman Catholic who brought others with him and a newspaper and read therein a tissue of falsehood against our principles.' (Palmer.) Between this visit and the next, some new missionaries arrived in the area, and Elder Palmer reported:

> We now visited Skenfrith again with our reinforcement of young troops. On the Monday following I baptized John Preece and William Williams in the River Monnow and delivered a public discourse the same evening at Brother Reed's.

Palmer also recorded that missionary attention was then focused on the 'fair town of Monmouth', where he and Elder James Morgan 'obtained a house for public worship'. (*Ibid.*)

Neither Elder Burnham in the north nor Elder Palmer in the south comments about any language barrier in teaching the Welsh. Since these initial proselytizing efforts were just over the Welsh border, it seems likely that those who listened to the elders were bilingual. In his journal entry of 19 February 1841, Elder Palmer describes his first encounter with some Welsh folk who were less than fluent in English:

> I crossed the Black Mountain to Llanthony with the view of preaching the gospel, but all doors were closed against us. I felt that thereafter if that people wanted my ministerial labours they would have to come and invite me after such cold treatment. They are what might be rightly called 'mongrel Welsh', as but few of them can speak the English or Welsh language correct [*sic*]. (*Ibid.*)

Strangely enough, it was only a short time before Elder Palmer underwent a major change of attitude towards the people of Llanthony. After preaching in nearby Longtown, he was approached by one Jacob Watkins, who questioned him about the gospel until 3.00 a.m. and was back at daybreak with more questions. A resident of Llanthony, Mr Watkins promised to have a houseful of listeners if Elder Palmer would come back for a second visit. Thus, on 1 March 1841, just ten days after his initial 'cold treatment' in Llanthony, Elder Palmer *was* 'invited' back to a house full of eager listeners – so many, in fact, that he had to preach in the doorway so that people both indoors and out could hear his message. He later recorded:

The Lord blessed me with great liberty of speach [*sic*] and his Holy Spirit thrilled through my system from head to foot, accompanying his word, manifesting to my understanding most assuredly that there were those present before me that would respond to the call as soon as they were properly instructed in God's divine law. The people here speak the Welsh as well as the English language. (*Ibid.*)

Nearly two years of proselytizing in the border towns of South Wales produced only forty-four members – a discouraging number when compared to the many conversions in North Wales during this same period. Eventually, however, these growth rates would reverse, and South Wales would yield large numbers of converts – as much as fifteen times as many as the North.

The last area of Wales to see LDS missionaries was the centre. In early 1843 an Englishman from Cornwall, Elder William Henshaw (who had been baptized two years earlier in Wolverhampton) was called to labour in Wales. He began in the Merthyr Tydfil area, in Penydarren. As Elder Henshaw spoke no Welsh and the people of Penydarren were not so bilingual as those nearer the border, he had to approach people who did speak English and then rely on bilingual converts to teach the gospel to their Welsh-speaking countrymen. Still, Elder Henshaw achieved some success, baptizing his first family – William Rees Davis, his wife Rachel and their two sons – on 19 February 1843. The Davises were followed by others, and by June there was a thriving branch of thirty-two members in Penydarren. Before the year was out, the Penydarren Branch grew to fifty members, and another branch was organized in nearby Rhymni.

As the early missionaries had reported, opposition in Wales generally grew as the Church did. Although most Welsh religious periodicals prior to this time had remained silent about the Mormons, there was one Baptist publication, the *Seren Gomer* (Star of Gomer) that had printed three articles on Mormonism. These presented a view of the Mormons as 'religious hotheads' who had been deceived into believing 'the most shameful superstition which has ever been proclaimed in a Christian country' and who, if properly ignored, would soon die out. One of the articles mentioned 'Thomas Margretts' (Margetts) and his 'escape' from Nauvoo earlier that year, but in none of them was there any reference to contemporary Welsh converts, and most of the writer's information had probably been gleaned from English publications. (*Seren Gomer*, Jan 1841, pp. 6–8; Dec 1841, pp. 373–4.)

Another Welsh religious periodical, *Y Diwygiwr* (The Reformer), published by the Congregationalists, carried an article about the supposed attempt of Joseph Smith to walk on water (*Y Diwygiwr*, Dec 1843, pp. 370–1), but the first publication to comment on Welsh Mormons was apparently *Y Bedyddiwr* (The Baptist), in an article written by 'Tobit ger y Bont' (Tobit near the Bridge), a pseudonym for the Rev. W. R. Davies. Mr Davies was a Baptist minister in Dowlais, about two miles from Merthyr Tydfil, and was the most vociferous opponent of Mormonism in Wales until his death in 1849. When his first article appeared in March 1844, the Mormons in the Merthyr Tydfil area numbered just over one hundred, enough to provoke the alarmed Davies into action. He warned the people:

> The foolish and madmen who call themselves 'Latter-day Saints' have arrived in Pendaran [*sic*]. They profess to work miracles, to prophesy, to speak in unknown tongues, yea, in a word to do everything which the apostles did. I am sorry to say that a number of the dregs of society are now believers. They baptize at night, and those receiving baptism must undress for them and go into the water stark naked! (*Y Bedyddiwr*, Mar 1844, p. 99; all Welsh-to-English translations are by Professor Ronald D. Dennis, Brigham Young University.)

As the Rev. Davies's article preceded the establishment of a Mormon periodical in Wales by over two years, Elder Henshaw and his new converts had no official vehicle through which they could defend themselves. Evidently some saints attempted to rebut these charges by writing letters to the editor of *Y Bedyddiwr*, but their letters were never published there or in any other religious periodicals of the time. Ironically, for lack of extant journals or records containing information concerning this early period of the Welsh Mormons, it is chiefly to the Rev. Davies and his series of articles in *Y Bedyddiwr* that we owe thanks for our present knowledge about these early events. Despite their heavily antagonistic bias,

Davies's four articles contain valuable information about this otherwise unknown era of Church history.

In his second article, published in April 1844, Davies presented what he called 'an account of their [the Mormons'] failure together with their success', the 'failure' being that the missionaries had not won any converts from amongst the Baptists, and the 'success' being that they had been able to baptize a few 'men of the sprinkle', as Davies calls them. He continued:

> With respect to this group of subjects of his Majesty [meaning Satan]... Penydaran is their main church; here dwells the head prophet [meaning Elder Henshaw ?]. They have striven and continue to strive to expand their boundaries and win proselytes, and among other places they are attacking is Merthyr, and they have set up their camp in an area of that place which is called Georgetown, near Nant-y-Gwenith. (*Y Bedyddiwr*, Apr 1844, p. 123.)

Davies then related how Dafydd Oliver, a Baptist in the Georgetown area, and James Wilkins, a Baptist minister, met the Mormons head-on in a series of three debates. According to Davies, the Mormon debater was easily shown to be a 'satanic and presumptuous wretch'. The minister's son, Henry Wilkins, later joined the Church, however.

Davies further stated:

> Next they moved their miraculous persons to Dowlais, and made their encampment in a residence near the Caersalem house of worship, where bodies and souls were fattened on the ministry of St. J—y T—m and St. J—m C—r. (*Ibid.*)

But their stay was short, said Davies, because of the strength of the many Baptists in that area. (Caersalem, incidentally, was Davies's own chapel.) He continued by relating two more 'campaigns' by the Mormons – in Twynyrodyn near Sion Chapel in Merthyr, and in Cefncoedycymer, about three miles from Merthyr – both again unsuccessful because they were opposed by the Baptists.

Finally, they 'camped near the men of the sprinkle, or the church of the Independents by the name of Bethesda, Merthyr'. Here they were opposed by 'an intelligent and gifted young man, a member in Bethesda and a deacon in the Sunday School'. The evidence indicates that this was Abel Evans, who later became a stalwart missionary for the Church. Mr Davies labelled this phase of the Mormon 'campaign' a success because the debate centred on infant baptism, a position the Independents were unable to defend. The result was that the 'intelligent and gifted young man' went from the scene of the debate to the river and was baptized by the Mormons. The young man's father was greatly distressed, but four days later he and another son and daughter were converted to Mormonism as well. 'Had they been Baptists,' observed Davies, 'they would have won the battle.' (*Y Bedyddiwr*, Apr 1844, pp. 124.)

For his third and fourth articles, Davies used 'I' as his pseudonym. The third appeared immediately following the second in the April 1844 issue of *Y Bedyddiwr*, and the fourth was printed the following month. These two, somewhat briefer than previous articles, dealt with the supposed failure of the Mormons to heal the diseased leg of a recent convert, and concluded that the Mormons were therefore 'nothing but heretics, wolves, false prophets and deceivers'. (*Ibid.*; see also May 1844, p. 160.)

Whilst Davies was attaching such epithets as 'Quack Henshaw', 'the great prophet', 'the high deceiver', and 'the Chief Apostle' to Elder William Henshaw, Church leaders in the April 1844 Liverpool conference voted to call him a conference president. (*MS* 4: 197.) Seven Welsh branches, all results of Elder Henshaw's efforts during the previous fifteen months, were to form the Merthyr Tydfil Conference: Beaufort, Tredegar, Merthyr Tydfil, Aberdare, Abersychan, Penydarren and Rhymni. The Abergavenny Branch was taken from the Garway Conference and added to the new Merthyr Tydfil Conference.

Y Bedyddiwr was silent about the LDS Church for two years following Mr Davies's articles. *Y Diwygiwr*, however, took up the attack in July 1844, publishing a letter from one Thomas Williams, originally from the Merthyr area, now living in Ohio, USA. He had written to his Welsh friends, he said, to warn them about the 'damnable and destructive heresy' of Mormonism that he had heard was being preached in his homeland by some 'cabbage-faced pygmies'. (*Y Diwygiwr*, Jul 1844, p. 213.) Also, the *Seren Gomer*, in its September issue, printed a paragraph about the assassination of Joseph Smith, in which the editor promised to give a full account of this 'deceiver' and his sect in the following issue. (*Seren Gomer*, Sep 1844, p. 287.)

The editor fulfilled his promise and did publish a seven-column history of Joseph Smith and the Mormons in the November 1844 issue of *Seren Gomer*. There is but brief mention, however, of the saints in Wales: 'These men have made their appearance lately in some places in Wales, and we heard one of them preaching a few nights ago in this town.' (*Seren Gomer*, Nov 1844, pp. 327–31.) 'This town' apparently referred to Carmarthen, since the *Seren Gomer* was published there, and thus it appears that by late 1844 the elders had begun to preach outside the Merthyr Tydfil area – as far away as Carmarthen, forty-five miles distant.

The year 1844 marks not only the expansion of the Welsh proselytizing effort beyond the counties of Monmouth and Glamorgan, but also the publication of the first Welsh-language materials printed by the Church. In a letter dated 3 September 1844, Reuben Hedlock wrote, 'The Church in South Wales is progressing rapidly. I have published a small pamphlet in the Welsh language on the first principles.' (JH, 3 Sep 1844.) Unfortunately, no further details about this pamphlet are known, as no copy of it has been found.

The year 1844 also marks the utterance of Joseph Smith's last recorded prophecy before his death – a prophecy that was given to a Welshman and had to do with the Church in Wales. The Welshman was Captain Dan Jones, and the prophecy was that he would live through the events at Carthage and fulfil the mission to Wales to which he had been called. Dan Jones was baptized in the icy waters of the Mississippi River, USA, in January 1843, just about the time William Henshaw began his mission in South Wales. Contrary to most printed accounts of Jones's conversion, it was three months *before* meeting Joseph Smith that he investigated the Church and was baptized. In May 1843, just a month after Brother Jones met the Prophet, he was called to serve a mission to his native land. But because of business details involving the *Maid of Iowa* (Jones's steamboat, which was eventually purchased by Joseph Smith), he did not leave for Wales until 28 August 1844, two months after Joseph's death. Dan Jones later wrote to Thomas Bullock about the Prophet's purchase of his boat:

> Brother Joseph never paid me the first dollar for the boat... A few days previous to being arrested he told me 'I have a check in the house for $1200; as soon as I can get it cashed you shall have $1100 of it, and then start for Wales, not with your fingers in your mouth but prepared to buy a Press and do business aright.' (D. Jones, letter to Thomas Bullock, 20 Jan 1855, p. 23.)

John S. Davis (1822–82), translator of the Standard Works into Welsh.

William Howells (1816–51), first Latter-day Saint missionary to France, 1849.

Dan Jones (1810–62), mission president in Wales 1845–9 and 1854–6.

John Parry (1789–1868), first conductor of the Mormon Tabernacle Choir, 1849.

William S. Phillips (1815–76), mission president in Wales 1849–53.

With Joseph's martyrdom and the resulting confusion, Jones never received his money, but he remained philosophical: 'Thrilled with prospects of my mission I left all, rejoicing in the exchange of a steamboat for an Eldership on the deck of the never-sinking ship of life.' (*Ibid.* p. 24.)

Captain Dan Jones was with the Prophet at Carthage gaol, just hours before Joseph and Hyrum Smith were killed. The previous night Dan and Joseph had lain side by side in the upper room of the gaol, and the others were apparently sleeping when Joseph had asked Dan in a whisper if he was afraid to die. 'Has that time come, think you?' Dan asked. 'Engaged in such a cause I do not think that death would have many terrors.' 'You will yet see Wales and fulfill the mission appointed you ere you die,' Joseph told him. (*Ibid.* p. 10; see also *BYU Studies 24*:95–104.)

In the following forty-eight hours, Dan Jones was delivered from the hands of his enemies three times. His first escape occurred in front of the Carthage gaol, where his horse was saddled and awaiting his departure with a letter he had received from the Prophet for a solicitor in Quincy, Illinois, some sixty miles down river from Nauvoo. The men in the mob, thinking the message to be a call for the Nauvoo Legion to come to Joseph's rescue, demanded that Jones hand over the letter. In the confusion that resulted when he refused to do so, Jones jumped on his horse and rode off, with bullets whistling on either side of him. He was unharmed.

Jones's second deliverance was just moments later, as he rode on his way towards Nauvoo, twenty miles to the north-east. He went, as it were, 'between two fires' – some of the mob from Carthage having gone off into the woods with rifles to waylay him, and another group of about three hundred 'painted assassins' waiting ahead on a prairie ridge for the opportune moment to ride into Carthage. Without knowing it, Jones threaded his way right between these two dangers.

But he was not safe, even then. Later that night, after reaching Nauvoo, Jones boarded a steamboat for Quincy. It was when the boat stopped at Warsaw that he first heard of the deaths of Joseph and Hyrum Smith, from a mob who were trying to convince people to prepare to defend themselves against a retaliatory attack by the Mormons. When Jones spoke up to explain that there was no need for such a defence, he immediately became a marked man. Nevertheless, he continued on the steamboat to Quincy, where he again lifted up his voice against the members of the mob, who were now trying to get the militia to go upstream to Warsaw. As he was about to take a steamer back to Nauvoo, Jones was warned by its captain to wait for the next boat, as some of the mob had concocted a plan to kill him. Accordingly, he took passage on the next steamer, the *Ohio*. But even on that boat were people who planned to hang him when they reached Warsaw. At Warsaw, Jones waited breathlessly underneath a mattress while the mob shouted, 'Where is Capt. Jones; where is he; bring him out; out with the d—d Mormon.' He could hear those on the shore also shouting, 'Bring him out, hang him up.' Captain Atchinson of the *Ohio* declared, however, that he had put Jones ashore below the town, and finally convinced the mob to desist. The gallows prepared for Jones on the shore went unused, and he was delivered from death a third time since Joseph's prophecy less than forty-eight hours earlier. (*Ibid.* p. 18.)

Two months later, Dan Jones and his wife Jane were on their way to Wales. They travelled in company with Wilford Woodruff, Hiram Clark and their wives, reaching Liverpool in early January 1845. Captain Jones, now Elder Jones, was first assigned to Wrexham in North Wales, an area he was well acquainted with, having spent his childhood just a few miles from there. Unable to purchase the press that Joseph Smith had wanted him to have, Elder Jones hired the press of William Bayley in Wrexham to print his first pamphlet, a 48-page work in Welsh, entitled *Y farw wedi ei chyfodi yn fyw: neu'r hen grefydd newydd* (The dead raised to life, or the old religion anew). For his later publications, however, he used the press of his brother, John Jones, who was a printer and Congregationalist minister in Rhydybont.

The date of the preface of Elder Jones's pamphlet, 4 April 1845, coincides with the date of the first meeting between Elders Jones and Henshaw – the date of a conference in Manchester. Elder William Henshaw, who still spoke no Welsh, reported the opening of five more branches in his conference during the previous year, and an increase of 195 convert baptisms, or about 16 per month. Jones, fluent in both Welsh and English, had neither baptisms nor branches to report, but he addressed the conference with such eloquence that, after taking down a few lines, the clerk wrote:

We would here remark that we are utterly incapable of doing anything like justice to the address of Captain Jones, for though delivered while struggling with disease, such was its effect upon ourselves, and we also believe upon others, that we ceased to write, in order to give way to the effect produced upon our feelings. (*MS* 5:170; the disease was probably Elder Jones's chronic lung ailment.)

During the next eight months, an average of twenty convert baptisms per month were reported in South Wales, under Elder Henshaw's leadership. Meanwhile, Elder Jones's efforts in North Wales, despite his gift for oratory in both Welsh and English, and despite his 48-page pamphlet, brought only three new members into the fold. His lack of success amongst his countrymen must certainly have caused some reflection on Jones's part. Having travelled from Nauvoo with Wilford Woodruff, he was no doubt aware of the phenomenal results Elder Woodruff had seen in Herefordshire some four years earlier, and that he had anticipated a similar experience himself is evident in a letter he wrote to Elder Woodruff after about seven weeks in North Wales: 'I have neglected writing until now, expecting to have better news to give you, because I had some forebodings of glorious consequences.' (D. Jones, letter to Wilford Woodruff, 24 Feb 1845.) Elder Jones's 'glorious consequences' would come, but not until he had spent nearly a year of frustration in North Wales.

In August 1845, some four months after the conference in Manchester where Elder Jones had first met Elder Henshaw, he went to South Wales for a visit. The reason for his visit is not clear from the surviving documents – perhaps he went to call on his brother John in Carmarthenshire, or perhaps he went to observe William Henshaw in action – but while Elder Jones was in Merthyr Tydfil, there was a colliery explosion in neighbouring Cwmbach, which claimed the lives of 28 men and boys. Elder Henshaw later reported that 'many of the Saints were at work in the pit at the time of the explosion, not one of whom was injured, for which they felt truly thankful to the Heavenly Father'. (*MS* 6:94.) Elder Jones, however, had a much more spectacular report concerning the tragedy. Reporting to Church leaders in Liverpool a few weeks later, he told them that the saints who were regularly employed in the pit were not there at the time of the explosion because they had been warned of the impending catastrophe in a vision. He also reported that those who had been killed had

> particularly distinguished themselves by disturbing a meeting of the Saints, and crying out for a sign, little deeming that their request would be granted so speedily, and in so awful a manner...[And] the services of the Saints...were [then] called into requisition to bring up the bodies of those that were destroyed, nor would the agents, or overlookers of the works attempt it, unless preceded and assisted by the Saints. (*MS* 6:110.)

Both Henshaw and Jones, however, agreed in their accounts that no Church members were hurt in the accident, even though several were employed at the pit. This fact alone would have caused members of the community to take notice of the growing numbers of Latter-day Saints in their midst.

The next occasion where Elders Jones and Henshaw met was the Manchester Conference in December 1845. During that conference, Elder Wilford Woodruff proposed that Dan Jones be appointed to preside over the branches in Wales, nearly all of which had been established by Henshaw. This proposal received unanimous approval (including Elder Henshaw's, even though it would put Elder Jones in a position of leadership over Elder Henshaw, who was to continue as president of the Merthyr Tydfil Conference).

When Elder Jones became the president of the Church in Wales (the title used at that time for mission president) there were approximately five hundred members, most of them in the Merthyr Tydfil area. One of Elder Jones's first objectives as their new president was to defend them and their faith against the increasing opposition from the Rev. Davies and his colleagues of the clergy. In addition to his eloquent verbal rebuttals, Jones also made use of the press to ensure that the Church was portrayed accurately to the reading public. One example of this phase of his defence was Jones's response when his pamphlet was attacked in thirty-two pages of invective published by a lay preacher named David Williams. Williams's title, *Twyll y Seintiau Diweddaf yn cael ei ddynoethi* (The fraud of the Latter Saints [*sic*] exposed), was mild compared to some comments in his text. His statement about *Annerchiad y Deuddeg Apostol* (Jones's Welsh translation of the 1845 *Proclamation of the Twelve Apostles*), is one example:

By the time I had glanced over the above treatise on the kingdom of God [Jones's pamphlet], yet another one [Jones's translation of the proclamation] came to my attention, one so presumptuous as if it had been written by the fingers of the devil, who had dipped his pen in the venom of dragons or in the fiery furnace itself, and had it printed in the gates of hell. (David Williams, p. 29.)

It is difficult to think of Rhydybont, the picturesque little village near Llanybydder where *Annerchiad* had been printed (on the Rev. John Jones's press), as 'the gates of hell'. Another anti-Mormon spokesman later attached the epithet 'prostitute press' to Mr Jones's Rhydybont operation, as it was the only press in Wales that printed LDS literature. (*Seren Gomer*, Dec 1847, p. 375.)

Elder Dan Jones's reaction to Williams's vitriolic pen was simply to put his own pen to paper and have his brother print a rebuttal. A translation of his title suggests the nature of the treatise: 'The scales, in which are seen David weighing Williams, and Williams weighing David; or David Williams, from Abercanaid, contradicting himself, caught in his deceit, and proved deistic'. The following segment illustrates Jones's style throughout all sixteen pages of his pamphlet:

Who says that? Williams, I think, for David in the previous two lines says the complete opposite to that in this admission... Which one do you believe? David or Williams? I believe David now... Well done, Williams! Although he lost before, he wins now, and is closer to the truth than David. (D. Jones, *Y glorian* [The scales], p. 5.)

In the March 1846 issue of *Y Bedyddiwr*, a headline proclaimed, 'A Miracle! A Miracle! At last!' and was followed by a two-column article ridiculing the Mormons' claim that William Hughes's broken leg had been healed by the laying on of hands. Although the article was signed with a pseudonym, the author obviously was the Rev. Davies again, this time on a rampage against 'the Latter-day Satanists' that would end only with his death three years later. Elder Jones immediately responded by sending a letter to the editor of *Y Bedyddiwr*, complete with the sworn testimony of William Hughes himself and the signed affidavits of non-LDS eyewitnesses to the healing, but these were never printed.

Jones's frustration at this and other editors' refusals to print anything in defence of Mormonism soon prompted him to initiate his own periodical, *Prophwyd y Jubili* (Prophet of the Jubilee). In the first issue (July 1846) Elder Jones declared to his compatriots:

You know how we have been accused of every evil, fraud, yes, and of every foolishness. To the periodicals which have accused us we have sent in the kindest manner convincing letters in defence of our innocence. But have they been printed? No! Have we been accused in the *Amserau* (Times), *Seren Gomer*, *Dysgedydd* (Educator), *Bedyddiwr*, etc.? Yes, indeed... Can everyone else raise up his magazine except us? Is the press closed to us? Is that the freedom of Wales in the 19th century? Have the periodicals been locked up? We shall open our own periodical, then. Has the press been defiled by slandering us? We shall cleanse it through defending ourselves, then. (*Prophwyd 1*: ii.)

This little periodical appeared regularly for the next thirty months, all but the last two issues being printed on the Rev. Jones's 'prostitute press'. Much of the untold history of the Welsh saints is nestled in the nearly 600 pages of this remarkable defender of the faith – hidden behind the formidable barrier of the Welsh language, now spoken by only twenty per cent of Wales's three million inhabitants.

The Welsh Mormons' claims of miracles being performed, as well as their assertion that theirs was the only true church of God, were disturbing to the Welsh nonconformists. To them, such claims were blasphemous, and they felt not merely justified but obliged to oppose and denounce the Mormons. In July 1846 Dan Jones recorded the incident of a young man who had a sore leg, from which twenty pieces of bone had been removed. For six months he had not been able to walk without a crutch, at which time Elder Jones reported:

When he believed the gospel, I told him he would be healed if he would obey; he walked about a mile with crutches. By the river side we prayed that he might be enabled to dispense with his crutch, and he walked into the water [to be baptized] without it – out again, and home – and so far as I have heard has never used it since. I carried his crutch home through the town on my back, the man telling them that he was healed, but strange to say they would neither believe him nor their own eyes, but cried out impostors, etc., and that he might have walked before!! although they knew better; but however, the man got a blessing, and when I left, the wounds in his leg were closing finely, and free from pain. (*MS 8*:40.)

There is evidence that in Carmarthenshire a minister tried to prove the 'fraud' of Mormonism by setting up a blind man for baptism. According to Thomas Jeremy, a convert from that area in March 1846, the blind man was a 'prepared Judas' who had been encouraged by his friends to request baptism and restoration of his sight. Then, when the Mormons were unable to restore his sight, it would prove that they were frauds. Suspecting the plot, Elder Jones announced a public baptism – a departure from the normal procedure of quiet, private services. He later reported:

> It was astonishing to see the crowds that came from the regions round about; both priests, preachers, persecutors, and people. Oh, what an opportunity that was to explain the whys and wherefores of Mormonism, sign seeking, etc. They all listened with the greatest attention for about two hours, although many had come on purpose to oppose, but I could not get a try out of any of them. I shewed them that our religion was true, whether the blind man got his sight or not; it was true before the blind man was heard of, that it would remain as true when he was dead and forgotten, and that it is eternally true, and I knew it. But after the baptism, while walking up to the house to be confirmed, it was amusing to hear the remarks as the crowd followed, crossing and re-crossing to peep at his eyes, to see whether his sight was restored; some said it was, some that he was blinder than before, and that was difficult. (*MS 8*:41.)

If it was true that the blind man was part of a plot to discredit the Church, it is also true that the plan backfired. For upon confirming him, Elders Dan Jones and Abel Evans anointed him and gave him a blessing, after which 'he shouted for joy in the presence of all, and testified that while hands were on his head he could "see the candle in the candlestick on the table"; that he was more than satisfied'. (*Ibid.*)

But the story did not have a happy ending. Following his baptism the man, whose name was Daniel, attended only two Church meetings and then proceeded to malign the Church. One of his 'backers', according to Elder Jones, was the Rev. Josiah Thomas Jones, editor of *Y Drysorfa Gynnulleidfaol* (The Congregationalist Treasury), and one of the results of Daniel's faithlessness was a vicious 12-page pamphlet, the publication of an interview between Daniel and the Rev. Josiah Thomas Jones. An eight-stanza poem at the beginning of the pamphlet stated Daniel's position and his obligation. Here is a translation of the last stanza:

> Now I must testify
> That the Saints do but deceive
> If you buy this, you shall have the complete story
> Of the way in which I was charmed.

In characteristic fashion, Elder Jones responded with a pamphlet of his own, entitled '*Haman' yn hongian ar ei grogbren ei hun*! ('Haman' hanging from his own gallows). Not long afterwards, Thomas Jeremy and Dan Jones were on their way back to Llanybydder when they had a chance meeting with Daniel on the road. Elder Jones asked him why he had become such a persecutor of the saints, and Daniel offered not a single reason in answer but only made it plain that he chose to remain an enemy. Brother Jeremy later wrote:

> Capt. Jones told him that if he continued to persecute and malign the Saints the hand of God would be upon him and his fate would be hotter than that of Korah, Dathan, and Abiram [the three who were swallowed up in the earth for opposing Moses]. He sternly told him the danger of persecuting and maligning the people of the Lord...[Afterwards] Daniel was stricken with a severe illness which caused him to feel his bowels igniting within him. He drank large quantities of water to extinguish the supposed fire from within, and also he would rush outside to immerse himself in water to cool down; but all was in vain. He died in this painful condition. (*Prophwyd 3*: 171.)

In spite of such opposition, the Church in Wales continued to grow. It was about this time, in fact, that a particular Welsh family joined the Church under rather unusual circumstances – a family that would later furnish the first conductor of what would become the Salt Lake Mormon Tabernacle Choir. Long before the missionaries arrived in Great Britain to preach the restored gospel, the Rev. John Parry was doing considerable preaching of his own, first as a Baptist, then as a Campbellite minister. North Wales was well acquainted with John Parry and his family of musically talented sons and daughters. In 1841 John's eldest son, Bernard, a portrait painter and piano teacher, contracted a fatal illness. His brother John later wrote about the extraordinary predictions that Bernard made just before his death:

> Two nights before he died he was very quiet in his bed about midnight while father and myself were sitting up with him; after a while he called father and myself to his bedside, and told us that the Lord had showed him great and marvelous things that should come to pass in our time. But he should not see them as he was to die very soon. Said he, 'The Lord is going to make a great work and a wonder upon the earth, and you shall be called to it, father, and you shall preach the everlasting gospel to thousands in Wales even yet.' And he said, 'And you, John, shall be called to it. And you shall preach the gospel to tens of thousands, and shall baptize many, even in the Vale of Clwyd here.' (Parry, pp. 4–5.)

It was another five years, however, before Bernard Parry's family came to understand the full implication of his mysterious prophecy. Once again it was a deathbed scene – that of Sarah, Bernard's younger sister. While living in Cheltenham with some relations, Sarah became converted to the Church but had declined baptism out of deference to her father. Again, her brother John wrote:

> And while upon her deathbed, she accused me and father in the following words: 'Father,' she said, 'your religion is worth nothing in the hour of death. I have lived it as faithful as mortal could do, and it is of no good to me now in death. I am going to utter darkness, even to hell. Therefore, look unto yourselves, and seek a religion that will support you and enable you to face death fearless, as the one that you have is of no value. You and John did persuade and hinder me from going to the Church of Jesus Christ. And now I am going to utter darkness.' I then fainted and fell down. (*Ibid.* p. 6.)

Five weeks later, Sarah Parry's brother John and their parents took her advice and were baptized. A sister and two other brothers soon followed.

The conversion of the Parry family in North Wales caused much jubilation amongst the Welsh saints. Dan Jones commented on it in the *Prophwyd*, expressing the hope that those who had followed the Rev. John Parry 'from darkness to degrees of light through frown and scorn' would follow Elder Parry further, 'to the midst of the fervent light of the eternal gospel'. In fulfilment of Bernard's prophecy five years earlier, both father and son were called to serve missions in North Wales, and they did indeed preach to thousands of their fellow Welshmen. Eventually, the senior John Parry's musical ability resulted in an invitation from President Brigham Young for him to institute a choir – the one that would evolve into the Tabernacle Choir.

Although record-keeping in the early days of the Welsh Church was irregular at best, and few of even those irregular records have survived to this day, it appears from the statistics in the *Millennial Star* and the *Prophwyd y Jubili* that about twenty converts per month joined the Church during 1845. In 1846 and the first half of 1847 this number doubled, and during the latter half of 1847 it more than trebled. Figures for the two-year period from July 1847 to July 1849 show an average of 140 convert baptisms per month in Wales. Of the many conversion stories recorded in the *Prophwyd* and the *Star*, there follow three that may serve as a representative sample.

In mid-July 1847 a Hindu, 'late from Bengal' and in his native dress, called at Dan Jones's door in Merthyr Tydfil for charity. President Jones felt an immediate attachment to the man, inasmuch as he had been in India as a youth – a stranger without a friend. Using the little Hindi that he could recall, Jones invited him in and began to preach the gospel to him. Somehow, in the midst of the Hindu's broken English and Jones's pidgin Hindi, communication took place well enough for the newcomer to request further information about the Church. At Elder Jones's invitation, he returned for several days in succession and 'appeared very thankful for the instructions he received'. In a letter dated 22 July 1847, Jones wrote to British Mission president Orson Spencer as follows:

I took him to our church meetings on Sunday, and requested the Saints to pray that the great dispenser of all spiritual gifts would cause him to be instructed in a language which he understood, and that it should be for a testimony to him. The gifts, and 'tongues' in particular, are profusely enjoyed here generally, but this time more abundantly, so that before the close of the meeting I knew, and all the Saints indeed knew, that he had heard a language which he understood, and great was our joy when he said that he had heard the great things of God taught him in that meeting in eight different languages of the east, which he understood more or less of. But what astonished him the most was, a song which one of the sisters sung [*sic*] in the Malabar language (as he called it), and another in the Malay; this so animated him, that he pulled a Hindoostanee hymn-book out of his pocket, and fain would sing in the meeting with them, supposing they could follow him in that too. (*MS* 9:238.)

One of the sisters who sang in tongues was Margaret Morris Mathews, a convert of about three years. The story of that event was preserved in her family, and years later her daughter recorded it as follows:

In the congregation there was a Hindu who, when my Mother started singing, took a small book from his pocket and sang with her, the tears streaming down his cheeks. After the meeting he asked my father who the lady was who sang so perfectly the song his mother sang to him when he was a boy. (Mathews.)

The next day, Elder Jones felt impressed to ask to his house several of the elders and brethren 'that had the gifts' and, as he recorded:

We covenanted in prayer to seek his conversion in the Lord's way further, and for the space of four hours the brethren, through the gifts of the spirit, taught him the gospel so plain and forcibly, that before he left the room he requested to be baptized. Sometimes he interpreted in English as well as he could, and the speakers again, by the gift of interpretation, in Welsh, in some instances almost *verbatim*. (*MS* 9:238.)

To test the depth of the Hindu's sincerity, Elder Jones invited him to live in his house free of cost and eat at his table, but he replied that all he wanted of Jones was 'good religion to please the great "Shurinah"'. On Wednesday, 21 July 1847, the man was baptized by Elder Dan Jones, thus becoming the first Hindu convert to the Church.

Another Welsh convert from this period became the first missionary to France. William Howells, a merchant and Baptist lay minister living in Aberdare, about seven miles from Merthyr Tydfil, had often heard the Rev. Davies and others pounding their pulpits and shouting about the 'great fraud, devilish hypocrisy, and miserable darkness of the Latter-day Satanists'. (*Ugdorn Seion 1*:93.) He had also read their pamphlets but had decided to suspend judgement until he could obtain better information than the invective of Davies, 'whose brain had no doubt been softened by the fire of the angry passion which was working to the point of boiling the frothy sweat of his forehead'. (*Ibid.*)

Mr Howells's grandson later wrote that, since Howells was too bashful and proud to go to any LDS meetings or speak with the missionaries, his first positive contact with the Church came when a widow who was supported by the poor fund of his parish presented him with a pamphlet written by Elder Dan Jones. (Howells, p. 3.) The pamphlet was Jones's reply to the opposition of yet another Baptist minister, the Rev. Edward Roberts of Rhymni, who had thunderously promised to kill Mormonism and bury it by Christmas. Howells later described the impact that Jones's pamphlet had on him:

> In a few hours [it] proved the religion I professed to be no other than a sandy foundation – all my false hopes fled, all human traditions that I had cleaved to appeared folly. I was convinced that the Saints were the only true church of God. (*MS 10*:175.)

Elder Jones was exultant as he wrote to President Orson Spencer:

> He came four miles purposely to be baptized, though he had never heard a sermon, only [read] my publications; especially my last reply...finished him entirely, and he came in as good a spirit as any one that I ever saw, and has just returned on his way rejoicing. (*MS* 9:364.)

And William Howells himself declared:

The first few hours I spent after having been baptized for the remission of my sins, by a servant who knew that he was sent by God to administer the ordinance, gave me more pleasure and knowledge of spiritual things, than during the twenty years with the Baptist connexion. (*MS 10*: 175.)

Because Howells had served a short mission to France as a Baptist lay minister, the Church leaders in Liverpool soon called him to go back to France, this time as an LDS missionary. During the year and a half before he began his mission on the Continent, he managed to baptize nearly one hundred of his Welsh compatriots. And when he stepped on to French soil on 9 July 1849, he also stepped into the history books as the first LDS missionary to France. (An account of his experiences in France is contained in Cannon and Whittaker, pp. 43–81.)

The most triumphant conversion story of the time, however, was that of Rees Price, a former Baptist who had worked closely with the Rev. Davies himself. It caused a good deal of excitement amongst the saints to have a high-ranking officer of the enemy camp defect from the Baptists and seek religious asylum with the Mormons, and Dan Jones was unabashedly exuberant as he wrote about it in the March 1848 *Prophwyd y Jubili*:

There have been nine baptized [in Dowlais, the home of Mr Davies's congregation] since the beginning of January, one of which was the 'right hand man' of the Rev. W. R. Davies! He was a scribe in his meeting-house, one of the 'trustees', etc., and very staunch in their sight. Their persecution and their endless lies are what caused him to look into Mormonism; and the honesty and the love which he has toward the truth caused him to embrace it as the treasure of all treasures. Two others of Mr Davies's members were baptized after him [the 'right hand man'], and several before that, although Mr Davies maintains that only one old woman left him for the Saints. (*Prophwyd 3*:45.)

Later Brother Price, a 33-year-old miner at the time of his conversion, also offered his viewpoint in the pages of the *Prophwyd*:

I was a member with the Baptists for close to nine years, living as righteously and zealously as I could and striving to the best of my ability to get a grasp on the comfort of the Holy Ghost, as promised in the scriptures. I received the best counsels of the Rev. W. R. Davies, Dowlais, for years. I heard his persecution and his continuous false accusations against the Latter-day Saints in meetings, from the pulpits, through the periodicals and throughout the houses and the streets; and I examined them carefully and without bias as well as I could; eventually

I became convinced that they were baseless and derived from a bad principle. And I perceived also that Mr Davies could not to my satisfaction disprove the principles espoused by the Saints. (*Prophwyd* 3:131.)

Price said he had also listened with interest to the anti-Mormon lectures of the Rev. Edward Roberts when Roberts came to Dowlais to 'kill Mormonism'. He similarly attended Dan Jones's rebuttal lecture and later read the 40-page pamphlet which Jones published about Roberts's shallow reasoning. He stated:

I heard and read the Saints' defense in the face of it all, whereupon I requested my excommunication from the Baptists and received baptism from the Saints. (*Ibid.* p. 132.)

Over the years, the Welsh saints had come to expect all kinds of continual opposition. However, like Rees Price, many new members bore testimony that their conversions had come after observing unfair treatment of the Mormons by their own religious leaders and by the press.

The opposition to the Latter-day Saints caused them to be all the more desirous of leaving 'Babylon' to go to their 'Zion' in America. Since Dan Jones was assigned to lead a group of Welsh emigrants in early 1849, a conference was scheduled for 31 December 1848 and New Years's Day 1849 in Merthyr Tydfil for his release. President Orson Pratt was to be there to reorganize the leadership in Wales. But when President Pratt did not arrive, President Jones went right ahead and conducted the business himself. According to instructions he had received from his leaders at Liverpool, he organized a presidency for Wales, as follows: 'Elder William Phillips, a sterling and tried man, president; Abel Evans, an indefatigable veteran, his first counsellor... ; Elder John Davies [actually Davis], who is a faithful man, to be his second counsellor.' (*Ibid.*)

For some months before this 'changing of the guard', extensive encouragement and instruction had been offered to potential emigrants in the *Prophwyd*. Many of the specifics of this life-changing venture were spelt out in nearly every issue of 1848, in an unmistakable spirit of optimism and enthusiasm on the part of the editor, Dan Jones. The attitude of their leaving Babylon for the promised land is plainly evident in 'Henffych California' (Hail to California), a song that appeared in the October issue and which was to be sung by the Welsh as they sailed away. (The name 'California' then applied also to the Rocky Mountains.) Perhaps the following two verses (in translation) will serve as a sample:

When pestilence is harvesting the countries,
Harvesting man like the grass of the field;
When its foul breeze blows,
Laying waste the green earth,
California –
Yonder across the distant seas, for me.

When the sharp, shining sword
Is bathed in blood;
Yes, blood – the warm blood of men,
In the worst battles ever fought,
California –
Yonder to the Rocky Mountains I shall go.

One comment by a non-believer just before the departure of the first Welsh emigrants was particularly amusing to the saints. It was published in the October 1848 issue of the *Seren Gomer*:

After receiving enough money to get a ship or ships to voyage to California, their Chief-President [Dan Jones] will sail them to Cuba, or some place like it, and will sell them as slaves, every jack one of them. It would serve them right for having such little respect for the book of Christ and giving it up for the books of Mormon. (*Seren Gomer 31*:305.)

The emigrants must have had a hearty chuckle as they went past Cuba on their way to New Orleans and thought of that ominous prediction.

Not all the anti-Mormon opposition could be met with a chuckle, however. Thomas Jeremy described a sort that required bodyguards and secrecy:

The life of our dear Brother Captain Jones was in such danger that his house was attacked almost every night for weeks before leaving Merthyr, so that his godly life was not safe in sleeping except between guards from among his brethren; and there were scoundrels so inhuman who had been paid to kill him as he left, so that he had to leave secretly the day before. (*Udgorn 1*:57.)

The emigration plan called for all Welsh saints to meet in Liverpool by 15 February 1849; saints from South Wales were to gather the day before in Swansea, to travel from there to Liverpool by steamer. Over 300 people packed trunks with all their remaining possessions and headed for Liverpool to board the *Buena Vista*, bound for New Orleans. Only 249 of these, however, would fit on board this rather small vessel; the remainder waited another week and travelled with some English saints on the *Hartley*. A group of Welsh ministers went amongst their emigrating compatriots at Liverpool in one last-ditch attempt to convince them of their folly. But these efforts did not yield them any results.

On 26 February 1849, after a few days' delay, all was ready for the *Buena Vista* to set sail. William Phillips and others who had gone to Liverpool to see off their fellow saints had brought oranges to hurl to the outstretched hands of the passengers as the ship was being towed from the Waterloo Dock. When the ship had gone too far to throw any more oranges, handkerchiefs were then waved as a final farewell. Tears of friendship and brotherhood flowed freely.

Fifty days later there were hearty cheers when the *Buena Vista* docked at New Orleans. There the saints boarded the *Constitution*, a steamer that would take them up the Mississippi River to St Louis. When they docked at St Louis, all gave thanks for having escaped the cholera epidemic that was raging up and down the shores of the Mississippi. The voyage from St Louis to Council Bluffs, on board the *Highland Mary*, proved tragic, however: over twenty per cent of them died of cholera. And the percentage was about the same for the Welsh saints who had crossed on the *Hartley*. Grief and mourning engulfed the survivors as they gathered at Council Bluffs.

The many who did not have enough money to continue directly from Council Bluffs to the Salt Lake Valley that summer remained in Council Bluffs to work and save. About eighty were able to get themselves 'outfitted' to cross the plains that same year, travelling in the George A. Smith company. In characteristic Welsh fashion, they sang their way to their promised land, and it was there that President Young asked John Parry to form a choir to sing at the next general conference. It was this choir, with its nucleus of Welsh saints, many of them non-English-speaking, that was the beginning of the far-famed Mormon Tabernacle Choir.

In the meantime, back in Wales the reins of leadership had been given into the hands of William S. Phillips, a 34-year-old father of four. He had been baptized five years earlier, when the Church was in its infancy in South Wales, with about eighty members. Now he was called to preside over nearly four thousand Welsh Mormons. William Howells, in comparing President Phillips with Dan Jones, characterized him as 'another Samson brought up amongst his brethren, flesh of their flesh, bone of their bone, who would fight the Philistines and cause their Dagon to fall more perplexed than ever'. (*MS 12*:90.)

President Phillips selected as his first counsellor one of his contemporaries, a stalwart by the name of Abel Evans. Evans, a 37-year-old bachelor, had distinguished himself as a highly successful missionary, and one who had the gift of healing. President Phillips's second counsellor was John S. Davis, a 27-year-old bachelor and master printer, who owned his own press.

With these three as the new leaders of the Church in Wales, the conversion rate continued at the same high level that had begun about eighteen months before. For unexplained reasons, however, perhaps because of the weakening effect of emigration, the numbers dropped considerably during 1852. And at the official announcement of the practice of polygamy (1853), even fewer baptisms were recorded.

With the change in leadership came a change in the title of the Church's Welsh publication. The *Prophwyd y Jubili* became *Udgorn Seion* (Zion's Trumpet), with Elder John S. Davis serving as both editor and printer. In his time as editor of this periodical, Elder Davis made several outstanding contributions to the growth of the Church in Wales, such as increasing the circulation of *Udgorn Seion* to 2,000 and printing it weekly during 1853. He also published three hymnals, some poetry, letters from the Welsh emigrants, and a host of doctrinal pamphlets. Perhaps his greatest contribution, however, was the translation of the scriptures into Welsh.

In August 1850 Elder Davis announced in the *Udgorn*: 'We have been counseled to translate the Doctrine and Covenants and we shall give further information about it.' By November, he had a plan to finance the publishing costs: all the book distributors in the branches throughout Wales were to take subscriptions from amongst their members, who would receive the book in sixteen-page instalments to appear every other week.

The first instalment came out on 22 February 1851, and the

succeeding ones appeared almost weekly rather than bi-weekly, until the last one six months later, on the 23rd of August. A similar approach was used for the Book of Mormon. The first segment was off the press by 20 September 1851, and by the 17th of April, just seven months later, 2,000 copies had been printed. As soon as the work was completed a copy was sent to the editor of the *Seren Gomer*, with the request that he give his opinion as to the accuracy of the translation. He returned it with the comment that 'it was a pity such valuable labor in producing so perfect a translation had been bestowed upon so worthless a work as the Book of Mormon'. (Whitney, *History*, 4:352.)

All told, more than eight hundred pages of scripture were translated into Welsh, printed and bound, in only twenty months' time – an amazing feat when one considers that nine months were required just to set the type for the 1830 edition of the Book of Mormon in English. A few months later, in October 1852, the Pearl of Great Price was off the press also, making Elder John Davis's Welsh translation of the standard works complete.

Meanwhile, the constant opposition to the Mormons became particularly intense in the Merthyr area in 1850, when a Baptist minister began to practise the laying on of hands for the gift of the Holy Ghost. Furthermore, he was re-baptizing Baptists, the second baptism being for the remission of sins. As might be expected, these 'heretical' practices came quickly to the attention of his fellow ministers, and they called a council and excommunicated him.

This colourful character was 'Dewi Elfed' Jones, his real name being David Bevan Jones. Beginning in early 1850, he had travelled and preached extensively to raise money for the building of a Baptist chapel in Cwmaman, a small town near Aberdare, both about seven miles from Merthyr Tydfil. It was shortly after the dedication of this building, which was called the Gwawr (Dawn) Chapel, that Dewi Elfed was investigated by his peers, judged guilty of heresy, and excommunicated.

Even after being excommunicated, however, he continued to preach from his pulpit for another six months before he accepted baptism and the laying on of hands from those who he decided truly had the authority to perform such ordinances – the Latter-day Saints. In early March 1851 Dewi Elfed requested a visit from the presiding elder of the Church in Wales, President William Phillips. A few days later, President Phillips wrote excitedly to President Franklin D. Richards of the British Mission:

Last week the minister sent for me and I went to him. He wanted us to take the chapel, as it was his, or rather he had a lease of it. I found therein a clause, stating that the Baptist doctrines were to be preached in it during the course of every year. We went to the landlord and talked with him about the clause; he said he would take his pen and strike that clause out, put Latter-day Saints doctrine in its stead, or renew the lease. (*MS 13*: 110.)

A few weeks later, on the 27th of April, President Phillips returned to Cwmaman and baptized David Bevan Jones, David Rees (another Baptist minister), and three of their flock. Following their baptisms, a meeting was held to proceed with their confirmations, the most curious feature of the meeting being that it was held in the formerly Baptist Gwawr Chapel. President Phillips wrote:

At two o'clock we entered the chapel again. I retook the minister's chair under the pulpit, and after opening the meeting we confirmed the two ministers, and the three others, in the large seat under the pulpit. Afterwards I moved, and it was seconded, and passed unanimously, that brother David Jones and David Rees be ordained priests, so we ordained them in the large pew also. (*MS 13*: 173.)

Gwawr Chapel was used as a Mormon chapel for the next several months, until a large group of Baptists, having established legal ownership, stormed the building, led by the Rev. Thomas Price, the chief of the Baptist ministers in that area. Price's biographer, the Rev. Benjamin Evans, gave a blow-by-blow account of the event:

On the 4th of November, 1851, about two thousand men came together to see the chapel re-possessed by the Baptists; but the wicked man, David Jones, together with some other false apostle, had locked themselves inside the chapel, and since the sheriff did not have the right to break the door, it appeared that the Saints might keep the chapel, although the law was against them. But Price, having fought a successful battle until then, was not about to be defeated by the two devil-saints who were keeping hold of the chapel...

Dewi [Welsh diminutive of David] and the apostle had locked and bolted the chapel door making it as secure as possible. Also they had nailed shut each of the windows, which were quite difficult to reach from the outside. The people were waiting expectantly for the scene, feeling to some extent angry with the usurpers who were in the temple. Then Price came, a wild look in his eye, walking quickly, a look of determination, and his every movement said the

Gwawr Chapel would shortly belong not to the Saints rather to the Baptists. (B. Evans, p. 110.)

Price tried the door, but to no avail; whereupon he shouted 'in an authoritative manner' to one of his deacons, Phillip John, and to David Grier, a carpenter, who happened to have a few tools with him at the time, and told them to open a window so he could 'go in after the devils'. All three men went into the chapel through the window.

The first thing they [the deacon and the carpenter] saw was Price chasing after Dewi and the apostle, around the chapel, up to the pulpit and down again. And after going around two or three times he trapped them in the lobby. Price grabbed them with a giant's grasp. He told Grier and John to open the door, which they did with considerable effort. At that the two rascals were literally kicked out of the chapel one after the other by Price, and they disappeared in the distance in the midst of the hurrahs of the large crowd which were eyewitnesses of the deed. (*Ibid.* pp. 110–11.)

Dewi Elfed, according to Price's biographer, made further attempts to regain legal possession of the Gwawr Chapel for the Mormons, and even threatened to sue Price for assault and battery, but nothing ever came of it.

During the five years of William Phillips's presidency (1849–53) the membership peaked at 5,244, in December 1851. Although there were about 88 convert baptisms per month during this period, the branches in Wales, as in other parts of Britain, were very much affected by the large numbers of saints who continued to emigrate to America.

The issues of *Udgorn Seion* are filled with interesting information about this period of Church history. A topic that the editor, John Davis, deemed to be of continual importance was emigration, a goal of every convert in Wales. And to encourage Church members to emigrate, Davis printed numerous letters from those who had arrived in the Great Salt Lake Valley, all of which gave glowing reports of the blessings that awaited those who could 'gather to Zion'.

There was great celebration amongst the Welsh saints when it was announced in *Udgorn Seion* that three of their brethren who had sailed on the *Buena Vista* in 1849 were now returning as missionaries to Wales. Dan Jones, Thomas Jeremy and Daniel Daniels were called by President Brigham Young in August 1852 to return to their native land. Dan Jones, of course, had already served as president of the Church in Wales, and both Thomas Jeremy and Daniel Daniels would serve in that position later on.

The Welsh saints expected that Dan Jones would replace President Phillips. Elder Jones, however, was called to serve as President Phillips's first counsellor until both Phillips and John Davis emigrated in early 1854, along with 262 other Welsh saints on board the *Golconda*. Just before their departure, Dan Jones was called as president of the Church in Wales and also as editor of *Udgorn Seion*, thus replacing William Phillips and John Davis just as they had replaced him five years earlier.

The Rev. W. R. Davies had died of cholera in 1849 and thus was no longer around to oppose Mormonism. The Rev. Edward Roberts, who had threatened to kill Mormonism back in 1847, had since been excommunicated by the Baptists for drunkenness and hence was far less visible. But other articulate individuals with antagonistic feelings towards the Mormons preached, published and polemicized against them. President Dan Jones and his missionary force proceeded to respond in kind.

In September 1854 the headquarters of the Church in Wales were removed from Merthyr to Swansea. The presses for printing *Udgorn Seion* and other Church publications, mainly pamphlets, were also removed. Reasons for this removal are not clear, but it may have been to place the headquarters in a more advantageous position to assist future emigrants, most of whom had to pass through Swansea on their way to Liverpool.

By the mid-1850s the work of the Church in Wales was beginning to wind down. The last great emigration of Welsh saints was in April 1856 on the *Samuel Curling*, when Captain Dan Jones, newly released from his second mission in Wales, led a group of 560 of his compatriots to the 'promised land'. After the departure of President Jones and this last large emigrant group, numbers of convert baptisms dwindled, but the publication of *Udgorn Seion* continued for another six years. At that time, 9 April 1862, William Ajax, the last editor of the *Udgorn*, wrote in his journal: 'The 14th No. of the "Udgorn" was the last issued, and no more will be issued until I will have become sufficiently strong in body, or a substitute can be found.' (Ajax, p. 61.) Ajax recovered from his illness but decided to emigrate to Utah rather than resume his publishing activities. No one took his place.

The demise of *Udgorn Seion* is somewhat symbolic of the near-demise of the Church in Wales during the nineteenth century. Although there would be missionaries there for the remainder of the century, they would not experience anything like the success and excitement of the 1840s and 1850s.

From the mid-1860s until the middle of the twentieth century, very few Welsh converts would come into the Church. Yet, because of the extraordinary success of the Church's early proselytizing efforts in Wales, there are today tens of thousands of Latter-day Saints who can point with pride to a Jones, Thomas, Davis or Williams line on their pedigree charts and thank the Lord for the courage of their ancestors who accepted the restored gospel somewhere in the hills of Wales.

9

The Ebb and Flow of the Church in Scotland

FREDERICK S. BUCHANAN

THE STORY of Mormonism in Scotland begins in Canada – not a surprising fact when one realizes that for thousands of Scots in the nineteenth century, Canada was a second homeland. Two Scots, Alexander Wright of Banffshire and Samuel Mulliner of Midlothian, had settled in Upper Canada (now known as Ontario) in the mid-1830s, and shortly thereafter were converted to the Church. In 1839 they were called to return to their native land – and the homeland of the Prophet Joseph's ancestor John Mack – as emissaries of the restored gospel.

In New York on 21 October 1839, they met Wilford Woodruff and a Brother Foster 'at sister grames to have some counsel consarning going to Scotland'. After raising funds in New Jersey and Long Island, they were set apart by Elders Wilford Woodruff and Parley P. Pratt to take their message to the land of John Knox and the Covenanters. On the 4th of November they left New York on the *Tarolinta* and arrived in Liverpool on the 3rd of December. After some delay caused by a lack of signed certificates, they were accepted as bona fide representatives of the Church, and Willard Richards permitted them to continue their mission to Scotland. Accordingly, they left Liverpool by ship and arrived in Glasgow on the 20th of December.

Their first contact person was supposed to be an Englishman (a timekeeper on the railway) who had joined the Church in Preston and had been transferred to Bishopton, near Glasgow. They were informed, however, that James Lea had been killed the previous summer. Leaving Mulliner's uncle to make enquiries about Lea, they left Glasgow and travelled to Edinburgh by canal boat, where they were joyously received by Samuel Mulliner's parents. The two pioneer missionaries lost no time in letting their relations and friends 'know our erand to Scotland' and thus began the first of 150 years of Mormon missionary activities in Scotland.

With Mulliner concentrating his attention on his friends and relations in Edinburgh, Wright undertook to spread the word amongst his relatives in Marnoch, Banffshire, walking most of the one hundred miles through the bitter Scottish winter. Smallpox plagued him en route, but he persisted and by the 28th of December he was at his parents' home in Marnoch. By 11 January 1840 he had sufficiently recovered to begin proselytizing, using as his vehicle Parley P. Pratt's *A Voice of Warning*, which he had sent to his father two years before.

His sister Jean had already given her employer, the local Presbyterian minister, a copy of Pratt's booklet. When Alexander visited her at the Manse, the minister expressed an interest in conversing with him about the new religion from America. Two hours of discussion in the minister's study did not convince him of Wright's claims, but he was relatively non-judgemental about the message: whilst the new ideas did not agree with what he already believed, yet 'he could not say it was not so'. However, he did warn Wright about religious schemes that were being introduced that were nothing but a delusion and referred in particular to the 'Irvingites' – a restorationist group popular in the west of Scotland in the 1830s and 1840s. Wright responded that he 'had seen and herd there [the Irvingites'] sistem tried and proved to be fals'. The discussion ended with the minister asking 'for a reed of the Book of mormon which I promised him the first opertunity'.

While Wright was trying to break new ground in the north-east, Samuel Mulliner received word in Edinburgh that James Lea was alive in Bishopton. Arriving there, Mulliner was introduced by Lea to Alexander and Jessie Hay on 9 January 1840, and five days later the Hays were baptized in the wintry waters of the River Clyde, becoming the first of more than 9,000 people who joined the Church in Scotland during the nineteenth century.

By the beginning of February, Mulliner and Wright had again joined forces, and after baptizing two men at Leith, they began concentrating their energies on preaching in the towns and villages in the vicinity of Bishopton, including Kilpatrick, Kilmacolm, Kilbarchan, Johnstone, Bridge of Weir and Houston. Contacts were also made in the larger population centres of Glasgow and Paisley. It was slow work, for by the 15th of February there were only three converts in Renfrewshire, and by the end of March a mere ten. However, by the end of April sixty-one people had joined the Church, and the pace began to pick up as increased numbers led to further contacts.

Success also led to persecution, and Wright and Mulliner were forced out of the village of Kilpatrick under a shower of stones and rubbish. In spite of such opposition, on the eve of Elder Orson Pratt's arrival in Scotland, the 3rd of May, twenty people were baptized, giving the Church a membership of eighty after about four months. Four days after his arrival, Elder Pratt organized the first Scottish branch of the Church at Paisley on 8 May 1840 – one of some one hundred branches to be organized in Scotland during the nineteenth century. (Wright; Scottish Mission History.)

Given Orson Pratt's disposition to things intellectual, it is perhaps not surprising that he eventually made his way to the 'Athens of the North', Edinburgh. Here he laboured hard amongst a citizenry that seemed to be characterized by prejudice and apathy, and 'numerous false teachers and imposters [*sic*] which infested the city'. Such conditions, according to Elder Pratt, made it 'almost impossible to awaken the attention of the people'. In a letter to Brigham Young, he expressed a mixture of hope and disappointment as he recounted his efforts in Edinburgh:

> I still remain in this city although the people here are very careless...There have never been more than 12, 15 or 20 present at any meetings but I have persevered, determined to plant the standard of truth in this city. I have baptized as yet only 30 here.

During this time Elder Pratt took to climbing Arthur's Seat, the rocky eminence above Edinburgh, where he 'often retired and lifted up [his] desires to heaven in behalf of the people of that city'. On his first climb it is reported that he pleaded with the Lord for 200 converts and in time he witnessed the Edinburgh Conference grow to more than 200, but not before he and his co-workers had laboured long and hard in the cause – sometimes addressing seven meetings on a Sunday. After a debate with a Methodist minister on two consecutive evenings there was an increase in the number of inquirers and 'the power of God rested upon them, and they spake with tongues, prophesied, saw visions, and some few sick were healed by the laying on of hands'. (*MS 2*:12; O. Pratt, letter.)

What Elder Pratt lacked in numbers of baptisms, however, he more than compensated for by his own immersion in the intellectual environment of the university city in which the Scottish 'Common Sense' school of philosophy prevailed; an environment which had an impact on his later writings. It was in Edinburgh, too, that Elder Pratt was inspired to write and publish in 1840 his own proselytizing tool entitled *An Interesting Account of Several Remarkable Visions, and of the Late Discovery of Ancient American Records Giving an Account of the Commencement of the Work of the Lord in This Generation*. This 31-page tract, which became a standard Church publication, contained the first published account of the Prophet Joseph's first vision, a relatively matter-of-fact account of the appearance of the Book of Mormon, and a summary of LDS beliefs which influenced Joseph Smith's later statement of the Articles of Faith. Perhaps appealing to the intellectual climate of Edinburgh, Elder Pratt's work has been characterized as an approach which 'expounds salvation in the tones of the mathematician'. Edinburgh, with its long tradition of intellectual inquiry, apparently provided a creative stimulus to the young apostle-philosopher from America. (England, pp. 65–71.)

In March 1841, after ten months of striving with Edinburgh's reluctant populace, Elder Pratt felt satisfied to leave more than 200 disciples in the care of Elder George D. Watt, an Anglo-Scot and the first person baptized in the British Isles. Other branches had been organized, including one in the industrial centre of Scotland, Glasgow, on 8 August 1840. By 1845, in far-off Nauvoo the *Times and Seasons* proclaimed: 'In Scotland the truth flourishes.' Indeed, the labours of Alexander Wright, Samuel Mulliner and Orson Pratt had helped write another chapter in Scotland's long religious history and had added a uniquely Scottish foundation-stone to the building of the latter-day Kingdom of God. (*MS 2*:12; Glasgow Conference minutes, 8 Aug 1840, *TS 6*:975.)

The events of history do not occur in a vacuum, however; in

human history, as in nature itself, as the Scottish-American naturalist John Muir so aptly phrased it, 'When we try to pick out anything by itself, we find it hitched to everything else in the universe.' (Murphy and Collins, p. 2.) Similarly, in order to understand the development of the Church in Scotland we need to put that experience in the perspective of the times by considering the conditions to which the restored gospel in nineteenth-century Scotland was 'hitched'.

Bernard Aspinwall has referred to the Scots as the 'shock troops of modernization' because Scotland was amongst the first of nations to undergo the political, economic and social trauma of the industrial revolution. (Aspinwall, p. 2.) To understand the Mormon experience in Scotland, the nostalgic and romantic idea of a land of tartan-clad clansmen and bagpipes must give way to a less ideal view of a land in turmoil over the changes which were being forced upon it by the new industrial order. Listen to Nathaniel Hawthorne describe the Canongate of Edinburgh – Walter Scott's 'mine own romantic town' – during an 1857 visit to 'auld reekie'. Hawthorne peeped:

> down the horrible vistas of the closes, which were swarming with dirty human life as some mould and half-decayed substance might swarm with insects; vistas down alleys where sin, sorrow, poverty, drunkenness, all manner of somber and sordid earthly circumstances, had imbued the stone, brick and wood of the habitations, for hundreds of years.

Night, he says, hides the reality of these Edinburgh slums – the home of 'layer upon layer of unfortunate humanity' – and the change from day to night symbolized for Hawthorne the difference between 'a poet's imagination of life in the past...and the sad reality'. (Hawthorne, pp. 535–6.) What, then, were some of the 'sad realities' that shaped the Scottish nation and prepared it for the message of the Mormon elders?

The emergence of large urban areas changed Scotland's geography considerably, as the need for more coal mines and factories crowded in on the once-rural shires of Midlothian, Lanark, Renfrew and Ayr. In place of villages where close-knit family life dominated the pace of living, formerly rural communities like Airdrie, Coatbridge and Wishaw became 'frontier towns' – seething conglomerations of squalor and poverty whose police forces were kept busy trying to maintain a semblance of law and order. Swollen to capacity by natural increase, the towns became magnets for other dispossessed persons from the Scottish highlands and from Ireland. Overcrowded conditions and frequent unemployment generated yet another set of problems: diseases such as cholera, high infant-mortality rates, and an alarming degree of drunkenness and crime.

Although the Rev. Thomas Chalmers, one of the leaders of the established Presbyterian church, had said that the greatest challenge to the church was the thousands of unchurched 'heathens' growing up in the slums of the 'frontier towns', the Kirk was unable or unwilling to use its influence to mitigate the evils of the industrial age. (Checkland, p. 6.) Its impotence in the face of the dramatic changes which were occurring in the land may have been caused by its own conservatism and by what *Blackwood's Edinburgh Magazine* referred to as 'the insane divisions of the Scotch church' – the traumatic disruption of the 1840s when a dispute over the role of the government in church affairs led to over 400 ministers leaving the established church. Presbyterianism was thus split into 'a three-cornered affair': the Official Church of Scotland, the Free Church of Scotland, and the United Presbyterian Church – a weak basis on which to meet the new and pressing theological, cultural, industrial and scientific challenges facing Scotland. (*Blackwood's*; Checkland, pp. 122–3; Mackinnon, pp. 151–4, 226.)

A variety of organizations arose in this period as a counter to the social and economic ills of the new age: temperance societies, co-operative unions, and more politically orientated organizations such as the Chartists – all of which attracted the attention of large numbers of working-class people. On the purely religious level in the late 1820s and early 1830s, the attention of Scotland's dispossessed was also attracted to the charismatic preaching of a young minister from Dumfries, the Rev. Edward Irving. His emphasis on the need for a return to primitive Christianity and upon the gifts of the Spirit drew large crowds in the west of Scotland, in Edinburgh and later in London. Indeed, in April 1830 when Joseph Smith was establishing the Church in upper New York, a great religious awakening involving spiritual manifestations also swept through the west of Scotland:

> among quite ordinary folk wonderful things had occurred; there were reports of miraculous healings, of human faith being answered by Divine action, of speech in unknown tongues, of ecstatic utterances in prayer, and of exposition of scripture, all in a power that was preternatural. (Davenport, pp. 17–18.)

This religious awakening has been interpreted as a reaction to the formalism and gloomy tendency of the old Calvinism which seemed to restrict the love of God and Christ's atonement to a few select individuals. One minister, the Rev. MacLeod Campbell of the Rhu Kirk in Helensburgh, began to preach a more humane theology, and of a God who was willing that all should be saved. Unfortunately for Irving and for Campbell, they were expelled from the Presbyterian ministry, but the revival of which they were a part sparked the development in Great Britain of the Catholic Apostolic Church. This group claimed that Christianity had apostatized and had lost the right to preach the gospel as it had been manifest in the Primitive Church. The sure sign of this apostate condition was that Christendom denied the need for the gifts of the Spirit, such as tongues, healings and prophecy. These gifts, some claimed, had now been restored as part of the 'signs of the times' which would culminate in the imminent second advent of Jesus Christ. (Davenport, pp. 29–35.)

Thus, when the Mormon missionaries came to Scotland in 1839, they were entering an arena that was ready for the message that God had spoken through 'very ordinary folk' and had restored the authority, practices and power of the primitive church. Apparently thousands of Scots were indeed ready for such a message, as during its first decade in Scotland the Church grew from eighty members and one organized branch to 3,257 members in more than fifty branches. This steady growth is shown in the graph opposite, and reflects a condition which was common in other parts of Britain.

From 1840 to 1855, some seventy branches were organized in Scotland, twenty-eight of them in the foremost industrialized shires of Lanark, Renfrew and Ayr. Most of the other branches were situated in the vicinity of Stirling, Fife, Clackmannan and Edinburgh: all in the Scottish lowlands, and all heavily involved in coal mining. (*MS 1*: 20; *10*: 253; *13*: 207; *14*: 15; *15*: 79; British Mission statistical records, 1855–76.)

In the highlands, very little was accomplished by way of conversions, although Peter McIntyre traversed Argyllshire and some

Scottish membership compared to British membership

of the Western Isles preaching to large groups in Gaelic (*c*. 1845). According to McIntyre, many listened and even agreed with the message, but refused to be baptized. When William MacKay offered in 1847 to preach Mormonism in Gaelic to the highland Scots, William Gibson expressed the hope that success would attend MacKay's efforts 'till the heather hills of old Scotland reverberate with the songs of Zion'. In 1850 some Gaelic tracts were even printed in Inverness under the title 'Do Suchd-siridh Kioghachd Dhe' (Seekers after the Kingdom of God). (McIntyre; *MS* 9: 362.)

Whilst a few 'hardy sons [and daughters] of the mountains' accepted the Mormon message, it was not the heather hills of the highlands but rather the chimney-stacks and crowded, dank alleys of industrial Scotland that echoed with the songs of Zion, and by 1855 there were four LDS conferences in Scotland: Glasgow, Edinburgh, Dundee and Kilmarnock. The relative size of these Church units can be seen in the table overleaf.

Naturally Glasgow, having a total population of 345,000 in 1851 (larger than the combined populations of Edinburgh, Dundee, Aberdeen, Paisley and Kilmarnock), led the other conferences

Comparison of Scottish Conferences

	Glasgow		Edinburgh		Dundee		Kilmarnock	
Year	Br.	Memb.	Br.	Memb.	Br.	Memb.	Br.	Memb.
1855	20	1,442	14	666	8	242	7	271
1856	18	916	12	536	8	210	7	222
1857	16	741	12	420	6	133	6	52
1858	21	783	10	446	6	123	*—	—
1859	19	731	10	386	4	107	—	—

BR = Branches; Memb. = Members.
*Amalgamated with Glasgow in 1857.

during this period – and throughout the nineteenth century – in numbers of branches and in membership, sometimes accounting for twice as many saints as all other areas combined. (Mackinnon, pp. 151–4.)

With such rapid and sustained growth, the *Millennial Star* could justly proclaim in 1848:

> Scotland is doing wonders; upwards of 400 baptized during the last quarter ...We hope to see thousands of her noble sons come forward as valiant men in this great and triumphant work of this last dispensation. (*MS 10*: 299.)

In the mining village of Hunterfield, near Edinburgh, a branch was established which by 1848 consisted of seventy members out of a total village population of ninety. In nearby Tranent the Mormon branch 'flourished to an extraordinary degree' in the 1850s and 1860s, meriting mention in a history of Tranent published in 1883. This brief reference to the Latter-day Saints in a local Scottish history also succinctly summed up what happened in many branches towards the end of the 1860s: 'the body is entirely defunct, all having renounced the doctrines of the Prophet, or flown to the land of promise'. (Hunterfield Branch History; P. M'Neil, pp. 79–80.)

After 1851 there began an irreversible decline in the total LDS membership and the number of local congregations. Between 1855 and 1859, for instance, there was an approximately fifty per cent decline in membership in the Glasgow, Edinburgh and Dundee Conferences. In the same period, Kilmarnock went from a mem-

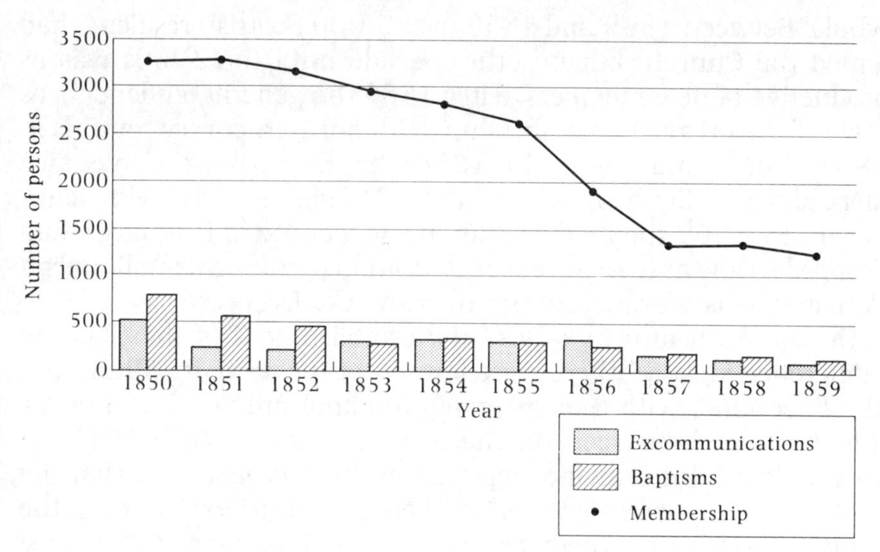

Scottish membership compared to baptisms and excommunications

bership of 271 to 52, an eighty per cent decline. Of course, the 'call of Zion' was a major factor in this decline as Scottish Mormons responded to the spirit of gathering. Between 1852 and 1856 more than 1,000 saints emigrated to America, and by the end of the century almost 5,000 Scots had 'gathered to Zion'. (Buchanan, 'Scots'.)

Another source of decline was the practice of 'cutting off' members who were not meeting the requirements of membership in the kingdom of God. In the period just cited, there were 1,441 excommunications. There were, of course, 1,308 baptisms, but the inflow of new converts hardly kept pace with the outflow of excommunicated members, as is shown in the graph above.)

These figures reflect the reality that in the late 1850s there was a church-wide 'reformation' in effect and the expectation was that only tried-and-true members should be affiliated with the Church. However, the disciplining of members and continuing emigration account for only part of the decline in membership; the most crucial factor contributing to the long-term decline of the Church was simply that apparently fewer Scots were being attracted to the message of the restoration. Baptisms declined from as high as 559 in the Edinburgh Conference (1848) to a low of 35 in *all* of Scotland (1873), a trend that seems typical of the United Kingdom as a whole. Between 1849 and 1859 over 3,000 Scottish residents had joined the Church, but no other decade until the 1960s was as productive of new members. After 1855 the general tendency was towards shrinkage in membership, with only temporary revivals in 1862, 1864 and 1868. In 1858 the Kilmarnock Conference merged with Glasgow, and in 1868 Dundee merged with Edinburgh. By 1869 the membership in the vicinity of Edinburgh had dropped so low as to require reorganization of the former Edinburgh Conference as a branch of the Glasgow Conference.

On the 35th anniversary of the establishment of the Glasgow Conference in 1875 there were but ten branches of the Church in all of Scotland, with a membership totalling only 482, a number that had not been seen on the Scottish records since 1841. In 1883, Elder John Crawford reported in the *Millennial Star* that the Scottish saints were 'few and far between, scattered all over the country, and most of them very poor. There is only one Conference in Scotland where there used to be four.' And to continue the dismal story further, by 1890 there were little more than 200 saints in what once had been one of the most fruitful fields of the British vineyard. These were indeed 'gie dreich' years for the Church in Scotland. (*MS*; British Mission statistical records; JH, John Crawford to Joseph Hall, 15 Dec 1882.)

But statistics are only part of the picture. The experience of the Scottish saints cannot be adequately understood and appreciated unless we get some sense of what it was like to become a Mormon in the middle of the nineteenth century. Who were these people who allied themselves with the strange doctrines from America? Why did they join such an unpopular group? What experiences did they have that confirmed them in their position? How were they viewed by the majority and why did so many fall away from the faith? By examining the journals, autobiographies and letters that these Scottish saints left, we can enliven the statistics and see these people as human beings rather than as entries in the cosmic ledger of births, baptisms, marriages, excommunications and deaths.

In terms of socio-economic class, the Scots who responded to the gospel message were neither the upper class nor the dregs of society that many of their critics claimed. The bulk of the LDS branches were situated in the industrialized shires of Lanark, Renfrew, Midlothian and Ayr: Scottish saints were solidly working class. Of

588 LDS Scottish males who are listed in the Liverpool emigration records, 40·6 per cent were identified as from the mining industry; 11·5 per cent were associated with the textile industry; labourers made up 7·8 per cent; and metal workers, including blacksmiths, accounted for 7·1 per cent, with the leather industry represented by 5·4 per cent. Three major industries thus accounted for three-quarters of the sample group, with the remaining 25 per cent consisting of carpenters, stonemasons, gardeners, farmers, bakers and ropemakers. Obviously the people who helped build the kingdom of God in nineteenth-century Scotland, and in Utah, were also the ones who had helped make Scotland the workshop of the world. (Emigration records, 1855–70.)

Most of the accounts of early converts give the impression that those who converted were from homes in which religious values were dominant. Alexander Baird recalled that his grandfather, who had died before the Church was established, had told his children that the 'true gospel' was not yet on the earth, but that some day it would be restored as in the days of Jesus. Baird himself was puzzled over the issue of how a good God would want to send 'bad boys' to hell, and he and his sister often prayed in the fields that this would not be their fate. After hearing a missionary's discourse about the LDS concept of God he 'knew' immediately that the doctrine was true and, at fourteen years of age, was baptized. (Baird.)

James Ure considered all the contending factions of Christianity corrupt and held aloof from them. But when he first heard Alexander Wright and Samuel Mulliner preach, he was astonished to find 'two plain, simple and seemingly illiterate men declaring and testifying to the truth of the plain, untarnished but potent principles of the Gospel...I unhesitatingly received their testimony, embraced the Gospel, went and was baptized.' (Ure, p. 1.)

John Duncan, a one-eyed, one-legged miner in Fife, was attracted by the practice of immersion which had always seemed to be the correct way to be baptized. (Duncan.) Alexander Gillespie was attracted to the Church in 1847 because he wanted to know more about an organization which could produce 'such excellent young men'. He applied the 'by-their-fruits-shall-ye-know-them' test in coming to a decision. (Rawlings.)

Robert Gillespie, who admitted that he had not been very reli-

Samuel Mulliner (1809–91) and Alexander Wright (1804–76), the first two LDS missionaries to Scotland, 1840.

Latter Day Saints.

The *Edinburgh Branch* of this Society now meet, for Public Worship, in

MR. M'PHERSON'S LARGE HALL,

No. 2, N. West Corner of Drummond Street,

Every Sabbath at 11 A. M., 2 P. M., and 6 Evening.

The Public are respectfully invited to attend.

N. B. As Dr. Lee thought proper, at the Meeting of the Edinburgh Presbytery, to assert that we taught principles so absurd, that even a Hottentot would not believe them,—we now give him an opportunity of proving, in Public Discussion, whether the Doctrines held by the Church of Scotland or those held by the Latter Day Saints are most consistent with Reason and the Word of God, as contained in the Scriptures of the Old and New Testaments. If he will not do this, then every candid mind will know what to think of such a man.

Mr. Samuel W. Richards, from America, is expected to preach on Sabbath the 6th curt.

Edinburgh's Latter-day Saints advertised their meetings in 1847 with this broadside and used the occasion to challenge the moderator of the Edinburgh Presbytery, Dr Robert Lee, to a public debate. (*Courtesy of Frederick S. Buchanan.*)

gious before his conversion, was convinced by the 'consistent and reasonable' arguments given in debates between LDS missionaries and their antagonists – the missionaries usually 'came out best' although they were unlearned. (Gillespie, p. 32.) When William McMaster first decided to attend a Mormon meeting he did so because he wanted to see whether all the things being said about Mulliner and Wright in Paisley were true. He heard Mulliner preach and was immediately converted. In that same meeting, he bore testimony and was baptized three weeks later, the thirty-second person to join the Church in Scotland. (McMaster.)

Joann Walker heard the message from her fellow factory worker, Elizabeth Stuart. At her first meeting she witnessed the gift of tongues, the interpretations of which indicated to her that she would join the Church and be gathered to Zion. She did both. (Richardson.) William McFarland and his friend Thomas Crooks had visited all the meeting-places in the town of Dysart, Fife, in 1842, seeking the true religion. When George D. Watt brought the message of the restored gospel to the village their response was: 'If angels appeared anciently, why not now?' MacFarland told Watt that if he could give him the knowledge that angels had indeed appeared to Joseph Smith he could 'dip him in any mudhole he pleased'. Watt did just that and both McFarland and Crooks were baptized. (MacFarland, p. 5.)

Most of the foregoing converts were young men in their late teens or early twenties, and their conversion accounts focus on the one idea or notion that seemed to attract them to the Church. Some joined because of the influence of family members or close friends, and some may have been baptized because of guilt feelings over sin or unworthiness. The great cholera plague of the late 1840s in the west of Scotland 'scared a great many into the church' – either because they believed they were in imminent danger of dying in a sinful state or out of a belief that being a Mormon would save them from the cholera. In fact, Eli Kelsey reported that there were significantly fewer deaths from cholera among the Latter-day Saints than amongst the population at large; he held out the promise that 'none will die of cholera who are Faithful & attend to the ordinances of the church'. (Richardson, p. 7; Glasgow Conference History, 1848–9; *MS 11*: 62; R. Watson.)

Fifty-two-year-old Peter McIntyre, a veteran of the 42nd Highland Regiment who had seen service in the Napoleonic Wars, gives more detailed insight into the conversion process. Shortly after his wife's death in 1838 he became an attendant to a Mr McKarle, a wealthy eccentric in Helensburgh, who had recently learned of the 'new religious sect called Mormons' and had sent for some literature. He told Peter McIntyre that he didn't believe the Book of Mormon was true because it mentioned compasses before compasses were invented, but he gave Peter the book and asked for his opinion. Peter recorded that 'I read earnestly till the time I was to give a judgment, when I told him the book was from God'. McKarle invited missionaries to his home and questioned them about speaking in tongues, but did not accept their message. However, his servant did, and told the elders that he believed they had been sent by God. He did not commit himself immediately, but consulted with an acquaintance, a Mr Dickie, who had been praying for apostles and prophets for six years. However, to Dickie the Mormons were impostors rather than answers to his prayers, and he considered McIntyre a 'poor deluded man' for listening to them. In August 1841 Peter decided to contact the Latter-day Saints 'as I can possess no peace till I join them'.

Finally, in Greenock, he attended a Mormon meeting and 'although the preachers were weak' he recognized the 'strength of the Spirit and power of the Gospel of peace'. At the home of a member that night he witnessed the gift of tongues, along with interpretations. During this meeting he prayed silently that God would give him counsel through those present. Immediately an Elder McBride delivered to him a verbal revelation commanding him to join the Church, warning him that if he did not, the Spirit would withdraw. According to McIntyre he had been 'led to the knowledge of the principles of the Gospel by revelation to prepare [him] for the Church'. In the months that followed his conversion he was so open in his proclamation of his new faith that he became known as the 'Angel of Helensburgh'. (McIntyre.)

In these accounts we can see that conversion to the restored Church was a process characterized by a great deal of diversity, ranging all the way from what appeared to be the plain logic of the Mormon position, which characterized Robert Gillespie's experience, to the ecstasy and almost mystical experience of Peter McIntyre. It is quite obvious that although the saints preached 'one Lord, one faith, one baptism', there was also a decidedly individualistic refrain in the testimonies which have been recorded: everyone seems to have come at his or her testimony from a slightly different perspective.

For some, however, the process of acquiring a testimony took place over a long period of time and involved a great deal of hesitation and self-doubt. William Carruth, for instance, believed 'without the least hesitation' after he heard the first sermon preached at his farmhouse in 1844, and after the meeting, 'I went aside by myself and gave vent to my feelings in tears'. In spite of this feeling, however, for almost eighteen months he vacillated between the urgings of his brother-in-law to join the Church and the urgings of his neighbours, who considered Mormonism the greatest blasphemy every heard, to reject it. According to Carruth, the devil whispered in his ear 'these Mormons are a poor, low, degraded set, hardly worth being noticed'. His brother-in-law's tears and pleadings persisted and William felt the chastening hand of God over him until he decided to be baptized. (Carruth.)

Some converts were actually active in the Church for many years without having received a testimony that it was true. This was the case with Robert McKinlay, who joined the Church with his parents in 1847, when he was fifteen. By 1854 he had married and was an active deacon in the Church. Late one Sunday evening, during a two-mile walk with the president of the Lochgelly Branch to their home in Cowdenbeath, the topic of why McKinlay never bore his testimony came up. Robert admitted that while he could say he believed the Church to be the work of God, he could not say that he 'knew' it was true as so many others seemed to be able to say, 'whether they know it or not'.

President Robert Cushnie counselled him to make it a matter of prayer, and both retired to the woods between Lochgelly and Cowdenbeath at almost midnight to pray that Robert would receive the sought-after testimony. For the next few months he continued to do as Cushnie counselled him, 'wrestling with the Lord in prayer night and morning'. Finally the answer came as he lay in bed one evening 'meditating upon nothing in particular'. He saw

> a very clear circle of light. Its brightness attracted my attention. It was bending its way toward the earth, and, as it drew near, its light filled the room where my wife and I slept, and a Being whose light it was stood by our bedside and said, 'Follow me.' Immediately I arose and followed him, enjoying the halo of light that surrounded him and walking in the same.

He reported that the 'Being' then took him to a spot halfway between Cowdenbeath and Lochgelly and showed him the land covered with what appeared to be a thick fog and directed his attention to the village of Lochgelly, where the saints met each Sunday. The streets were lined with people trying to get into their churches unsuccessfully, because they were surrounded by a thick wall of impenetrable darkness. The 'Being' then told Robert to look into the centre of the town, and there he saw the members of the Lochgelly Branch, bathed in the same bright light, walking down the middle of the street right into the Latter-day Saint meeting-place. This experience was enough to convince young Robert McKinlay, and thereafter he was able to testify that he 'knew' the restored Church was true, concluding that 'this writing is true as God is my witness'. (McKinlay.)

Although such dramatic affirmation seems unusual, it demonstrates that not all saints who were active and committed to the Church in the nineteenth century were absolutely convinced of its truth until some years after baptism. For some, a testimony was as much a process of *becoming* a convinced Latter-day Saint as it was a final destination.

It would be an unbalanced interpretation of the existing documents if we were to conclude that all saints maintained an unswerving testimony from the moment of conversion until their demise. From a perusal of the *Millennial Star* and early Church records, we know that some of the early converts did not stay in the Church and that in the 1840s there were several former Latter-day Saints, such as Andrew Robertson and Andrew Hepburn, touring Scotland claiming to expose the supposed fallacies of the Mormon beliefs. These dissidents were energetically rebutted at every stop by local and American missionaries. And of course, they were excommunicated for apostasy. (R. Campbell, journal, 30 Jun 1842; Gibson, p. 8.)

However, some of the excommunications were, according to

the *Millennial Star*, related to 'excess of zeal, a desire of showing authority [and] personal pique' on the part of branch officers, which led to a too-strenous striving for unquestioned obedience. Some local leaders even used their authority to the point of requiring members to support the conference officers financially on pain of being cut-off. (*MS 23*: 170; Stuart.)

There can be no doubt, however, that conversion was not a matter to be taken lightly. The minutes of the Edinburgh Conference in 1851 express great concern over the large number of people being excommunicated, the mission leaders regarding it as evidence that new converts were joining the Church *before* they had a clear conception of what it meant to follow the 'laws of God'. In those early years 'keeping company with the world', 'treating the servants of God with contempt', 'drunkenness', 'neglect of duty', and 'apostasy and sacrilegious conduct' were viewed as sufficient reasons for questioning the standing of Church members. One member was called before the Dundee Council because he had opened his shop on the Sabbath, while another brother was accused of 'not comming [*sic*] to his duty, he had objections in regard to plurality of wives'. In 1852 a 'Priest Adamson' was charged with 'rebellion' when he argued with the presiding officer in the Falkirk Council meeting. He was 'cut off', but a fellow backslider, John Frew, was forgiven when he came before the council and confessed his failure to attend meetings. He didn't like being deprived of his *Millennial Star*, and addressing the council, he said: 'I ask your forgiveness and desire an interest in your faith and prayers for I am determined to go on and be saved.' (Falkirk Branch; Edinburgh Conference History. See also Sprowl; Glasgow Conference minutes; and *MS 11*:92.)

If disciplining came quickly, so too did forgiveness; great efforts were made to retrieve those who had deviated from the faith, and most of the members of the Girvan and Dalry Branches were rebaptized shortly after they had been dis-fellowshipped in 1849. Alexander Gillespie recorded that much of his time as president of the Cowdenbeath Branch was spent working with saints who had, in his opinion, been cut off prematurely. For many he succeeded in 'keeping the flickering light that was in them aglow'. One gets a keen sense of the personal concern that Alexander Gillespie felt not only for the eternal welfare of these people, but also for their values as human beings who deserved to be treated with respect. (Rawlings.)

The purpose of membership in the Church in the nineteenth century was, of course, not primarily to give people a sense of belonging or provide a support system or even to help them get ahead through emigration, though these may have figured in some conversions. Essentially, the purpose was to save oneself before the Judgement Day and to prepare for the imminent Second Coming. This sense of urgency about the Second Coming is seen in the blessings given to infants, Margaret McDonald and David Hutcheson, in the Dalry Branch in 1850, just a year after the members of the branch had been reinstated in the Church. These children were blessed and promised that they would 'see Jesus come in his glory and reign with him on earth'. Henry Hamilton expressed the common hope that the 'day will soon be here when the children of men will have no power over the servents of the leaving God, when he will overthrough the wicked and the saints will [reign] with the Lord God a [thousand] years on the earth and may it soon be accomplished'. (Dalry Branch, Apr 1850; Hamilton, 16 Sep 1852.)

It must be remembered, however, that these pioneer Scottish saints, whilst they endeavoured to be not *of* the world, were in fact very much *in* the world. They carried on their daily work, family affairs and leisure activities as well as trying to build the kingdom of God. In their journals we find evidence of some who took part in the leadership of coalminers' unions, even to the extent of being labelled as troublemakers by the management. Alexander Baird, one of the first 'international' Latter-day Saints, signed up as a cabin-boy on a Clydeside sailing ship and spent the next decade sailing the seven seas. He was a member of the U.S. naval contingent which accompanied Commodore Perry to Japan in 1854. Wherever he went he took with him his commitment to the Church, and was continually meeting fellow saints in Asia, Africa or America. In spite of his rough, seagoing ways, Alexander Baird kept the faith and was active in the Church in Paisley before emigrating to Utah in the 1860s. (Gillespie, pp. 37–8; Richardson, p. 14; Baird.)

The Gillespie brothers, Robert and Alexander, were champion

quoit players in 1852, and travelled throughout England and Scotland in competition matches. In Dundee, the members of that branch organized a thirteen-member flute band under the direction of James McNaughton, and in Tranent the Mormon miners had a brass band of some renown.

Weddings and soirées featuring locally produced music and poetry and 'many joaks made' by leaders such as Rob Campbell and Jock Lyon contributed to the amusement of a people who, whilst they were serious about their religious life, knew how to enjoy themselves. In 1849 six hundred Glasgow saints spent eight hours together in a New Year's Day party which had been made free so that all could attend. No doubt this type of event was designed to help the Scottish saints through the difficult days of a Scottish Hogmanay celebration, at which excessive drinking was the norm. And long before the Mutual Improvement Association became a Church institution, the Dundee saints organized the 'Mormon Mutual Improvement Society' so that they could improve themselves socially as well as spiritually. Scottish Mormons never lost sight of the fact that eternal salvation was inextricably tied up with life on earth and that spirituality did not mean a dour manner. (Gillespie, p. 34; Hamilton, 2 Nov 1852 and p. 33; Richardson, p. 13; P. McNeil, pp. 79–80; Eli Kelsey, 1 Jan 1849.)

Indeed, the Scots seem to exhibit a sense of humour in their approach to their religious commitment, no better expressed than in the many original Mormon songs which were set to old Scottish folk tunes. Particularly creative in this respect was Matthew Rowan, a relatively well-educated Scot who joined the Church in the 1840s and served as a missionary in Scotland and England. He took Burns's rollicking 'Duncan Gray' and transformed it into a light-hearted celebration of the message of the restoration, capturing the enthusiasm of the converts, then combined it with a familiar Scottish cultural artefact – a folk melody:

Bab'lon is declining fast,
  Woe! Woe! to Babylon:
Her cup's nigh full, her die is cast,
  Woe! Woe! to Babylon.
Lo! Mormonism grows so strong,
  While Bab'lon's bigots cry ''Tis wrong';
And Mormons chant this truthful song,
  Woe! Woe! to Babylon.

Saints are hast'nin' to the West,
Woe! Woe! to Babylon.
While here, their lives were sore opprest,
Woe! Woe! to Babylon.
Let priests rage on, and bigots rail,
And publish many a spurious tale;
Yet TRUTH, triumphant, will prevail;
Woe! Woe! to Babylon.

When emigration was reinstated in 1850, Rowan wrote some verses which helped connect the converts with the ultimate aim of gathering to Zion and helped them relate to the far-off centre of the Church in the Great Salt Lake Valley. It was sung to the popular tune 'The Campbells Are Coming'.

O, heard ye what news from the valley has come?
O, heard ye what news from the valley has come?
All we who are faithful are soon to go home;
O 'tis glorious news, from the valley that's come.

Long, long we have cried for the help of the Lord,
A day of deliverance, the true Saint's reward,
But his word, through the prophet, has opened the way,
So, gladly and promptly his voice we'll obey.

. . .

God bless Brigham Young and his Counsellors, too,
And long live the Twelve, who are faithful and true,
And all worthy saints, both at home and abroad,
Salvation to them, and all honour to God.

Such songs were often used in the social and religious gatherings of the Scottish saints and no doubt played a role in integrating their new religion into their own cultural traditions. (Buchanan, 'Immigrants and the Muse'.) The Scottish motif also came into play as the saints said farewell to their departing mission leaders. Parties held in their honour often included the presentation of paisley shawls, plaids, Scottish bonnets complete with thistle badges, and tartan material for wives in America. The saints in Glasgow, for instance, dressed Eli Kelsey in a plaid and bonnet, proclaimed him 'a braw Scotch lad' and contributed £85 toward his return to his family in Winter Quarters. In later years Samuel Richards remembered the Scottish saints' kindness to him during his mission by claiming, when asked his nationality, that he was actually 'Scotch' because his life had been saved during an attack of smallpox by the ministrations of the Scottish saints. Even Brigham Young received from Henry Baxter and Robert Campbell, by courier, a plaid and an 'elegantly bound' copy of the songs of Robert Burns (although there is no evidence that President Young ever quoted the Bard). (Glasgow Conference History, 27 Dec 1847, 24 Jun 1849; Richardson, p. 10; R. Cannon, p. 10; R. Campbell, letter.)

If the Scottish Latter-day Saints could take a joyful view of the truthfulness of their commitments and feel at ease mingling the truths of the gospel with their Scottish culture, the official Presbyterian response to the saints' concern with the 'dispensation of the fullness of times' was to dismiss it as not being a genuine religious experience. For the established church, ignorance, credulity, poverty and despair were at the roots of Mormon success. In 1847 the LDS Church figured in a debate in the Edinburgh Presbytery on the question of church support of state aid to schools in Scotland. In the course of the debate, the moderator, the Rev. Dr Robert Lee, referred to the 'fearful ignorance that prevailed' in the 'manufacturing parishes' that he had under his care. Too many in the Church of Scotland, he said, overlooked ignorance in Scotland by saying it was not as serious as in England. Lee went on to note that much had been made in Scotland of the ignorance in the county of Kent, where a man named Thoms had claimed to be the Messiah and had collected a following. However, Scotland had its ignorant masses too:

> When Mormonism was first preached in the west of Scotland, there appeared there a man who preached absurdities so gross that one wondered that any man, even a Hottentot, could receive them and believe them. And what was the result, even in the midst of all their parish schools and educational institutions! It was a fact that hundreds of persons were baptized in the faith of Joe Smith, and that scores of Scotchmen were at present expiating the follies of which they were then guilty at Nauvoo. With facts like these, would any man pretend that nothing was wanted in the education of Scotland! (*The Scotsman*, 1 May 1847.)

Such negative appraisal of the motives for joining the Church is common in the literature originating amongst Scottish non-members and, of course, it may be discounted because it is highly anti-Mormon in tone. However, it can also be seen as a typically intellectual and secular response of a Church of Scotland which in many ways had lost touch with its New Testament roots. The established church had become very respectable, rational and institutional in its interpretation of Christianity. After all, if the Kirk could brand some of its own sons as heretics for encouraging the 'millennialist' and 'restorationist' movement in the west of Scotland in April 1830, is it any wonder that they considered the saints' claims to spiritual power as counterfeit and founded in credulity and ignorance? Similarly, the emphasis on the 'gifts of the Spirit' amongst the saints was enough to brand them as fanatics in the eyes of the official Kirk. Church members were, of course, well aware of the fact that they were outside the pale of 'orthodox' Christianity. Indeed, their espousal of a radically different theology and church practice was one factor in their initial success in Scotland as well as in other areas of the United Kingdom. (Thorp, 'Religious Backgrounds'.)

The difference in emphasis between the Latter-day Saints and the older churches also contributed to some of the persecution and disorder that accompanied LDS proselytizing efforts. Missionaries were stoned in Kilpatrick and mobbed in Busby, and Joseph Smith's effigy was burned at the toll booth in Clackmannan in 1842. (Jenson, *Church Chronology 1*: 349; Gibson, p. 109.) At Crosshill in Ayrshire in 1849 a mob of 300 men, women and children surrounded the house in which a meeting was being held and disturbed the assembled saints by howling and throwing stones. After the meeting adjourned, about a hundred members of the mob followed the Mormons to Maybole, throwing stones and abusing them. (Eli Kelsey, 9 May 1849.) In 1844 Robert Campbell reported that a number of investigators in Ayrshire were prevented from joining the Church because of being 'bound down by their tyrannical employers', who threatened to dismiss persons who joined the Church. So threatening did the disruptions become in Edinburgh that it was found necessary to publish in the *Quarterly Report of the Edinburgh Conference* the official British law which prohibited the disruption of religious assemblies. When a mob broke up a Mormon meeting in Paisley, its leaders were arrested for disturbing the peace. The magistrate promised that he would mete out heavy punishment if they attempted to disturb another Mormon meeting, asserting that Scottish law would protect the preacher in the barn as well as the one in the pulpit. (R. Campbell, journal, 3 Jul 1844; *Quarterly Report of the Edinburgh Conference*, 1851; Gibson, p. 8.)

However, the law did get involved against the saints when Elder Thomas Stewart's reliance on the healing gifts of the Spirit led to his being charged with culpable homicide in the deaths of two young LDS women, Elizabeth and Mary Murray. The *Glasgow Herald*, reporting the case under the headline 'Extraordinary Case: Cholera Treatment by the Latter-day Saints', said it did not know whether to characterize the affair as one of 'inhumanity, barbarism, or fanaticism'. The report criticized the elders for failing to call medical aid for the two women and belittled the efforts of the elders to cure cholera through prayer and anointing. According to the newspaper report, a group of Church members consisting of a belt-maker (Thomas Stewart), a preacher, two weavers, a clerk, a sawyer and a collier, 'with sisters to match...ranted around the bed of the poor girls all night till they died, instead of sending for a doctor'. Although a charge of culpable homicide was made against Stewart, the *Millennial Star* reported that when he was brought before the magistrates, 'he bore himself nobly, faced his accusers boldly, preached the Gospel to them in his defence, until they were ashamed of themselves, and were glad to dismiss the matter'. (*Glasgow Herald*, Feb 1849; *MS 11*:61.)

This incident, in which members of the Church are portrayed as relying more on the power of prayer than on the power of physicians or the existence of a professional clergy, points up one of the major distinctions between the established churches of the day and the saints: amongst the saints there was no need for a professional clergy or professional healers. Priesthood power was viewed as being sufficient for both functions.

In listing the trades of the participants in this case, the press demonstrated an elitist bias – as if to say, how can such common people assume to act as intermediaries in place of physicians? But that was a basic assumption of early saints in Scotland and elsewhere: they could. The purely religious press of the day was no less critical of these upstarts from America. That such a system founded on superstition could manage to find adherents 'even in

Glasgow' was something of a puzzle to rational Presbyterians who also saw a 'striking analogy betwixt Mormonism and Popery, between Joe Smith and Pius the Ninth'. Both churches were perceived as 'of human or rather of Satanic origin'; both added to the scriptures, practised despotism, controlled their people through physical force and made great profession of religion. Ultimately, said the editor of *The Bulwark*: 'Mormons and Papists will probably unite; but at all events they are only two branches of Satan's great army against the truth and liberty of the gospel of Christ'. Interestingly enough, this anti-Mormon piece was written in response to one which appeared in the Jesuit *Dublin Review*, which had claimed that the emergence of Mormonism was an example of what was wrong with Protestantism! (*The Free Church Magazine 8*: 364–8; *The Bulwark 2*: 166.)

With such published criticism, it was probable that many were turned away from the message of the restoration – how many we do not know. What we do know, however, is that in spite of a 'poor press', being characterized as superstitious, ignorant, credulous and under the complete control of their leaders, the Latter-day Saints attracted thousands of Scots who listened, believed the message, covenanted to be saints and kept the faith that was 'once delivered to the saints' and was now delivered in its purity to them. As one reads the journals that these people left, one cannot escape the conclusion that what they had accepted became an important part of their personal value system, gave them a deep sense of their place in the world, and contributed to their perception of themselves as a people with a mission – to build the kingdom of God in the last days. Although John Knox might have been dismayed by their particular beliefs, he might also have appreciated the zeal and energy that they put into their Zionistic vision.

In the early years, the LDS Church in Scotland grew in part because of the unfavourable economic climate of the times, the political protest movements and unsettled religious conditions. In addition, the Latter-day Saint emphasis on the establishment of a Zion here and now, in which religious values and material concerns are interwoven, struck a respondent note in the hearts and minds of the working-class people who joined the Church. What, then, explains the shrinkage in membership?

Although one must be careful in explaining conversions (or their lack) by reference to economic and social conditions, the decline in the attractiveness of the restored Church may, to some degree, be attributed to the relative betterment in social and economic conditions in the latter part of the nineteenth century. Although 'economic pressure and sheer frustration' were still potent factors in promoting emigration, the improvement in political and social conditions and in Scottish prosperity meant that the United States was pulling fewer Scots to its shores. The decrease in Mormon conversions may have shared in this overall decline for similar reasons. (Brander, p. 73; Mitchison, pp. 380–98.)

Whatever role social and economic conditions played in reducing the numbers of Scots who joined the Church, there are other factors which may have contributed to the decline – factors that have their origin in peculiarly LDS issues. One was the controversy over plural marriage. This seems to have been the stimulus for an anti-Mormon editorial in the *United Presbyterian Magazine* in 1852. Admitting that it was with some reluctance that it made any reference at all to Mormonism, the magazine felt justified in devoting space to the subject only because such publication 'might perhaps do good in warning some thoughtless persons meditating emigration to the great theocratic settlement in America'. The October 1853 issue of the same magazine observed that Mormonism was growing rapidly in the United States and that it was 'not a little humbling to observe that while this increase is occasioned by importations from Europe, the largest number go from Britain'. (*United Presbyterian Magazine*, March 1852, October 1853.) Although no records exist telling us how many Scots were 'saved' from the Mormons by the 'exposés' in the anti-Mormon press, it is nevertheless likely that the anti-polygamy movement played a role in reducing the numbers of converts.

Another factor that may have reduced the flow of Mormon converts not only to Utah, but also into the Church in Scotland, was the change in Utah's economy, which by this time was not able to absorb many emigrants. The promise of opportunity and a better life no longer existed. Under these circumstances, reports that came from Utah in letters to Scotland may have dampened some of the enthusiasm for the Church and emigration. That is the impression received from the examination of a collection of Scottish LDS emigrant letters sent from the United States between 1857 and 1890. These documents give a picture of life in Utah quite at odds with the successful heroic struggle to conquer the desert portrayed in some pioneer epics.

Of the three brothers in the MacNeil–Thomson family who left Scotland between 1857 and 1872, the eldest, John Thomson, never arrived in Utah but joined the Reorganized LDS Church in Illinois, and then lost his life in a coalmine accident. The next brother, John MacNeil, joined the Church a few days before leaving Scotland, experienced numerous economic difficulties, and shortly after marrying in the Endowment House, announced to his family that he no longer considered himself a member of the Church. His life ended in the cave-in of a silver mine in Park City, Utah, in 1903. The youngest of the trio, James MacNeil, was converted and baptized after he came to Utah. James persisted in the faith and was contemplating a mission to Scotland when he was drowned in the swollen Gila River in Arizona in 1884. All of these letters paint a picture of life in Utah in very realistic terms and it is clear that there is, in the experience of these Scottish Mormon emigrants, more of Burns's sentiment 'That man was made to mourn' than the Latter-day Saint belief that 'Man is that he might have joy'. (Buchanan, *Good Time Comin'*.)

These reports, like the anti-Mormon press, may also have had a negative impact on the Church's proselytizing efforts. Especially if combined with such 'exposés' as the one by the former Scottish Mission leader, T. B. H. Stenhouse, whose *Rocky Mountain Saints* was selling at a discount in the Glasgow bookshops in the 1870s. Commented Elder A. F. MacDonald: 'the Preachers' Trade Union wish to give premiums for misrepresenting' the saints. (*MS 40*: 220.) Of some eleven members of the MacNeil–Thomson family who were involved in the Church in Scotland in 1850, not one of the first generation had any connection with the Church fifty years later. In fact, when Ann MacNeil wrote to her niece in Utah in 1910, she seemed unaware that the family had ever had an LDS background, although she and her family had all been blessed in the Church when they were children, and some had been baptized.

The existence of such an informal communications network as the MacNeil family correspondence may therefore have contributed to the decline in numbers of baptisms and total membership in the latter half of the nineteenth century, as word spread that Zion was not necessarily what the elders may have painted it to be; it was made up of real human beings, with real problems, not a perfect 'Zion society'.

If the 1840s and 1850s were viewed as hopeful years and gave Scotland the appearance of a field ready to harvest, the 1870s and 1880s presented a dismal picture of hopelessness and the appearance of a pasture well trodden over. Some even went so far as to imply that all the 'believing blood' had been gathered out of Scotland in the early years and that the downturn in conversion was a sign of the nearness of the 'end of the age'. (*MS 20*: 715.) More pragmatically, there were meetings of missionaries with mission leaders designed to find out what the problem was and why so few were being converted. (*MS 34*: 475; *35*: 379.) Of course, converts continued to be made, but it was more a matter of 'one of a family and two of a city' than the large numbers in single communities that joined during the early years. Still, a small-but-faithful remnant persisted, and if the reports in the *Millennial Star* reflect fewer and fewer baptisms, they also exhibit an air of hopefulness that better times lay ahead and that there was still some believing blood amongst the natives of Caledonia. (*MS 26*: 318; *33*: 233; *41*: 672.) However, the reality is that the 'better times' did not appear until the 1960s, when once again the number of Latter-day Saints in Scotland climbed beyond the benchmark of 3,300 set in 1851.

It should be remembered, however, that large numbers are not a necessary part of missionary success. Indeed, the notion that where two or three are gathered in Jesus' name, there he will be, is evident in the lives of individual saints even during the discouraging, 'gie dreich' years of the late nineteenth and early twentieth centuries. And out of the experience of these saints there have arisen accounts of conversions just as dramatic and moving as those in the early years. For instance, when George Gordon Campbell, a respected elder in the Church of Scotland in the village of Galston, returned from a walk on Galston Moor about New Year 1879, he little realized that the strangers speaking at the village cross would have any impact on him or his family. He stopped to listen to what they said, and later recounted that at that moment a distinct voice spoke to him, saying: 'This is the gospel of Jesus Christ; accept it and you will be saved; reject it and you will be damned.' He turned to see who spoke to him, but saw no one. He moved closer to the strangers and listened to their message. Within a few weeks he was baptized and set in motion events which changed him for ever, as well as a large segment of his family – including where they would live, the kind of lives they would lead, and the work they would do. The power of conversion, commitment and gathering to Zion was still at work, even if it was not as widespread. And the experiences of George Campbell were being held in remembrance among the scattered Ayrshire saints many years after he left Scotland. (Erskine; J. Campbell, pp. 4–5.)

It was also during these bleak years of the Scottish Mission that a young missionary from Utah returned to the land of his fathers to try and stir up the embers of the dormant gospel fire. Elder David O. McKay, upon whom the challenge of missionary work in Scotland lay heavily, became discouraged while working in Stirling. After all, there were only about 338 members of the Church in Scotland, scattered amongst nine branches. Perhaps only about 150 members could be considered active, and in the year 1897 there had only been 55 baptisms – including children of members. He had good reason to be discouraged. During a long ramble along the streets of Stirling in the shadow of the ancient castle, Elder McKay received what he perceived to be an answer to his prayers – there above the lintel of a new home being constructed were the words: 'What-e'er thou art, act well thy part'. It galvanized the homesick David into realizing that, even if circumstances were not the best and people were suspicious of his motives, he still had an obligation to do his duty. Eventually, at a priesthood meeting in Glasgow, Elder McKay, then president of the Scottish Conference, received confirmation of his commitment to the Church and a portent for the future. During the meeting a number of elders reported that angelic visitors were in attendance, and President James L. McMurrin is reported to have turned to young David and said: 'Let me say to you, Brother David, Satan hath desired you that he may sift you as wheat, but God is mindful of you. If you will keep the faith, you will yet sit in the leading councils of the Church.' (Scottish Conference History, 29 May 1899; Middlemiss, pp. 11–15, 174–5; J. Campbell, pp. 7–10.)

Elder David O. McKay (1873–1970) served as a missionary to Scotland, 1897–9. (*Courtesy of David O. McKay family.*)

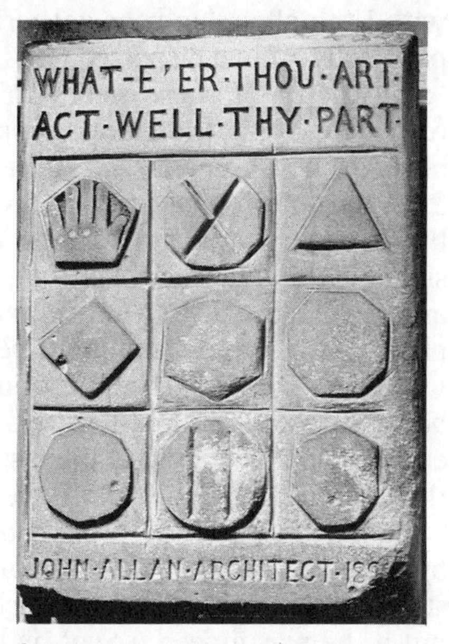

The inscription Elder McKay saw in Stirling, which inspired him by its message. (*Courtesy of the LDS Museum of Church History and Arts.*)

The years following David O. McKay's tenure as president of the Scottish Conference are rather uneventful as far as the Church as an institution is concerned. Of course, a few converts continued to be made and some did their best to raise their families within the Latter-day Saint heritage, in spite of a decidedly hostile environment. Officially, members were encouraged to build up the Church in Scotland, but there was still the persistent emigration of those who might have given it the leadership it needed. This, combined with a low conversion rate (it was only 1·5 baptisms per missionary in the United Kingdom around 1900), kept the Church in a continual crisis of leadership at the local level. This lack of leadership, as well as petty personality conflicts and a degree of insularity, all combined around the turn of the century to make the Church in Scotland a mere shadow of its former self. (Scottish Conference minutes, *passim*; Alexander, p. 222.)

The decades following 1890 have been characterized as transition years for the Church, as it moved away from a major concern with Utah affairs and the gathering of the saints to take on a wider perspective and a dispersed and international body of believers. The 'dreichness' of these years in Scotland are in some degree a response to this transitional period, as the Church sought to stabilize itself in a new order of reality. (Alexander, see especially pp. 212–38.) In time, of course, David O. McKay, whose forebears had been 'dippit i' the burn' near Thurso in Caithness, became president of the Church and initiated an era of international expansion and development. In a sense, we might say that the international phase of Church development began on the day that David McKay was given a sense of what lay in his future. And it is fitting that it began in 'dear auld Glesga toon', the workshop of the British empire. As a people who have spread themselves and their culture throughout the globe, and have played a role in world affairs that is significant out of all proportion to their numbers, the Scots are, by second nature, internationalists. Nor are Scottish saints strangers to the concept of a world-wide church. As Robert Gillespie put it, he was indeed a Scot by birth, but 'my religion teaches me the idea that the earth is my home and to do good [is] my religion. A nation is too small for [the] home or aspirations of the human heart.' (Gillespie, p. 24.)

Today, in the Museum of Church History in Salt Lake City, stands the very piece of Scottish sandstone from Stirling on which David O. McKay saw inscribed the words which made a difference to him in 1898: 'What-e'er thou art, act well thy part'. This epigram still presents a challenge to individual Latter-day Saints wherever they live. It also stands as a visible reminder of the role that the Kingdom of Scotland has played in the affairs of the Kingdom of God since the earliest days. The Scots have acted well the part that history has assigned to them.

10

The Irish Experience

BRENT A. BARLOW

EVEN BEFORE the first LDS missionaries arrived in Ireland in 1840, events had occurred that would have great impact upon the future of the Church. On 15 August 1745, for instance, William Lee had been born in Carrickfergus. Twenty-five years later he sailed for America, landing in Philadelphia in 1770. Within a year he married Susannah Chaffings and moved with his bride to North Carolina where, over the next few years, four sons were born to them. Tragically for the young family, Susannah died in April 1775, shortly after the birth of their fourth son, Samuel. Though none of them could have known it at the time, Samuel Lee would eventually become the great-great-great-grandfather of Harold B. Lee, eleventh president and prophet of The Church of Jesus Christ of Latter-day Saints. (Goates, p. 8.) It is worthy of note that every country in the British Isles has produced a prophet/leader of the Church, and Ireland is no exception.

In 1839, two years after Elder Heber C. Kimball and his companions had first brought the restored gospel to the British Isles, President Joseph Smith directed members of the Quorum of the Twelve Apostles to go to Britain again. Elder John Taylor, one of the apostles, arrived in Liverpool on 11 January 1840. By April he had organized a branch of the Church there, having thirty members.

Some of Elder Taylor's converts in Liverpool were actually Irish by birth, which was not unusual considering that one in every seven people in that city was an Irish emigrant. One of these Irish converts was James McGuffie who, after his own baptism, probably urged Elder Taylor to take the gospel to his native land and undoubtedly volunteered to go with him. In the weeks that followed, the apostle gave serious thought to the possibility of proselytizing in Ireland. (Barlow, p. 17.)

Other LDS missionaries also were thinking about Ireland. Elder Reuben Hedlock, who had accompanied the apostles to England, boarded a ship bound for Belfast on 22 May 1840. Arriving the following morning, he became the first known LDS missionary to go to Ireland. He stayed three days, during which time he recorded his impressions:

> [Belfast] is a fine flourishing town, containing about 54,000 inhabitants. Here I met (as I passed through the streets) the rich enjoying their abundance and the poor in rags begging for a morsel of food to sustain life. I had never before witnessed such scenes of suffering, and I say in my heart, has the Gospel of Jesus Christ lost its power among those who profess it, so that one part of the human family must drag out a miserable existence, and die in wretchedness and want while the other can live in pride and plenty all their days? (*MS* 2:92.)

After his three-day visit to Belfast, Elder Hedlock sailed for Paisley. The Irish had met a Mormon.

At a conference held in Manchester on 7 July 1840, William Black was officially called as a missionary to Ireland. (Joseph Smith, *HC* 4:150.) A native Irishman, William had been born at Lisburn on 20 August 1784, the son of William and Mary Gardiner Black. In 1838 he had moved with his wife Jane to Manchester, where they soon afterwards met Elder William Clayton at a place called 'Harris Cellar'. Elder Clayton baptized both William and Jane Black on 14 January 1839. (Black, pp. 10–11.)

In the meantime, Elder John Taylor had also decided to go, and on 27 July 1840 took passage for Ireland with William Black. Accompanying the two missionaries were the aforementioned James McGuffie. Before their departure, Elder Taylor had met a farmer named Thomas Tait, who he had prophesied would be the first person to be baptized in Ireland – which he was.

Thus Elder John Taylor, with James McGuffie and William Black, arrived in Ireland on 28 July 1840. Their steamer docked at Warren's Point, a relatively new town of 2,000 people, at the head of Carlingford Lough. From there they walked the seven miles to Newry, possibly the birthplace of McGuffie and certainly a place where he had friends and connections. Brother McGuffie arranged

William Black (1784–1873) accompanied Elder John Taylor when the first baptism in Ireland was performed on 31 July 1840 at Loughbrickland.

Harold B. Lee, eleventh president of the Church, whose 4th great-grandfather, William Lee, was born in Carrickfergus in 1745.

for them to use the town hall that evening and also engaged the bellman to advertise a meeting at 7 p.m. More than six hundred of Newry's inhabitants gathered to hear Elder Taylor preach the restored gospel for the first time in Ireland, on the evening of 28 July 1840.

The next night another meeting was held, but only a few people turned out, which prompted Elder Taylor to conduct an informal discussion. The next morning Elder Taylor left James McGuffie to proselytize in Newry and, taking William Black and Thomas Tait, hired a 'jaunting car' (a two-wheeled open carriage pulled by a horse) and set out for Lisburn, the home of Brother Black. Along the way, however, they decided to stop at a place called Fourtowns, where a farmer named Mr Wyllie allowed them to conduct a meeting that evening in his barn. The meeting was held, but with limited success in either attendance or interest.

Early the next morning, 31 July 1840, the threesome began

walking towards Lisburn. During their journey Elder Taylor began to talk with Thomas Tait about the gospel. As they approached Loughbrickland, they came to the crest of a hill and found themselves looking down on the village and a nearby lake. Seeing the water, Thomas Tait exclaimed: 'There is the water; what doth hinder me being baptized?' Thus, upon coming to the lake, he and Elder Taylor went into the water, and John Taylor's prophecy about Thomas Tait was fulfilled. (Roberts, *Taylor*, pp. 84–7.)

Having performed the first LDS baptism in Ireland, the missionaries continued on their way to Lisburn, passing through Hillsborough where a few months later the first Irish branch of the Church would be organized. Upon reaching Lisburn, Elder Taylor created considerable interest by preaching several times in the market-place. Many of those attending undoubtedly recognized their former townsman, William Black.

After ten days in Ireland, John Taylor sailed for Scotland on 6 August 1840. Before leaving he learned that James McGuffie had performed some baptisms in Newry, but later indications are that McGuffie and Black soon followed Elder Taylor back to England.

Two months after the gospel had been introduced in Ireland, Elder Theodore Curtis was assigned there as a missionary. Arriving in September 1840, he chose to begin his labours in the town of Hillsborough. Elder Reuben Hedlock, who had first visited Ireland in May, made a second trip in October and spent some time with Elder Curtis in Hillsborough. While there, he attended a six-hour debate between Elder Curtis and a gentleman who had 'sixteen things to prove about or against the Mormons'. In addition, Elder Hedlock himself preached twice to small congregations in Belfast before leaving for Glasgow on the 20th of October. By the time Elder Curtis was transferred back to England in May 1841, he reported thirty-five members of the Church in Hillsborough.

Early in December 1840 a Mr and Mrs Bell left Ireland and travelled to Paisley being 'led by the spirit' to investigate the Church there. The Bells stayed with the missionaries in Scotland for a day and a half before being baptized, then returned to their home in Ireland, saying that if any LDS missionary wanted to labour in the Hollywood or Bangor area, he could have lodgings with them. Elder David Wilkie was later sent to Ireland to replace

Elder Theodore Curtis and apparently accepted this offer from the Bells. He began proselytizing and soon organized the Crawfordsburn Branch in that vicinity. By 21 July 1841 he reported twenty-two members in the Crawfordsburn Branch who, when counted with the saints in Hillsborough, brought the total to fifty-one members of the Church in Ireland.

Elder James Carigan then arrived to assist Elder Wilkie, and by July 1842 the membership had risen to seventy-one. At that time Elders Wilkie and Carigan left Ireland, and many of the Crawfordsburn and Hillsborough saints emigrated first to England and then to America. During the next few years the membership steadily declined. (Barlow, pp. 22–3.)

Elder James Sloan, an Irishman by birth and a personal friend of the Prophet Joseph Smith, arrived in Ireland with his wife in September 1843 to try to revive proselytizing there. But they met little success, reporting in January 1844 that there were 'few Saints from Ireland'. A few months later, in April 1844, Elder Sloan was assigned to labour in England. He reported, upon his departure, that they had been able to organize a small branch at Melusk, but that there were only fifty-two members of the Church in all of Ireland. (*MS* 4:195.)

Little proselytizing was done in Ireland during the height of the famine (1845–7). Paul Harrison, an Irishman who had been converted in England, laboured with his countrymen from April to December 1845, but still the membership declined. During the famine, Ireland became part of the Glasgow Conference in Scotland, and Elder Peter McCue reported on 31 May 1846 that there were only forty-five saints then. Most of those members soon emigrated, leaving only a handful of Church members in Ireland. (British Mission history, 31 May 1846.) Between 1840 and 1850, fewer than 200 converts joined the Church in Ireland, mostly because of the political, religious and economic turmoil of the time. Still, Irish people *did* join the Church in relatively large numbers during that decade, but the conversions occurred in England, Scotland, Wales and other countries where thousands of Irish people had emigrated.

One factor that made the Irish potato famine so severe was the density of the population. Shortly before the turn of the nineteenth century Ireland's population began to increase at a rate previously unknown in the history of Europe. Between 1779 and 1841 there was a 172 per cent increase, resulting in a total of 8·2 million people. Of those, nearly 5·5 million, or two-thirds, depended on agriculture for a livelihood. Half the population were living in windowless, one-room mud cabins and trying to make a living on their allotted land of less than five acres per family. (Edwards and Williams, p. 89.)

In 1845–7 conditions grew even worse as the famine swept through Ireland. During these years the average life expectancy in rural Ireland was nineteen years. Not one person in five lived beyond forty, and fewer than one in twenty reached the age of sixty. As one might expect under such conditions, hunger, illness, pillage, murder and anarchy were rampant. (Adams, p. 377.)

The LDS people were aware that in the last days there would be 'famines, and pestilences...in divers places'. (Matthew 24:7.) Some twenty years earlier, the angel Moroni had told Joseph Smith 'of great judgments which were coming upon the earth, with great desolations by famine, sword, and pestilence; and that these grievous judgments would come on the earth in this generation' (Joseph Smith—History 1:45); and other latter-day scriptures state that in the last days, God would warn the nations of the earth 'by the mouth of my servants...and by the voice of famines'. (D&C 43:25.) In the light of these prophecies the missionaries were naturally anticipating such judgements; and they were seldom hesitant about making their beliefs known.

During January 1839 a tremendous wind in Ireland and other portions of Britain unroofed many houses and turned hundreds out of their homes. Ports were damaged and many lives were lost on both land and sea. President Joseph Smith noted, 'Such a wind had not been witnessed by anyone living and some began to think that the judgments were about to follow the Elders' preaching.' (*HC* 3:245–6).

A similar statement appeared in the *Millennial Star* in 1840 under the heading 'Signs of the Times'. The article mentioned some of the recent earthquakes and rumours of war, then described in detail the economic distress of the people of Ireland. Editor Parley P. Pratt added, 'When we see prophecy fulfilling, were are bound to acknowledge that those who uttered it were directed by the spirit of truth'. (*TS* 2:231.)

That same year Elder Heber C. Kimball wrote to President Joseph Smith about the economic turmoil, the unemployment and the thousands starving in Ireland:

> This scene of things is passing before our eyes daily, and we look upon it with sorrow and regret; *at the same time it is that which is spoken of by the mouths of prophets*, and we feel to pray without ceasing that God may roll on his work and restore that which is lost and establish peace...that the knowledge of God may cover the earth as the waters cover the sea. (*TS 6*:862–3 [my italics].)

Elder Kimball also quoted a newspaper article telling in great detail about the critical situation in Ireland, then added:

> These things are coming upon the inhabitants, yet they are blind and cannot see it; they appear to exult over the saints, and when a few fine days come (which are indeed scarce) they cry out to the saints, 'where is [*sic*] your famines, pestilences and judgments you have predicted'; then we tell them to wait a little while and they shall see them, and they shall know that we have told the truth. (*Ibid.*)

To Elder Kimball, the famine was inevitable.

When the famine reached its peak in 1845, Elder Parley P. Pratt claimed that the awaited judgements had begun in Ireland. His editorial in the *Millennial Star* declared the following:

> And why did the potato crop...in Ireland perish and rot in a night?...Because the angel hath flown in the midst of heaven, having the everlasting gospel to preach to them that dwell on earth; and to every nation, kindred, tongue and people saying with a loud voice, fear God, and give glory to Him, for the hour of his judgment is come. (*MS 8*:100; see Revelation 14:6–7.)

In 1847 Orson Pratt also made a significant statement regarding the gospel in Ireland:

> If Ireland [will] receive this gospel, judgment shall be turned away from their land, and the earth shall bring forth in its strength, and plenty shall crown their labors, and the Lord shall bring favour unto them. But if they reject the fullness of the gospel, and the great message now offered to them, the hand of the Lord shall be against them until they are wasted away in sorrow and wretchedness. (*MS 10*:299.)

In the ten years from 1840 to 1850 Ireland's population decreased by half – from eight to four million people. Upwards of one million died of starvation and three million emigrated to other countries, particularly England, Scotland and Wales.

During the 1840s one-tenth of Manchester's and one-seventh of

Liverpool's population were Irish emigrants. (Barlow, p. 17.) By actual count, the Liverpool Branch records of the LDS Church for 1840–55 show that there were nearly 2,000 converts in Liverpool during this period, and of those who reported their places of birth, 9 per cent, or about 180 converts, were born in Ireland. (*Liverpool Branch Records.*) As to the large number who recorded no birth-place, one British historian concludes that many of Liverpool's converts were transients, which fairly accurately describes the Irish refugees in that city. (P. Taylor, p. 149.)

During the famine years large numbers of Irish people also emigrated to Glasgow, where it was reported that the streets were 'literally swarming' with Irish men and women fleeing the ravages of the potato famine in their homeland. The Glasgow Branch records for 1840–51 indicate 1,240 converts during that time. Of those who indicated their birth place, 228, or 18 per cent, were born in Ireland. (*Glasgow Branch Records.*) Another study found that during the years of 1845–7 about one of every three converts in Glasgow was actually Irish. (Platt, pp. 6–7.) On 4 January 1862 George Q. Cannon of the British Mission presidency wrote:

> I understand there are more Saints in Glasgow and Western Scotland who are Irish and of Irish extraction than there are of Scotch: and this proves that they [the Irish] are susceptible to the truth when circumstances are favourable for their receiving it. (*MS 24*:134.)

Many of the Irish fleeing the famine also sailed for Swansea, Cardiff and Newport in Wales. The poor-law inspector for the Welsh coast reported that 'great numbers of Irish landed...but the number could not be ascertained or even guessed'. (C. W. Smith, pp. 279–80.) Considering this statement, it is interesting that Elder Dan Jones reported from Wales, on 17 October 1846 that more than one thousand converts had joined the Church there during the past eighteen months. (Jenson, *Church Chronology*, p. 31.) Many of these 'Welsh' converts were probably Irish. Perhaps similar numbers of Irish people found the gospel in other countries as they were scattered from the homeland and gathered to the restored gospel.

Still, though the famine may have led to greater numbers of Irish converts in other lands, it seriously hampered the Church's progress in Ireland. As the first missionaries had arrived there just five years before the famine began, proselytizing had scarcely started when the famine temporarily interrupted the work. In 1850 Franklin D. Richards, mission president in Britain, was aware of the lack of progress in Ireland and commented on it in the *Millennial Star*.

At several different times efforts have been made in the vicinity of Belfast, and a few have been added to the Church, a part of whom were turned out of employment because of their faith, and were obliged to flee to England for subsistence. (*MS 12*:254.)

President Richards then announced that missionaries had returned to Ireland for a new effort, and added, 'It is earnestly hoped the present may prove the dawning of a better day to the seed of promise in the Emerald Isle.' (*Ibid.*)

On 20 June 1850, when Elders Gilbert Clements and John Lindsay arrived in Belfast to revive the flagging missionary work, they found the branch somewhat disorganized, and reported to President Richards that they had no public place for workship. Elder Clements then explained that they had rectified the problem, having obtained a commodious chapel on King Street formerly occupied by the Baptists.

Within a month the two missionaries had toured their area, and Elder Clements remarked:

I have visited a small branch of the church at Hyde Park, a village six miles from Belfast. There are seven members, including two priests, all in good standing, and rejoicing in the work of God...There is another branch at Kilachey, ten miles from Belfast, consisting of six members, including one priest, all in good standing. Belfast branch numbers about thirty-three members, including four elders, three priests, and one teacher. We can scarcely find out one-third of the Belfast branch, it has become so scattered and disorganized. (*MS 12*:253–4.)

At the conclusion of the report, however, Elder Clements indicated that he had succeeded in bringing the saints together, and after much preaching and teaching the members were beginning to feel and enjoy 'the sweet influence of the Spirit of God'.

But Belfast was not the only area opened to missionary work at this time. Contemporary with the departure of Elders Clements and Lindsay for Belfast, Elders Sutherland and Bowering had set out for Dublin. Elder Edward Sutherland was a native of Dublin who had emigrated to London, joined the Church, and then been assigned to preach the gospel in the Dublin region. Arriving in the city in mid-June 1850, he was surprised to find how little the Dubliners knew about the Church. To remedy the situation he posted up notices announcing a public lecture on 'the Restored Gospel of Jesus Christ', and word soon got round that the 'Mormons' had arrived in Dublin.

The first lecture was attended by several hundred irate Irish. According to Sutherland:

> Many thought I should have been killed, the disturbance was so great at the close of the meeting. But, however, the God of heaven, in whose work I was engaged, protected my life. (*Ibid*, p. 312.)

By 1 September 1850, Elder Sutherland had managed to organize a branch of six converts in Dublin, mostly his relations.

This first reception the two elders encountered in Dublin was typical of what followed during the next two years. Surprisingly, much of the opposition came not from the many Catholics in that vicinity, but from the Protestant minority at Trinity College. Of this group, Sutherland related, 'the difficulties with which I have had to contend have been considerable...[I have been] tossed about with bigotry and prejudice on every hand.' He then commented:

> For several weeks past they attended our week-night meetings for no other object but to prevent us worshipping in peace. Last night a large number of the students came, and before the meeting had been long commenced, you would have thought that the powers of hell had been let loose. To continue the meeting was impossible, and the fury, to all appearances, could only be appeased by tearing me to pieces. But, however, the Lord preserved me, and the brethren that were with me, till at length, through the aid of the police, the hall was cleared. Similar proceedings have characterized our week-night meetings for several weeks past, and we try to console ourselves by expecting we are only in the commencement of our persecution, for I believe we shall have to meet it on every hand. (*MS 14*:269–70.)

Difficulties in Dublin were not limited to opponents from Trinity College, however. The missionaries had obtained a small office building at 4 Aungier Street and established a bookshop, selling their pamphlets and other Church publications. They reported these efforts to their mission president during March 1853, but five months later a second letter regarding the bookshop followed:

> A sad misfortune happened to our [book] depot. A fire broke out in the paper-hanger's next door and burned the establishment to the ground. The crowd, as

they are always officious on such an occasion, rushed in...and threw out books, tracts, stationery, etc., etc., into the street. Many were unfit for use. The loss was considerable. (*MS 15*: 573.)

After proselytizing for three years in southern Ireland, the missionaries had established five small branches with a combined membership of fifty-six. There was the 'Travelling Branch' at Athlone, King's County, consisting of a number of soldiers belonging to the 62nd Regiment stationed in southern Ireland. In Gurteen, near Tullamore, King's County, Elder Sutherland had converted his parents, and at Rathkeale, in the vicinity of Limerick, another soldier, Elder Allen of the 14th Regiment, helped convert a few people. Elder Sutherland had also spent some time in Carrickmacross, near Dundalk, and gained five converts in that area. But most of the Church members in southern Ireland were in Dublin.

In 1853 most of the LDS missionaries in Ireland left for America, but the work continued under the direction of a local member, Patrick Lynch. A year later, on 25 June 1854, he attended a conference in England and gave the following remarks:

I cannot give a very flattering account of the Church in Ireland. When I went to the Dublin Conference, it was said to number fifty-seven members. Now there are but twenty-seven. Some have emigrated, some have gone to the Eastern [Crimean] War, and others have removed to other places. I have applied for leave to preach in the open air, but have been refused the privilege. The Conference is in debt, and the religious ministers use all their influence against us. (*MS 16*:467.)

At the same conference, Brother Lynch reported that in all of Ireland there were but six branches and eighty-seven members, sixteen members having emigrated since the beginning of the year.

Unknown to the discouraged Brother Lynch, five elders from Salt Lake City were already on their way to Ireland. On 6 April 1854, at General Conference in Utah, Elders John D. T. McAllister, James Bond, Matthias Cowley and John Croston had been called to serve missions in Ireland, with Elder James B. Ferguson, a native Irishman, being appointed as presiding elder. Arriving in late July 1854, Elder Ferguson and the four other missionaries baptized ten new converts in the first two months, and on the 23rd of September Elder Ferguson reported: 'Prospects are still more encouraging for the future.' (*Ibid.* p. 601.) He noted three weeks later that the Church was increasing in faith and numbers, in that seventeen had joined since the first part of August. Adding that they had obtained a new meeting-hall, Elder Ferguson asked for more labourers in Ireland.

With the native Irishman Ferguson leading the missionaries, Church membership increased in Ireland during 1855–6, and total membership grew to over two hundred members. During the seventeen months that Elder Ferguson presided, nearly one hundred converts were added, though the new Church members in Ireland accounted for less than three per cent of all members in Great Britain. (JH, letter from Erastus Snow to W. C. Flagg, 21 Mar 1855.) Indicative of Ferguson's enthusiastic leadership was the Belfast Branch excursion to Cavehill overlooking the city of Belfast. Of that occasion, Elder McAllister recorded in his journal:

> On Monday, the day following our Conference, we went up to a mountain called Cave Hill...and when we reached the summit, brother Ferguson led off three times three cheers for the advancement of 'Mormonism' in Ireland. The brethren and sisters joined, and we made it echo again and again. (McAllister, pp. 334–5.)

During this time, new hope seemed to abound throughout the whole British Mission for the establishment of the Church in Ireland, as indicated by the following *Millennial Star* editorial:

> We receive cheering accounts of the progress of the Gospel from various places. The Lord is greatly blessing the labours of the Elders in Ireland. Repeated efforts have been made to give the work strength and permanency in that land, but with very limited success. We feel that a brighter day is now dawning upon Erin. (*MS 17*: 314.)

With this upsurge of optimism in Ireland, the missionaries in the north began investigating other areas besides Belfast for proselytizing. In mid-1855 Elders Ferguson and Bond were labouring in Belfast, whilst Elder McAllister toured among the scattered saints. A sixth missionary, Elder Reid, arrived and was assigned to labour in Londonderry, and Elder Croston proselytized in Fermanagh and Monaghan. When Elder Samuel Kerr arrived, he began his work in Down and Armagh.

When the missionaries visited Dublin occasionally, they found organized opposition from the London Tract Society, a group publishing much anti-Mormon literature. Elder James Bond reported that the saints there had responded to this by organizing an 'LDS Tract Society', but that

opportunities for spreading out very fast are very limited here at the present, yet we feel assured that the Lord will direct us in gathering out the honest in heart, and bring many noble sons and daughters of Erin from the thraldom of priestcraft and bigotry to the light of the Gospel. (*MS 17*: 349.)

As a recommitment to the gospel, all the saints in Dublin and Belfast were re-baptized during the summer of 1855. A new branch was organized in Lisburn, and the Church health laws found in the Word of Wisdom were re-emphasized, as was the gathering to Zion. Indeed, interest in emigration to Utah grew amongst the Irish saints, and their leaders reported:

the priesthood and members feel alive in 'Mormonism' and from the oldest to the youngest, all feel Zionward, and are, at the present time, rejoicing in the anticipation of pulling or pushing a handcart to their home in the west. (*MS 18*: 47.)

On 8 December 1855 Elder James B. Ferguson was released from his mission to Ireland, and upon his departure was presented with a silver sword from the Belfast Branch members, an act of love that moved Elder Ferguson to tears. Nevertheless, the Belfast saints were quite naturally grateful: it was largely due to the efforts of Elder Ferguson and his colleagues that missionary work in Ireland had passed through a difficult period into one of its most productive seasons.

Having thus attained considerable success in Ireland during 1855, the missionaries were anxious to maintain this momentum – and they managed to do so, as in the following year nearly a hundred new converts were gained. Church membership grew to 210, a record in Ireland. Reports were that 'prospects look brighter for Ireland than they have done in years past', and Elder Ferguson's successor, Elder John Scott, gave an interesting account of Church activities at the conference he attended in Birmingham on 21 July 1856:

When brothers James Ferguson and J. D. T. McAllister, and those who worked with them left Ireland, they left things in a flourishing condition, and I am thankful to be able to say that things are moving nicely along. There has been added to the Church in the north of Ireland about 30 persons, since our last report. The spirit and feelings of the Saints are good, those of the clergy about as we expect them – pretty severe against us. (*Ibid.* pp. 561–2.)

Elder Scott further reported to President Orson Pratt of the British Mission that the law of tithing had been introduced in Ireland and that many of the saints, though they had very little to give, would pay their tithing and only wished that they could pay more.

In addition, the LDS Tract Society was prospering in its publication of the written word, and in the latter part of the year mission authorities decided that the work should be extended beyond Belfast on a more permanent basis. Thus on 16 December 1856, Elder E. T. Benson visited Ireland and decided that if Elder Scott could cut back his expenses in Belfast, the money saved could be used to send more missionaries into the smaller towns and villages.

Such plans were halted, however, by a crisis that had developed in the Salt Lake Valley during the summer of 1857. Due to misunderstandings between the Church, now headquartered in the Utah Territory, and USA officials sent to govern them, an army of 2,500 United States soldiers had been dispatched to Utah to settle the 'Mormon Question'. This began what came to be known as the 'Utah War'. As the Church made preparations to confront the approaching army, the call came from Church headquarters for all the available brethren scattered throughout the world to return home. Missionaries serving in the United States and Canada had already begun the trek towards the Great Salt Lake Valley by the time Elder Samuel W. Richards was dispatched to England carrying instructions to President Orson Pratt and Elder Ezra T. Benson (both members of The Quorum of the Twelve Apostles) that all the American elders were to return home. (Roberts, *CHC* 4:240–1.)

Thus the work in Ireland halted abruptly. Missionary work again declined, ending the recent surge. And, due to the intensified efforts of the missionaries outside the greater Belfast area, the saints in the Belfast Conference had become scattered throughout the province of Ulster. Ireland would be without missionaries from Utah for four years. None would return until 1861.

Thomas Ward, a local member representing the Church in Ireland, gave a rather dismal report of his stewardship at conference at Birmingham in 1859.

> I will do my best to give you a true representation of the Irish Mission. It has its own peculiarities. The Saints there are very much scattered, and can't very well be visited, in consequence of some part of the families being out of the Church. This is the case in a great many instances. They can't attend meetings. There is

no real organization of the Church in that mission, with the exception of one or two places. There are two Conferences. In the Dublin Conference there are only 13 members altogether... The Saints in the Belfast Conference are more scattered than in Dublin. Many of them are unable to be visited, except now and then, when some who are opposed to us are out of the way. (*MS 21*:82.)

Since there were no missionaries in Ireland from 1857 to 1861, there were very few converts in either the Belfast or the Dublin Conferences. During August 1860 two elders from England visited Ireland and commented that they sympathized with the saints in Ireland because of the many unfavourable circumstances there. One year later, the Belfast Branch president claimed that from January 1859 to April 1861, 'only 30 had been baptized'. The Church membership in Ireland declined to seventy-seven, and except for occasional visits from missionaries in England the Irish saints had very little contact with the Church.

Then, on 30 July 1861, Elder Jacob G. Bigler was transferred from England to Ireland to assist the local leadership and to do as much missionary work as possible. As the only missionary, he visited the branches in Londonderry and Dublin and reported only a few faithful members in those localities. After appraising the progress of the gospel in Ireland, he reported during October as follows:

The work of the Lord does not appear to flourish so much in this country as in many others, yet we are increasing in numbers slowly. It is a difficult matter to get people to hear us; they all seem to be on guard day and night, each one guarding his party or creed. There is a powerful religious party-spirit here between the different religious denominations, and many battles have been fought and much blood shed; and the spirits of those who have been slain in these religious struggles are prompting and binding their parties. (*MS 23*:679.)

Elder Bigler reported similar conditions four months later in conference: 'The saints are few in number, the whole mission containing but about 100, who are scattered over the country from Cork to Londonderry.' He also noted strong desires among the Irish saints to emigrate, but their economic status prevented them at that time. After he left, Church membership in Ireland fell to a scant fifty-five.

As proselytizing efforts once again began to wane in Ireland, there arose some scepticism among the missionaries about Ireland and the Irish receiving the gospel. President George Q. Cannon of the British Mission presidency gave an insight on the Church amongst the Irish on 4 January 1862:

I will say a few words about the fields that different Elders have to labour in. I was very pleased to hear the report of brother Bigler, and to see the spirit that animated him concerning his field of labour...What is the reason, then, that they have not received the Gospel in Ireland, as they have in Wales and Scotland? The reason is obvious. Because they have not been surrounded by as favourable circumstances. I look at the people here and see that England and Scotland have been favoured by circumstances; and if I could see Ireland in the same position that Wales is in, I have every confidence that the Irish would receive the Gospel the same as the Welsh or any other portions of the Celtic race have done...In *thousands of instances* where the people would receive the truth, they have had the alternative of remaining as they are or in houseless poverty, if they embrace the Gospel for they would be turned out of doors and out of employment if they dared to exercise free thought and openly receive the truth. [my italics] (*MS 24*: 134–5.)

Missionary work in Ireland gradually came to a halt between 1863 and 1867. Branch Presidents Robert Brown of Dublin and John Reid of Belfast put forth their best efforts to keep their small groups functioning. The few saints in Dublin, fewer than twelve, held their meetings for a short time, until the members either emigrated or lost interest in the Church. That same year, 1863, John Reid reported from Belfast:

This season has been very severe on the members here for work without exception; we have not had work half the time. I had to bring the Saints to meet in my house on account of not being able to pay hall rent; but they are feeling well and intend, by the help of God, to do their duty...We have had priestcraft in all its horrors to contend with here. (British Mission History, 31 Dec 1863.)

On 9 October 1863 Elder George Halliday visited Ireland for thirteen days and met each member of the Church. Thereafter he reported: 'The total number of Latter-day Saints in Ireland does not exceeed forty and they are very much scattered.' (*MS 27*: 882.) He also relayed the desire of the Irish saints to have a 'missionary from Zion' in their midst. But mission leaders apparently did not feel they should send missionaries to Ireland, and by 31 December 1863 the Irish Mission had been geographically reorganized to be included in the Bristol Conference, which meant that Church affairs in Ireland would be administered from Bristol. (British Mission History, 26 Aug 1867.)

Two years later (in 1865) an editorial in the *Millennial Star* lamented: 'Ireland is a dead beat, those who desire persecution have only to declare themselves Latter-day Saints and the multitudes are more relentless in their pursuit than if they were chasing mad dogs.' (Barlow, p. 62.) And in 1867 Thomas Allen of Belfast claimed that the work there was at a standstill and that there were only about thirty members. (British Mission History, 16 Aug 1867.) In September 1867 President Charles W. Penrose of the British Mission sailed for Ireland, and held a conference with the Belfast saints on the 25th of October. Apparently he thought it best for the saints to emigrate and to close the Irish Mission altogether, for by the end of 1867 both the Dublin and the Belfast Conferences had been discontinued. (Jenson, *Encyclopedic History*, p. 368.) The few Church members remaining in Ireland were placed under the immediate jurisdiction of the British Mission presidency and, except for occasional visits from Church leaders and missionaries in England, the Irish members had little contact with the Church.

Thus ended the second LDS missionary effort in Ireland. And for the next seventeen years the Emerald Isle would have no more missionaries from America.

On 8 September 1882 an article in the *Millennial Star* mentioned Ireland again:

> For several years Ireland has been without representatives of the Kingdom of God, and what efforts that have been put forth to introduce the revealed Gospel have been fruitless. It must be a matter of regret to all who have received the Gospel of Jesus, that in so fair a land, containing, as it does, so many generous and noble spirits, there should be so few to step forward and accept the latter-day Gospel committed to man by former-day beings. So near to Ireland are these kindred lands, one would think that every little zephyr [wind] would waft the falling seeds and spread them on her bosom, so that the growing trees would send their growing roots across the narrow sea to become embedded in the Sister isle, and bring forth life and life fruits. (*MS* 44:680.)

Not long after this report, John Henry Smith, then president of the British Mission, saw a need to launch a third missionary effort in Ireland. This he did in 1884. In proselytizing work before that time, Church leaders had often called upon native Irish members to return to their homeland as missionaries, and this third campaign in Ireland was no exception. This time, Elders Robert Marshall and George Wilson received the assignment.

These two Irishmen arrived in Belfast in May 1884. By then most of the Irish members had emigrated, and there were no known Latter-day Saints in Belfast. The elders commenced by holding open-air meetings on the Custom House steps in Belfast and by so doing established a meeting-place still associated with the Church. Since the two men entered Belfast unnoticed, they met no immediate opposition. (*MS 46*: 379.) But by the end of June 1884 Elder Marshall stated that 'old Babylon' was beginning to awake from her slumbers: 'My name as a "Mormon missionary" is on every tongue,' he said, 'and many chide my friends for harboring me.' (*Ibid.* p. 475.)

Elder Marshall proceeded to Doagh, a town twelve miles from Belfast, where he had some acquaintances whom he hoped to convert to the Church. On the 23rd of June he held a lively meeting in the centre of the country town, and many gathered to hear their Mormon friend who had previously been a Protestant minister in England. After exhorting and preaching until past midnight, Elder Marshall commented:

Many of my old friends were in the crowd and recognized me while I was addressing them...This was very favourable to me, and was very much to the contrary to my adversaries who were greatly blamed by very many for their interruptions. God bless the people, and may the seed sown take deep root. (*Ibid.* p. 479.)

By the 26th of August the two missionaries had converted six of their countrymen to the new faith, but not without much persistence. 'One of the greatest difficulties in the way,' said Elder Wilson, 'is in getting access to their houses, but once in, we are like a severe cold, hard to get out.' (*Ibid.* p. 572.) With such concentrated efforts, the two men converted thirteen more people during the next three weeks, and by the 17th of September there were nineteen members of the Church in Belfast.

The unusual success of these elders was undoubtedly due not only to their persistence, but also to the positive attitude they held towards their work. Elder Wilson declared the following just four months after his arrival in Ireland:

It cannot be asserted in truth any more that we cannot get a foothold in this country. We have demonstrated beyond a shadow of a doubt that the Gospel can be preached in this country as well as elsewhere. It is true they [the Irish] are a very impulsive but at the same time a generous people, and although they would jostle you about, they would the next hour take you in their domiciles and administer to your wants, proving that...the heart is kind, and we must forgive the little faults of a warm and generous nature. (*Ibid.* p. 667.)

The two Irish elders did indeed prove that the gospel could be preached as successfully in Ireland as in other parts of the world. By the 20th of October, just five months after arriving, they had re-established a branch in Belfast, with twenty-nine members. With the help of two more missionaries, the work continued to prosper until, by the end of 1884, the Belfast Branch had a membership of fifty Irish saints. (JH, p. 4.)

January 1885 proved to be another highlight for the Church in Ireland – the four missionaries gained thirteen converts in just one month. And in eight months Elder Robert Marshall had converted thirty people, an unheard-of accomplishment before that time. (*MS* 47:142.)

Not only were numbers increasing, however; the faith and courage of the saints were also growing. An example of this greater commitment was a baptism that took place one cold winter night in Belfast. Shortly after the missionaries had arrived in the city, they had met and taught the gospel to some people living in nearby White Well. Towards the latter part of November 1884 the two elders urged baptism, and the candidates said it could be done in the very near future. Then on the 1st of December, Elder Robert Marshall wrote from Belfast:

On Sunday evening, while holding a meeting at Fortingale Street, judge my surprise when Mrs Garlick came in accompanied by her two sisters; and judge still more of my astonishment and amazement to find that Mrs [Ellen] Maybin, the sick lady who had been nearly at the point of death a few days ago, had walked the entire distance to White Well – nearly twenty miles, and landed there at ten o'clock on Saturday night without a soul with her. Surely the Spirit of God was in the heart of this noble 'Mormon lady'.

But my surprise did not rest here, for her sister of White Well proposed to go out to the Fourth [*sic*] river through the storm and snow – the snow being four inches deep, and at that hour of night, be baptized by me. But was this all? No indeed, for young Mr Berry, Mrs Garlick's son-in-law, also proposed to go into the water at this inclement hour and be baptized. And who do you think had the grit to propose to baptize him? Why none other than Elder Greenwell, with his sick chest and throat. Well, while the meeting was being held I sat and wept like a child with happiness and gratitude to God. (*MS* 46:779–80.)

Elder Marshall concluded, 'Many are getting ready... The work rolls.'

Much of Elder Marshall's proselytizing was in Edenvale, just outside Belfast, and it was there he converted the aforementioned Mrs Ellen Maybin, an acquaintance he had made before leaving Ireland. This elderly lady was living with her son and daughter-in-law, who both later joined the Church. Six months after her own conversion, Sister Maybin died. She had previously asked that the elders preach at her funeral – an unusual request, since no one in Edenvale had yet witnessed a 'Mormon' funeral service.

When Sister Maybin died, Elders Marshall and Francis went immediately to Edenvale at the request of the family and, during that February night in 1885, held a wake, sitting up with the body. Many curious mourners attended the wake and argued the doctrines of the Church until nine o'clock the next morning. The elders later remarked that 'the dear old lady who slept in death had preached a greater sermon in her departure, than many had done during a long lifetime, for she had, by her death, brought many together to listen to the Truth who would never have heard it in any other way'. (*DN*, 10 Apr 1885; see also JH, pp. 4–5; and *MS 47*:91–2.)

The day after the wake, the funeral was held under the direction of the two elders. That afternoon a long train of vehicles accompanied the two missionaries and Sister Maybin's body to the cemetery, seven miles out of town. The elders wrote of this occasion:

> The country was in a fever, and those attending the funeral felt a smothered excitement all the way. Many of her friends raged in their hearts and smiled with their faces, and some fumed and frowned without disguise while all were deeply mortified to find two Mormon Elders and a company of converts escorting their aged sister's remains to their last resting place, and this Sister was a near relative to all present. (*DN*, 10 Apr 1885.)

Not long after the funeral, it was rumoured that Mrs Maybin had drowned while being baptized in a 'lint dam'. In reality, she had been baptized in a clear stream six months before her death. 'Everywhere I go,' Elder Marshall said, 'this lie about her baptism being the cause of her death meets me. It has passed from mouth to mouth like lightning.' (*Ibid.*) It seemed as though some of the saints in Ireland were the object of persecution even after death.

Even though the missionaries had experienced considerable success during the two years after their return to Ireland, the intense political disturbances in Belfast during the summer of 1886 limited their progress. Elder Joseph D. Smith, who presided over the Church in Ireland during that summer, later wrote, 'This summer has been quite unfavourable to the work in Ireland, so much political strife and bloodshed that but little outdoor speaking could be done.' (*MS 48*: 748.) The turmoil began early in the summer as the annual Twelfth of July celebration approached. Elder Smith explained why he had decided to refrain from preaching:

> Our out-door preaching will be very much interfered with this summer, for almost all the business men consider things will be quite unsettled until after the 12th of July, which is the day the Protestants march in memory of the battle of the Boyne. If it passes quietly, it may secure peace again for a short time, but I see in the near future another election. This is well calculated to inflame the minds of the rough element who seem to know nothing but what their ministers and priests tell them.
>
> Eight bodies were buried today. I believe our street was protected across the ends by soldiers to prevent any trouble. The eight were all killed within 300 yards of this address, and many were wounded. (*Ibid.* p. 413.)

Elder Smith also reported that he and his companions had to stay inside their house at night to avoid the disturbance, even though the city was well protected with soldiers who were guarding the police against irate citizens. Apparently, such riots only heightened the desire of the new LDS converts to leave their country. In the following month (August), it was noted that 'the Belfast branch will be somewhat weakened when the boat sails for Zion'. (*Ibid.* p. 251.)

But the political unrest in Belfast was only one aspect of Church history during this period. A highlight in Ireland about this time was the return of Elder Charles A. Callis, who had been born in Dublin and would later become an apostle. Elder Callis served his mission in 1893–4, and in November 1894 was appointed president of the Irish Conference. During his administration in his native land, the Church prospered, as the membership in the Belfast Branch grew by fifty per cent.

Elder Callis was born on 4 May 1865, a son of John and Susannah Quilliam Callis, who had recently moved to Dublin from Liverpool. Unfortunately Charles's father died on 25 February 1867, and later that summer the widowed Susannah moved with her three children back to Liverpool. Susannah Callis later accepted the gospel, as did Charles at the age of ten. He was baptized on 12 September 1875, and a short time later emigrated to Utah with his family, where they settled in the town of Bountiful.

After serving his first mission in 1893–4, Elder Callis returned to Utah, where he became a lawyer and served as the Summit County Attorney for six years, city councilman of Coalville for a number of years, and was a member of the Second Utah Legislature.

At the age of thirty-seven he married Grace C. Pack, in September 1902, and they later became parents of eight children. In 1906 Elder and Sister Callis were called as missionaries to the Southern States Mission. In 1908 Elder Callis was appointed to succeed President Ben E. Rich as president of that mission, where the Callises served for more than twenty-five years. He was then called to give the rest of his life to the full-time service of the Lord, and was confirmed as a member of the Quorum of Twelve Apostles at the October 1933 General Conference. Elder Callis, a Dubliner by birth, died on 21 January 1947 at Jacksonville, Florida, where, as a general authority, he had gone to organize a new stake. (Carter, *13*:364–5.)

One reason for the generally slow growth of the Church in Ireland was the continued 'gathering to Zion'. From 1884 until 1900, for instance, there were 214 people baptized into the Church in Northern Ireland, but about ninety of these emigrated to America – and death and excommunication claimed another twenty-eight – so that only half these converts remained in the Belfast Branch. Indeed it was difficult to build a strong branch with such factors working against the missionaries. In fact, in this sixteen-year period the highest membership in Belfast was 139, which occurred in 1898. (*MS 60*:795.)

Even though there was only one branch in Belfast, the work extended to Ballymoney, Londonderry, Magherafelt, Edenvale, White Well, Ballyclare, Lurgan, Newtownards and Portadown during this period. In Portadown considerable interest in the Church was generated during 1889–90 by a series of debates on LDS theology, which were published in the *Portadown* and *Lurgan News*. (*MS* 52:20–3.) But no new branches were organized.

Another important event occurred on 11 August 1889, when

the first conference of the Irish Mission was held in Dickson's Hall at 1 Independence Street, Belfast. Still, by the turn of the century, the Belfast Branch had seen comparatively little growth since its re-establishment in 1884.

There were several reasons why the Church in Ireland had failed to flourish since the first missionaries arrived in 1840, and one of these was the nearly constant opposition the missionaries encountered. The term 'opposition' is preferable to 'persecution' because the latter implies physical violence, and the Irish have seldom inflicted any physical harm upon the saints. One minor incident did occur in 1908 when a missionary was struck on the shoulder and neck by an Irishman 'who gave unmistakable signs of having imbibed freely in Irish Whiskey'. (*MS 70*: 380.) Except for a few minor occurrences like this, the missionaries and members in Ireland had not been subjected to violence in the early years, which is remarkable when one considers the many lives lost in Ireland because of religious differences.

Commenting on the violence experienced by LDS missionary elders in different parts of Europe, President George Q. Cannon of the British Mission presidency wrote in 1862, 'Germany has up till now rejected the Gospel as much as France or Ireland. Elders have had to run for their lives there which they have not had to do in Ireland.' (*MS 24*: 134.) Still, as has been shown, the Church had not been unopposed in Ireland. On the contrary, those desiring that the gospel should not be taught in Ireland have used a variety of ways to hinder the work – one of which was amassing large crowds.

Remarkably, three or four missionaries often attracted huge crowds of Irishmen. Perhaps out of curiosity, or maybe to harass, the Irish often attended open-air meetings and formal Church services in force. This was true from the beginning.

On 29 July 1840, for instance, Elder John Taylor and his two companions arrived in Newry. After obtaining the use of the courthouse for a meeting that evening, they sent a man through the town to announce the proposed gathering, and a congregation of seven hundred people from Newry and surrounding areas turned out to hear the first sermon in Ireland on 'the Restored Gospel of Jesus Christ'. (Roberts, *Taylor*, pp. 84–5.)

Elder Edward Sutherland reported a similar though more lively incident when the gospel was preached for the first time in Dublin. On 28 September 1850 he wrote:

I lost no time in adopting a plan I thought likely to spread a knowledge of the principles of eternal truth; I announced a public meeting by placarding the city, which lecture was attended by many hundreds. (*MS 12*:312.)

President John Henry Smith of the British Mission visited Belfast on 9 October 1884 and advertised that he would preach that evening in a rented hall. In spite of inclement weather, the hall was filled to capacity, and many were turned away disappointed. Nevertheless, not everyone who attended anticipated being converted to the gospel:

Many doubtless came from curiosity and possibly some were there with the express intention of creating a disturbance. To say the least the rowdy element was well represented, and the interruptions caused thereby were so frequent throughout the evening that the services were not very satisfactory... There was a rollicking good humor, however, about the disturbers and an evident desire for frolic. (*MS 46*:665.)

Open-air meetings attracted even larger and more unruly crowds. On the evening of 5 August 1885 Elder Charles W. Penrose, an apostle, visited Ireland and with the aid of three other missionaries tried to conduct an outdoor meeting. Elder Penrose addressed between two and three thousand Irishmen on the principles of the gospel 'amidst derisive cries and interruptions from the assembled multitude'. The crowd finally became impatient and rushed the speaker, forcing him off the Custom House steps. This in turn brought the Belfast police to the scene, who cautioned the Church leaders not to proceed with their meeting. Elder Penrose and his associates sought refuge in a tramcar amidst jeers and taunts that 'Mormons made a great mistake if they imagine they could convert the people of Belfast to their objectionable form of religion.' The meeting was cancelled for the evening. (Barlow, p. 93.)

A public challenge to debate gospel principles in an open-air meeting attracted a similar crowd in Belfast on 21 May 1896, where a Mr Marshall had challenged Elder Stephen W. Ross to debate 'Mormonism, Past, Present, and Future'. Several hundred Irishmen were waiting for the elders that evening, and before long the listeners numbered two thousand. During the controversial debate, someone shouted, 'Let's shift them!' The crowd rushed forward and soon had the missionaries on the move. Through the aid of two police officers, the elders escaped without injury, but were followed down the street by nearly a thousand jeering Irishmen. (*MS 62*: 374–9.)

Vast numbers of Irish not only disrupted LDS Church services and open-air meetings, but tried to interfere with the elders' tracting as well. Near the turn of the century, two missionaries went to Dundalk, a city of eleven thousand Catholics and some two thousand Protestants. Not much happened until the day the two elders were accused of slander and arrested. Then a group named the 'Hibernian Society' met, and decided to drive the missionaries from the town – though they agreed the young men were not to be harmed physically. Upon being released from two days' confinement in gaol, the elders were advised to proceed to Newry. This they did, but much to their surprise, as they left Dundalk, they were accompanied by three hundred Irishmen. Elder T. J. Bennett commented,

> It was certainly laughable to see the elders leading a bunch of men all through the town and out into the country. For two days the missionaries walked them almost to death, visiting friends out in the country. They [the Hibernian Society] would go up to the doors with the elders and when a tract was given, the men would grab it from the elders' hands and tear it up. Every time the elders would go out they would have from two to three hundred people following them. It was certainly great advertisement. Every man, woman, and child in that section knew there were 'Mormons' there. (*MS 70*: 844–5.)

But huge and unruly crowds were not the only form of opposition the Church encountered in Ireland. Perhaps the most difficult sort came from the landowners, often non-Irish, who rented farms and homes to the Irishmen. These landowners sometimes teamed up with members of the local clergy, thus presenting the double threat of eviction and excommunication to anyone who listened to or in any way assisted Mormon missionaries. In 1844 Elder James Sloan, who had been a missionary in Ireland, expressed his feelings on this matter:

> I got little opportunity to preach in Ireland, for it is pretty generally the case there that the tenants have not any leases, and the nobles, etc., in many places have notified them that in any case they received, entertained, or heard me preach, they might rise up and leave the place or they would be dispossessed,

and the clergy of the day have traveled assiduously to places where they had not been for months and years before, threatening excommunication if they received or heard me. (Sloan.)

A year later, Elder Reuben Hedlock again expressed his views on the Church in Ireland:

There has not been much done in Ireland, the people are so bound by poverty, and so dependent upon their landlords, that they dare not admit any one to preach in their neighborhoods or to keep them overnight if the reader of the parish forbids them; if they disobeyed his orders, he would inform the bishops and overseers of the parish, and they, the landlords, and the people would forfeit their homes and employment, *and this is the great reason why the gospel does not spread more in Ireland.* (*TS* 6:988 [my italics].)

LDS Church historian Andrew Jenson also noted this occurrence in his statement about the first decade of missionary work in Ireland:

Considerable difficulty was experienced by the missionaries in Ireland on account of the great poverty which prevailed. Most of the farmers occupied their land and depended for their livelihood upon the goodwill of their landlords, who being mostly Catholics, disapproved of the introduction of a new religion into their midst, and intimidated their tenants by withholding coal and other free distributions and threatened loss of employment and eviction from their homes and farms if they disobeyed the local Catholic priests by attending meetings of the Latter-day Saints. (Jenson, *Encyclopedic History*, pp. 368–9.)

By 1862 the missionary work in Ireland had again come to a standstill, and realizing that the missionaries had made little progress in that country in comparison to other parts of Britain, President George Q. Cannon wrote, on 4 January 1862:

In thousands of instances where the people would receive the truth, they have had the alternative of remaining as they are or in houseless poverty if they embrace the Gospel; *for they would be turned out of doors and out of employment if they dared to exercise free thought and openly receive the truth.* (*MS* 24:135 [my italics].)

Thus we can only guess where the gospel in Ireland would be today had those 'thousands' been allowed to choose their own religious beliefs and follow them.

Besides the pressures exerted upon LDS converts by landowners, the missionaries themselves would often be harassed, and one form of harassment was stone-throwing. That is, stones would be thrown at missionaries, but as far as we know no major injury or damage ever occurred. For example, Elder William Butler, an Irishman converted to the Church in Utah, returned to his native country as a missionary in 1854. Upon arriving in Gary, he held an open-air meeting on one of the town corners, and a large crowd soon gathered. While he was preaching, a few burly Irishmen pushed him into the street and began throwing stones. 'There was a constant shower of rocks,' he reported, 'but none hit me.' As the stones were falling about him, Elder Butler saw a woman standing by the gate in front of her cottage. As he walked towards the woman, she started to close the gate as if she detected his intentions. In so doing she was hit by a stone meant for Butler and knocked to the ground. A small boy took the missionary to his home just as the police arrived to disperse the crowd. Neither the young boy nor Elder Butler sustained any injury. (Butler.)

In another incident, this time in 1904, the elders in Newtown Hamilton, Co. Armagh, were holding meetings in the loft of a flax barn, 'the only available place in the vicinity'. Elder George Tolley reported that 'while one of the meetings was in progress, some boys threw stones in through the door, but no one was hurt. Since then we have not been molested, save by words.' (*MS* 66:91–2.)

With such treatment, however, the missionaries were not always content to turn the other cheek, especially if they themselves were Irish. During December 1885, Elders Edward Clyde and James Sloan, both Irishmen, returned to their native country as missionaries for the Church. One evening as they were on their way home they were assaulted by four other Irishmen, who threw a volley of stones and chased them. While the attackers were gathering more stones, the two elders decided to defend themselves, and Elder Clyde recorded this rather humorous incident as follows:

> They came so near, we found it necessary either to run, fight, or be pelted with the stones. To stand and be beaten with stones seemed altogether out of reason. To run would have hurt our feelings worse than the stones possibly could have done. So, being both of Irish descent, we concluded to share the pleasure of stone throwing.
>
> The conflict was kept up for about twenty minutes, each party loading and reloading to his best advantage. We had no desire of gaining a victory, but were earnest in our efforts for self-defense. Being experts at the stone throwing, we were able to keep our assailants at a good distance from us, and by great exertion we reached our place of destination without injury. From the threats and actions

of our Christian friends, we have concluded it would be more healthy and agreeable for us to pay our visits a little earlier in the day. (*MS 48*:44–5.)

And yet there were still more original forms of opposition directed against the missionaries in Ireland. Towards the latter part of February 1908, five elders proceeded to Omagh to hold their first meeting in that city. They rented a hall and announced the service for 3.30 p.m. A large crowd gathered at three o'clock and advised people not to go to the meeting, so the elders sought police protection, which was refused. The missionaries began their meeting at the appointed hour with about forty people in attendance.

During the second hymn, thirty men and boys entered the building and sat down in the rear of the hall. Within a few minutes everyone in the meeting started coughing and sneezing, which temporarily disrupted the meeting. The elders soon discovered that burning rolls of cloth containing cayenne pepper had been conveniently placed throughout the hall by one of the 'guests'. After the room had been aired, a few visitors returned to the meeting, but minutes later the missionaries discovered smoke rising through the cracks in the floor. Their opponents had gone underneath the building and were 'smoking out the Mormons'. Everyone, missionaries included, left the hall at this second interruption.

When the smoke cleared, the elders went back into the building, since they 'felt safer inside than out'. The meeting continued as the missionaries sang hymns and bore testimony in the midst of constant confusion. Not satisfied with the burning pepper or the smoke, the ruffians poured sheep-dip (a liquid preparation used to destroy parasites in sheep) all over the floor, which brought applause from hundreds of onlookers in the street. The putrid odour caused the disappointed missionaries to terminate the meeting, but only after vowing to return to Omagh in the near future. (*MS 71*:163–5.)

Cayenne pepper had also been an effective way to disrupt earlier Mormon meetings in Ireland. In February 1886 missionaries advertised a meeting in Ballyclare for 7.30 p.m. and arrived to find a congregation of three hundred awaiting the service. After the usual hymn and prayer, Elder Edward Clyde addressed the group, but he had not spoken five minutes when everyone began coughing violently. The elders thought it to be a prearranged plan to interrupt their meeting, but soon the smell of cayenne pepper reached them. 'Some conscienceless cur had sprinkled this disagreeable pungent pepper on the floor', wrote an elder, 'and for about twenty minutes the people were running to the windows for a breath of fresh air, holding their handkerchiefs over their mouths and noses, and coughing as though they would tear their lungs asunder.'

When the audience had quietened down, the same missionary tried to continue, but again some playful Irishman performed the same deed. The house went into an uproar for the second time. Not wanting to gratify the perpetrators, the elders tried not to cough, but finally one of them could not refrain any longer, and his coughing received a rousing cheer from the audience, 'not withstanding it was Sunday night'. Most of the crowd soon left, fully convinced that the Mormons would hesitate before trying to hold another meeting in 'sweet Ballyclare'. (*MS 48*: 122–3.)

Still another creative means used to inhibit the missionaries was the foghorn. Elder Charles A. Callis reported that the device was used in Belfast during December 1894 while he was president of the Irish Conference:

> Our open-air meetings, although well attended, have not been noted for the courtesy our listeners have shown us. While we were addressing one of these gatherings recently we were interrupted in a provoking but effectual manner. An individual armed with an unappreciated instrument known as a fog-horn came close to where we were speaking and blew a blast so long and loud that it was impossible for us to be heard. Others encouraged and added to the hideous noise which continued until they succeeded in abruptly terminating our meeting. (*MS 46*: 827.)

Thus another missionary meeting was forced to close.

As the Church progressed in Ireland and employed more efficient proselytizing techniques, the opposition also became more skilled. During August 1913 there were several anti-Mormon plays at Belfast theatres. These productions were probably the same ones used in England during 1911, depicting what supposedly happened to those who joined the Mormon Church. (*MS 73*: 808–11.)

Another problem for the missionaries – a problem related to the other difficulties with landlords – was finding a place for the saints to meet. Since the Church did not own a meeting-hall in Ireland until 1948, they were at the mercy of others for a meeting-place, which was often a great disadvantage. Missionaries held meetings in barns and flax lofts, and on hillsides. And they were shifted from building to building by indignant building owners.

As mentioned earlier, when the missionaries returned to Belfast in 1850, they reported no central meeting-place. (*MS 12*:253.) During the following decade they moved in and out of buildings almost yearly. On 4 February 1853 the elders in Dublin conceded:

> The public mind is much embittered against us; so much so that every place we have hitherto occupied had been taken from us through the influence of our enemies. This has been a great drawback to the work of God in this city. (*MS 15*:141.)

It was noted again, on 1 January 1859, that there was 'no regular place of meeting' in Belfast, and two years later the elders stated that 'for some three years past there has been no public hall occupied by the Saints'. (*MS 23*:254.)

But even when a hall was found, there was rent to pay. Patrick Lynch reported in 1854 that there were not enough Church members in Ireland to redeem his watch, which he had pawned for three pounds to pay the 'rint'. (*DN*, 5 Oct 1854, p. 2.) The women pawned their shawls and the men their watches and rings, and even the furniture out of their homes, to help pay the expenses for a meeting-place for the Belfast Branch. (*MS 18*: 562.)

Meeting-hall refusal occurred as late as 1908 in Belfast, when members of the Church applied for the use of the Ulster Minor Hall, a well-known building in the city. It was scheduled for a half-yearly conference on 28 September 1908. The elders made a down payment, and by Saturday the 27th of September the final payment had been made, for which the town clerk issued a receipt. But by midday on Saturday the presiding elder received a refusal notice. (*MS 70*:632–6.)

The refusal was a severe disappointment to the members and missionaries in Belfast, who had placed several large posters around the city and distributed thousands of circulars advertising their meeting. On Sunday the 28th of September, more than 300 people gathered for the meeting at the Ulster Minor Hall only to be told by the missionaries that the meeting had been cancelled. (*Ibid.*)

Thus, by many and varied means, Church growth was hampered in Ireland for decades. Though Mormon missionaries in Ireland were seldom injured physically, as they sometimes were in other countries, these 'harmless' methods of opposition were apparently very effective. Although Church growth was slowed for many years by such strategies, it did begin to improve around the turn of the twentieth century. As mentioned earlier, the Belfast Branch was reopened in 1884 when missionaries returned to Ireland after a seventeen-year absence. The Dublin Branch, however, had continued to function for little more than a decade after its organization in 1850, even though a few members still lived in that city. Then on 29 April 1900 the Dublin Branch was reopened, as several LDS families of German descent settled there. (Irish Conference History, 18 May 1903 to 28 Mar 1915; the Dublin Branch was apparently reorganized on 24 Mar 1901.) The Dimlers, Horlachers and Mogerlys were typical of the families who formed this branch after 1900.

A few years before the turn of the century, Fredrick A. Dimler and Babette Henrich had emigrated separately from Wurtemberg to England. They both obtained employment with meat merchants and eventually married and settled in Hull. The Dimlers had two daughters, one of whom later married Christian Steele, also of German parentage, and a convert to the Church. Brother Steele proceeded to teach his wife the gospel, and when she joined the Church, she in turn taught the gospel to her parents. They also were baptized and then moved to Dublin, with their daughter and son-in-law, to carry on their trade as pork butchers. (*MS 98*: 148–50.)

Similarly, about 1900, Herman Horlacher left Wurtemberg for Dublin and became involved in the meat industry, whilst Lena Brenner left Germany about the same time, moved to Dublin, and met and married Horlacher. His brother had also emigrated from Germany, had joined the Church, and was later influential in converting both Herman and Lena Horlacher to his new faith. (*Ibid.*) Meanwhile Henry Mogerly, also born in Germany, had emigrated to England, where he married Mary Pratt. They both joined the Church in England, moved to Dublin, and became members of the Dublin Branch. (*Ibid.*)

These three families were just a few of the pork-butcher Mormons comprising the Dublin congregation. So rapid was the growth of the Dublin Branch that the first half-yearly conference

Loughbrickland, site of the first baptism in Ireland. Elder John Taylor baptized Thomas Tait on 31 July 1840.

The Dublin Branch, Irish Free State District, 11 May 1924.

in Dublin was held on 4 December 1904 at 45 Lower Sackville Street. (*MS 66*: 778.) By 1905 Church leaders were noting that most of the saints in Dublin were German rather than Irish. On 20 May 1905 President Heber J. Grant of the British Mission visited Dublin and reported the following:

> There is a thriving branch of the Church in Dublin, most of the members not being Irish, but Germans. A number of enterprising German Saints, having found it profitable business to sell pork in all its varied forms and grindings to the inhabitants of Dublin, have invited others of their fellow countrymen to come over and partake of their good fortune and opportunities, and so there is quite a colony of German pork butchers in the capital of the Emerald Isle. (*Instructor*, 14: 32.)

Soon after the turn of the twentieth century, branches of the Church had been established once again in both Belfast and Dublin. By 1920 there were about 225 members in the Belfast Conference and approximately 60 members in and around Dublin. The LDS members and missionaries could be justly proud of their accomplishments.

In 1884 Elder John Henry Smith, a member of the Quorum of the Twelve Apostles, visited Ireland. Following this visit, he said, 'I am inclined to believe there are hundreds and thousands of people in Ireland who will receive the Gospel . . . I trust that the Gospel may spread in that land and that thousands may receive its truth.' (*JD 26*: 176–7.)

Similarly, Elder John T. D. McAllister, undoubtedly representing the sentiments of the many LDS missionaries who laboured in Ireland, wrote the following:

> While walking the roads, I felt to bless the people, for I could see Ephraim all through my travels . . . Royal blood flows in the veins of Ireland's noble sons and daughters, and when they have the privilege of hearing the Gospel, they will embrace it. Well, the time to favor Erin has come, and I rejoice that I have been counted worthy to work in the field known as the Belfast Conference. (*MS 17*: 474.)

Truly, 'the time to favor Erin has come'.

Looking Forward

CONTEMPORARY HISTORY is the most difficult sort to write, as we have not the benefit of time's sifting of events into their order of importance. Yet we struggle to see the pattern, that we may look forward, because history that looks back and not forward is a failure. In a world that has forgotten its own parentage, we assert that Israel has an unbroken lineage and a sacred history that goes back to when the world was new. But lineage alone is not enough. (Matthew 3:9.) We are required to do the works of righteouness if we would be faithful heirs. We are given the names of our righteous parents that we may remember their works and pattern our lives upon theirs. (Helaman 5:6–7.) There are, in the history of the Church in Britain, many noble patterns for our lives.

This is the second time we have celebrated a year of jubilee in Britain. Once again we have the opportunity to 'do [his] statutes, and keep [his] judgments, and do them', that we may dwell safely in this land. (See Leviticus 25.) It is a new start, a time of re-dedication, a time of forgiving, repenting and growing.

The first section of the Doctrine and Covenants, given by the Lord as a preface to that work, serves equally well as a prologue to our work in Britain for the next fifty years: it is still expected of us, as Latter-day Saints, 'that every man might speak in the name of God the Lord, even the Savior of the world; that faith might also increase in the earth; that mine everlasting covenant might be established...'. (D&C 1:20–2.) Sometimes it seems painful to read of attempts by 'the weak and the simple' to proclaim the fullness of the gospel. But we are the weak and simple of our generation, to whom the same charge has been given.

And so we read of the persecutions and the bleak war years and wonder what it means. Those of us who remember President Hugh B. Brown and others of the men and women chronicled here know that from the hardships of those years came faith-building stories that are today the bedrock of our testimonies.

We sometimes heard missionaries before the Second World War report that the 'harvest' was over. Yet those who survived that war to become new missionaries preached the gospel with a vitality that brought a spiritual response in their hearers. Thus, at a time when other churches are standing empty, the saints are building new chapels in Britain.

So what of the history of the Church in our lifetimes? What will we contribute to the building of Zion? These concluding chapters give us the opportunity for reflection and re-dedication.

11

The First World War and the Great Depression 1914–39

Louis B. Cardon

The two world wars, coming as they did within a single generation and affecting virtually every major aspect of British life, could not fail to influence the history of the Church in Britain. Even so, they do not totally dominate that history. The British Mission was also affected by other external developments such as the economic depression of the inter-war decades and the alternate waxing and waning of religious persecution and religious apathy. Moreover, the mission possessed strong leadership and other dynamic internal forces. These helped to produce growth even amidst difficulties, and brought changes in proselytizing methods as well as in the roles of both missionaries and local members.

The First World War, commonly called 'The Great War' by the generation that experienced it, was indeed a 'great divide' for Britain. It separated a century of unprecedented world leadership from a century of unprecedented challenges to that status, as well as to the very livelihood of the British people. Some of Britain's problems in the post-war era, such as increased commercial competition from rising industrial countries like the United States and Japan, would probably have come early in the twentieth century even without the war. But by its financial demands and its interruption of industrial production for world markets, the First World War accelerated the process. At the time, however, few people had much concern for these long-term effects; the war itself placed too many urgent demands upon their time and energies.

For the first two years of the war, the spiritual leader of the saints was Elder Hyrum Mack Smith, president of both the British and European Missions of the Church. Like most of the British Mission presidents before him, President Smith was a member of the Quorum of the Twelve Apostles. He was also the son of Joseph F. Smith, who was then president of the Church, and was a respected Church leader in his own right. Mission presidents did not at that time have counsellors, but President Hyrum Smith had a particularly able assistant in Elder J. M. Sjodahl, who had been editor of the *Deseret News* and then served very capably as associate editor of the *Millennial Star*. (*MS 76*: 638; *81*: 95–265.)

Early in the war, the *Star* published an address by President Joseph F. Smith delivered at Cardston, Alberta, Canada, reminding the saints that patriotism was part of their religion. (See *MS 76*: 664–5.) Nevertheless, the British saints were also urged, through the pages of the *Millennial Star* and through President Hyrum Smith's district conference addresses, to avoid letting their hearts become hardened towards the enemy. 'Love your enemies' was Christ's commandment, and those called into the armed forces were asked to remember that they were soldiers of the faith as well as of the nation. They should go to war

> with the idea of establishing righteousness in the world... and not with the thought of murder in their hearts, or even hate... [Though] members of the Church must and will bear their part of fighting for the country of which they are an integral part, let them go... pure in heart, even as go forth the thousands of elders who are called to preach the gospel; let them keep pure and remember always the teachings of the gospel. (*MS 76*: 612–14; 664–5; *79*: 274–5.)

As the war continued and became more horrible, with loss of life exceeding anything previously known in history, many British saints wondered, along with other Christians, how a loving God could permit such slaughter. Answers came from President Hyrum Smith, Elder Sjodahl, and Church leaders in General Conference, all printed in the *Millennial Star*. This war, wrote President Hyrum Smith, was clearly a continuing fulfilment of Joseph Smith's prophecy that war would be 'poured out upon all nations' prior to Christ's second coming. (D&C 87: 2.) However, this did not mean that God willed or caused the war. It came because men generally had rejected the gospel of Jesus Christ. Yet in the end, war could prove one means of preparing the world for the reign of peace. (*MS 76*:693; 714–16; *78*:264–5; *79*:248–9.)

Besides the other hardships imposed on British saints by the war, there was a drastic reduction in the number of missionaries coming from North America. This naturally diminished proselytizing and, together with the wartime shortage of adult men in local branches, caused severe difficulties in maintaining the organization of the Church. Though the missionaries were not summarily called home (as they would be in the Second World War), those who were released throughout the first years of the war were replaced by few new ones.

From a missionary force of 258 in 1913, the number had dropped to just 31 by 1919. Still, though the number of missionaries quickly decreased, it seemed that in some ways the proselytizing of remaining missionaries might actually be aided by wartime circumstances. In his October 1914 conference address in Salt Lake City, President Joseph F. Smith said:

> Reports that we receive from England, notwithstanding the conditions of war that exist there, are that our elders are in safety at present, and that the field is opening before them with somewhat better prospects than heretofore. A great many people are beginning to feel the necessity of prayer for deliverance and safety, and as the spirit of prayer rests upon their minds, they begin to feel after their spiritual as well as their temporal welfare. (*MS 76*:770.)

This report of a moderate increase in proselytizing success was borne out by the 1914 statistics. The number of baptisms (399) was the highest for several years, and there were corresponding increases in other proselytizing statistics. Despite the lack of missionaries, baptisms remained at about 300 per year until 1918, when they dropped slightly, to 248. (*MS 78*:72.)

President Hyrum M. Smith and his successor, President George F. Richards, spread their dwindling numbers of missionaries throughout the fourteen conferences of the mission as best they could. They used them as conference and branch presidents in many cases, instructing them to give first priority to the needs of the approximately 8,000 British saints, who were divided among some seventy branches. Since many of these members lived some distance from any branch meeting-place, and since wartime restrictions often impeded travel, it was difficult for the missionaries and the few local adult priesthood-holders to keep in touch with all the members. (*MS 77–80, passim.*)

Nevertheless, President Smith came to feel that the shortage of missionaries, though unfortunate in many ways, was not altogether without benefit. Early in 1916 he wrote in his diary:

The situation is serious and the saints are suffering and grieving because of the absence of the elders. It may prove a good thing in some cases as the saints will of a necessity place greater trust in the Lord and rely upon him rather than men...(H. M. Smith, vol. 5, 10 May, 12 Aug 1916; *MS 78*:72–3.)

The British saints made great efforts to remain faithful during wartime, and President Smith recognized this diligence in his final editorial in the *Millennial Star* of 24 August 1916.

Notwithstanding these unfavourable conditions, the saints are generally very faithful. Some branches have been closed, while others are ably presided over by local brethren, and the work is going on splendidly...I believe that never before have the saints kept the Word of Wisdom, paid their tithes and offerings, and endeavored to do just what is right, with greater zeal and faithfulness than they are doing now. (*MS 81*:538.)

In this same final report, President Smith pinpointed one of the principal causes for the excellent wartime record of the British Mission, both in personal faithfulness and in proselytizing:

Much of the unity and strength of the saints is due to the activities of the Relief Societies, which were never better organized, or more energetic and efficient, than at the present time. (*Ibid.*)

To this commendation Sister Ida B. Smith, mission Relief Society president, added her observation:

In the past two years we have seen a great reawakening of interest in the Relief Society cause. The organizations, some of which had become more or less listless, have been aroused and rejuvenated. Many new organizations have been effected...(*Ibid.* p. 541.)

Mission statistics bear out this statement. At the end of the war there were at least ten more Relief Societies in the mission than at the beginning, and average attendance at Relief Society meetings in some periods exceeded 80 per cent.

One reason for this increased vitality was the challenge the Relief Society had received early in the war to assist in the national effort – a challenge they met, in part, by sewing and knitting mufflers and other articles of clothing for British soldiers and sailors. These were produced both during work meetings and by individual labour at home. But the Relief Society sisters also performed many other services, including caring for the wounded and ill, collecting books and magazines for use by soldiers in convalescent stations and behind the front lines, and observing 'Egg Sundays', when eggs were collected and delivered to war hospitals. (*MS 76*: 637; 653–4; 763; *77*:12–15; *78*:431; *80*:87; *81*:299.)

Many of the women in the British Mission – besides working in Relief Society, contributing to the national war effort, caring for their own families, and performing individual part-time volunteer work – also assisted in the proselytizing work of the mission during the last two years of the war. At first this was apparently done informally and on local initiative, for on 12 August 1916 President Smith noted in his diary, following a visit to the Leeds Conference: 'Many of the sisters have taken up tracting and have met with considerable success.' (H. M. Smith, 12 Aug 1916.) Two weeks later, at President Smith's final interview with his conference presidents, it was reported that, in other conferences too, local sisters – and a few available brethren as well – were helping with the proselytizing work. (*MS 78*: 561–7.) About the same time Sister Smith, in her final message as mission Relief Society president, declared:

> Now that the elders are so few, there is need of the help of the women, who might find time to distribute a few tracts occasionally. This has been done in a few instances with splendid effect. Many doors have been opened for the preaching of the gospel in this way. (*MS 78*: 540–2.)

Soon thereafter, on the 7th of September, President Smith was replaced as British and European Mission president by Elder George F. Richards, also a member of the Quorum of the Twelve Apostles. At this time there were still over fifty missionaries from America in Britain; but in 1917 only one new missionary arrived, and from 1918 until the middle of 1919 there were no replacements at all for the missionaries being released. Consequently, in June 1919, shortly before President Richards's release, there were only five missionaries from North America in all of Great Britain. Even so, baptisms rose slightly in 1917 (from 297 to 319) and then dropped only moderately (to 248) in 1918.

President Richards gave credit for this record to the corps of more than three hundred British sisters that he called into part-time missionary service shortly after his arrival. These sisters were formally set apart as missionaries and replaced as needed throughout President Richards's administration. Together with a few local male missionaries, they distributed about half as many tracts and copies of the Book of Mormon in 1917 as did the full-time missionaries from America, and held about half as many 'gospel conversations'. In 1918 they did approximately two-thirds of this work and in 1919 over three-quarters. (*CR*, Richards, Apr 1932; R. Evans, p. 217; *MS 82*: 721; *78–83*, statistical reports, *passim*.)

There was one challenge of the war era, however, that neither began nor ended with the war itself, and that was the continuing prevalence of anti-Mormon sentiment in England. During the war, in fact, most of the crusaders against the Church temporarily gave up the effort to attract the public's attention to the 'Mormon peril'. The one notable exception was Winifred Graham, who continued her series of anti-Mormon novels and occasionally still made headlines with her sensational accusations, even during the war years. To the customary story of Mormon missionaries seducing girls in order to maintain the practice of polygamy in Utah, she added the charge that the Mormons were behind the German war effort. The *Millennial Star*'s lists of LDS war casualties were actually *German* war dead, she claimed. (Thorp, 'Winifred Graham'.) President Richards and other British Mission spokesmen regularly refuted such charges through the pages of the *Star*, but what was most encouraging was that they were also frequently able to refute them in the very newspapers which had printed Graham's stories. In addition, other papers now sometimes printed factual articles about the Church on their own initiative, and occasionally published interviews with Church members. With the end of the war, the saints began to hope for unharassed proselytizing and the return of a large corps of full-time missionaries. (*MS 76*: 593–7; *77*: 586–7; *79*: 88–95, 267–71, 280–1, 341–3, 458–9, 504–6, 520–3; H. M. Smith, 4: 158–60, 5: 99–100.)

Unfortunately, however, the war's end did not bring immediate relief from the shortage of missionaries in Britain. Only one new missionary came to the British Mission during the six months following the armistice of November 1918, and this was Elder Junius F. Wells, appointed in April 1919 to succeed Elder Sjodahl in editing the *Millennial Star*. Elder Wells, a mature Church worker of sixty-four, had served an earlier mission to Britain (1872–4) and in 1875 had been assigned by President Brigham Young to organize the first Young Men's Mutual Improvement Association (YMMIA) in the Church. (*MS 81*: 232–3.)

In addition to this valuable new assistant, President Richards continued to have the services of two other particularly capable and faithful missionaries: John E. Cottam and James Gunn McKay. Elder Cottam arrived in June 1915, and before his six-year mission ended in March 1921, he served as secretary to three British Mission presidents: Hyrum M. Smith, George F. Richards and George Albert Smith. Elder McKay arrived in December 1915 and was soon appointed president of the London Conference. Here he laboured for over five years, during which time the conference grew in size from six to thirteen branches. Elder McKay was a pioneer in using the local sisters as missionaries, and just after the war he developed a popular slide lecture called 'Utah and Her People'. (*MS 83*: 154–5.)

Thus, in the early months of 1919, President George F. Richards had the assistance of a small but effective four-member missionary corps. All the branches in the mission were under the care of local leaders and almost all the proselytizing was being done by local missionaries, most of them women. Then, about the time of the June arrival of a new mission president, George Albert Smith, the missionary force was augmented by a dozen new missionaries from America. After this, however, it was another year before additional missionaries were permitted to enter Britain. (*MS 82*: 721, *83*: 123–4.)

These long delays in the arrival of new missionaries were due only in part to the natural aftermath of war and the shortage of shipping berths between England and America. Such problems were alleviated within months of the armistice. After that, the barriers were primarily political ones, as the British government refused to grant visas to Mormon missionaries. (Thorp, 'British Government'.)

This abrupt change in the government's position was a shock to the Church, especially in the light of the fair-minded attitude that the Home Secretary, Winston Churchill, had maintained throughout the 1910–14 anti-Mormon campaign. During the war, however, there had been a considerable shift in the political orientation of the British government, even though no general election had been held. At the end of the war there was a new Home Secretary, Edward Shortt, and several other officials who were apparently opposed to the re-admission of Mormon missionaries into England. As stated in a memorandum from the Home Office's assistant secretary for legal matters:

> Most people consider them as no better than white slave traders. Perhaps this does them an injustice: but...I think the [Foreign Office] sh[oul]d be told that their presence here w[oul]d be strongly resented by large classes of the community and w[oul]d be likely to lead to hostile demonstrations. (*Ibid.* p. 315.)

To this the Home Secretary added his opinion: 'I agree. A Mormon [can] come here on business, but Mormon missionaries w[oul]d certainly lend to disorder.' (*Ibid.*) Possibly this opinion was influenced by Mr Shortt's residence in Sunderland in 1912, when that city had been characterized as the 'storm centre' of anti-Mormon agitation in the North.

The new British Mission president, George Albert Smith, pointed out that the missionaries had proselytized in Britain for eighty-two years without any such treatment by the government, and that the Church had voluntarily withdrawn them during the war only to further the common effort of Britain and the United States. The Latter-day Saints had served honourably in the armed forces of both countries and, as testified by Herbert Hoover with respect to USA war relief for England and Europe, 'none did more in proportion to their numbers than the Utah Mormons'. (*Ibid.* pp. 314–16.) In view of this record, President Smith concluded:

> We cannot believe in return it is the deliberate intention of the British government to do us the great injustice of denying the resumption of our labors here, now that the war is over; or to deprive the British members of our Church of the services of their necessary and customary missionary force. Should such treatment be fair? (*Ibid.*)

But his appeal seemed to fall on deaf ears, and President Smith turned to American political leaders for help, particularly the two Utah senators, Reed Smoot and William H. King. Soon Senator Smoot was able to enlist the aid of the acting U.S. Secretary of

State, Frank L. Polk, and following his intercession the Home Office at last agreed to grant the missionary visas.

President George Albert Smith was informed of this decision on 27 May 1920, and in July the first twelve missionaries arrived. Thirty-four more came that year, and more than a hundred arrived the next. Hence by the time President Smith was released in July 1921, the missionary force was beginning to resemble the 'normal' force of the pre-war era. (*Ibid.* p. 321; *MS 82*:490–1; R. Evans, p. 243.)

Contrary to the expectations of the government, the anti-Mormon campaign that started in 1921 never gained much momentum. Inflammatory newspaper accounts, lurid novels and even anti-Mormon dramas and films were rife for a year or two, but only a small part of the British public paid any heed. In fact, an unexpected result came from this campaign: *defenders* of the Mormons began to protest about unfounded press attacks and to denounce mob action. By 1924 the defenders, who included an increasing number of newspaper editors and reporters, began to outnumber the attackers, and the most far-reaching result of this last major anti-Mormon campaign was to bring 'Mormonism' to the attention of more people – and in a more favourable light.

Nevertheless, when substantial numbers of American missionaries began to arrive in 1920, no one knew exactly what to expect, and the particular proselytizing activity that seemed most likely to provoke trouble was the 'street meeting'. When anti-Mormon campaigns stirred up antagonism, street meetings could become dangerous, as they were obviously a prime place for instigating mob action. The missionaries had to exercise great caution, and there were even some periods when mission leaders, sensing potential trouble, instructed missionaries not to hold street meetings for a while. One such time occurred when Elder Ezra Taft Benson, as a young missionary, was labouring in Sunderland in 1923. Years later, as president of the Church, he recalled:

> One time we received a letter from mission headquarters instructing us that we should discontinue all street meetings... When that instruction arrived, we already had a meeting scheduled for the following Sunday night. So we reasoned that we would hold that meeting and then discontinue street meetings thereafter. That's where we made our mistake!

President and Sister David O. McKay seated front row, centre, at the Newcastle annual conference, Gateshead-on-Tyne, 13 May 1923. Elder McKay was serving as President of the European Mission. Elder Ezra Taft Benson, then a young missionary, is seated front row, first person on the right.

The next Sunday evening we held our street meeting as scheduled. The crowd was large and unruly…

When the saloons closed, the rougher, coarser element came out on the streets, many under the influence of liquor…

Soon an attempt was made to trample us under their feet…During the excitement, my companion and I became separated…Then a big husky fellow came up to me…and said, 'Young man, I believe every word you said tonight!'

By this time a British policeman had worked his way through the crowd. He took me by the arm and…led me several blocks and then ordered, 'Now you get to your lodge and don't come out anymore tonight.'

When I arrived at the lodge, I found that my companion was not yet there. I worried and then prayed and waited. I became so concerned about him that I decided to disguise my appearance by putting on an old American cap and taking off my topcoat. Then I went out to try to find him.

As I neared the place of the meeting, a man recognized me and asked, 'Have you seen your companion?'

I said, 'No. Where is he?'

He responded, 'He's down on the other side of the railway station with one side of his head mashed in.'

This frightened me greatly, and I sprinted to the site as fast as I could. Before I reached the railway station, however, I met the same policeman again. He said, 'I thought I told you to stay in...'

I replied, 'You did, officer. But I'm concerned about my companion. Do you know where he is?'

He replied, 'Yes, he got a nasty blow on the side of his head, but he's gone to the lodge now...'

So I went back to the lodge and found my companion disguising himself in order to go out and look for me. We threw our arms around each other and knelt together in prayer. From that experience I learned always to follow counsel, and that lesson has followed me all the days of my life. (*CR*, Apr 1985, pp. 48–9.)

Still, the street meeting was too effective a proselytizing tool to be given up permanently. As anti-Mormon sentiment waned and the crowds became friendlier, missionaries were soon using the outdoor meeting again in many parts of Britain. In London, such meetings sometimes attracted over a thousand people. During several of these meetings, a group of about a dozen young hecklers seemed antagonistic, but within weeks one of their ring-leaders became a serious investigator and was baptized. After that he helped at the meetings by distributing tracts, and several of his comrades also became investigators. (*MS 82*: 712–13.)

In the spring conferences of 1921, President George Albert Smith noted that the country was 'now more open for the teaching of the gospel than in several years past'. He also commented on the fact that reputable newspapers were now willing to print fair, descriptive articles regarding the Church, and spoke of the friendly attitude he had found in the well-informed public officials with whom he had contact. (*MS 83*: 234; *82*: 712–13; *83*: 408–9.)

At last the Church, instead of being connected only with polygamy, was beginning to be recognized for a diversity of accomplishments. One evidence of this new image was a well-illustrated article in the April 1921 issue of the *Millgate Monthly*, the official organ of the British Co-operative Society, which had its headquarters in Manchester. Based on the writer's research in Utah, the article read, in part:

The Mormons have been somewhat to the front of late; not as aggressive members of society or as crazy followers of a despised creed, but rather because of their exemplary character and genius, in solving some of the great problems of today. First there is the patriotism and generosity which they displayed in the war. No class in America came forward more energetically to fight in Europe than the Mormons of Utah; and no citizens of America subscribed more liberally to the various war charities than the people of Salt Lake City. This is certainly to their credit; but their presence, here and in France, has enabled us to better judge the people, and, incidentally, learn something of their methods in grappling with social and economical problems.

For instance, one of the burning questions of today is the housing problem, which has become so acute that an Inter-Allied housing and town-planning congress, consisting of architects from the Allied countries, has been appointed to deal with it. They met recently in London, and to the astonishment of our architects, and also those of France and Belgium, they found the Mormons could give the world many valuable hints in town planning, sanitation, heating, and in the creation of artistic dwellings for the people.

A deeper study of the subject reveals the fact that many of the newer cities of the West have been modelled after...Salt Lake City. It is the same in regard to education, and also in the matter of health, and in the encouragement of suitable means of recreation for the people. Not least they have developed the principles of co-operation to a fine art, and much of their prosperity to-day can be traced to their belief in co-operative methods of trading. (*MS 83*: 232–4.)

Thus this latest anti-Mormon campaign took an unusual turn. Thousands of people were beginning to be sceptical of the sensational 'true' stories, and some were even led to a personal investigation of the Church. Others went further than mere enquiry. Time and again, a malicious press account would be refuted by letters from better-informed or fairer-minded members of the community. And if the offending editor would not publish the refutation (which was often the case) there were now other editors who would. (*MS 84*: 71.)

An excellent example of such a defence was a series of letters written by a member of 'the Baptist denomination' to the *Swindon Evening Advertiser* and published therein on the 16th and 18th of January 1922:

Sir – permit me space in your columns to reply to the notes of your contributor, 'Wayfarer', upon Mormons and Mormonism. I hold no brief for them, I do not accept their theology, but I believe in fair play and toleration...

I made the acquaintance of Mormon missionaries in Swindon prior to the war. I found them well-educated and intelligent...I questioned them and probed them...I found them honest and sincere...My opinion of them was confirmed by those with whom they lived when in Swindon. I have recently met the present two who are now at their work in the town and I find them no exception to their predecessors. Your writer speaks of one of them as 'an oily individual'. Why I cannot imagine.

Now for their principles. 'Wayfarer' charges them with luring girls to Utah, and refers to what he calls their filthy wages. As a matter of fact, they draw no wages; every missionary pays his own expenses, or the money is found by members of his own family. He must not touch alcoholics, nor smoke, neither may he drink tea or coffee...

Writing in the *Daily News* last November, Helen Macdonald said: 'Salt Lake City isn't polygamous now any more than London or Paris – and I investigated as thoroughly as was possible – but the Mormons have discovered the secret of national vitality. Everywhere in the state were healthy, happy families.' In the same paper of last Friday's date appeared the report of an interview with the President of the London Mission. He said: 'Polygamy is not practiced by Mormons. It is forbidden by the United States Government and is now contrary to our principles. It is not true that we press for women converts more than men. It is not a condition that converts go to Utah; they do this at their own choice, and we advise them that if their circumstances are satisfactory in this country they should not make the change. We do not provide free passages, and we do not guarantee employment on arrival.'

Mr Whitney, President of the European Mission, said last week that 'from their headquarters in Liverpool a reward of £200 has been offered since 1911, but not claimed by anyone producing evidence of induced emigration of women or girls as alleged'.

'Wayfarer' asks, 'Why should Swindon tolerate them?' I would point out to him that his request for their violent migration can only be carried out by the police or the mob. The police must have a 'case' before they can act...If the appeal is to the mob, then I blush for the *Swindon Advertiser*...

'Wayfarer' appeals to the 'Free Churches' of Swindon to help him in his crusade. I belong to the Baptist denomination, a body that has always placed religious liberty in the forefront and has suffered heavily in that cause, and the appeal only repels me.

In a second letter, this defender of the Mormon missionaries wrote:

Sir – 'Wayfarer' does not meet my points, nor my facts, but...charges me with 'gullibility that could hardly be excelled' because I happen to be that curious type of person who likes to know both sides of a question before he expresses an opinion and to stand up for fair play for people whose views he cannot accept but whose good points he is prepared to admit.

My appeal is to reason and enquiry – that of 'Wayfarer' is to brute force. I have seen the unthinking mob...It was my dread of...such brutality towards two very mild, inoffensive American citizens that urged me to utter my protest.

Wild charges are always made against the pioneers of every religion... Prejudice and ignorance will believe and invent the worst against others...

If you accuse a man of crime give the specific details as you would be bound to do in a court of law. How is it that...no one comes forward with a case but shields themselves behind fearfully abusive generalities...? Who is the one guilty of 'gullibility that can hardly be excelled'?

If any of your readers are sufficiently interested I would suggest that when the opportunity occurs they should discuss first-hand with these 'oily individuals'. I don't for a moment think they will accept Mormon views any more than I do myself, but they will be less inclined to heave half a brick at them (*Ibid.* pp. 65–8.)

Although there were still incidents of antagonism and even violence directed at Church members throughout England during the next two years, intelligent public reaction was generally the same: disgust at the perpetrators and sympathy for the Mormons.

President Orson F. Whitney presided over the mission from July 1921 to November 1922, when he was released due to ill health. His successor, Elder David O. McKay, was of Scottish and Welsh descent. He had come to the British Isles for his first mission in 1897, and he never thereafter lost his missionary zeal. During his administration, world-wide demands upon the missionary resources of the Church brought a temporary decrease in the number of missionaries coming to England, so the missionary corps dropped from more than 150 to just over a hundred. Nevertheless President McKay – according to his successor, Elder James E. Talmage – 'carried the standard of missionary work in Great Britain to a height never before reached'. (*MS 86*: 744–5.) One of President McKay's later contributions to the Church as a whole would be to increase the involvement of local members in proselytizing. In fact, the slogan 'Every member a missionary', now familiar to Mormons throughout the world, is a product of President McKay's term as president of the British Mission, where it was adopted as a theme in 1923. (*MS 86*: 792–5.)

It was during the presidency of Elder James E. Talmage (1924–8) that the last major anti-Mormon crusade came to its inglorious conclusion. President Talmage was particularly fitted to lead the counter-campaign for reasonable and fair treatment of the saints. Born and raised in England, he had joined the Church and then emigrated to Utah at the age of fourteen. There he earned widespread respect both in and outside the LDS community as a man of God and as a scholar.

President Talmage chose the direct approach in dealing with newspaper editors. When, within a fortnight of his arrival, a journal in the Leeds district began a prejudiced serial story about the Mormons and reported that a 'secret' Mormon baptism was soon to take place in the public baths, President Talmage immediately responded by spending several days in Leeds, interviewing newspaper editors. Consequently, there were several reporters present at the baptism, as well as at every session of the district conference held just afterwards; and dozens of papers, in Leeds and elsewhere, later carried favourable articles on both the baptismal service and the conference, some even publishing photographs and interviews. The newspaper which had initially carried the adverse publicity was one of these – along with the *Manchester Guardian* and the leading papers of Leeds, Liverpool and Birmingham. From that time forward, they accorded fair treatment to the Latter-day Saints. (*MS 86*: 776–9; *87*: 27–8.)

During the next year, President Talmage extended his personal campaign to some of the London papers. Early in 1926, following a two-hour interview with Lord Beaverbrook and Viscount Castlerosse, who between them controlled several London dailies, President Talmage received the pledge of both men that they would henceforth guard against any harassment of the Mormons in their papers. In an article in the *Sunday Express* of 14 February 1926, Castlerosse admitted that his opinion of the Mormons had previously been based on highly coloured and prejudiced stories. 'Such stories', he noted, 'have been published in most of the great London daily newspapers.' After some investigation, however, he had been very favourably impressed by the Mormon mission president, Dr James E. Talmage, 'a member of the Philosophical Society and a man of unquestioned distinction and integrity', as well as by Senator Reed Smoot, a man of 'calm judgement' and 'weighty reasoning'. The viscount said he now felt it 'absurd to stigmatise a religion to which [such men] belonged as one consisting of crazy or immoral fanatics', and concluded:

> It appears to me, therefore, that the Mormons, whose creed debars the persecution of other religions, have not had fair play in this country owing to popular misconceptions. (Thorp, 'Winifred Graham', p. 114.)

It was particularly gratifying to the Latter-day Saints to receive a similar pledge of fair treatment from Lord Beaverbrook, inasmuch as his journals included the *Daily Express*, which had led most of the anti-Mormon news campaigns since 1910. (*MS 88*:122–5.)

At the end of his presidency in 1928, President Talmage summed up his experience with the British newspapers in an appreciative spirit and without any indication of his own considerable contribution to the Church's new relationship with them:

> I have had wide experience with the British editors, and regard them as a very honourable body of men. Some of those whom I met were at the head of publications of a somewhat sensational character; and misrepresentation of our Church and people had been made through contributions to such papers and magazines. But, when the misrepresentation was pointed out and demonstrated, in almost every instance the editor extended a courteous invitation to us to make reply, giving freely of their space... In Great Britain the proclaiming of the gospel message is now regarded with toleration and with a great measure of respect. (*MS 90*: 242–3.)

President Talmage's successor was another of the Church's best-known authors and scientists, Elder John A. Widtsoe. Soon after he assumed his new duties in January 1928, however, President Widtsoe and the First Presidency came to feel that the task of supervising the ten growing European missions *and* tending to the affairs of the Church in Britain had grown to the point that two separate offices were now needed. Thus, for the first time in its history, the British Mission had its own full-time president, beginning in December 1928. Whilst President Widtsoe continued, until October 1933, to preside over the European missions (which included the British Mission), Elder A. William Lund served as president of the British Mission from December 1928 to January 1932. (*MS 90*: 8–9.)

Unlike many of his predecessors in the British Mission presidency, President Lund was not an apostle. He was, none the less, a man with broad experience in the Church, including a mission to Britain twenty years earlier. He had been an assistant historian of the Church since 1911 and also served as a director of the Genealogical Society of Utah. In January 1929, early in President Lund's administration, a separate headquarters for the British Mission was established at 23 Booth Street, Handsworth, Birmingham, whilst the European Mission and *Millennial Star* editorial offices continued at Durham House, 295 Edge Lane, Liverpool. (*MS 90*: 728–9; *94*: 56–7; *91*: 8–9.)

The second president of the separated British Mission, President James H. Douglas, was a notably successful businessman and a prominent member of Rotary International. In 1932, the first year of his presidency, the mission headquarters were moved to London, at 43 Tavistock Square. Then in 1933, just months before his release, President Widtsoe secured spacious new quarters for the European Mission office at 5 Gordon Square, London. A year later, in 1934, President Douglas moved the British Mission office into this same four-storey building. Thus after five years of separation the two headquarters, along with the *Millennial Star* office, were reunited under one roof – but in London rather than in Liverpool.

In 1933 President Widtsoe was replaced as European Mission president by Elder Joseph F. Merrill, another member of the Quorum of the Twelve. A former professor of physics and engineering, President Merrill had also served as Commissioner of Education for the Church. From December 1934 to July 1937, Joseph J. Cannon served as British Mission president. President Cannon had previously been editor of the *Millennial Star* (1902–4) and editor of the *Deseret News* (1930–4). At 5 Gordon Square he had the company of President Merrill until September 1936, and then of Elder Richard R. Lyman of the Quorum of the Twelve. (*MS 94*: 88–9; 95:616–17; *96*:760; *98*:629–30.)

The decade of the 1920s brought hardship to many of the British saints. During the war, Britain's concentration on war industries had interrupted her production of manufactured goods, whereupon countries like the United States and Japan, less involved in the war and favoured with rapidly growing economies, had taken over many former British markets. As many members' employment had been linked directly or indirectly to Britain's textile factories, coal mines and other export industries, they were now experiencing very hard times.

One of the harder pressed areas was Wales, where the livelihood of many Church members depended on the coal-mining industry. In 1925–6 the Welsh miners faced their greatest crisis. The report of a royal commission indicated that many of the mines simply could not compete with the cheaper coal produced in other countries nor with the rising petroleum industry, and when the pit owners threatened a cut in wages, the long-suffering miners went on strike – for seven long months. After that, as many drifted back to work (at lower wages and longer hours), others found their mines permanently closed and themselves out of work.

President James E. Talmage, in this crisis, called upon Church members to maintain a conciliatory spirit, and complimented them on their abstinence from violence:

> Members of the Church have been directly involved; yet, so far as we know, none of them have been guilty of individual lawlessness. This is as it should be; for it is a cardinal doctrine of the Church, and a required observance on the part of its members, that they shall be orderly and law abiding. (*MS 88*: 312–13.)

Further advice was forthcoming at the October 1926 conference of the Welsh district, meeting in Varteg, a small coal-mining town in South Wales. At this time there were 120 members in the entire district, and only twenty of them priesthood-holders. Pontypool and Abercarn were the only fully organized branches, though regular meetings were also being held in several additional towns and cities. At the conference, President Talmage addressed the timely subject of 'practical religion', detailing the proper role of religion as a guide through life:

> What can religion do for us in the present state of national disturbance and distress? Deprivation of the ordinary comforts of life, the pangs of hunger and the chill of fireless homes are realities that test the souls of men and women.
>
> Religion should teach us to stand for the right and at the same time to be mindful of the rights of others. There can be no industrial stability, no real progress in civilization, no rising from the earthly to the heavenly, when capitalism oppresses labour and labour wars with capital. Neither of these can say to the other, 'I have no need of thee.' The Gospel of Jesus Christ comprises the teachings of the Savior, and these will save if men will only put them into practice in their lives. (*MS 88*: 716–17.)

Exemplifying the 'practical religion' President Talmage advocated, the British Mission's Relief Societies did yeoman service that autumn and winter. As reported in March 1927:

> The stress and struggle incident to and resulting from the great strike brought both opportunity and responsibility to Relief Societies. In many branches treasuries were depleted in affording relief to those whose distress was greatest... Our hearts were made glad by the response...to the suggestion...that those [Relief Societies] who had a surplus should help their sister organizations who had little or nothing. A beautiful spirit of self-sacrifice was shown...(*MS 89*: 148–9.)

When the USA stock market crash of 1929 widened into a

world-wide depression, Britain, with her dependence on international trade, proved vulnerable. By 1933 national unemployment had jumped to three million, its highest level in history. As a guide to the British saints in these trying conditions, the *Millennial Star* of 12 October 1933 published the 'Relief Message of the First Presidency', presenting the Church's welfare programme. Its fundamental principles included self-reliance, caring for one another within the Church community, avoidance of charity that offered 'something for nothing', and the performance of some service in return for aid. It also urged upon the saints

> the paramount necessity of living righteously, of avoiding extravagance, of cultivating habits of thrift, economy and industry, of living strictly within our means, and of laying aside something, however small it may be, for the times of greater stress that may come. (*MS* 95:664–5.)

By observing these principles, the British saints not only survived the 1930s but grew strong in the process. In fact, the degree to which they rose above the mere struggle for necessities was evidenced by the chapel-acquisition programme. For instance, during the coal-mining crisis in the mid-1920s, a new chapel was acquired at Norwich; and at the very depth of the Great Depression, in 1933, the saints in Hull succeeded in building a chapel. In this case, a large donation from one person was a major factor of their success, however. Sister Julia Foster and her husband had worked and saved for many years to emigrate to Utah. But when her husband died just before their hopes were to be realized, Sister Foster decided to contribute her savings to the branch building fund. (*MS 87*:249; *95*:757–8.)

The next year, all the branches in the British Mission competed to develop the best plan for a branch building-fund programme. Sheffield Branch's prize-winning plan relied principally on an individual assessment, to be agreed upon between each branch member and the branch president, according to the member's ability to contribute. By such means, and with aid from Church headquarters, Sheffield and several other branches were able to realize their dreams within just a few years. (*MS 96*:428–9; *97*: 76–7; *98*:54–5.)

By 1935, twelve chapels formed the 'growing circle... expanding toward the realization of a mission-wide ideal, a Church-owned chapel with attendant facilities for every branch in the British Mission'. The twelve fortunate branches were Kidderminster, Northampton, Handsworth, Oldham, Manchester, Sunderland, Sheffield, Lowestoft, Norwich, West Hartlepool, Hull and Burnley. Twenty-one branches, of the seventy-three in the mission, had established building funds. (*Ibid.*)

In 1937, at the peak of the chapel-acquisition programme, the saints in Britain took advantage of the centennial visit of the prophet, President Heber J. Grant, to dedicate seven new and recently acquired chapels. In addition to Burnley, completed in 1935, the dedications included Bradford, Rochdale, Merthyr Tydfil, Liverpool, South-west London and North London. Of special note were the chapels at Merthyr Tydfil (the first in Wales) and the one at 301 Edge Lane, Liverpool. The latter was just a few steps from Durham House, which had been acquired for the Church in 1906 by President Heber J. Grant when he was British Mission president and which had been the European Mission headquarters until 1933. (*MS 99*:485–6, 569–9.)

The chapel acquisitions of the 1920s–1930s were in keeping with a new objective of the British Mission in the post-war era: 'Build Zion in Britain'. The long-standing desire of British saints to emigrate to 'Zion' had apparently not been diminished by the war. Although there was naturally little emigration during the war itself, many people had better incomes than in peacetime, and some had saved enough to move to America after the war. Consequently, emigration reached three hundred in 1920 alone – the highest number for years.

The next year, however, President Orson F. Whitney announced an important change in policy. Whilst the principle of gathering was not rescinded, it was to be put in abeyance. (*MS 82*:840–1; *83*:584–6.) Emigration did not halt abruptly, but it gradually slowed, leaving the British branches with more and more members to take over leadership responsibilities.

Thus, when the number of American missionaries again declined after 1932, local saints were more prepared to take over missionary duties. Priesthood-holders began to proselytize part-time, much as the sisters had done during the First World War. Under branch supervision they tracted and held meetings. By 1934 there were seventeen full-time local missionaries. In addition, local members largely staffed mission auxiliary boards and headed almost all branch auxiliaries, and sixty of the eighty branch presidents were British. With emigration to America greatly reduced after 1929, British Mission leaders began to encourage their people to put aside thoughts of emigration indefinitely:

What are Church converts to do? The answer is plain – stay where they are; live the Gospel truly, and enjoy the rewards for so living...Zion is where live the pure in heart. The Church is to be built up in these missions...

No longer are the emigrant ships carrying saints from these shores. Zion in the West has been built up. The ringing challenge on these Isles today has become: 'Build Zion in Britain', (Kerr, pp. 37–9; *MS 89*:42–3; *95*:152–3, 840–1; *96*: 312–13; *98*:54–5.)

In the summer of 1937 the British Mission was one hundred years old. A remarkable celebration of that event took place in July, which graphically demonstrated how well the converts of that first century, along with the 5,947 missionaries who had served in the mission, had succeeded in building Zion in Britain. Though incomplete, records showed that over 52,000 of the 126,593 persons baptized in the British Mission during that first century had emigrated to America, thus playing an indispensable role in the building of Zion there. But those converts who had lived out their lives in Britain, helping the foreign missionaries and edifying themselves and their families by gospel living, had also erected the solid foundation, organization and physical edifices that the Church proudly displayed during that centennial celebration.

In observance of the centennial, Church president Heber J. Grant arrived in England on 19 July 1937, just one hundred years after the arrival of Elder Heber C. Kimball and his six companions. President Grant was accompanied by his grandson, Elder Richard G. Smith; his secretary, Joseph Anderson; and Elder Hugh B. Brown, who came to replace President Joseph J. Cannon of the British Mission. Within the next two days, President Grant's first counsellor, J. Reuben Clark, Jr, with Sister Clark and a contingent of more than fifty Church leaders, arrived in England to participate in two weeks of festivities and conferences. (*IE*, Sep 1937, pp. 540–2, 576; *MS 99*, *passim*.)

Highlights of the ten days of preliminary activities were the dedications of several chapels by President Grant, beginning with the recently acquired building in Liverpool. This was dedicated on the 20th of July. Over the next seven days five more chapels were dedicated, ending with the one in Merthyr Tydfil. The seventh chapel to be dedicated was at Rochdale. It was here and in nearby Preston, site of the first proselytizing activities in Britain, that the four-day centennial conference was held.

The activities began on Friday the 30th of July, with the dedication of a commemorative plaque on the banks of the River Ribble, scene of the mission's first baptisms; and they ended on Monday the 2nd of August, with an impressive MIA sports tournament and a centennial ball. The Rochdale town hall, with a seating capacity of one thousand, could not contain the audience which assembled on Saturday evening for the presentation of a pageant by a cast of 200. A repeat performance had to be scheduled the following evening for the hundreds turned away. The three Sunday conference sessions also overflowed the town hall and, by means of a public address system, additional hundreds in the car-park and garden listened to memorable messages from their Church and mission leaders. (*Ibid.*)

Two years before the centennial celebration, another kind of all-mission gathering had been inaugurated: the first mission-wide MIA conference. Under the direction of Elder G. Homer Durham, superintendent of the mission Young Men's MIA, and taking as its theme 'Build Zion Today', this first MIA conference met for three days in June 1935 at Kidderminster, Worcestershire. Approximately 300 attended, including 91 missionaries, 40 members of branch presidencies and 15 members of district presidencies. The response of those who participated in this conference was so enthusiastic that for several years it was an annual event. (*MS 97*: 362–3.) The last of these conferences was in June 1939, when more than seven hundred participants met at Sheffield. Speakers included President Hugh B. Brown of the British Mission and Elder Joseph Fielding Smith of the Council of the Twelve Apostles. In keeping with the growing apprehension of the times, the theme of this last pre-war conference was 'Peace, Purpose and Power through Applied Christianity'. (*MS 101*: 370–2.)

At this 1939 MIA conference were displayed two new instruments the British Mission had developed for putting the Church before a larger public. These exhibits were a baseball game between two missionary teams and a musical programme by a missionary chorus. What made these events unusual was the fact that the groups involved were not just hastily organized for this conference: the Rochdale Greys and the All Stars were top teams in the national baseball league, and the Millennial Chorus was a nationally recognized singing group.

Of all the activities of Latter-day Saints in Britain in the 1930s, perhaps those that best promoted a favourable image for the Church were the ones involving baseball, basketball and the Millennial Chorus. In 1935, the first year of organized league baseball in Britain, two teams composed of Mormon missionaries rose to prominence. In the national finals, the London missionary team, known as the Latter-day Saints, defeated the Rochdale missionary team for the title, becoming England's first national baseball champions. The next year the National Baseball Association decided to establish two professional leagues, and six of London's largest stadiums sponsored teams in the London Major League, with Catford Stadium in south-east London sponsoring the Latter-day Saints. The Catford Saints, as they then came to be called, were the only amateur team participating in their circuit, as were the Rochdale Greys in the North of England League.

In 1936, and again in 1937, the Rochdale Greys won the North of England championship. On 31 July 1937, this same team played (and defeated) the Liverpool Caledonians in a Saturday afternoon league game featured as part of the British Mission centennial. President Heber J. Grant, a lifetime baseball fan and still vigorous at 80, joined the team in their pre-game 'battle song' and pitched the first ball (*IE*, Feb 1938, pp. 86–8, 117; *MS 98*:666–9.)

In Rochdale, the LDS baseball players were well known by this time:

'Bobbies' on the street corners ask them how the prospects for the next game look...The town paper, which three years ago wouldn't accept a paid advertisement from the 'Mormons', last year devoted an entire page to the team and its activities. In less than a year there have been almost fifty new members converted to the Church in Rochdale. (*IE*, *ibid.*)

Nor was the Rochdale team's fame limited to one city. An article in the *Daily Mirror* observed:

Rochdale Greys – Champions of the North of England League – are a team of missionaries. Baseball followers know them as fine players and sportsmen, but how many know them as religious teachers? These boys are missionaries of the Church of Jesus Christ of Latter-day Saints, in other words, Mormons. They have worked and played themselves right into the hearts of the people. Not one of them is more than 23, and not one gets a cent remuneration or expenses. (*MS 94*: 109–10.)

In the London area, however, the Catford Saints were the favourites. In the 1936 baseball season they reached the finals of the National Cup, but were defeated by the White City team in the huge White City Stadium, site of the 1908 Olympic Games. Later, Elder Wendell J. Ashton, manager and player for the Catford Saints, received a letter from the secretary of the White City team:

We always hoped and needed to play our best game against our L.D.S. friends. Most important of all, however, was the sporting spirit in which every game was played, and I regard those games in which I was privileged to participate against you last year as ample reward for the work which has devolved upon me in connection with baseball.

Although you came to this country as missionaries of your Church, your success as ambassadors of goodwill has earned a special debt of gratitude from the general public both here and in the States. (*MS 98*:666–9.)

In the 1937 season the Catford Saints reached the national quarter-finals, and in 1938 the Rochdale Greys won the national championship. By 1938 the Hull, Bradford, Rochdale and Birmingham M-Men teams, composed of local Saints and missionaries, were competing in amateur leagues. 'Do you know that the Rochdale M-Men train on our "American Specials"?' proclaimed a sign in a local milk bar, which also offered a drink called the 'M-Men Special'. (*IE, ibid.*; *MS, ibid.*)

In the late 1930s LDS basketball teams became as well known as the baseball teams. Like baseball, basketball was a relatively new sport in Britain. The National Basketball Association was formed in 1935, and in the 1936 season a London LDS basketball team, made up of missionaries who worked in the London district and the British Mission office, won the London League championship. In March 1937, they defeated the Hoylake YMCA 1936 national champions; and to a listening radio audience of millions, announcer Dick Cartwright observed: 'These Latter-day Saints neither drink nor smoke, and their condition shows it.' Although defeated by the same YMCA team for the 1937 national championship, the

Saints went on to achieve their greatest basketball successes in 1938. (*Ibid.*)

In order to take advantage of the Catford Saints' baseball fame, the London missionaries' basketball team assumed that same name. With several players from the baseball team, the Mormon missionary basketball Saints also rose to prominence, playing in the British national basketball championship games held in Wembley Stadium in April 1938. (And the other finalist team was none other than the Rochdale Greys, who had also expanded successfully from baseball into basketball and had retained the same team name.) By winning that championship, the Catford Saints earned the right to represent England and Wales in international competition against Germany, France and Belgium. Successful against the German team in the first round (whilst the French defeated the Belgians), the Catford Saints went on to win 'The Grand International Tourney of Basketball' by defeating the French team at Lille. Upon the team's return to Britain, their manager Mr Browning reported to the national committee:

> It was a pleasure to accompany such an exemplary group of young men on this trip as manager. Their conduct at all times was above reproach. On the basketball floor their clean play and sportsmanship made them very popular with the large crowds who saw them play... They were a distinct credit to the highest traditions of British sportsmanship. (*IE*, Aug 1938, pp. 476, 502–3; *MS 100*: 292.)

Even as these LDS-missionary baseball and basketball teams were winning renown for the Mormons in the eyes of British sports fans, an LDS-missionary singing group known as the Millennial Chorus was winning the applause of other thousands throughout Britain. This group had been organized during the memorable first mission-wide MIA conference at Kidderminster. At the direction of President Joseph J. Cannon, sixteen of the ninety missionaries in attendance were chosen for a special assignment. For several months they tracted by day and then sang at nightly street meetings and at district conferences. In August they began to present concerts in schools and churches, then at cinemas, and several times on the radio. By 1938 the chorus had become a polished singing group with several outstanding soloists, and an article in the *Millennial Star* of 18 August 1938 concluded:

With two or three performances each day...before audiences of up to two and three thousand each session, it is not over-estimating to say that in one week more than 25,000 people are coming in contact with these singing ambassadors...[–people who] cannot help but admire the views and conduct of this outstanding group of young men...There is not a more effective means of making friends for the Church in Britain than through the efforts of the members of the Millennial Chorus...(*IE*, Feb 1937, pp. 92–5; *MS 100*: 520–1.)

As these LDS athletic and choral groups had been well known in Britain for several years, it was no surprise to the British saints, though it must have been particularly gratifying, to read on 25 August 1938 in the *Daily Express* (one of the erstwhile leaders of anti-Mormon campaigns):

The faith of the Mormons, which began in ridicule, now stands in dignity and respect. They have created a worthy and useful institution whose members do good by teaching and by the example of their upright lives.

And two days after the *Express* article, the British news magazine *Cavalcade* presented a similar opinion of the Church, in an article about the Mormon baseball teams. It concluded:

Since [the Mormons] arrived in this country one hundred years ago they have had to fight against blind prejudice brought about by untrue stories...In the years that have passed they have succeeded in living down this calumny...(*IE*, Dec 1938, pp. 719, 758; *MS 100*: 556–7.)

Obviously the days of persecution and violence against the saints in Britain were past, and the Church's prospects for future expansion looked bright. However, within a month of the *Express* and *Cavalcade* articles about the Church, British papers were filled with news of a different sort: accounts of the September 1938 Munich conferences of Prime Minister Neville Chamberlain with the Italian prime minister, Benito Mussolini, and the German chancellor, Adolf Hitler. In one more year, Germany would invade Poland, Britain would go to war, and the Church baseball and basketball teams, the Millennial Chorus and, to a large extent, the Church's proselytizing work in Britain, would come to an abrupt halt.

12

War and Recovery, 1939–1950

LOUIS B. CARDON

AT THE BEGINNING of the Second World War, the withdrawal of the American missionaries from the British Mission was sudden and complete. Less than three weeks after Britain's declaration of war in September 1939, all American missionaries were back in the States, except for a very few who, with mission president Hugh B. Brown, were ordered home soon afterward.

Precipitous as it seemed at the time, the evacuation of missionaries from Europe had actually been foreseen, and preparations had been made for it some time before the outbreak of war. President Heber J. Grant, before and after his participation in the British Mission centennial in 1937, had visited a number of the missions on the Continent, and though favourably impressed by conditions in the missions, he had been disturbed by Germany's armaments programme and by the prospect of troubled times ahead. With prophetic insight, he began to urge the European saints not to be dependent upon the missionaries and to assume more Church and priesthood responsibilities. (*CR*, Apr 1940, p. 20.)

In the summer of 1938 President Grant sent his first counsellor, the experienced diplomat J. Reuben Clark, Jr, to tour the European missions. During this tour President Clark assembled the mission presidents for a conference in Berlin and there discussed the possible need to recall the missionaries. He instructed each president to formulate a detailed plan for such an evacuation, and suggested that Switzerland, the Netherlands and the Scandinavian countries might be the best avenues for leaving the Continent. (Murdock, p. 116.)

Within six weeks of this conference the first test of the new evacuation plans occurred, as the Sudetenland crisis brought Europe to the brink of war. The missionaries from the German and Czechoslovakian Missions were quickly withdrawn to neutral countries, according to plan, but then were allowed to return to their fields of labour two weeks later when the Munich Conference alleviated the prospect of immediate war. It was only a year after this 'drill', however, that Poland was invaded and the general evacuation plans were activated in earnest. Although troop movements were under way before the withdrawal could be completed, and great courage and ingenuity were required to bring the operation to its successful conclusion, most of the missionaries were back in America soon after the order to evacuate.

Orderliness in this complicated process was aided by the presence of Elder Joseph Fielding Smith in Europe during the final crisis. As a member of the Quorum of the Twelve Apostles, he had been visiting the European missions throughout the summer of 1939, and on the 24th of August was conducting a conference in the West German Mission. That day President Heber J. Grant, in Salt Lake City, recorded in his journal:

> Last night telegrams were sent warning our mission presidents in Europe to be ready at a moment's notice to leave. The dispatches today showed that war seems to be almost inevitable and that England and France are recommending that Americans leave for home at once. (Boone, p. 14.)

The following day, the 25th of August, Elder Smith received another telegram, instructing him to direct the evacuation of all missionaries from the areas threatened by war, starting with the Czechoslovakian and German Missions. He immediately set up headquarters in the Netherlands and proceeded to carry out these instructions.

Within another ten days Germany had invaded Poland – and Great Britain was at war. But before that declaration of war on 3 September 1939 the missionaries had already been evacuated from the most endangered countries, and evacuation from the others was under way. In view of the chaotic conditions prevailing in Europe's transportation and communications networks during those few days, this was an amazing accomplishment, but the success of the operation had been greatly facilitated by the advance warning received through Church leaders. (*Ibid.* pp. 12–15.)

Back in Britain, President Hugh B. Brown was conducting a conference in Edinburgh when news of the crisis on the Continent reached him. He immediately returned to London and there, on the 23rd of August, he found a telegram from the First Presidency instructing him to arrange immediate passage to the United States for all seventeen of his sister missionaries, as well as his own wife and children. Fortunately, having followed earlier instructions, President Brown had already reserved 100 spaces on the United States Lines, to be used when needed. Thus, at a moment when thousands of people in London were trying to book passage to America, President Brown and his transportation secretary simply bypassed the long ticket queues and picked up their reservations. (*Ibid.* pp. 99–100.)

In consultation with Elder Smith, President Brown decided that it would be wiser to send his missionaries home directly from Britain rather than to have them assemble with the other European missionaries in neutral Scandinavian countries. So, despite the sisters' great reluctance to leave Britain when no war was actually under way, they boarded an American ship at Southampton on the 31st of August.

By this time the elders were already assembling at the London mission home in preparation for their return home. The members of the Millennial Chorus, on tour in Scotland when President Brown's telegram reached them, were among the last to arrive, but last of all were the ten Ireland-based elders. They had originally been instructed to depart directly from the Irish port of Cobh, near Cork, on a British ship, but after Britain declared herself at war on the 3rd of September, President Brown thought it safer to bring them to London and put them on an American ship with the other missionaries. (*Ibid.* pp. 100–5.)

The elders who had reached London by the 3rd of September (a Sunday) gathered in President Brown's office at 11.15 that morning to hear the Prime Minister, Neville Chamberlain, announce to the world Britain's declaration of war. It was obvious, some of them later recalled, that President Brown was the member of the group most affected by the announcement. Having fought in the

First World War as a Canadian officer and knowing too well the horrors to which Britain would be subjected again, he seemed to 'age five years' before their eyes. They also recalled, however, that amidst the hectic activities of those first days of the war, as anti-aircraft guns and balloons were being set up around London, gas masks issued, buildings sandbagged, and the missionaries themselves detailed to dig a bomb shelter behind the south London Ravenslea chapel, President Brown often talked informally with them about marriage, family life and other subjects far removed from war. These sessions, in which he shared his experiences and thoughts with them, helped these young men to keep their perspective on life and fortified them for the trials that some of them would soon face. (*Ibid.* pp. 105–11.)

On the 12th of September, following a final testimony meeting and a farewell song by the Millennial Chorus, the 107 elders who were returning to America boarded the crowded U.S.S. *Washington.* (The president himself, and a select staff of six experienced missionaries, remained a few weeks longer to complete arrangements for the transfer of mission direction to local members.) The passengers on the *Washington* (including the U.S. Ambassador Joseph P. Kennedy and his sons John, Robert and Edward) had some tense moments when they were stopped by a German submarine verifying the ship's nationality, but there were also some more relaxed moments as the LDS Millennial Chorus presented its last performances before being disbanded in America. (*Ibid.* pp. 111–13.)

The departing missionaries were part of a general exodus of foreigners from Britain, resulting both from the dangers which lay ahead and from the specific request of the British government. President Brown took care to let the British saints know that the missionaries were not leaving by their own choice, or even because of Church directives based primarily on concern for their safety. In a *Millennial Star* editorial of 14 September 1939 he explained:

> We are sure the saints and friends will receive word of this evacuation with sorrow. No one, however, will be as deeply affected by the order as the missionaries themselves. To many it means an early termination of their missionary service; to others, a transfer into new fields of labour; and to all, departure from a land and a people they have learned to love.
>
> Both the lady missionaries and the elders have expressed deep regret. Each would have preferred to stay at his post and carry on.

> The decision of the general authorities of the Church to withdraw the missionaries was reached after consultation with the government officials. In making the decision the welfare of the saints and of the Church in the British Isles was uppermost in the mind of the presiding brethren.
>
> Neutral nations, and especially friendly nations, endeavor to avoid adding to the burdens or increasing the difficulties of the nations that are involved in war...Britain...concurs [that] Americans could best serve the cause by returning home.
>
> Thus, the decision to evacuate the missionaries was reached by the government and Church authorities not, primarily, to safeguard the lives of those concerned, but rather as being the wise and proper thing to do under the circumstances. (Campbell and Poll, p. 138; *MS 101*:584–5.)

It was not long before the transition staff of six missionaries and President Brown were also called home. Three of the missionaries left in October and the remaining three with President Brown on 15 January 1940.

Three days before, on the 12th of January, President Brown had set apart three British elders as the acting presidency of the mission. The three men chosen for this challenging assignment had previously been serving as the presidency of the London District. President Andre K. Anastasiou (who changed his name to 'Anastasion' when he emigrated to Utah in 1945), the acting mission president, had been born in Russia but had come to England at the age of nineteen. Shortly thereafter he was introduced to the Church through a business associate. He was baptized in 1918, filled a short-term mission near the end of the First World War, married a young LDS woman, and had since served in many Church offices, including those of branch and district president. (Anastasion, autobiography, *passim.*)

President Anastasiou was fortunate to have particularly capable and loyal counsellors. James P. Hill served for a time as first counsellor and also directed publication of the *Millennial Star*. After a few months he was replaced as counsellor by George H. Bailey, president of the Sheffield District, but he continued to edit the *Star* throughout the war, and even after the release of the Anastasiou presidency. James R. Cunningham was the second counsellor, with special responsibility for the Sunday School and for genealogical work. (Anastasion, *ibid.* pp. 82, 84; *MS 102*:48.)

President Anastasiou's position was considered a full-time missionary calling, but at first the two counsellors continued in their

Andre K. Anastasiou – Acting British Mission president, 1940–4.

Selvoy J. Boyer – British Mission president, 1946–50; London Temple president, 1958–64; director of the British Mission's post-Second World War recovery.

professions and performed their Church work on a part-time basis. The demands upon their time were so great, however, that both soon decided to accept President Anastasiou's call to devote all their time to Church service. For President Cunningham, that involved particular sacrifice, as he was obliged to sell his home and furniture to finance his mission. For a time his family (and President Hill's) lived in the Gordon Square mission headquarters; after that was damaged by bombs, they moved to the large Ravenslea building where the Anastasious already lived. Later in the war, when enough short-term missionaries had been called to lessen the demands upon the presidency's time, President Cunningham worked in an aircraft factory twelve hours a day. (R. West collection: James R. Cunningham interview, 27 Nov 1985; notes of an address by same, 4 Jul 1985, Sutton Coldfield Stake.)

When President Brown and the last three American missionaries left in January 1940, it was the first time in the 103-year history of the Church in Britain that the mission was totally without missionaries from the USA. The first missionary, Elder Heber C. Kimball, had prophesied, however, that the day would come when the missionaries would leave and the British saints would be on their own. More recently, President Heber J. Grant, at the time of the 1937 centennial, had made a similar prophecy. Still, many of the saints were shocked when this actually occurred. As President Anastasiou later said:

> They felt depressed, unhappy, full of uncertainty and even foreboding. No longer could we call upon our Missionaries to come here and go there; to organize this, that, and the other Branch meeting, Sunday School, M.I.A., etc.; to visit the sick, to heal and comfort, to baptise new converts, and be the staff and protection of those who depended so much upon them. The Church and the Saints were left to stand on their own feet, so to speak, and to depend upon each other and carry on as best they could. A number of our members felt that they were being deserted, especially in a time like this, when the strongest in the faith were expected to stay and look after them. Some even stopped coming to meetings. Little these members knew that every Missionary sent here from Zion...was willing to stand by the Saints and stay on, whatever happened... They had to go in compliance with the orders of both Governments. (Boone, p. 118; *MS 102*:143; *104*:242–3.)

Even as President Brown issued his last challenge to the saints to live the gospel and care for each other, he seemed apprehensive that Church activities might have to be seriously curtailed. He counselled President Anastasiou 'to hold the fort and not move out very much'. According to the latter, President Brown also 'was very doubtful as to whether the *Millennial Star* could be continued by local brethren with only spare time at their disposal'. However, the general authorities were strongly in favour of its continuance if at all possible, since it was the oldest Church publication and an established bulwark of the faith in Britain. (Anastasion, autobiography, p. 84; *MS 102*:346.) As President Anastasiou admitted later:

> The scope and magnitude of the work seemed tremendous, the responsibility great and even awe-inspiring... For about three months we sat 'holding the fort', but in the meantime, the monthly reports from the 68 branches of the church scattered throughout the cities of England, Wales, Scotland and Ireland, were coming in and we had to organize ourselves to carry on the British Mission. (Anastasion, *op. cit.* p. 84; *MS 104*:242–3.)

The reports showed that many members were carrying on the activities of the branches and looking after each other's needs as well as they could, but it was also evident that other members, particularly those isolated from branch centres or living in small branches that had given up their leaders to the call of national service, had lost contact with the Church.

During the First World War, when a similar shortage of branch leaders had developed, a test case had been tried in the British courts to determine whether an LDS branch president was entitled to ministerial exemption from war service. Although the case took nearly two years to work its way through the courts, the verdict had been in favour of the Church, the court recognizing that The Church of Jesus Christ of Latter-day Saints was a legitimate religious denomination in Britain and that its branch presidents were legitimate ministers. By the time this verdict was rendered, the First World War was almost over and there was no need for the Church (even if so inclined) to seek general exemption for branch presidents. (*MS 79*: 238–9, 300–1, 312–13, 764–5; *80*: 42–3.)

Early in 1940, however, President Anastasiou felt that the dearth of priesthood leadership was becoming critical:

> Our...men, ordained and working in the ministry, were being called to serve their Country... We had to realize that sooner or later we should have none left to take care of our Branches and Districts. I went to the Ministry of Labour and National Service to put our cause and our case before them. I received very sympathetic and very kind attention... The senior official...courteously but firmly said to me: 'We need every man and woman to serve the Country.' I agreed. 'We as a Church are alive to the situation. Most of our men have gone; those who remain shall go when called, but the King of Kings needs a few men to do His will and take care of His Church.' The conversation continued. Finally he said: 'I agree with your point of view. How many men do you need to carry on the work of your Church?' I gave him the number needed to sustain the Districts and the Branches of our Mission, and it was communicated to me later that our Elders, engaged in the Ministry of the Church, ordained in the Higher Priesthood, are recognized Ministers of Religion, or Men in Holy Orders, and entitled to exemption in accordance with the laws and provisions of the Acts of Parliament. (Anastasion, 'King of Kings', *passim*; *MS 104*: 243–4.)

Although the government's decision thus made it possible for any British Melchizedek Priesthood-holder to claim ministerial exemption from war duty, members of the Church were instructed that only branch and district leaders and those working in the mission office were expected to request this exemption. President Anastasiou later observed that even some of those who *might* have claimed exemption from military service on such grounds nevertheless volunteered to join the armed forces or, if they remained at their Church posts, also performed war work on weekdays. (During the first year after the war's end, while obligatory registration for military service was still in effect, President Selvoy Boyer, first post-war British Mission president, instituted strict controls to ensure that no LDS priesthood-holders except branch and district presidents *would* utilize the ministerial exemption. Its use was terminated altogether soon after that.) (Anastasion, *op. cit.*; British Mission History, 29 Sep 1946; R. West collection, *passim.*)

It was a relief to the mission presidency and to the district presidents, in 1940, to know that some priesthood-holders would continue to be available to serve as branch leaders. Over the next three years the presidency even found it possible to re-organize several branches that had been disbanded early in the war for lack of leadership. In some cases one priesthood-holder would serve two congregations, conducting services in one on Sunday morning and then travelling to the other in time to conduct services in the afternoon. (Anastasion, *op. cit.*)

Still, there were isolated small groups, families and individuals who could seldom attend any branch meetings. In order to provide these members with some contact with the Church, and in order to renew at least small-scale proselytizing in Britain, President Anastasiou decided to call a corps of local full-time missionaries. Just two days before President Hugh B. Brown had left Britain in January 1940, he had called two such missionaries to work in the mission office and help the new mission presidency. With the approval of the First Presidency, President Anastasiou called a dozen more local members on six-month full-time missions before the end of 1940. As was the case during the First World War, these were generally women, boys not yet old enough for military service, or men with health or disability deferments. By the middle of 1941 this missionary force had grown to twenty-seven, and it reached a peak of just over forty in September. After this, with increasing war demands for labour in war industries as well as in the military, the number of missionaries dropped to thirty-one at the end of 1941 and twenty-nine at the end of 1942. (*MS 103*:440–1, 579; *104*: 10, 839; *105*:40–1.)

With an average of just one pair of missionaries for each of the fourteen districts, or one pair for five branches, the mission leaders developed a rotation system that enabled each branch in the mission to have missionaries assigned to it periodically. A pair of missionaries would remain in one branch for four or five weeks, visiting the outlying members, contributing to the meetings, and proselytizing as time permitted. Then they would move on to another branch. Thus all the branches in the mission would be visited at least twice a year and some contact would be maintained with the isolated members. In April 1942 President Anastasiou was happy to report:

> These British missionaries...have covered the Branches of the Mission several times and have restored to a very great extent the spirit and the pulse of our Branches almost to a pre-war condition... The parents of all these Missionaries forget their own problems and trials when they hear of the fine Missionary work their children are doing.

Naturally it was often difficult for parents (or the missionaries themselves) to finance a mission. But the *Millennial Star* editorials of President Anastasiou, as well as the published letters of many missionaries, often told of generous gifts from unexpected sources or even full sponsorship by non-related members of modest means. In some branches members would pool their resources in order to send one of their number on a mission. And it was not infrequent for missionaries, after fulfilling one six-month term, to be provided with support for a second or even a third term. (*Ibid.*)

Despite such efforts, there were few persons in the British Mission during the war years who were able to serve a full-time mission. There were hundreds of others, however, who had a 'missionary spirit' and were willing to serve as missionaries for a few hours a week. President Anastasiou recognized this, and in the spring conferences of 1941 he started to call part-time 'home missionaries' to supplement the work of the full-time corps. The response to this new programme exceeded his expectations; in early July he reported:

> The faithful members have responded magnificently... We hope our force of Home Missionaries will exceed two hundred by the end of August... These Home Missionaries [are] sent forth...to preach the Gospel to their neighbors, relatives, families and friends, to visit the inactive members, to build up Sunday Schools, Mutual Improvement Associations, Relief Societies, Beehives and Primaries and generally proclaim the message of the Restored Gospel. (*MS 103*:440–1.)

By the middle of August there were 250 home missionaries in service, some working four hours and others as many as eighteen hours per week. In September President Anastasiou reported:

The outstanding feature of all the annual Conferences has been the enthusiastic response to the call for Home Missionaries. Beginning with five Home Missionaries set apart at the Belfast Conference, every other District responded to the call with joy and readiness.

Mission and District Presidents went almost without food setting apart Home Missionaries between the Conference sessions. The hands that were lifted up presented a sight in almost every Conference that will forever live in memory. Birmingham contributed 45 Home Missionaries, Bristol 11, Hull 15, Leeds 44, Liverpool 23, London 75, Newcastle 20, Manchester 25, Nottingham 22, Sheffield 34, Scottish 20, Welsh 9, and Norwich yet to report.

358 Home Missionaries have been set apart for the sacred work in the Branches of the British Mission. Each one has received a letter of appointment; each one's record is kept in the Mission Office. (*MS 103*: 522–3, 603.)

Enthusiasm for home missionary work continued throughout President Anastasiou's administration. The number of members so engaged stood at 403 in 1942 and 433 in 1943. A brief training programme had been developed for them, special supervisors had been established, weekly reports were sent to the mission office, and the home missionaries met their district president monthly. Their first responsibility, like that of the full-time missionaries, was to visit the members, particularly the isolated or inactive ones, but they also tracted – and reported a generally cordial reception. (R. West collection: Joseph Hamstead letter, 1985; Edna Smith letter; *MS 104*: 10, 839, 92.)

For almost all the saints in Britain, the war brought many changes in everyday routines as well as in Church activities. Some members still have vivid memories of these wartime experiences today, more than forty years after the war's end. For instance, Bert Martins of the Norwich Branch recalls that wartime meetings were attended mostly by mothers with children. If a priesthood-holder was present, he might conduct the meeting, bless and pass the sacrament, *and* be the principal speaker. Sometimes the branch president 'would be the first speaker at the Lowestoft Branch, then travel 30 miles by train to be the final speaker in the Norwich Branch'. Some members were assigned a regular monthly circuit to serve as speakers for smaller groups in the district, and would travel to those meetings by bicycle or train. (R. West collection: Bert Martins interview notes.)

Veronica O. Bettinson of the Chiswick Branch recalls that branch meetings were held for a time in a small art studio with a smoky cast-iron stove that produced very little heat. When the skylights in the studio were broken in the air raids of September 1940, meetings were held in the eight-by-twelve-foot kitchen:

> Since we had only about 6–8 members coming out, that wasn't a great problem. Alf Willmott [the branch president] and Rachel, his wife, and children came clear from Enfield [across London] every Sunday. And, Alf came every Tuesday night. We had Relief Society and then MIA back-to-back, regardless of air raids. Often, when the [tube and train] lines were bombed, Alf would spend a lot of time trying to get home on foot... to Enfield.

Later in the war the Chiswick Branch was consolidated with the South London Branch, which met at the beautiful old mansion of Ravenslea. When the attendance increased with visiting servicemen, the resulting large group provided a welcome change for the branch members. (R. West collection: Veronica O. Bettinson letter, 1985.)

For some of the saints, Ravenslea – the mission home and South London chapel – played somewhat the same role in the Second World War that Deseret, the London District headquarters, had played in the First. Deseret, designated by President Penrose in his 1908 dedicatory prayer as 'a refuge in time of danger', had actually served as such during the First World War bombing raids on London. Under the direction of Elder James Gunn McKay it had served as a shelter for more than a thousand people during some of those raids. It came through the war unscathed – and Elder McKay attributed twenty conversions to the close associations and gospel conversations of those perilous occasions. (*MS 95*: 25–8.)

In the Second World War, when Britain suffered longer and more destructive air raids than in the First, an air-raid shelter was built in the basement of Ravenslea. During intensive raids on London this sometimes served as the common sleeping quarters of the mission presidency's families, the mission office staff, and others. Actually, according to the later recollection of President Cunningham, there was little sleep possible on some of those nights, because of the 'terrible noise of the bombing', but he recalls 'sitting on a blanket on the hard floor, reading aloud the Book of Mormon in turn'. Although Ravenslea did suffer some damage late in the war, it received no direct hits and there were no injuries among those who used it for refuge. (*MS 106*: 695–6; R. West collection: James R. Cunningham address.)

One of the British missionaries who served on the mission office staff at Ravenslea was Elder Ralph S. Mount. Having given up a well-paid foreman's position to accept his mission call, Elder Mount served in several areas of the mission for over two years (1941–3), ending with an assignment in the Hull Branch. There he and his companion, Elder James Martin of Scotland, repaired the bombed-out windows in the chapel, restored the heating system to operation, and by visiting inactive members were able to raise meeting attendance from fifteen to forty. (R. West collection: Ralph S. Mount letter.)

Because of its importance as a strategic port on the North Sea, Hull was one of the more heavily bombed British cities. Nora English, a member of the nearby Beverley Branch, recalls:

> It was terrible for anyone living in Hull. We could go to the bottom of our garden in Morton Lane and see the sky lit up with fires in Hull after there had been an air-raid nearly every night for weeks. (R. West collection.)

Thus Elder Mount, when asked by the mission president at the time of his release if he would remain in Hull and be its branch president, 'knew what [he] was taking on':

> My last job had been and now would continue to be the welfare, spiritually, socially, and physically of the Saints... I had [shared] and could continue sharing their bomb shelters with them during air raids until the war ended.
>
> Fear challenged faith many times; Hull was bombed continuously. But the members, even though their homes were bombed still 'kept the faith'. We became, if anything, more united than ever. (R. West collection.)

Elder Mount had observed at the outset of the war that 'with the departure of the American Elders some members thought the Church was finished'. But as 'hurried arrangements were made for local worthy brethren and sister[s] to take their places...we the British Saints...felt that this was the time to prove ourselves'. Evaluating his wartime experience forty years later, when he was patriarch of the St Albans Stake, Brother Mount affirmed:

I can bear testimony to this vital fact – that the Church is here to stay until the 'end'. This particular period of time proved that without any doubt whatsoever. (*Ibid.*)

The experiences of the war also proved the ability of the British people to endure danger, hardship and heartache without complaint. During the most intense air raids (after France had fallen) mission leaders made plans to evacuate members' children to LDS homes in Alberta, Canada, so that the parents might be relieved of at least that concern. Although the plans were changed and the children evacuated to the countryside rather than overseas, it was none the less heart-rending to separate the children from their parents under such uncertain circumstances. For President Cunningham, who was in charge of arranging the evacuation of LDS children from London, four decades could not erase the vivid memory of tearful farewells at railway stations between parents and 'little boys and girls with labels tied to them'. Nevertheless, as he testified later: 'Out of the crucible came great bishops, stake presidents, patriarchs, regional representatives, and temple presidents.' (R. West collection: James R. Cunningham address notes; *MS 102*: 535, 619.)

Although the saints were on their own, they were not completely without the presence of Church members from overseas. Beginning early in the war, some British branches were visited by increasing numbers of Church members in the Allied armed forces stationed in Britain. In the first two years of the war, most of these were Canadian volunteers, but after 1942 most were Americans – in Britain as part of the preparations to invade North Africa and the Continent.

Contacts with these foreign saints made an enjoyable and mutually sustaining relationship. For the servicemen, branch meeting-halls and the homes of many British members afforded an atmosphere of 'belonging' that they appreciated. As one soldier in the Royal Canadian Army Medical Corps testified:

I was in England several months before I found Ravenslea, but having...once felt the spirit that permeates the Mission Home, it has become a magnet to me. It has brought me into contact with 'my people'...and since they all have the same ideals as I have, then my being with them helps me to do as they do. (*MS 103*: 533–4.)

Edna Smith, who served as assistant mission secretary during part of the war, recalled forty years later:

[A] great influx of American Servicemen...filled the branches and helped by their spirit. Many of these young men were given assignments to visit outlying branches and willingly undertook to do what they could. We also took them with us to cottage meetings. (R. West collection.)

In several cases, where there were no British branches conveniently located, members in the armed forces organized their own Sunday meeting groups. Such was the case in Lancashire, Cambridgeshire, Norfolk, Suffolk, Gloucestershire and Hampshire. In other cases, as at Salisbury, the British Mission presidency organized a special branch for members in the forces, presided over by ex-missionary servicemen or by local members. Long after the war, Henrietta Martin Squire recalled the regular meetings held in her home in Aldershot for the servicemen stationed at the nearby base. She and her husband, Henry Squire, were the only resident members of the Aldershot Branch, created in 1941 especially to provide a place of worship for these servicemen. Henry was the branch president, Henrietta was a home missionary, and their home was an 'open house' for the LDS soldiers to visit any time they wanted. (R. West collection; *MS 106*:641.)

The mission presidency also organized periodic armed forces conferences. More than 120 Mormon servicemen, mostly American, attended such a conference for two days in September 1943 at the British Mission headquarters. The 137 members attending a similar conference at Wigan a month later were welcomed by the mayor of Wigan, who commented:

I met your missionary choir at the Liverpool University before the war, and never have I heard such a fine presentation by such fine, clean young men. You have got something good. (*MS 105*:536, 585.)

Encouraged by the response to these conferences, the mission MIA boards sponsored a larger armed forces conference in Birmingham in January 1944. Complete with basketball matches, grand concert, and Gold-and-Green Ball, this conference attracted over 400 participants in spite of transportation difficulties. Attended by many young British saints as well as LDS servicemen, this was doubtless the most spirited Church gathering in Britain since the pre-war mission-wide MIA conferences. (*MS 106*: 631–2.)

But there were darker moments connected with the presence of LDS servicemen from abroad. Particularly poignant was the news of the death of Hugh C. Brown, son of President Hugh B. Brown. This young man had served as a missionary in Britain just before the war when his father was presiding over the mission. With the coming of the war he had been sent home in the general missionary exodus, but less than two years later he was back in England as a volunteer airman. What happened then was described in the *American Outpost*, an armed forces newsletter in Britain:

> We first heard of him through three Eagle squadron airmen who visited the *Outpost*. They told of a young minister – a fighter-pilot in their unit. 'He makes religion real. We all think he's great.' So we asked him for a short article which we published in Letter No. 27.
>
> On leave in London thereafter, he remarked that of the 29 trained men who had crossed the Atlantic with him in August 1941 to join the R.A.F., there were only three left. The winning of the Battle of Britain, the continuing defence of these shores, the assault on the war-production of the enemy are costly business.
>
> His leave ended, he left London on March 15th. Next morning at his aerodrome he volunteered for patrol duty. On the squadron's return journey, they flew into a bank of fog. The pond-like sea was deceptive. Apparently he flew too low, striking the water at 240 miles per hour. His friends called to him. No reply. For hours they searched. Of the 29 brave airmen there now remain but two.

At the memorial service conducted by the mission presidency, a poem written by Hugh B. Brown, 'A Father's Salute to His Son', was read. The two remaining airmen of the group of 29 were planning to attend the service, but were killed just before it. (*MS 104*: 256, 523, 576–7.)

Even with the heavy losses in the R.A.F. and some other branches of the British forces, loss of life in the British military during the Second World War was considerably lighter than that produced by the trench warfare of the First. Property losses in Britain from the air raids in the Second World War were much greater than those of the First, but a good advance warning system and the air-raid shelters kept the loss of civilian life also surprisingly low, given the magnitude of the bombardments.

Throughout both wars the *Millennial Star* regularly reported the deaths of Latter-day Saints killed in action and published as well a 'Roll of Honour' at the end of the War. These records show that war fatalities among the British saints totalled about 65 in the First World War and 23 in the Second. This was approximately proportionate to the death toll for the British people as a whole. In neither war were there any civilian fatalities among the active Latter-day Saints, although in the Second World War one member-of-record, long dissociated from the Church, was killed in an air raid. At war's end, despite the great sadness for loved ones lost and injured, there was also a widespread feeling among the saints that they had been preserved by the hand of the Lord. President Anastasiou later testified: 'Every month we had more than one report of bombings among the members, but no casualties, and we were always grateful for the Lord's protection of His saints.' (Anastasion, autobiography, pp. 89–91; *MS 108*: 303; *109*: 75; *76–81* and *101–8, passim.*)

The end of the war came in May 1945 in Europe, and three months later in the Pacific. About a year earlier, in May 1944, an epoch came to an end for the British Mission, with the return of President Hugh B. Brown and the release of the acting mission presidency. President Anastasiou had served as acting president for four years and five months. James R. Cunningham had served throughout this period as second counsellor, and continued for a time to supervise the Sunday School and genealogy activities in the mission. George W. Bailey, former president of the Sheffield District, had served as first counsellor in the mission presidency for over four years. Throughout the whole period of the war, and even after the release of President Brown in 1946, James P. Hill maintained the perfect record of the *Millennial Star* editors: over a century with never an issue missed.

Thus President Brown, upon resuming his presidency in May 1944, was giving more than perfunctory praise when he commended these four men for having met the 'multitudinous and at times almost baffling' demands of their calling with 'courage and fortitude'. President Brown had given the 68 branches of the mission into their keeping at a time of bleak prospects. Knowing that the mission would probably have to be self-supporting during the war in finances as well as in personnel, President Brown had left President Anastasiou the meagre £200 remainder of the mission fund with the recommendation that he husband it carefully ('you may not get any more'). Four and a half years later, President

Anastasiou was able to turn the mission over to President Brown with a justifiable sense of satisfaction:

Every department of the Mission carried on its work regularly and in accordance with Church procedures. Monthly accounts and reports were sent to Salt Lake City without interruption... The number of branches increased from 68 to 75, and at the end of my 4 years mission, we had over $80,000 [£20,000] surplus in tithes and offerings. The mission prospered, our prayers were answered.

President Brown's praise extended to the entire mission membership:

In spite of the ravages of war...in spite of bombings and losses and death, in the midst of fear and anxiety and bereavement, these men and the Saints generally have held high the banners and standards of the Church, have given generously of time and money, and have shown their faith by their works. (Anastasion, autobiography, pp. 84–9, 99; *MS 106*: 718–19.)

As for President Anastasiou, he had planned to return to the firm where he had previously worked for eighteen years but instead accepted the suggestion of President Brown: 'Why don't you and your family go to Zion? You may be called on another mission.' This prediction proved true. After emigrating to Utah in 1945, Andre Anastasion (as he then spelled his name) served a two-year mission in France, and then translated the Doctrine and Covenants, the Pearl of Great Price, and fifteen Church pamphlets into Russian (having previously translated the Book of Mormon into Russian upon President Talmage's request). After a full life, at the age of nearly eighty, he fulfilled an assignment from the First Presidency to go to Russia and Yugoslavia to investigate the possibilities for missionary work in those countries. Small wonder that his former counsellor, James Cunningham, remembered him decades later as 'the hardest worker I have met in this land' and testified of his war-time mission presidency: 'He did a remarkable job in a difficult time.' (Anastasion, autobiography, pp. 107–19; R. West collection.)

During most of the four-year period that President Anastasiou was looking after the spiritual needs of several thousand Church members in Britain, Hugh B. Brown, back in the United States, was called as LDS servicemen's co-ordinator, to look after the spiritual needs of increasing tens of thousands of Church members in the armed forces. In 1944, when many saints in military units were being sent to Britain in preparation for launching a mammoth new front in Europe, Elder Brown was released from his assignment as general servicemen's co-ordinator to resume his post as British Mission president. He continued, however, to be a member of the Church's general servicemen's committee, and along with presiding over the British Mission, served as field co-ordinator for LDS servicemen throughout Europe.

In his first *Millennial Star* editorial after his return to Britain, President Brown declared himself

> pleased and grateful to find the mission in a healthy and prosperous condition. The districts and branches are all well officered, the mission is self-supporting, and everywhere there is evidence of faith and devotion.

But the war was not over yet, and despite the efforts of the acting presidency, the mission's supply of qualified leaders was low. At the end of March 1944, when President Brown took over from President Anastasiou, fewer than half a dozen full-time missionaries (all of them women) were available to help maintain contact with the branches. The mission president could still make his rounds for district conferences, but with many of the district presidents heavily involved in war work, there were many tiny branches operating largely on their own.

Under these circumstances, it is not surprising that inexperienced priesthood leaders, some of them very recent converts from other faiths, should have occasionally improvised some meeting procedures or simply 'borrowed' practices from their former churches. For some time after the war there were stories in circulation about wartime deviations from standard LDS practice. Though these stories had some basis in fact, most of the unorthodox practices in Britain were restricted to the smaller, more isolated branches and were quite innocuous.

In one case, a potential problem was quashed in an amusing but effective manner by President Brown. In the Preston branch some of the members had come to regard the sacrament table itself as a sacred object and wanted to erect a brass rail around it to protect it from careless contamination. Before this could be done, however, President Brown visited the branch. Following the meeting and the clearing of the sacrament trays, while talking to some members he *sat* on the table. As one member reported later, there were 'no more requests for the brass rail!'. (R. West collection: Eveline Foster.)

For President Brown and his post-war successor, President Selvoy Boyer, there were much greater concerns than a few easily corrected procedural problems, however. For one thing, the loss of contact with the Church had made some of the younger adults particularly vulnerable to sexual immorality and other serious sins. Several of President Brown's *Millennial Star* editorials addressed this concern; in one he wrote:

> War is disruptive, distracting, scattering in its effects, and one of the needs of the time is some cohesive, uniting, gathering influence which will offset this chaotic aftermath. Several small branches have carried on through the war years and have had their numbers steadily reduced until meeting together was an act of loyalty without much hope of benefit.
>
> It is easy under such conditions to get 'out of focus' and to come to feel that the church is small and ineffective and to begin to look about for other organizations and groups with which to associate. These times have driven some people back into Babylon and the church has lost members while the members have lost faith and deprived themselves of the blessings of the Gospel. (*MS 107*: 304–5.)

To help correct this condition, President Brown implemented a major restructuring of the mission by consolidating some of the smaller branches. During the two years of his 'second presidency' (April 1944 to July 1946) the number of branches in the mission shrank from seventy-five to twenty-nine. In Norwich District, for example, 'the drawing of many young members, male and female, into the services of their country...left the District operating with but seven active members of the Priesthood, and brought about the closing of its branches at Great Yarmouth and Thurlton'. In the Sheffield District, 'two small branches, Barnsley and Rawmarsh, were closed. Their members attended meetings in the Sheffield chapel. Work was found for them to do.' In the Birmingham District, where there had been seven branches, four were consolidated into one branch, called the Birmingham Branch. This branch held its meetings in the Handsworth chapel, with an average attendance of about seventy persons. In another typical district, Liverpool, nine branches were consolidated into four. The most extreme example of consolidation, however, was the Leeds District, where seven branches were reduced to one. (*MS 107*: 107, 126, 169; *109*: 141, 232, 328.)

The feelings of the saints affected by such consolidations were mixed. For a young person like Veronica Bettinson who, with her mother, had attended meetings through much of the war in the 'two-family' Chiswick Branch, it was a pleasant change for the branch to be absorbed, along with three other London branches, into one consolidated London Branch, meeting at Ravenslea. In such a case it was easy to see the realization of the ideal stated by President Brown:

> The larger branches make possible the organization of priesthood quorums, auxiliaries, activity groups, choirs, etc., and give opportunity to all to participate... (R. West collection; *MS 107*: 304–5, 186–7; *109*: 73.)

In other cases, however, some saints lost even the limited association they had had with other Church members. A post-war report from President George W. Bruerton of the Manchester District refers to this problem:

> When the policy of consolidating the branches in the British Mission was completed, the Manchester District had shrunk from seven to two, the remaining ones being Rochdale and Oldham. The chapel owned by the church in Manchester was sold and the members were expected to travel to one of the remaining branches for services, Sunday School, etc.
>
> Transportation difficulties caused many to stay away and these are numbered among the 'lost members'. The task of seeking them out and reviving them is a difficult one. (*MS 109*: 360.)

President Brown's 'second' presidency was served under a number of complicating circumstances. To help him meet these problems he had a small but able circle of helpers. James R. Cunningham was supervising the mission Sunday Schools and genealogy work. James P. Hill, in addition to continuing his work on the *Star*, was called by President Brown to be superintendent of the mission YMMIA. Norman Dunn, president of the Birmingham Branch, was recruited as mission secretary and became President Brown's right-hand man. Florence Dunn, his wife, became mission Relief Society president, inasmuch as Sister Zina Brown had not yet been able to join her husband in England. (Campbell and Poll, p. 167; *MS 106*: 806–7; *107*: 11.)

Scarcely two months after President Brown's return, the smooth functioning of this staff suffered some serious setbacks, due to the V–1 flying bombs launched from occupied France. Highly destructive, these 'buzz-bombs' were also nerve-shattering because they struck at all hours and without warning. The mission staff at

Ravenslea were shaken several times by the concussion of near misses, and President Brown wrote in his journal that he was often reminded of a line from a well-known hymn: 'When the earth begins to tremble, bid our fearful thoughts be still.' Finally, a particularly close explosion shattered the mission home's windows and caved in part of the roof. With that, President Brown decided that the time had come to evacuate. The chapel at Handsworth, Birmingham, was chosen as the new headquarters, and the removal made in July 1944.

Though Allied capture of the major bases ended the raids in September, Ravenslea was not sufficiently repaired for re-occupation until May 1945. In the meantime, the mission staff worked in cramped, unheated quarters at Handsworth, sharing the chapel with the consolidated Birmingham Branch. Despite the difficult circumstances, however, President Brown testified that 'never before, not even in the tabernacle itself, had he felt so strongly the Spirit of God' as when he served under these conditions with what remained of the British Mission staff. (British Mission History, Aug 1944; Campbell and Poll, pp. 171–4; *MS 106*: 833.)

At the end of 1944 President Brown experienced another, more personal impediment: the recurrence of a painful affliction in his facial nerves, a tic douloureux. When medical treatment in wartime Britain proved difficult to obtain, the First Presidency advised him to fly back to Salt Lake City for an operation. Although the surgery was successful, his convalescence and his servicemen's committee assignments in the United States delayed his return until May 1945. In the meantime, the mission staff carried on in their respective duties, with secretary Norman Dunn handling general mission affairs from 1 January until 22 May 1945. (Campbell and Poll, pp. 176–80; *MS 107*: 11.)

Two weeks before President Brown's return to England, on 8 May 1945, Germany surrendered, and the war in Europe was over. Just after his arrival, President Brown wrote home:

> There is a spirit everywhere of good cheer and the kind of happiness which is known only to those who have suffered much and lived in fear, who have known dread and sleepless apprehension and are then released, freed, liberated and made to feel that all is well. (Campbell and Poll, p. 180.)

Two months later Sister Zina Brown arrived from America, with

Elder Ezra Taft Benson, President of the European Mission, January 1946, examining welfare shipments to war-ravaged saints.

their daughters Margaret and Carol. Sister Brown, of course, was already known to the British saints and quickly resumed her role as Relief Society president and 'mission mother'. Margaret, the elder daughter, was called as the first American missionary in England since the beginning of the war and assigned to the mission office. After that, however, as after the First World War, getting more missionaries from the USA proved painfully slow. During the next year only two couples and one sister came from Utah. They were immediately assigned to labour in districts with especially critical needs. In addition, two British sisters were still serving full-time missions and working in the mission office, but these few, in spite of President Brown's repeated requests for more missionaries, were his only full-time helpers during the last year of his presidency. (*Ibid.* p. 182; *MS 108*:116.)

Evidently the chief cause for this second delay in obtaining missionary visas was the continuation of wartime shortages of food, transport and other necessities. As a matter of fact, the British people, despite a brief euphoria at the end of the fighting, were facing more bleak years of hardship.

To help with the most pressing needs of the British saints (and with the even more desperate needs of the saints on the Continent) the First Presidency, in January 1946, called Elder Ezra Taft Benson of the Council of the Twelve Apostles to serve as president of the European Mission. With his extensive experience in agriculture, from field labour to national farm co-operative administration, this future U.S. Secretary of Agriculture was a natural choice for this assignment requiring special attention to the organizing of emergency food relief. Although President Benson spent less than a year in Europe, at the time of his departure in December 1945 the work of the Church was firmly re-established throughout Europe, with fully organized missions and with welfare supplies moving efficiently. (*MS 108*: 80–1.)

Upon his arrival President Benson was pained to see the harsh living conditions in Britain:

> Food and clothing are very strictly rationed and housing and living conditions are even more critical than during the war years... The contrast of conditions here with conditions in the States makes one feel that he is truly in another world. Everything seems short including patience. England has truly felt the effects of this terrible war.

He observed further that, though the British people generally were downcast and apprehensive, Church members were more optimistic. At his first meeting with the saints in London, President Benson encouraged them to look forward to growth of the Church in Britain:

> The most effective way to teach the gospel is to live it, and I feel that you Saints and the hundreds of true Latter-day Saint servicemen who have been among you have preached the gospel most effectively. We may look forward to a great period of missionary work as a result of the many favorable contacts that have been made by you during the war years. (European Mission History, 1946, p. 2.)

In April, President Benson took advantage of the opportunity afforded by a meeting of all the district presidents in the mission to explain and inaugurate the Church welfare programme 'on a basis adapted to the needs and capacities of the mission'. He was pleased with the prospects for this programme:

> Although many branches have been forced to consolidate with other larger branches, due to lack of priesthood members, full cooperation in the plans and

objectives of this program was assured and reports indicated that most districts have been anxiously awaiting the plan presented to them and are prepared to initiate the proposed welfare activities. With the present critical world food situation such a program will do much to meet the needs of this mission. (*Ibid.* p. 26.)

It was also in April that President Benson had an opportunity to attend a Newcastle District conference in Sunderland. This was the district where he had served as president twenty-three years earlier, and he was greeted joyfully by the saints who remembered him. At this conference too, the president's message was one of encouragement and promise. He contrasted the favourable press treatment given his present relief mission with the persecution he and his companion had encountered on that first mission – including a mobbing at a street meeting near the Sunderland railway station. (*Ibid.*; see pp. 343–5 herein.)

If the Church was to begin the post-war expansion that Presidents Brown and Benson confidently promised, it needed a new missionary force. (In response to President Brown's requests, the First Presidency had called several dozen missionaries to serve in the British Mission, but their arrival was being delayed for want of British visas.) On the 8th of May President Brown presented a discouraging report to President Benson. The British government had just ruled that 'aliens coming to England will not be permitted to stay longer than two months'. The best that President Brown had been able to obtain, as a concession from the Home Office, was an extension of this period to six months in the case of Mormon missionaries. As President Benson observed:

This, of course, will help very little. We hope to look into this matter further... However, in view of the serious food situation in all Europe and the fact that it is becoming increasingly serious in England, it is quite likely that the British government will discourage foreigners coming to the country for some months to come. (*Ibid.* p. 31.)

But soon a breakthrough came – achieved by the efforts of several people, including a friendly Member of Parliament. The Home Office was persuaded to grant missionary visas, first to the new mission president, Selvoy Boyer, in May 1946, and then to the waiting missionaries in America, beginning in July. (British Mission History, vol. 31, 17 May 1934–2 Feb 1954; Boyer, p. 7.) In the meantime, President Brown's mission was drawing to a close, as

President Boyer arrived to replace him in the middle of May. When the Browns took their leave, on the 4th of June, it was with the heartfelt love of the British saints. (Campbell and Poll, p. 186.)

Selvoy J. Boyer, prior to his call to the British Mission, had extensive experience at the ward and stake level, as well as in civic affairs. Grandson of a Utah pioneer and son of an English mother from Norwich, President Boyer had been mayor of Springville, Utah, and was bishop of a Springville ward at the time he was called to preside in Britain. Sister Boyer had also had experience in the welfare programme as a member of the stake Relief Society presidency, and these practical qualifications were welcomed by the British saints. Also welcomed was President Boyer's open, frank manner and his direct, enthusiastic approach to all kinds of challenges. Like most British Mission presidents of the twentieth century, President Boyer had seen previous missionary service in England: for eighteen months in 1923–5 he had been president of the Nottingham District. (*MS 108*:212–13; European Mission History, 1946, p. 60.)

When President Boyer assumed the mission presidency, he had only seven missionaries (five American and two British) to aid him. But he and President Benson were encouraged that month as they attended the first post-war mission-wide conference. Organized by President Brown before his departure and featuring presentations by the various mission auxiliaries, it was entitled the 'Thanksgiving Conference'. Three days of festivities, attended by more than five hundred members and friends, included a Gold-and-Green Ball, a pageant written by a local member, and impressive marching in the town square by a large group of LDS scouts and Beehive girls, accompanied by a twenty-piece drum-and-bugle corps. 'It was a conference that was thrilling and soul-satisfying in every particular,' President Benson said.

> The expressions of testimony and gratitude manifest in the general priesthood and Relief Society meetings...are evidence that the spirit of the conference had been received and that a new era for the gospel in Great Britain had been inaugurated. This conference has been most successful not only in winning the love and confidence of the people, but in lifting the Saints from their spirit of war depression to new heights of enthusiastic missionary endeavor. A new era of expansion is on the threshold. (European Mission History, 1946, pp. 35–6.)

A still larger mission-wide conference was conducted in Birmingham four months later, in October 1946. This marked the first time in the history of the British Mission that two such conferences had been convened in one year. By this time, forty-three missionaries from America had been added to the five who had come before President Brown had left. Since word had been received that President Benson, his emergency mission completed, was soon to be released as European Mission president, this conference also served as a farewell for him. Perhaps to set an example for the British branch and district leaders who would soon be involved in extensive leadership re-assignments, he declared to the conference audience his willingness to serve wherever he might be called, though expressing also his regret at having to leave his work amongst the saints of Europe. (*Ibid.* pp. 80–1.)

President Benson's replacement as president of the European Mission was Alma Sonne, a prominent banker, businessman and Church leader from Cache Valley, Utah. He too had filled a mission in Britain (1910–12), and, following service in Logan (Utah) bishoprics and stake presidencies, had been named an Assistant to the Council of the Twelve in 1941. In the words of Selvoy Boyer, decades later: 'President Sonne was a marvelous man and had the gospel at heart. He could guide and direct... He helped me tremendously.' (*CN*, 27 Jul 1946; European Mission History, 1946, p. 62; Boyer, p. 8.)

President Sonne and President Boyer made a good team and, by their exceptional industriousness, provided more than three years of inspiring guidance to the missionaries and members of the British Mission. Although President Sonne spent much of his time on the Continent directing the post-war development of the European missions, he always arranged to be in England to accompany President Boyer on his twice-yearly rounds of district conferences. Between these conference visits, President Boyer consistently arranged to meet his missionaries individually once a month. After May 1947 President Boyer also had the help of counsellors. This was in accordance with a directive from the First Presidency suggesting that henceforth each mission president should select two counsellors, one an outstanding missionary and the other an experienced local member. President Boyer's first British counsellor was George F. Poole, London District president. When he and his family emigrated to Utah, William O. Chipping, superintendent of the mission Sunday School, took his place. Missionary counsellors were Elders Wallace R. Reid and Melvin Russell Ballard. (Boyer, pp. 10, 15; European Mission History, 1946–50, pp. 261, 90–260 *passim*.)

Presidents Sonne and Boyer received a harsh introduction, during their first winter in London, to the rigours of English weather and to the deprivations that had become commonplace to the British saints. With the 'worst blizzards in fifty years', economic conditions in Britain became so critical in February 1947 that the crisis was frequently called 'the second Dunkirk'. Coal supplies were so depleted that electricity had to be cut off several hours daily, first in London and then throughout Great Britain. Periodicals were forced to suspend publication for several weeks. Soon, floods followed the blizzards in thirty-four of England's forty counties, and the food outlook grew darker still with the drowning of thousands of cattle and sheep. Most of the British people felt more depressed than during the war. (European Mission History, 1946–50, pp. 103–5.)

Although the LDS Church in Britain had survived the war in comparatively good condition, just after the war LDS Church activity was far below its normal level. With a continuing shortage of leadership, and with 'consolidated' branches having responsibility for large and dispersed memberships, over 50 per cent of the members in some areas had fallen into complete inactivity. As the first post-war missionaries commenced their work in the autumn and winter of 1946–7, even some of them were briefly affected by the general feeling of 'bankruptcy and gloom' prevalent at the time amongst the British people. Hence, combating discouragement became one of the principal concerns of Presidents Boyer and Sonne as they visited the districts during this period. (European Mission History, 1946–50, pp. 93, 98, 103, 105.)

Even in the harsh winter months of January to March 1947, however, there were signs that a post-war recovery period was already under way for the British Mission. In many branches the return of members from the armed services or from distant war-production plants provided new vitality. A member of the Norwich District presidency, for example, reported in April:

> Norwich Branch...commenced its work of reorganization by bringing into offices the young members returning to the Branch. Twelve of these young people, called into the service of their Country, returned with a burning testi-

mony of the Gospel. The M.I.A.... now is set up under its Young Men's and Young Women's presidencies. Relief Society and Sunday School underwent modifications, and with the help of the two lady missionaries laboring in this branch, a Primary organization was set up and now brings in many children from the homes of non-members. (*MS 109*: 107.)

With the aid of priesthood holders returning to their homes and of the newly arrived missionaries – most of them mature young men who had served in the armed forces and had considerable experience in the Church – many of the branches which had been disbanded or consolidated were being reorganized. (European Mission History, 1946–50, p. 109.) Improvements were also being made in branch meeting facilities. Mission-owned buildings had generally been in a very poor state of repair at the end of the war, some of them damaged by the bombings and others deteriorating from lack of regular maintenance. Many of the rented meeting-halls were in such shabby or poorly situated buildings that President Benson reported in October 1946:

I am really ashamed of most of the halls in which our people are meeting in Great Britain today. Never has there been so much favorable sentiment towards the Church and such opportunities to interest people in our message. It would help so much to have suitable places in which to meet. (Benson, 13 Aug, 17 Oct.)

President Benson had already authorized President Boyer to proceed with the more urgent building repairs and, in October 1946, he and President Boyer decided to purchase a fine building in the Nottingham District, the first ever owned by the Church in that area. President Benson expressed the hope that this would be just the first step in a general programme of acquiring new meeting-places for British branches – and such a programme did, in fact, gain momentum in 1947. In addition to the upgrading of rented buildings, five new properties were purchased or dedicated in the course of that year; and during the entire term of President Boyer (ending in February 1950) twenty-six new properties were acquired. Most of these included a building appropriate to the immediate needs of a branch, with sufficient land for construction of a chapel later. A large portion of the cost of these properties came from the tithes and other contributions of the British members, accumulated in part during the war. (Benson, *ibid.*; European Mission History, 1946–50, pp. 121, 164–5; Boyer, pp. 13–14.)

Even more heartening than the improvements in branch meeting facilities, however, was the improvement in meeting attendance that started in 1946 and continued even through the harsh winter of 1947. As reported in January 1947:

> The number in attendance at all meetings is taking a sharp and steady rise; the number of auxiliary organizations is constantly increasing; and enthusiasm over Church activities is mounting... Many new branches are being reopened... The old principle of 'divide and multiply' is working well, and as a result the total active Church membership is increasing rapidly.

When President Sonne accompanied President Boyer on his rounds of district conferences in March 1947, he was pleased to note that, in spite of the cold weather, meeting-houses were filled to capacity. Attendance at the conferences was approximately double that of the preceding autumn conferences, and the three-day mission-wide conference held in Bradford at the end of May similarly registered an attendance approximately double that of the previous October. It was described in President Sonne's report as a conference 'successful from every angle', and as 'an occasion that will live long in the memories of the British saints and missionaries'. (*MS 109*: 10, 176–7; European Mission History, 1914–50, Jun 1947 report, p. 122.)

A principal cause of this surge of optimism in the mission was that, for the first time in many years, a large number of investigators and new converts were appearing in the branch meetings and conferences. After a rather slow start in the winter of 1946–7 (due to exceptionally bad weather, even for England) proselytizing was at last beginning to produce excellent results. At some district conferences, a third of those attending were investigators. President Sonne reported that prospects for Church growth were good: the 125 missionaries now in Britain were full of enthusiasm, the people were open-minded and friendly, newspaper comments were favourable, and reporters eager for information. (*Ibid.*)

The number of convert baptisms continued to climb during the rest of that decade. In 1949 there were 366 convert baptisms, a higher number than in any year since before the First World War, and in 1950 the number of converts rose still further, to 593, and then exceeded a thousand, at last, in 1951. The era of the 'post-World-War-II recovery' had finally given way to the era of the 'great awakening'. (*Ibid.*)

These spectacular increases in convert baptisms in the last years of the 1940s were achieved, in part, by reviving some of the most effective proselytizing methods of the 1930s, as well as by experimentation with new ideas. Taking advantage of the widespread attraction of the cinema in Britain, the British Mission began, in the summer of 1947, to present a film-lecture on 'Utah and Mormonism' to audiences throughout the country. In addition, the Millennial Chorus and the LDS sports teams were reconstituted, and proved just as successful as they had been before the war. Even though the missionary teams were restricted by President Boyer to one game or practice per week, in 1948 and again in 1949 a missionary basketball team won the national championship of England and Wales. Such successes were again producing much favourable publicity and many proselytizing opportunities. These and other missionary activities were described by President Boyer in 1949, just a few months before his release:

> Various means of propagating the Gospel have been tried over the years, and it has been demonstrated that the growth of the Church comes...from a steady stream of personal contacts made by members and missionaries alike... Results are being obtained in the British Mission today...through the faithfulness of the Church membership and missionaries who are doing their duty and living their religion.
>
> Even though emphasis has been placed upon tracting, open-air meetings, and cottage meetings, new means for making Gospel contacts have not been shunned. Utilizing the traditional British market day, many elders have rented market stalls to display attractive posters and literature in town and city market squares.
>
> Posters have been used successfully in the underground railway system of London. Millions of Londoners and visitors travelling daily in the 'tubes' have seen the colorful Book of Mormon posters, [and] many...have sought further information.
>
> For many years basketball has been used to advantage in placing the name of the Church before sporting fans of the world.
>
> Over the B.B.C. of Newcastle and Glasgow, in the Sheffield football stadium, to multitudes gathered in public markets, in Hyde Park, in theatres, schools, hospitals, clubs...in all parts of Britain the newly-formed Millennial Chorus have made a lasting impression with their tuneful renditions of the songs of Zion and other favorites.
>
> Pursuing this course has brought steady progress to the British Mission. Since the close of the late war, fully organized branches in Britain have increased in number from twenty-nine to seventy-one, each giving opportunity to the membership for spiritual growth through participation in all the organizations. (*MS 111*:196–7.)

The one remaining obstacle to the growth of the British Mission was the post-war renewed flow of emigrants to North America. Recognizing the natural tendency of faithful Latter-day Saints to 'gather', Church leaders in Utah and in Britain had never definitely opposed the emigration of British saints. They had, however, repeatedly advised against moving to America primarily for economic reasons or without full consideration of the advantages which might accrue to the mission and to individual families when active members remained in Britain to build up Zion there. And in fact, some prominent members of the Church in Britain were electing to remain in their homeland. As James Cunningham stated in a conference in 1950:

I feel I have a debt to pay to my fellow countrymen in Great Britain. My repayment consists in giving the Gospel that I have received to others... What field [of labor] more fitting than among my own fellow countrymen? (Boyer, pp. 22–4; *MS 107*: 304–5; *112*: 198–9.)

Hundreds of other saints, however, chose to emigrate to America in the early post-war period. As a result, for several years the number of branches having missionaries as branch presidents steadily increased. But the new members flooding into the branches by the end of the 1940s would soon be prepared to reverse this trend. By the end of 1952, only 20 per cent of the branches were headed by missionaries; in the other 80 per cent, local leadership was in place.

Just at the end of the 1940s the number of members in the British Mission began to increase substantially. In 1935–45 the number had hovered in the vicinity of 6,000, even though the number of *active* members had decreased during the war. Then in the post-war years of 1946–8 membership dipped to about 5,600 when some of the 'lost' members were cleared from the rolls and the number of emigrants to America approximately equalled the number of new converts. Beginning in 1949, however, mission membership began to build. From 5,846 in that year, the number grew to 8,397 by 1952. Obviously the long-standing restriction on British Mission growth caused by emigration had finally been overcome. (*Ibid.*)

In February 1950 President Sonne was released as European Mission president and was not replaced, as the First Presidency had decided to supervise the European missions by having general authorities tour the missions from time to time. President Sonne was accompanied on his homeward trip by President Boyer, who had been replaced as British Mission president by Stayner Richards.

It was clear by this time that the post-war recovery of the British Mission was complete. Almost as evident were the beginnings of a new era of unprecedented growth for the Church in Britain, far surpassing anything previously experienced in the twentieth century. For the first time in the history of the mission, a high conversion rate was beginning to coincide with a relatively low emigration rate. The resulting 'explosion' of Church membership would usher in the era of fully organized wards, multiple stakes, and a temple in Britain – blessings perhaps only dimly anticipated by most members in 1950. But they were also blessings that had been repeatedly prophesied by Church leaders in the British Isles throughout the difficult era of the Great Wars. And they were blessings that would be welcomed both by those saints who remained in Britain and by those who had emigrated to America – without, however, forgetting their British roots.

13

The Great Awakening

James R. Moss

On 9 April 1951 David O. McKay, direct descendant of the Clan McKay in the northern highlands of Scotland, was sustained as the ninth president of The Church of Jesus Christ of Latter-day Saints. In fact, two British ancestral lines came together in President McKay, as his father, David, had joined the Church in Thurso, Scotland, whilst his mother, Jennette Evans, had come into the Church in Merthyr Tydfil, Wales, both in the year 1850.

President McKay knew the British Isles well at the time he became president of the Church. In 1897 he had been called as a missionary to Britain, and had served as president of the Scottish Conference. Years later he came back as an apostle, during a 1921 world-wide tour of the missions of the Church. Within a year he returned as president of the European Mission, at the same time serving as president of the British Mission. Upon his release he reported to Church leaders that they should visit Britain more frequently, and that suitable buildings were sorely needed there.

It was thus no surprise that one who so loved and understood the British people should be the one to help bring about a great awakening for the Church in Britain. In 1951, at the time David O. McKay became president of the Church, there was only one mission in the British Isles – but by 1971 there were seven missions and, for a time, there had been nine. Similarly, in 1951 there were no stakes in Britain, and most of the branches met in rented halls or in converted homes that were ill-suited to Church activities; by 1971 there were in the British Isles nine stakes, more than a hundred new chapels and, perhaps the greatest symbol of the spiritual awakening, a temple of the Lord.

In fact, the two decades between 1951 and 1971 saw greater changes for the Church in Britain than in any period since the apostolic missions of the 1830s and 1840s. Following a long night of struggle in its first century, the Church in Britain began to see the light of a new day in the 1950s, building upon the heritage it had forged through years of faithfulness in the face of persecution and sacrifice. By 1971 it had come of age as a fully developed and vital part of the world-wide Church.

The growth of the Church during this period was both external and internal. From the devastation of the Second World War, the saints grew both in number and in maturity. After a hundred years of serving primarily as a source of immigrants for the Church in North America, the Church in Britain at last attained all the spiritual, intellectual, social and temporal advantages of the full Church programme, and could look to a future of building the kingdom in a way that was distinctly British.

In 1945, as a member of the First Presidency, David O. McKay had counselled the British saints not to leave their homeland for America because of the war. The Presidency wrote:

> Let the Saints, one and all, regard it as their moral and religious duty to do all they possibly can to assist the missionary elders in building up the branches and maintaining them with a view to the perpetuation of such organizations, so that peradventure, there may always be some left ready to receive the missionaries and to render them the necessary assistance to enable them to still reach out and open up new fields of ministerial labour; and thus, by Saints and missionaries working harmoniously together, branches may be continued in their organized capacity by constant additions to their rolls of membership, which otherwise might become broken up and cease to exist through unwise emigration. (*MS 112*:198–9; First Presidency letter, 28 Aug 1945.)

Although emigration did continue to deplete the membership in Britain after the war, more and more saints began to remain in place and were thus prepared to revitalize the Church in the years ahead. On 17 April 1952, in a meeting of the First Presidency and Quorum of the Twelve Apostles, President McKay authorized the search for two temple sites in Europe, one in Switzerland and one in Britain. This momentous step was the first of many President McKay would take to begin the great awakening. In June 1952 he flew to Glasgow, where he dedicated the first chapel for the Church in Scotland. Two days later he also dedicated the Edinburgh chapel.

In his remarks at the Edinburgh dedication, President McKay reflected on the events that had brought him to Scotland over the years, and mentioned the Scottish missionary service of three generations of McKays:

And so as I look back in reminiscent mood upon those events, and many others that have crowded my mind, there is gratitude in my heart that a humble elder, a hundred years ago, knocked on a door in Thurso, and testified that the Gospel of Jesus Christ had been restored. I am thankful that my grandfather and grandmother believed that, because that was the beginning of the events that have happened in the century leading to this moment. (Morrell, p. 109.)

Following his visit to Scotland, President McKay flew to London for several days of meetings. At this time he also visited the prospective temple site near Lingfield, Surrey, and encouraged the mission president to purchase it. After a visit to the Continent, President McKay returned to London and from there went to Merthyr Tydfil to visit the home of his mother. He later wrote: 'I thought, as Sister McKay and I stood in that small bedroom, how different life would be now if two humble elders had not knocked at that door a hundred years ago.' (*DN*, *Church News*, 6 Sep 1952, p. 4.)

President McKay then travelled to Glasgow again where, on 22 July 1952, he announced the purchase of property in Berne for the first European temple of the Church. The British saints immediately grasped the significance of that announcement, and even though no publicity had been given to the search for a British temple site, they knew it would be only a matter of time before they too would have a temple.

The next three years saw the beginnings of major growth for the Church in Britain, with the number of convert baptisms increasing dramatically. Then, in 1955, several events combined to make it a special year: much larger elders' quorums were organized throughout the country, Elder Spencer W. Kimball of the Quorum of the Twelve Apostles visited Britain, the far-famed Salt Lake Mormon Tabernacle Choir came on tour, and President McKay returned to break ground for the new temple.

The first of these events occurred during the spring, when the elders from fourteen districts in Britain were united into five quorums covering the entire country. The size of these quorums was extremely large (one covered Newcastle and all of Scotland; another included Liverpool, Manchester and all of Ireland; a third covered Birmingham, Nottingham, and all of Wales) but the change caused the quorums to activate local priesthood holders and provide greater fellowship and leadership opportunities. By May 1955 more than 500 elders throughout Britain were functioning in their new quorums, beginning to learn from each other and to feel the strength of priesthood. From these quorums and the training they provided came the genesis of the future stakes of the Church in the British Isles.

The second event of importance in 1955 was the visit of Elder Spencer W. Kimball of the Quorum of the Twelve. Many members of the Church in Britain had never met an apostle, and many of the more remote branches had not been visited by a general authority of the Church for many years. Elder Kimball arrived in London on the 22nd of June, and in the following twenty-three days he covered 2,200 miles throughout England, Ireland, Scotland and Wales; interviewed 158 missionaries; met the saints in twenty public meetings; and held many other meetings with branch and district leaders. Between meetings, Elder Kimball visited historic Church sites in more than twenty cities. His schedule was exhausting, but Elder Kimball carried on without stopping, encouraging the saints wherever he went. He dedicated new chapels in Preston, Liverpool and Grimsby, and paid a special visit to Lincoln College, Oxford, where his son Spencer L. Kimball had studied.

In his addresses, Elder Kimball challenged the British saints to prepare for stakehood. He encouraged them to achieve total activity and full-hearted devotion in every member, to develop an expanded missionary programme using local part-time and full-time missionaries, and to have large families. He also stressed the need for the saints to remain in Britain and not move to America, and for members to assume leadership roles in business and society. (*MS 117*: 249.) The British saints' following of Elder Kimball's counsel was a major factor in their preparation for stakehood five years later.

The third noteworthy event of 1955 was the Tabernacle Choir tour of the British Isles, the first time this group had visited Britain. In announcing the tour to members of the Choir, President McKay stressed the missionary value of their travel to Britain:

Uninformed people in the world have had prejudices against the Church. Some still have them. No work has been more effective in removing such prejudices than the work here on Temple Square. Here the people learn that the Church stands for the highest and the best.

No organization has contributed more to informing and enlightening the people than has the Tabernacle Choir. The First Presidency would like to extend your influence and give the world outside the boundaries of the United States opportunity to partake of your influence and spirit and hear the famous Tabernacle Choir. To that end the First Presidency would like to take steps to have you take a trip to Europe.

There can be no greater missionary work than to have you sing for the cultured people of Europe the songs of Zion... You are chosen to represent the Church because of your abilities to sing and because of your personal characters and conduct. God bless you and protect you and guide you as you prepare for this great missionary effort. (*MS 116*: 322.)

The Choir arrived at Greenock at 6 a.m. on the 19th of August aboard the liner *Saxonia*. With them were their conductors, J. Spencer Cornwall and Richard P. Condie; organist Alexander Schreiner; and Elder Richard L. Evans, a member of the Quorum of the Twelve who was to supervise the British receptions for the choir and 'The Spoken Word' at all concerts. They were met by President and Sister McKay and their party, who had flown to Scotland from New York. Also on hand was a Scots bagpipe band who greeted them with 'The Mist-Covered Mountains' and 'My Home'. The Choir responded with 'The Bonnie Banks of Loch Lomond', 'Come, Come Ye Saints', and 'The Battle Hymn of the Republic'.

From Greenock, the Choir travelled to Glasgow, where they performed on the 20th of August, then to Manchester on the 22nd, to Cardiff on the 24th, and finally to London on the 28th. The response of the British press was overwhelming:

Glasgow thrilled at their singing, which is magnificent in volume and expression. (*Scottish Sunday Express*.)

Outstanding! The features of this choir were opulence and real beauty of tone and the perfection of its balance. What a pleasure it was to listen to a choir of this size which had completely adequate male resources. (*The Scotsman*.)

The singing itself was admirable; the tone quality was outstandingly beautiful in piano passages, when the sopranos, in particular, could float their voices with an ethereal purity of effect, while the bases retained an eviable mellowness no matter how low their voices. (*The Times*.)

The response of the British public was no less exciting. During the concert in Manchester, Elder Evans asked all members of the Choir who had British ancestry to stand, and when practically the entire choir arose, the applause from the audience was deafening. At the concert in Cardiff the audience broke into the programme twice, to join in singing 'Men of Harlech' and 'Cwm Rhondda' – an appropriate response, since the Tabernacle Choir was itself of Welsh descent, its original corps of singers having been Welsh immigrants in Utah under the direction of John Parry, a native of Flintshire. (See pp. 254–5, 261.)

But the warm reception was not limited to the Choir. President McKay travelled with them much of the time and was received wherever he went with kindness and dignity. In Scotland, for instance, the Lord Provost of Glasgow held a formal reception for President McKay and the Choir before their first concert; and in London the American ambassador entertained President McKay at a dinner with the Lord Mayor of London and editors of the London press. That these gestures of recognition and friendship affected President McKay is evident from his remarks in Edinburgh on the 21st of August:

> Nobody knows or can tell what this great choir missionary endeavor means to the Church. You can understand...how deeply this affects me when I tell you of my own missionary labours here 57 years ago. Nearly every day when I passed St George's Square in Glasgow and looked into marble halls, cords and guards barred my passage. Friday, together with this great choir of 400 members, we were welcomed in that great hall with highest honors, and received by the Lord Provost. A half century ago we were attacked and vilified in street meetings by professed ministers of the gospel and members of congregations. What changes have occurred in these 57 years. (Thomas, p. 96.)

The Choir's tour of the British Isles had a tremendous effect, building faith and confidence in the saints as well as opening new doors of acceptance in British society. Its value is perhaps best summarized by Elder Evans's appraisal following the concert in London:

> We are deeply pleased at the way the people of great Britain have opened arms and hearts to us. The friendships formed, understandings established with high officials and among all classes are beyond our highest expectations, and significant far beyond our ability to calculate. (*Ibid.* p. 123.)

The fourth major event of 1955 was the ground-breaking for the London Temple – a fulfilment of prophecies from leaders both in and outside the Church in Britain. In 1852 the president of the British Mission, Elder Franklin D. Richards, had written:

As the ancient worthies appreciated the ordinances, the revelations, the ministrations, and the powers of the Lord's House in their midst, so do the Latter-day Saints...Hundreds have secured unto themselves and their posterity the glorious promise of eternal life, and have obtained power to build up the Kingdom of God in the earth, and become Saviours upon Mount Zion. Having thus made their calling and election sure, they labour with increasing assiduity, and all the faithful may become partakers of the same glory; and this must be effected by the same means, viz., in the House built unto the Lord. Therefore, Saints in the British Isles, let us arise and build! (*MS 14*:9–10.)

President McKay repeated this admonition to the British saints when he served as European Mission president, and a third witness was added when Elder Richard L. Evans concluded his book, *A Century of 'Mormonism' in Great Britain*, with the challenge:

Every Latter-day Saint in the British Isles must strive toward that day when the Church of God shall be mighty in Britain, and when the spires of a Temple of the Lord shall pierce British skies, for 'Zion is the pure in heart'. (R. Evans, p. 241.)

These modern prophets and apostles were repeating an earlier inspired declaration by one of Britain's most famous Reformers, George Wishart, who said, before being burned at the stake for heresy:

This realm shall be illuminated with the light of Christ's [gospel], as clearly as ever was any realm since the days of the apostles. The house of God shall be builded in it; yea, it shall not lack the very copestone. (*IE*, Oct 1958, p. 719.)

The search that had begun in 1952 ended with an announcement to the British saints in 1953 that the Church had purchased a temple site. President McKay wrote, of this event:

This is the beginning of another great blessing for the faithful Latter-day Saints in this land, for the Saints can enjoy all the blessings that are available anywhere in the world. Here it is that another great branch of the Kingdom of God will be built by the faith and courage and righteousness of the sons and daughters of God. It is evidence that the Lord loves his children here, and desires that they shall be prepared with the fulness of the blessings that he has prepared for them. (*MS 115*:170.)

The London Temple, announced 1 August 1953, dedicated 7–9 September 1958, first ordinances performed 10 September 1958.

On 3 August 1953, President McKay arrived in London. After spending a day selecting the exact location of the temple on the property, he flew to Berne to dedicate the temple site there. Following that dedicatory service, he recorded in his journal, 'I want to bring the temple to the people.' (Gibbons, *McKay*, p. 323.) He then returned to England to dedicate the London temple site on the 10th of August. During this visit to Britain he also attended district conferences in Belfast and visited Thurso, his father's childhood home.

Plans for the temple developed rapidly. In January President McKay dedicated the Ravenslea chapel in London. While in England, he visited the temple site again, conferred with local Church leaders, and informed the saints that architectural plans were almost complete. A month earlier, the First Presidency had acquired the services of Sir Thomas Bennett of London as consulting architect for the temple, beginning a long and friendly association between Sir Thomas and the Church. The ground-breaking ceremony was held on 27 August 1955, music for the occasion being provided by the Tabernacle Choir, and construction began the following spring. By 1957 work had progressed enough for Elder Richard L. Evans to return to Britain for the laying of the cornerstone, which took place on the 11th of May with more than a thousand saints in attendance. The standard works of the Church, current Church periodicals, cuttings, photographs and other mementoes were placed in a copper box and sealed inside the cornerstone. In his address Elder Evans reviewed the history of the Church in Britain and noted that this would be the fourteenth temple of this dispensation, 'the first such temple to be built in Great Britain, the second in Europe, and the third in the British Empire, there being one also in Canada, and another under construction in New Zealand'. (*IE*, Jul 1957, p. 501.) He also paid tribute to the great heritage of the British saints in his dedicatory prayer:

> We are grateful that from this land have come tens of thousands of faithful men and women who, having heard the truth, have accepted it. We are grateful for those who have stayed here to strengthen the Church; and for those who have left to live in other lands, and whose sons and grandsons have come back to carry Thy word and to continue Thy work in this, the land of their fathers. (*MS 119*:175.)

After this laying of the cornerstone, the finishing work proceeded rapidly. In landscaping the thirty-two acres of land surrounding the temple, several ancient oaks on the property were retained and protected. One of these, standing near the highway, was named the 'David O. McKay Oak', as it symbolized for many saints the strengths of the prophet himself.

By mid-August 1958 the temple was ready for an open house. From the 16th of August to the 3rd of September, more than 76,000 people toured the temple before it was dedicated. Many of these were not members of the Church, and their impressions of the building did much to encourage good relationships between them and their LDS neighbours. Following the open house, the temple was closed to make final preparations for the dedication.

The temple in Britain was dedicated on 7–9 September 1958, with President David O. McKay presiding, speaking at the services, and offering the dedicatory prayers. Six dedicatory sessions were held during these three days, and more than 12,000 members of the Church were able to attend. In his dedicatory prayer, President

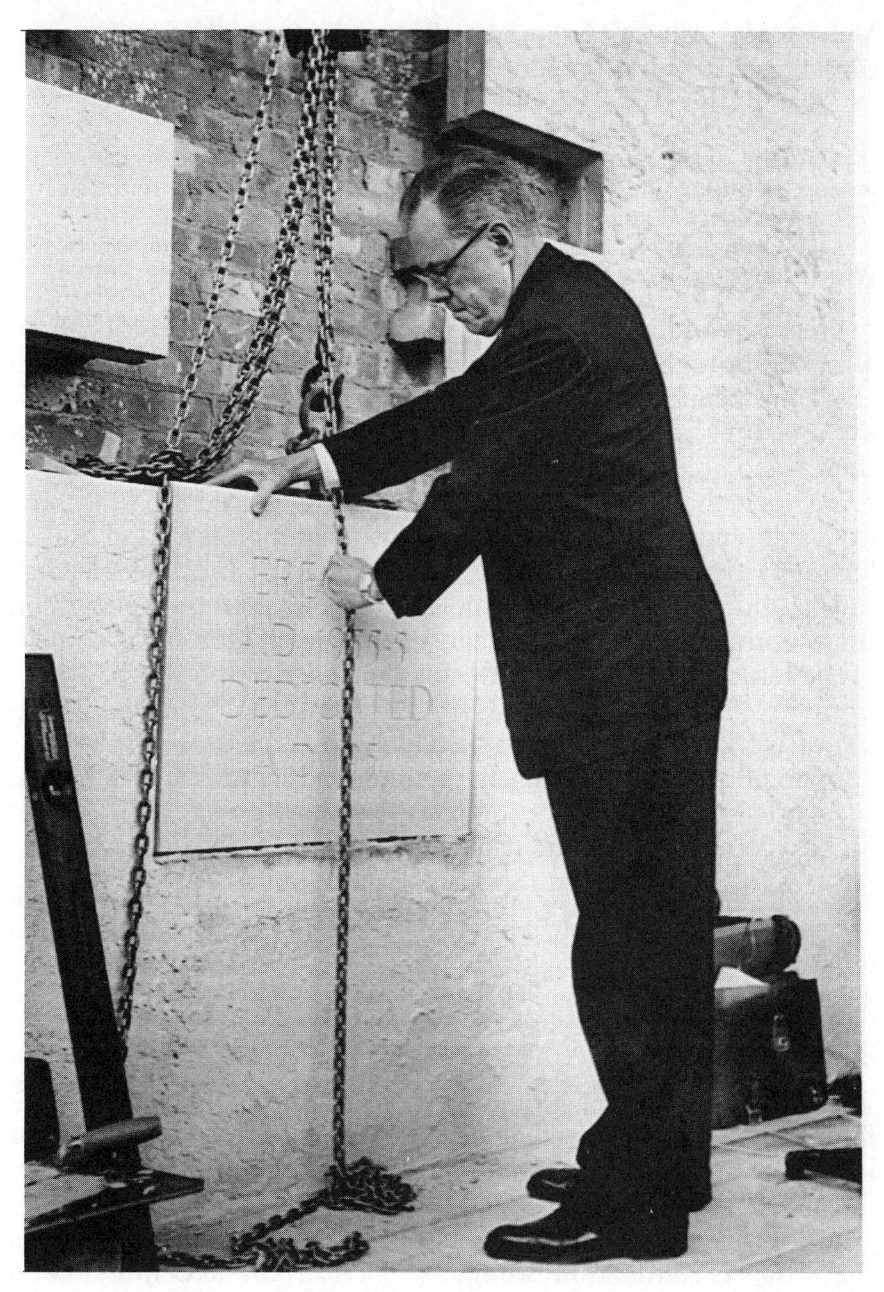

Elder Richard L. Evans lays the cornerstone of the London Temple, 11 May 1957.

McKay paid tribute to the great British heritage that had carried Christianity through its long years of preparation for the full restoration of the gospel, saying:

When in the Middle Ages the church departed from Christ's teachings thou didst inspire honest, upright men here in Great Britain to raise their voices against corrupt practices. Mingling with the denunciatory messages of Luther and Melanchthon in Germany, and Swingli in Switzerland, were the voices of George Wishart and later John Knox of Scotland. (*IE 61*: 719.)

President McKay also expressed gratitude in his prayer for those who had brought the gospel to Britain, and for the priesthood and auxiliary leaders in the Church throughout the British Isles, praying that they would know 'that they are trusted leaders, and that they are to hold sacred that trust as they treasure their lives'. (*Ibid.* p. 775.) He thanked the Lord for the blessings of freedom that came from the Magna Charta and the English common law, and prayed for the Queen, the Members of Parliament, and civic leaders throughout the land. He concluded his prayer with the recognition that, 'with this prayer, we rededicate our lives to the establishment of the kingdom of God on earth for the peace of the world, and to thy glory forever'. (*Ibid.* p. 778.) Following the dedication, ordinance work began almost immediately in the temple.

In addition to the British saints, thousands of others throughout the world hailed the dedication of the London Temple. As President McKay commented at the dedication:

This is a great day not only for the members of the Church in Great Britain, but for the tens of thousands of others who are now looking reminiscently upon their experiences here before they left, and are recalling in sacred memory their ancestors. Members of the Church in all parts of the world are centering their thoughts and offering their prayerful wishes this day upon you who are assembled in this dedication service. (*Ibid.* p. 748.)

Evidence of this international interest in the temple dedication is found in the fact that dedicatory sessions were held especially for members and missionaries from Scandinavia, the Netherlands, Germany and France.

In the years since ordinance work began in the London Temple, thousands of saints from Britain as well as from the Continent and the rest of the world have enjoyed its blessings. To missionaries far from their homes, it has offered spiritual contentment and a haven of peace to be found nowhere else; to saints it offers insights into the gospel plan and ordinances of salvation and exaltation both for themselves and for their ancestors. Truly it has been a blessing to the Church in the British Isles.

Unfortunately, the story of the London Temple would be incomplete without reference to one further trial the saints faced in ensuring its continued operation. On 16 January 1961, Lands Tribunal Officer J. P. C. Done held that the temple was exempt from rating – and therefore from paying taxes – as a place of public religious worship under the Rating and Valuation Act of 1955, despite the fact that the temple was open only to members of the Church 'in good standing'. The valuation office then took the case to the Court of Appeal where, on 11 July 1962, the lower court's decision was reversed and the temple held to be taxable. Leave was granted the Church to appeal to the House of Lords, and on 31 May 1963, the case was brought before that body.

The principal argument in the case centred on whether or not the temple was a place of 'public' religious worship. It was readily admitted that it was a place of religious worship, but the distinctions between regular LDS services in the seventy-five chapels in Britain and those of the temple were noted as sufficient to exempt the first group and not the second. Lord Pearce spoke for the majority of the court in reasoning:

> Since the Church of England worshipped with open doors and its worship was in that sense public, it was unlikely that the legislators intended by the word 'public' some more subjective meaning which would embrace in the phrase 'public religious worship' any congregational worship observed behind doors closed to the public. Furthermore, exempting from rating, though not necessarily consistent, showed a general pattern of intention to benefit those activities which were for the good of the general public. (*The Times*, 31 May 1963, p. 7.)

As a result of the Parliamentary decision that the Church must pay rates on the temple, there was some speculation that the building would have to be closed, considering the financial struggles the Church had faced for many years in Britain. However, through a greater effort on the part of the British saints to pay their tithes, and with support from the general funds of the Church, the required amount was paid to enable the temple to remain in operation.

In 1968 the temple completed a decade of service to the saints in Britain. In May of that year the First Presidency called a new president of the temple, following Selvoy J. Boyer, G. Eugene calling. Dougald McKeown of the London Stake became the fourth president of the temple, following Selvoy J. Boyer, G. Eugene England and LeRoy J. Buckmiller.

In June 1969 a new Visitors' Centre was dedicated by Elder John Longden in services conducted by Joseph Hamstead, president of the London Stake. Elder Longden, himself born in Britain, was an Assistant to the Quorum of the Twelve. In his remarks prior to dedicating the building, Elder Longden emphasized the spiritual message of the Church:

> There are many here today who have searched and received, for as the Saviour said in his Sermon on the Mount, 'blessed are they who do hunger and thirst after righteousness, for they shall be filled.' We are here today to testify that the Church of Jesus Christ is on the earth. (*MS 131*: 24.)

Special guests at the dedication of the Visitors' Centre included many neighbours from the surrounding area, and prominent government officials. Eric Rushman, vice-chairman of the East Grinstead District Council, welcomed the saints to the area, saying, 'We are glad to see them and we are glad to be here today. We hold a great deal of respect for the members we have been acquainted with. We are happy to have you in our midst.' (*MS 131*: 30.) With the dedication of the new centre, the temple became not only a place of importance for Latter-day Saints, but also a focal point of new missionary activity, as thousands of visitors came to learn more about the work of the Church.

It is unusual for a temple to be dedicated in a country before the first stake has been organized, yet it was so in Britain. In many ways, however, the dedication of the temple helped bring about the creation of the first stake two years later. It was on 17 March 1960 that the Manchester Stake was organized, when Elder Harold B. Lee of the Quorum of the Twelve Apostles came to Manchester with Elder Alvin R. Dyer, an Assistant to the Quorum of the Twelve. After explaining the significance of a stake of the Church, Elder Lee reviewed the progress that had been made in Britain to that point. He noted that from 1837 to 1960, 7,398 missionaries had served in the British Isles, in addition to the thousands of part-time member-missionaries who had shared the gospel with their friends and neighbours. As a result of those efforts, Elder Lee reported that 138,016 people had been baptized into the Church in Britain. This in turn had led to the building and dedication of the beautiful temple that had now been functioning for nearly two years. Summarizing this march of progress, Elder Lee said:

> And now with the commencement of the organization of stakes, it is expected that our saints will feel themselves more established, and therefore feel more content to remain here and become, as I have used the term before, the seed-corn, to reach out to their friends and neighbours and to encourage others to accept the Gospel of Jesus Christ while it is yet day. (*MS 122*:193.)

At the same time that Elder Lee organized the Manchester Stake he also divided the British Mission. From the time of its beginning in 1837 until 1960, all the British Isles had been in one mission. Now, with the organization of the first stake in Britain, the time also came to expand the missionary efforts of the Church and divide the country into two separate missions. Called to preside over the new North British Mission was Bernard P. Brockbank, later to serve as an Assistant to the Quorum of the Twelve. This mission division began a series of further divisions that eventually saw a total of nine missions in the British Isles (later reduced to seven to consolidate proselytizing efforts). In 1961 the North British Mission was divided and a new Scottish–Irish Mission was formed, as well as the Northeast British and the North Scottish Missions. In 1964, the British South Mission was created.

With the organization of these additional missions in Britain, the Church also increased the number of missionaries serving in them. In 1960 there were only 308 missionaries serving in the British Isles. By 1961 that number had grown to 821, and the following year it nearly doubled, to 1,613. For the next five years the number of missionaries in the British missions remained around 1,400, with the average number per mission between 175 and 225. As should be expected from this increase in missionaries, conversions to the Church also increased significantly during this period. In 1960, 2,434 people were baptized as converts. The following year, 13,187 joined the Church, and in 1962 a total of 15,692 were baptized. This tremendous growth contrasted markedly with the previous decade, when only 593 were baptized in 1950.

The growth of missions in Britain in the early 1960s saw great development for the Church, and it was only natural that a period of consolidation was necessary thereafter to solidify the missions and ensure that the gains were permanent. A source of some concern for Church members during those years was the great number of young people who joined the Church. Using a variety of youth programmes, missionaries brought thousands of young men and women into the Church who were impressed with the vitality and spiritual uplift of the gospel message. In some cases, however, the younger members of the branches came to exceed the older adults, causing some difficulty in effectively assimilating the new converts into the established Church units. Also, it seemed, some were less committed than others, and many of these young people soon left the Church to return to their former ways. As a result, the Church experienced some negative publicity in this period, but the young people who remained true to their faith during this time emerged a generation later to provide strong leadership for the growing stakes and wards.

With the expansion of missions and growth in membership, additional stakes were soon formed in Britain. On 26 February 1961 President David O. McKay dedicated the new Hyde Park chapel in London, and at the same time presided at the organization of the London Stake. The following month, on 5 March 1961, the Leicester Stake was formed from the old Nottingham and Birmingham Districts and the newer Leicester District. This was followed two weeks later by the organization of the Leeds Stake, at a division of the Manchester Stake presided over by President Hugh B. Brown. The organization of these three additional stakes in Britain in 1961 marked real growth for the Church. The presidents of the stakes were Donald W. Hemingway in London, Derek A. Cuthbert in Leicester and Dennis Livesey in Leeds, while Robert G. Larsen remained stake president in Manchester.

On 26 August 1962 Scotland received its first stake, when President David O. McKay organized the Glasgow Stake with the assistance of President N. Eldon Tanner of the West European Mission and President Marion D. Hanks of the British Mission. Meeting in St Andrew's Hall on Berkeley Street in Glasgow, some 2,700 members of the Church were thrilled to witness the return of President McKay to Scotland – exactly sixty-five years after he had first set foot on Scottish soil as a young missionary in 1897. Commenting on that important milestone and the progress that had been made in the interim, President McKay told the saints:

> God bless you, my brothers and sisters, for the action you have taken today. God bless you in all that you have done in contributing to the increased membership in Scotland. It thrills my heart to see how many of you have come into the Church just during the last year. Sixty-five years ago, we humble missionaries did not dream, when we went through these streets distributing tracts, of such a gathering as we have this morning. (*MS 132*:252.)

Additional stakes were organized in 1963 in Sunderland, in 1970 in the North London area, and in 1971 in East Anglia. President Archibald Richardson in Glasgow, President Fred W. Oates in Sunderland, President Thomas Hill in London North Stake, and President Dennis R. Reeves in East Anglia Stake provided strong leadership for these new stakes. And in 1969 the Birmingham Stake was created with President Derek A. Cuthbert as president, the second stake over which Elder Cuthbert was to preside prior to his calling as mission president, regional representative of the Twelve, and eventually as a member of the First Quorum of Seventy.

This brought the number of stakes in Britain to nine, besides the many districts of the British missions. Since 1955, when the five large elders' quorums were organized, great leadership had emerged, developed and made itself felt in the Church in Britain. By 1971 the responsibility for directing the ecclesiastical units of the Church had essentially passed from the hands of American mission presidents and missionaries to local British leaders, who now built upon the heritage of the past but also moved the Church vigorously into the future.

In the 1960s there were several important events in the Church in addition to the growth of membership, organization of new missions and creation of new stakes. In June and July 1961, for instance, the Church conducted its first seminar for mission presidents throughout the world, at which a new missionary teaching plan of six discussions was introduced. 'Every member a missionary' was the theme at that seminar, and the renewed emphasis on member-missionary work was felt throughout Britain.

In 1964 a new home teaching programme was initiated, in which renewed emphasis was given to visiting the home of every member and family in the Church. The new programme stressed the importance of spiritually uplifting those visited, of sharing a gospel message, and of praying with the family. The next year, the Family Home Evening programme was inaugurated. Although weekly home evenings had been encouraged in the past, Church leaders now stressed formal home evenings on a regular basis. In October 1970, Monday evening was appointed for this purpose, and Church leaders were instructed to hold no other Church activities on Mondays, so that the evening could be reserved for family activities. New family home evening manuals were published, with interesting and uplifting lessons for families.

A major organizational change took place on 29 September 1967, when regional representatives of the Twelve were appointed to serve under the direction of the Quorum of the Twelve in training the local leaders of the Church. Initially assigned as regional representative for Britain was A. Ray Curtis, a former mission president who had served in the Southwest British Mission in 1962–5. He was followed by Elder Derek Cuthbert.

The 1960s also saw a second triumphal tour of Britain by an LDS musical group, this time the Singing Mothers. In February 1961 forty-eight LDS women gave a concert at the Royal Albert Hall in London, as well as concerts in Manchester, Nottingham, Cardiff, Newcastle, Glasgow and Belfast. As had been the case in the Tabernacle Choir tour of 1955, the Singing Mothers tour of 1961 brought both critical acclaim and renewed interest in the Church. Under the direction of Dr Florence Jepperson Madsen, 'for the first time in the 119 years since the Relief Society was organised the miles separating the old world from the new had been bridged in song'. (*MS 123*: 147.) The Singing Mothers provided the music for the dedication of the Hyde Park Chapel in London on the 26th of February, and also visited saints in several other locations during their tour. This tour had many benefits for Church members in Britain, but even more gratifying were the comments that came from non-LDS sources. Only one of many, the following report from Newcastle shows the public's acceptance of the Singing Mothers:

> The whole concept is remarkable – 50 American singers who have come over specially for these events joined with 200 British singers, who have formed a choir whose performance was an absolute object lesson in choral singing. Apart from the obvious fact that every member was thoroughly cognizant of the

> music – the whole exacting programme was sung without reference to copies – credit must be given to the expert training and inspiring conducting of Dr Madsen, whose idea this was...
>
> Of the contribution of the choir to the programme one can only speak in the highest terms. Helped by the absence of copies, there was absolute unanimity in everything they did...They sang with artistic expression and never lost vitality...[but] it was that rare quality in singing, splendid enunciation, which struck me most. Such clarity, such care with adequate stresses, left the audience in no doubt about the words. (*Sunderland Echo*, 4 Mar 1961.)

The advertising company that worked with the Church in promoting this tour estimated that the Singing Mothers received four times more public comment than the Tabernacle Choir had received six years earlier. It was a great addition to missionary work in Britain.

Another significant event in the 1960s was the opening of Deseret Enterprises, Ltd, in January 1962. This company was set up by the First Presidency to handle the distribution of Church books and supplies for the saints in the British Isles. Located on London Road in Mitcham, Surrey, the building was named Deseret House, with Deseret Enterprises on the ground floor and flats in the upper storeys. Appointed as general manager of the company was Derek A. Cuthbert. The bookshop was officially opened by Elders Spencer W. Kimball and Howard W. Hunter of the Quorum of the Twelve Apostles, with about 150 people in attendance. This bookshop was a major step forward in providing the British saints with their own distribution centre, and would eventually lead to the establishment of an official Church Distribution Centre in Britain.

In 1967 three Regional Relief Society conferences were held in Britain: in Manchester, Edinburgh and London. Under the direction of Elder Mark E. Petersen of the Quorum of the Twelve Apostles, the conferences were conducted and addressed by the entire general presidency of the Relief Society, assisted by local Relief Society committees. Members of stake presidencies and other priesthood and auxiliary leaders also participated in leadership training sessions.

Two additional events during the 1960s involved visits from members of the First Presidency. In 1961 and 1963 President McKay came to Britain and in 1966 President Hugh B. Brown, first counsellor in the First Presidency, also visited.

President McKay's 1961 visit was in conjunction with the dedication of the Hyde Park chapel in London. He arrived on Friday the 24th of February and held a press conference that morning, attended an organ recital by Dr Frank W. Asper the following evening in the new chapel, then dedicated the building on the 26th. On the 27th he attended the opening concert of the Singing Mothers in the Royal Albert Hall, then left for Manchester and a brief visit to Scotland. Everywhere he went, President McKay's prophetic stature was evident, and the media coverage of his visit provided excellent publicity for the Church. A special part of this trip for President McKay was a visit to Merthyr Tydfil on the 2nd of March, to attend the unveiling of a plaque commemorating his mother's birthplace, and to conduct the ground-breaking ceremony for the Merthyr chapel and stake centre.

President McKay's 1963 visit to Britain also centred on Merthyr Tydfil, as he came specifically to dedicate the new stake centre on the 25th of August. The saints there had donated more than 30,000 hours of labour to help complete the building in time. Prior to the dedication, organ recitals had been offered by Dr Robert Cundick, then organist for the Hyde Park chapel in London. The organ itself was a special gift from more than six hundred businessmen in Salt Lake City, who had donated it to the Merthyr stake centre in honour of President McKay's mother.

In President McKay's dedicatory prayer he honoured 'the memory of the many thousands who, in the face of misunderstanding, bigotry, misrepresentation, accepted the truth of the restored Gospel, and found the peace that follows obedience to the principles thereof'. He then dedicated the building as 'a place of worship, a house of learning, a centre of wholesome and spiritual enlightenment', concluding with a plea to God: 'It is Thine; let it be held sacred.' (*MS 125*:267–8.)

The two visits to Merthyr Tydfil by President McKay and the Church leaders who accompanied him were a great blessing to the saints in Wales. Many were able to meet the prophet personally, and the instruction and inspiration he provided were a source of strength to them for years afterwards. These visits marked a new period of growth and maturity for the Church in Wales.

President Hugh B. Brown had accompanied President McKay on his 1961 visit to Britain. In 1966 he returned to dedicate chapels at Norwich and Poole and to attend the official opening of the new district centre in Bristol. A major benefit of this visit were his interviews on consecutive days on ITV and the BBC, in which President Brown was able to reach about four million viewers. Within days of these interviews, the British media became much more positive in their reports about the Church, printing articles such as the following:

Sensational Sunday papers have hardly been fair to the Mormons. The gentle Americans have, in the past years, brought a new religion to this country which has given new lives, higher principles, and spiritual peace to many for whom other forms of religion have no appeal. There is no mystery about the Mormon faith. It's a 'with-it' version of what could be compared with a combination of our Nonconformist churches. (*MS 128*:211, quoting *Poole and Dorset Herald*.)

In the early 1960s a massive building programme was begun for the Church in Britain. Officially started on 1 September 1961, the programme had actually begun several months earlier when the Hyde Park chapel in London was dedicated. The dedication of this chapel signalled a major effort by the Church to provide adequate buildings for the British members and also to use the buildings as a proselytizing tool by encouraging interest and attendance of non-members. In 1955 President McKay had said, 'There is a great need particularly in the great city of London for a chapel, a church edifice that will be a credit to the Church, that will accommodate those who are now seeking the truth and about to join the Church.' (*IE*, Apr 1961.)

The Hyde Park Chapel was no ordinary undertaking for the Church in Britain, for it was designed to provide a spiritual show-place for the Church in the minds of those living in the London area. Built in one of the city's most exclusive districts, only a short walk from the major museums and a focal point for many visitors to London, the chapel was specifically designed to serve a proselytizing function and to help the British people know the Church was in Britain to stay.

Sir Thomas Bennett, who had been consulting architect for the London Temple, was appointed by the First Presidency as architect for the chapel in April 1959. On 3 August 1959 Elder Marion G. Romney officiated at the ground-breaking ceremonies. Eighteen months of construction followed, and the building was ready for dedication when President McKay arrived on 24 February 1961. In his remarks at the dedication, President McKay observed:

We need these meeting-houses, these chapels, wherein men and women who are converted may meet in their own houses of worship. In 1922, 1923, 1924, when Sister McKay and I were in the British Mission, they had to meet in rented halls. People would ask, 'Where is your meeting place?'...We [would] say, it is in hall so-and-so, giving the impression to an investigator that the Church was not permanently established. (*MS 123*: 176.)

But the dedication of the Hyde Park chapel was not the only important step forward in the Church building programme in the 1960s. A decade earlier, the First Presidency had given permission for either the planning or purchase or construction of twenty buildings in Britain. The Church had started by buying large houses and converting them into chapels where missionaries or older LDS couples lived to retain the residential character of the building in accordance with government regulations. Four such houses were purchased in 1950–1. Then, in the autumn of 1950, work commenced on the first post-war chapel to be built in Britain. The rapid increase of construction in 1961–2 was the culmination of these earlier efforts.

Between May 1961 and August 1962 thirty-seven new chapels were begun all over Britain, from Belfast and Ayr to Merthyr and Cambridge. By 1963 forty-six chapels were under construction, with plans to complete twenty-five of them by the end of that year. On 17 November 1963 the Holywood chapel in Belfast was the site of thanksgiving services conducted by mission president Stephen R. Covey, and Ireland had its first LDS chapel specifically constructed for the Church. The 1960s saw a major shift in physical facilities for the Church, from the rented halls and converted homes to the beautiful new chapels now found throughout the British Isles.

A major factor in the construction of these chapels was the 'building missionary' programme. Begun a few years earlier in the South Pacific, this programme utilized the volunteer labour of construction supervisors who were called by the Church, usually from the United States or Canada, to provide leadership in the construction effort. These capable and experienced builders in turn supervised the work of local 'building missionaries', who were called specifically to work on the new chapels. Many supervisors and building missionaries worked on several chapels during this period, their efforts being supplemented by the work of local members, who contributed some of the labour on the buildings, as well as by full-time proselytizing missionaries who frequently worked in the chapels during their weekly 'preparation day'.

The building missionaries also assisted the proselytizing missionaries in the evenings after their construction work was finished for the day. Typical of their experience in this labour was that of James Laurie, who wrote:

> Through the men that I was directed by, I learned to work, not just to earn a living, but to work...I wasn't a very intelligent boy at school, but in the last three years I believe that I have learned more than I did in the whole rest of my life. My desire to learn is greater, my desire to love the Lord is greater, to serve him. I just cannot contain the blessings he has given me. (*MS 127*: 307.)

Many of the young men who first served building missions for the Church later accepted calls to serve as proselytizing missionaries. This changed the pattern of generally relying upon American missionaries to do the proselytizing in Britain, and introduced the first large group of local British members serving full-time proselytizing missions.

Another programme affecting young men and women in the Church in the 1960s was the organization of the British Athletics Association (BAA). This was inaugurated on 22 October 1966, when G. Carlos Smith, general superintendent of YMMIA, held a meeting at the Manchester stake centre with stake and mission leaders from throughout the British Isles. President William Bates of the Manchester Stake was called to chair the new programme, supervising all Church athletic programmes in Britain.

The first year's efforts of the BAA resulted in a tournament at Manchester in 1967. Accommodation was provided at Manchester University, and sports events were held at the Manchester Stake centre and in a nearby park. More than 200 young people from stakes and missions all over Britain competed in the tournament and attended the dance in the evening. Derek Plumbley, then chairman of the BAA, noted that many inactive young men and women had been inspired to new spiritual activity in the Church through their athletic associations, and in addition that many non-members had come into contact with the Church through the programme. (*MS 129*: 27–8.)

The following year the BAA was reorganized, with President Dennis Livesey of the Leeds Stake as the new chairman. That year over 400 young people participated in the annual tournament, with excellent competition and a wonderful feeling of sportsmanship pervading the events. Sixty-three individual events and fourteen team events provided a wide range of activities and opportunities for participation. For several years the BAA continued to provide excellent competition as well as fellowship and spiritual companionship within the framework of athletics.

Yet another programme that affected young adults in the 1960s was the formation of the LDS Student Association (LDSSA) in 1968. The LDSSA was a Church-wide programme officially begun in the United States, but it had its real beginnings in Britain in the Deseret Club at Oxford University. Several LDS students who were attending Oxford (such as Peter Joyce and Gilbert McCabe) felt a need for some organized LDS activities and therefore formed their own club. Extending their efforts to reach out to other LDS college and university students in Britain, they helped organize an LDSSA convention at the Leicester stake centre in March 1968. Although relatively few of the LDS students attended that first convention, it was successful enough to plan another one the following year at Sunderland.

In preparation for the second convention, Peter Joyce conducted a survey to identify every LDS student in the British Isles. Elder Spencer W. Kimball of the Quorum of the Twelve, then supervisor of the Church in Britain, encouraged Peter's effort, and through it nearly all LDS college and university students were contacted and invited to the convention, and more than fifty attended. The theme of the convention was 'Must We Compromise?' and Elder Marion D. Hanks of the First Quorum of the Seventy addressed that theme, encouraging those in attendance to reach out to their non-member friends and provide leadership in setting and maintaining LDS standards. With the initiation of the LDS Institute programme in 1970, the LDSSA was merged with the Church Educational System to provide an integrated social, educational and spiritual programme for LDS college and university students.

The Institute programme was an extension of the LDS Seminary programme begun in Britain in 1968 under the direction of John

Madsen. Brother Madsen was one of several men sent throughout the world at this time to expand the Church's religious education programmes to its international membership. For many years the Seminary and Institute programmes had functioned in the United States and Canada, where large numbers of LDS students took time from their regular school classes to study the scriptures, Church history, or other doctrinal subjects for an hour each day. But until the 1960s these programmes had been structured to serve the concentrated Church membership and not the scattered members of Britain. Under the inspired direction of William E. Berrett, then administrator of the Church education programmes, a new home-study system was developed that enabled both the Seminary and Institute programmes to be expanded and developed in areas where only a few students were LDS in each school or college.

The home-study programme proved an immediate and tremendous success in Britain. From the three areas begun by Brother Madsen in 1968, the work was expanded the following year throughout England, Wales and Scotland, with Ireland receiving the programme a year later. Using a system of independent study combined with weekly classes under the direction of a Seminary or Institute teacher who was called by the bishop or branch president, these educational programmes had a profound effect upon the Church in Britain, strengthening the gospel understanding and testimonies of entire families. The distribution of the curriculum material into the homes of students gave parents and other family members access to a type of gospel instruction they had never had before, and other Church programmes also began to use the Seminary and Institute materials. Before long, the first regular Institute of Religion was started in London at the Hyde Park chapel. There, classes for both college students and interested adults were offered on a wide range of gospel topics.

Programmes for adult members also developed in the 1960s. Education Days were held in several stakes, at which a day-long series of lectures on gospel topics was presented. With the addition of such adult programmes, members of the Church both young and old were served by a strong educational support system that augmented the Sunday instruction they received. Maintaining a close working relationship with local priesthood leaders and gradually turning direction of the programmes over to local members, the Church Educational System proved a great blessing to the saints of the British Isles.

The increasing flow of Church educational materials into Britain soon required the establishment of a Church Distribution Centre there, an expansion of the LDS bookshop begun at Deseret House in Mitcham in 1962. Prior to the establishment of the Distribution Centre, Church units ordered their supplies directly from Church headquarters in Salt Lake City, and individual members often had to order their Church magazines themselves. The cost of shipping materials on this individual-unit basis was excessive, and the lack of co-ordinated efforts often meant supplies arrived late. The Distribution Centre provided a unified programme for ordering supplies, and stocked all necessary materials in Britain, so that Church members had only to order from the Centre rather than from America. As a result of this new programme, Church supplies became more easily available, and at a much reduced cost.

Other programmes such as Church Public Relations also developed in the 1960s, with individuals called in stakes, missions and districts to establish a rapport with the local media and to involve non-members more in Church activities. Because of the growth of Church activity in Britain during the 1960s, it also became necessary to establish a more formal and unified location for Church offices, where the financial, construction, real estate, genealogical and maintenance departments could be housed. Initially this was established near Epsom, Surrey, but as the programmes and staff continued to grow the offices were moved to their present location at Solihull, near Birmingham.

The combination of all these Church programmes provided a support network for Church members in Britain. By 1970 they had a wide range of services to assist them in their intellectual, physical, social and spiritual growth. For the priesthood programmes of missionary work, genealogy, welfare services, and home and family teaching, these auxiliary programmes and activities provided strength and encouragement. By 1970 nearly every service available to Church members anywhere in the world was also available to members in the British Isles.

In the early 1970s Church leaders decided that with the worldwide growth in membership it would be wise to hold a series of area conferences at selected locations throughout the world, where general authorities of the Church would meet local leaders and members to train them in their duties and to strengthen them spiritually. The encouragement for this type of training came largely from the correlation programme under the direction of Elder Harold B. Lee of the Quorum of the Twelve. In November 1970 Elder Lee presented a plan to hold the first of such conferences in Britain the following year. (Goates, p. 420.) With the approval of the First Presidency, the announcement was made that the area conference would be held, and Elder Derek Cuthbert, the regional representative of the Twelve for Britain, was given the responsibility of organizing it.

Elder Cuthbert organized a planning committee that immediately set to work. It was decided to hold the conference in Manchester, both because of its central location and because of the historical associations it had with the early LDS missions in the British Isles. A BBC team travelled to Salt Lake City to produce a programme on the Church in preparation for the conference, and the news media also published a series of articles on the planning effort.

The conference was held in several halls in Manchester, with an LDSSA convention on the day before the conference. Sessions for youths and adults were held in King's Hall at the Bellevue Sports Centre, and other sessions were held in the Trade Hall. Approximately 10,000 people attended the general sessions of the conference held on Sunday, 29 August 1971.

Presiding over the conference was President Joseph Fielding Smith, the president of the Church. Assisting him were President Harold B. Lee of the First Presidency, seven members of the Quorum of the Twelve, and other general priesthood and auxiliary leaders, together with nine stake presidents, seven mission presidents and Elder Cuthbert as chairman of the local arrangements. Upon his arrival in Britain, President Smith said, 'I hope this becomes a pattern for what shall be held in other nations and places.' He added that he 'deemed it fitting that the British Isles should be the scene of the Church's first such area general conference, since from the early days Great Britain has contributed thousands of members – and leaders – to the Church'. (*DN*, *Church News*, 28 Aug 1971, p. 3.)

The opening hymn of the conference was a most fitting beginning: 'The Morning Breaks' had been written by Elder Parley P. Pratt for the front cover of the first issue of the *Millennial Star*, first published in Britain in May 1840. As it had heralded a new beginning for the Church in the British Isles, so its singing at the beginning of this first area conference for the Church 131 years later also marked a major milestone of Church history in Britain.

President Smith's opening remarks set the tone for the conference when he declared:

> We are members of a world church, a church that has the plan of life and salvation, a church set up by the Lord himself in these last days to carry his message of salvation to all his children in all the earth. The day is long since past when informed people think of us as a peculiar group in the tops of the Rocky Mountains in America... Now we are coming of age as a church and as a people. We have attained the stature and strength that are enabling us to fulfill the commission given us by the Lord through the Prophet Joseph Smith that we should carry the glad tidings of the restoration to every nation and to all people. (British Area Conference Report, p. 5.)

During the conference, the general authorities and auxiliary leaders echoed this theme and reinforced the growing awareness that the LDS Church had indeed become an international Church and had fully arrived in Britain.

Elder Spencer W. Kimball of the Quorum of the Twelve Apostles referred to the great strength that had come out of Britain to bless the entire Church. He said,

> We remember particularly the Willie handcart company. One of many, these were Britishers who, with all of their belongings and little two-wheeled carts, climbed the mountains, forded the rivers, braved other dangers, buried their dead, and crossed a great country to the West where they finally came to have even greater problems for some time. Here they built houses out of mud, and they dug sego roots out of the hills to survive upon. These were Britishers; these are a great people with a great heart, a great devotion. We must not ever forget. (*Ibid*. p. 22.)

In another address to the conference, Elder Kimball reflected on the great contributions that had been made by those who had come to Britain to share the gospel with others:

> My brothers and sisters, I have been pondering on the past a bit. I find myself thinking that perhaps today many interested eyes may be looking down on this assembly with pride and satisfaction – the Heber C. Kimballs, the Wilford Woodruffs, the presidents of the Church, the numerous missionaries who have served

in this land and perhaps are grateful for the improvement, the accomplishments, and the hopes. (*Ibid.* p. 78.)

Of special note in regard to Elder Kimball's comments was the fact that the general authorities who were in Britain for the 1971 area conference held a special meeting at which seven members of the Quorum of the Twelve Apostles were in attendance. The last time such a meeting of that quorum had been held in Britain had been in April 1841, when Brigham Young had assembled the nine members of the Twelve then serving together as missionaries in Britain. It seemed altogether appropriate for a similar meeting of the Twelve to be held after 131 years. After reports from each member of the Twelve on their recent labours, President Joseph Fielding Smith gave those assembled some excellent instruction and then President Lee closed the meeting with prayer, all those present kneeling around a long table in the room. This meeting provided a strong foundation for the rest of the conference.

In their addresses, the general authorities offered powerful spiritual instruction and encouragement to the British saints, and as the conference came to a close, the concluding comments of Presidents Joseph Fielding Smith and Harold B. Lee provided a fitting climax to three days of inspiration and edification. President Smith confirmed his feeling that 'the Church will prosper in Great Britain to a far greater degree than has been the case in the past', then added:

Several stakes of Zion, a temple dedicated to the Lord, a considerable number of ward and stake buildings, and some highly successful missionary work – all testify to the fact that the Church is coming of age in Great Britain and is being built up and strengthened here among some of the best people on earth.

We expect to see this growth continue until the gospel becomes a leavening, sanctifying influence throughout this whole land. The gospel is for all men, and the Church shall be established everywhere, in all nations, even the ends of the earth, before the second coming of the son of Man. (*Ibid.* pp. 176–7.)

The impact of the 1971 area conference was felt throughout the British Isles. Many of the general authorities remained in Britain the following week, staying in the homes of the members and local leaders for several days to further strengthen them and continue their instruction. The brethren visited the temple, the stake centres and ward chapels, participated in family home evenings, and provided many personal spiritual experiences for the saints. The measure of their spiritual power can be sensed from comments made by those who attended the area conference. Sheila King from the England Central Mission reported, 'I ate little, slept less, shed many ounces, and even more tears. And I feel great! May I never recover from conference!' Kathryn M. Jones from the Whitefield Ward said, 'The florist arranging the flowers prior to the conference commented on the atmosphere. She said that she did not know what it was, but the feeling was wonderful, and she had never been in an atmosphere quite like it before.' Mary Tolley of the Manchester Ward reported, 'Walking home from a morning session, I saw people shopping, and I thought, Oh, is life still going on? I had forgotten it was Friday in the ordinary world.' Lynn Ball of the North London Ward wrote, 'It's hard to put into words what that lump in my throat means.'

Jeff Davis of the Woodsetton Branch reported:

> It was the most amazing experience of my life to see the prophet. He stood there, a man of 95, with intelligence and ability, physically and mentally, to address young people and interest them. I thought he was marvelous. I only had to look at him, and I knew he was the prophet. If I had stood him amongst everybody else, I would have known he was the prophet.

And John Hill of the Northfield Branch perhaps summed up the experience that most of those who attended the conference would remember longest: 'In the future, instead of saying there is a prophet, I can say that I have seen the prophet.' (*New Era*, November 1971, pp. 39–41.)

And so the great awakening of the Church in Britain had taken place. From the struggles of 1951 when the Church members were still trying to recover from the tragedy of the Second World War, it had come of age in twenty years. The membership had grown to nearly 70,000. A temple had been dedicated. Stakes had been organized. Missions had been divided and created. Church programmes had been developed and were fully functioning. And the membership of the Church had come out of obscurity into the full light of acceptance by their non-LDS friends and neighbours.

One of the most significant measures of the growth of the Church in Britain by 1971 was the fact that ever-increasing numbers of Latter-day Saints were being given important responsibilities in education, business, government and civic affairs. No longer did the fact of being a Mormon disqualify a person from significant service or responsibility in society. Now members of the Church were looked to for their leadership ability and understanding of social relationships, as people throughout Britain recognized the value of LDS Church programmes and training.

The Church itself also went through a significant internal change in this twenty-year period. For many years the leadership of the Church had rested either with the American missionaries or with a seasoned and experienced generation of leaders who had been required to shoulder a heavy load of persecution and harassment from the outside world. As the Church came of age in Britain between 1951 and 1971, a new generation of leaders emerged, younger and more confident, as they were able to concentrate more of their energies on outward expansion and less on inward retrenchment. Made possible by the changing social conditions and greater acceptance of the Church in Britain, this new generation of Church leaders was able to build on the solid foundations of the past and assume the direction of the new stakes and wards created during this period.

As the Church members in Britain looked forward to their 150th anniversary in 1987, just sixteen years ahead, they shared the testimony of President Joseph Fielding Smith as he brought their remarkable area conference to a close:

> God's work cannot be stopped. You have had and will have difficulties to overcome, obstacles to surmount, but the Lord's work shall triumph and his purposes shall prevail. Truth always prevails in the end, and this work is true. (British Area Conference Report, p. 176.)

14

The Contemporary Church

ANNE S. PERRY

THE HISTORY of the Church in the British Isles from 1971 to 1987 is a story of fulfilment – the rebirth of the British Church that began during the late 1950s and 1960s. Prophetic calls to stay and build the kingdom, coupled with the opening of the London Temple in 1958 and the organization of the first stake (Manchester, 1960), led to dramatic growth for the Church in the British Isles. A surge in missionary work contributed to a tenfold increase in Church membership between 1950 and 1970. (See Appendix A.) Unlike the nineteenth century when converts were called to emigrate and help build up Zion in America, during the late twentieth century the Church in Britain was being built to last, built to stay.

Although the Church has continued to grow since 1971, the increase has come at a slower rate. This has been more a time of consolidation and strengthening. In his keynote address at the area conference held at Manchester in 1971, Joseph Fielding Smith, then president of the Church, declared:

> We want the Church to grow and flourish here. You already have a temple dedicated to the Lord in which you can receive those ordinances and blessings out of which exaltation grows. We hope to see the day when there will be stakes of Zion in every part of the land… (British Area Conference Report, p. 6.)

During the next decade and a half, that prophecy would be fulfilled, numbers would increase, the saints' spiritual understanding would deepen, and major new programmes would be introduced.

The Church was growing and expanding once more, but this time – in the words of a song written especially for the 1971 Manchester conference, and rousingly sung during its concluding session:

The Quorum of the Twelve Apostles, December 1986. Seated, from left, are President Marion G. Romney, Acting President Howard W. Hunter, Elders Boyd K. Packer, Marvin J. Ashton and L. Tom Perry; standing, from left, are Elders David B. Haight, James E. Faust, Neal A. Maxwell, Russell M. Nelson, Dallin H. Oaks, M. Russell Ballard and Joseph B. Wirthlin.

This is our place, here we will stay,
To build, to strengthen ward and stake.
Until the Lord supreme shall reign,
This is our place; here we will serve. (Hewitt.)

The 1971 area conference provided an unprecedented opportunity for the British saints to have personal contact with a large group of general authorities and to be blessed by their spirit. Such an opportunity came again five years later when three area conferences were conducted in Britain. This was the first time that more than one such gathering convened during a given year in the same nation; they took place simultaneously in London, Manchester and Glasgow during the weekend of 19–22 June 1976. Thanks to careful planning of schedules, President Spencer W.

Kimball was able to attend some meetings in all three locations. He expressed confidence that instructions given at these conferences would bring 'an upgrading of the Church in Great Britain'. The need to increase missionary work was an oft-repeated theme throughout the sessions. For months the saints had eagerly anticipated these conferences, arranged time off from work, organized bus excursions and made other arrangements to attend. Some ten thousand crowded into the Empire Pool Stadium in London, and large crowds were likewise present in the other two cities. (*DN, Church News*, 26 Jun 1976, pp. 3–5.)

Church leaders maintained contact with the Church in Britain in yet another way. Beginning in the 1960s a general authority, typically an Assistant to the Twelve or member of the First Quorum of the Seventy, was assigned to live in Britain. In 1972 the Presiding Bishopric established administrative offices in Lichfield, and the Church departments were all brought together into this one location. In 1977 these Church offices were moved to Solihull. From 1978 to 1983 John H. Cox, a Briton, served as the Presiding Bishopric's area supervisor. The pattern of having a resident general authority in Britain continued until 1984, when areas worldwide were reduced in number and enlarged to include a broader territory. At this same time area presidencies were formed, consisting of three members of the First Quorum of the Seventy. Britain became part of the Europe Area with headquarters at Frankfurt. One member of the area presidency was assigned to give particular attention to the Church in the British Isles.

Under the inspired leadership of these authorities, the Church in Britain flourished. The establishment of new stakes is probably a better measure of true Church progress than is a mere increase in membership. Comparing latter-day Zion to a large tent, the Prophet Isaiah referred to 'stakes' as sources of strength. (Isaiah 54:2.) In contrast to a mission district which generally must *receive* strength *from* the Church, a stake is able to *give* strength and stability *to* the Church, just as stakes support a tent. Church leaders have pointed out that 'stakehood' is the ideal for which every mission district is preparing. Before stakes can be organized, there must be more than just sufficient membership. Leaders and members must be trained and experienced in conducting the full programmes of the Church. (Cowan, pp. 163–6.) Hence the formation of stakes in Britain is a reliable measure of maturity and development in Church activity as well as spirituality.

East Anglia became the ninth stake of the Church in the British Isles in 1971. At that time there was only one stake in Scotland and none in Wales or Ireland. (The Belfast and Merthyr Tydfil Stakes would be organized in 1974 and 1975, respectively.) On 28 May 1978 5,000 saints attended a special meeting in the Royal Albert Hall in which six London-area stakes were realigned and three new ones formed. Then, on 12 October 1980, some 2,600 saints came from all over Scotland for a conference in Edinburgh's Usher Hall. On this occasion three stakes were formed, completely covering Scotland with stakes. Elder David B. Haight of the Quorum of the Twelve Apostles (and former president of the Scottish Mission) declared to the group that this would be 'one of the most significant dates in Scottish history'. (*DN*, *Church News*, 8 Nov 1980, p. 5.) Finally, by 1982 the whole of the United Kingdom was covered by stakes of Zion. Only the Republic of Ireland was still served by mission districts. In the mid-1980s there were forty stakes in Britain: thirty-two in England, five in Scotland, two in Wales, and one in Northern Ireland. (See Appendix D.)

As these stakes were organized, a new generation of Church members was prepared to assume leadership responsibilities. Alexander Cumming is a fine example of such a man. He was born in Edinburgh in 1934 but grew up in Glasgow. At twenty-one he found himself looking for some spiritual values and meaning he had not yet found. Eventually, through friends who were members of the Church he was taught by missionaries. He accepted the gospel at once and was baptized. The year after his baptism, Elder Cumming was called as Bishop of the Glasgow Ward; a few years later, after a move of house, he became president of the Kilmarnock District presidency. In October 1977 he was called as Glasgow Stake president, where he served until he was called as regional representative of the Twelve for Scotland in 1986. His ambition is to see the Church extended into every township in Scotland. (Cumming.)

These new local leaders received the orientation and training needed to enable them to serve effectively. The first area priesthood leadership meeting was held in July 1979, and similar training meetings have been held annually since then. In June 1981 a seminar was held for stake and district presidencies, all increasing the standard of leadership in the British Isles. Much of this training has been provided by regional representatives of the Twelve, typically men who have gained experience as stake presidents. Leslie Thomas Norton of Hereford was one of the original regional representatives called in 1967. William Roberts of Manchester was called to this office in 1969, as was Derek A. Cuthbert of Nottingham the following year. Since then, other experienced Britons have been called regularly to this service. On 16 October 1983 the first multi-regional conference in the world was held at the Royal Albert Hall, attended by Church members from six south-east England stakes,

The best measure of the success of the Church is the growth of individuals and families. The lay nature of the Church provides opportunities for everyone, whatever their abilities. Boys may hold the priesthood from the age of twelve, with its attendant responsibilities, and boys and girls may lead classes and teach. Young men and women may also lead or teach, and all have the chance to visit other members in their homes and to practise compassionate service. Church members of all ages learn important organizational skills through participation in Church activities. Everyone has the opportunity to bear testimony once a month, and all are invited from time to time to speak to the congregation at Sacrament meetings, usually for a few minutes at first, then for a longer time if they are willing. Many people who were once nervous and unsure of themselves have discovered that they are able to express their feelings with dignity and eloquence. People who had considered themselves very ordinary often acquire confidence and leadership skills that they would not have aspired to before.

One member became the first LDS mayor in the West Midlands. Another had a distinguished career in local government that spanned more than a quarter of a century. Even though he had attended many management-training seminars, he insisted: 'Nowhere have I received better management skill training than in the Church. Corporate management can be at its height when holding ward bishopric, correlation and council and Priesthood Executive Committee meetings.'

In 1980 the Church purchased a 305-acre farm at Kington, Worcestershire. Three full-time employees operated it, with additional help from ward members, as necessary. The farm included a dairy herd, beef cattle, and a flock of sheep, with all produce going to the Bishop's storehouse for distribution to needy Church members.

On 7 July 1980 the Bishop's Central Storehouse opened in Birmingham, and four days later the first unemployed member came to receive food for his family. In September the first 'Mobile Bishop's Storehouse' delivered food to Gloucester, Bristol and Plymouth. Between 1981 and 1983 other Bishop's storehouses were opened in Glasgow, Sheffield, Stevenage, Bristol, Reading and Crawley. Others followed in rapid succession. The Church's expanded Welfare Services programme also included employment centres, a licensed adoption agency and professional counselling for individuals or families with critical needs.

The Church Educational System also expanded its offerings. Seminaries and Institutes of Religion provided part-time religious instruction for high school and university students respectively and enrolment in both programmes expanded during the 1970s and 1980s. Many of these students became Church leaders in later years.

Originally, seminaries were of the home-study variety – the young people studying materials on their own during the week and coming together for a class weekly. Later, when there were more students available in certain concentrated areas, early-morning seminaries were introduced – classes convening in a centrally located home or chapel before school each weekday. Another arrangement was designed to overcome the problem of travelling long distances, particularly in early mornings when public transport either was not running or was impractical because of time. A sister in Gillingham welcomed six students in her home at 6.20 a.m., and two others joined in by special telephone link to the Isle of Sheppey. Previously the telephone students had had to rise at 4 a.m., walk more than a mile to the station, catch a train to the mainland, then walk another mile to the teacher's home. The return journey to school was even longer. With special voice-amplifying boxes fitted to the telephones at both ends, the class could be united in discussions, questions and scripture study.

In 1976 Seminary leaders in Liverpool and Preston organized a major commemorative project telling the story of the first missionaries to land in England, and the events leading up to the first baptism in the River Ribble in July 1937. Branches in the Liverpool District re-created an English Fayre of the period with appropriate stalls, and a drama was performed based on Charles Dickens's account of an emigrant ship. (See pp. 184–5.) Nearly 200 young people and adults attended, all in early Victorian dress, and Southport Branch constructed a set of stocks to discipline those who turned up in modern clothes. The following afternoon they re-enacted the first baptism and preached a sermon on the bank of the Ribble. Naturally this excellent weekend of youth honouring such a heritage commanded considerable attention from the press.

In March 1986 a new group of 240 Seminary students dressed in period costume again re-lived some of those early events in Liverpool and Preston, and tasted the flavour of their heritage. They visited the new Maritime Museum at the docklands in Liverpool, which show how the emigrants of that time were transported to the new world. 'We had to run from one place to the next,' one Seminary student recalled. 'I found this difficult in a long dress although I did begin to understand how women in the 1840s must have felt.' (Wade.)

They were also told of the race between two men across the bridge to the baptismal site, each of them eager to be the first person baptized in Britain. (See pp. 78–9.) 'When we saw the River Ribble where the early saints were baptized, I realized how strong their testimonies must have been,' another student remarked. 'I would certainly not relish the thought of getting baptized in there, yet they did.' (Pallet.) 'This experience helped me remember those valiant saints who have set a tremendous example of faith,' yet another student testified. (Eldridge.) 'I had to get up at six o'clock; I think it was well worth it,' a student from Nottingham concluded. 'I have often thought of our Church as an American project, but looking at British Church history made me realize that our Church is a worldwide organization and can be found anywhere.' (Poole.)

A filmstrip at the start of the 1981 Seminary course featured President Spencer W. Kimball challenging students to study the scriptures every day. He also suggested they might read through the Doctrine and Covenants several times if they were able. That year the stakes around London encouraged students to read the book through as many times as possible. One student read it more than twenty times, whilst quite a few others read it more than a dozen times.

Many young people found that Seminary studies improved their general study for school and career. In Bangor, Northern Ireland, an eighteen-year-old girl got up at 4 a.m. to study Seminary before going on to schoolwork, and then, following graduation, studied scriptures before work. A fifteen-year-old boy in Dublin got up at 5 a.m. to work at Seminary before maths and science for school, becoming one of the many who have earned thousand-day-consecutive-study certificates. Thus, through Seminary, the Church has encouraged daily scripture study not just for the duration of a course, but for life. A fine example of this was a member of the Kingston Ward, Staines, who continued to read her scriptures daily long after graduating from Seminary. She felt this commitment to be so important that, in giving birth to one of their children at 11.55 p.m. after several hours of labour, she asked for her scriptures – she had not read for the day and did not want to break her habit!

Not all British saints live in areas where there are organized wards and stakes and where the full programmes of the Church are available. Faithful members are to be found even on isolated islands. There has long been a branch in Douglas on the Isle of Man, and on the Isle of Wight. Jersey in the Channel Isles has a ward, but on the smaller island of Guernsey there are only four loyal members – two women and two children – who keep the faith in spite of having no Church organization. For some time a devoted brother travelled weekly from Jersey, when the weather permitted, to conduct their meetings and bless the sacrament. They held meetings together in their home, and welcomed all visitors. One of them wrote: 'We pray that before very long we will see missionary work go forward once again, and that we will, one day, have a chapel here. Until that time we know that the Lord loves us, and knows our needs.' (Langford.) In 1986 missionaries returned to Guernsey.

Similarly, three members live at Kirkwall in Orkney, a two-hour journey across the Pentland Firth from the Scottish mainland. They meet faithfully every Sunday in one of their homes, and hold

Relief Society, Sunday School, and Sacrament meeting. There are a few other members scattered on the other islands, but communication is difficult, and travel can be accomplished only in small boats and on foot. One of the members used to worry that they could not manage, then one day she heard the Spirit speak to her quite distinctly, saying 'I am God. I am stronger than the Devil, and nothing can bring my Church down.' Her anxiety vanished.

One of the major elements in the recent growth of the Church in the British Isles was the opening of the London Temple. (See pp. 400–405.) In the past, patrons travelling long distances who wished to remain overnight have stayed at Edenbrook House some miles from the Temple, but in 1979 a new Accommodation Centre was opened in the Temple grounds with 69 rooms, some double, most for three people, and a few for four, five and even six. There are kitchen facilities, a laundry, a small convenience shop and a centre for the distribution of temple garments.

One of the most successful achievements of the last fifteen years has been the continuing acquisition and preservation of genealogical records. In 1969 Jeffrey F. Packe accepted the responsiblity of directing this work in the British Isles, to seek out the records and to persuade their custodians to have them microfilmed, thus preserving them for the future.

At first the prospects seemed very exciting, but within a month he found difficulties in breaking down the prejudices of the many religious bodies with whom he had to negotiate. Latter-day Saint tenets seemed foreign to the various clergy, and at times hostile articles appeared in the national and local press. Therefore, permission was granted only sparingly. Archivists could see the benefit of microfilming their records, but seemed unable to help because of opposition from the clergy.

In 1969 some twenty-eight archives had agreed to microfilming. Brother Packe spent a great deal of time motoring around the countryside to various parish churches, sometimes through very bad weather, gathering the registers to bring them in for microfilming. In gathering one set of registers the vicar of the church asked what kind of insurance would be given for the collection to be taken some seventeen miles to the archives. Brother Packe asked him, 'How much insurance cover would you like? A thousand pounds? Ten thousand? More?' Then he tried to explain that the greatest insurance of all lay in having the register filmed for posterity, rather than left on paper which was subject to the wear of constant use, and the risk of damage by flood, fire or vandalism.

Then, in 1972, the Federation of Family History Societies came into being and Brother Packe arranged for them to have access to the Church's computerized genealogical files, which heretofore had been provided only to archives where the Church had filmed. This was the beginning of an excellent relationship with family historians all over the country. In due course Brother Packe visited each society in turn to talk about the records in the Salt Lake City Library, and to demonstrate how to use the Index. Realizing that something had to be done to protect the original records, the archivists themselves called for action in the preservation of these documents, and then the breakthrough came: the Parochial Records Measure of 1979 required parish documents to be deposited in central records offices. Doors which had been closed for years were now opened, and permission was obtained for microfilming many additional records. All archivists have played an important part in the work. There have been those who have written 'perfect' letters to appropriate Anglican bishops. One archivist made it possible for Brother Packe to meet with a school of the clergy to plead his case, and during the enquiry the archivist scolded them for their shortsightedness. Another archivist called Brother Packe every four or five years to tell him each time he had prepared another collection to be filmed. Another was a guide and friend with answers to the Church's problems, questions on points of law, always willing to give advice. Some have even felt themselves compelled by honour to reply to inaccurate articles printed by the newspapers.

From 1969 until 1985 three microfilmers were working in the British Isles. As more permissions were received, the work expanded; and by 1986 thirteen microfilm operators were at work. Training programmes and seminars are held annually to update the operators on the latest developments in technique, and they are trained in archival procedures in order to establish good relations with the staff of the various archives. Each operator is carefully selected for the work – they are ambassadors for the Church, and their behaviour must be exemplary.

The Church has established thirty-three branch genealogical libraries throughout Britain. These make available copies of the key records at the Church's main library in Salt Lake City. Especially important is the International Genealogical Index (IGI). Nearly half of its eighty million names are from the British Isles, and an ever-increasing demand from the public has meant that the libraries have done much to create a positive attitude toward the Church.

Billy Stewart, librarian and genealogist in Belfast, has many stories of people who were at first wary of making any contact with the Church, but after finding nothing through the civil records, approached the library at last. The people met with courtesy, skilled help and frequently outstanding success. One visitor from Australia had been unable to trace even his own parents in the civil records, and was advised by the civil authorities to 'try the Mormons'. He did so, and the library found many of his ancestors, including his present family, and brought about a family reunion. A couple visiting from the USA had been unable to discover an ancestor most important to them, until they came to the Holywood Road Library, and there, in the book of gravestone inscriptions, was their 'missing person'. The regional genealogical library (based in the Hyde Park chapel, London) has attracted the attention of many dignitaries who have been deeply impressed by the co-operation and help received.

One of the obstacles still standing in the way of the Church's growth is the fact that most people in Britain harbour mistaken ideas regarding its doctrines and activities. There has always been a certain amount of coverage in the media, especially the newspapers, though some of it has been marred by prejudice or sensationalism. The Church feels that its enemy is not publicity or public attention, but rather silence and public ignorance.

To meet this need a public communications office was organized in 1975. This office, as well as the public communications director at the local level, submits stories as regularly as possible to the media. Many excellent pieces have been published about members' achievements in the Church and community, missionary service, new chapels and genealogical libraries, human interest features, Church activities, celebrations, fund-raising and outings. All these help to heighten public awareness of the Church. A feature article in the *Evening Herald* of Chelmsford described a family who paid their tithing and supported a son on a mission even though they did not have a lot of money. It also praised the Mormons' clean life style. (*DN*, *Church News*, 16 May 1981, p. 12.) Similar favourable publicity resulted when the Surrey *Herald Weekly* selected a member of the Kingston Branch as 'Super Mum'. (*DN*, *Church News*, 5 Aug 1984, p. 11.)

The public communications programme has proved that when people do write articles attacking the Church nowadays, others will frequently come to the saints' defence and be more effective because they are seen to be impartial. For example, in the *Surrey and Hants News* of September 1981, the following letter from John Kay appeared:

There is something vaguely distasteful about the smooth-suited young men with the short back and sides seen in town centres locally waylaying passers-by to peddle their own particular brand of philosophy as Mormons.

At a time when a growing number of their contemporaries in Britain are unable to get work, these well-heeled fellows are kept in the manner to which they have been accustomed just so that they can try to convert the ungodly. I would be far more convinced of their sincerity if the [money] spent on sending them over here from the United States were ploughed into some worthwhile relief work, in the Third World, say, and [if] these young men followed [that money] out to the underprivileged countries concerned, to take off their smooth suits, roll up their sleeves and get down to some practical work to help mankind.

It is a way of getting over the Christian message that appears to have worked for some 2,000 years.

The following reply came in the *Camberley News* a few days later:

I have no connection whatsoever with the Mormon Church. Having studied Mormon beliefs in some detail, I would have to admit, if pressed, that I find them strange and impossible to accept. However I have always been deeply impressed with the Mormons I have met – both in this country and in North America. Without exception they have proved themselves polite, courteous, generous and friendly. Even when promoting their beliefs, they are sincere and not at all aggressive. They exhibit no inclination to impose their creed on anyone. So why they should cause John Kay to foam at the mouth is completely beyond me. John Kay seems to find it objectionable that some Mormons choose to conduct their missionary activities in Britain rather than in the Third World. What he does not say is that 'these well-heeled fellows' have volunteered to give up two years of their life without any financial reward in order to share their beliefs with anyone in this country who will listen to them. Is this something to be condemned?

John Kay claims there is something 'distasteful' about these 'smooth-suited young men with the short back and sides'. In reply, I can only conclude that there is something very distasteful about John Kay if, in this sick and degenerate world, he finds it necessary to vent his anger on a group of people who, in their own way, are trying to make it a better place in which to live. Jack Pigden, Pine Drive, Hawley.

Added attention was focused on the Church when ITV broadcast a programme on 'The Mormon Conquest' as part of a popular series in prime-time Sunday evening. It included an interview with Bryan Grant, the Church's director of public communications in Britain, featured the London Temple, and described how Mormon bishops provide help through the Church welfare programme. Missionaries invited their investigators to watch, and at least thirty-one baptisms resulted. (*DN, Church News*, 24 Oct 1981, p. 5.)

Another excellent story with national and local coverage in 1985 was that of Fred Bishop, the fire officer who rescued Conservative Cabinet Minister, Norman Tebbit, from the Grand Hotel fire in Brighton. Bishop, a high councillor in the Crawley Stake, subsequently went to Buckingham Palace to receive an MBE for heroism from HM the Queen. A touch of humour was added when Mr Tebbit sent Brother Bishop a bottle of malt whiskey as a token of appreciation for having saved his life, and Brother Bishop explained that he and his family had been Latter-day Saints for twenty-five years and abstained from alcohol. The *Sunday Mirror* of 18 August 1985 headlined it: 'Thought that counts, Norm'.

Great strides have been made in public relations. In July 1983 there were fifty-five column-inches over the nation, half of them negative, and sixteen minutes of radio time. In April 1986 the increase was immense: 1,223 column-inches, a mere 1·5 of them negative, and forty-one minutes of radio time. These successful public relations activities have helped to improve the climate in which missionaries have taught the restored gospel to the people of Britain. Over the years most of these missionaries were young men from North America. At a press conference in Manchester the day before the 1976 area conference began, the reporters asked President Spencer W. Kimball 'why all the missionaries of the Church in England were Americans'. He smiled as he replied: 'That's the point we expect to stress in conferences tomorrow and the next few days'. (*DN, Church News*, 26 Jun 1976, p. 3.)

The number of British-born missionaries has increased steadily over the last fifteen years. In 1975, the first year for which figures are available, there were 109 young men and 48 young women in the field; by 1983 there were over 400. For example, ten missionaries were serving at once from a north London ward of only 280 members. Three of these, all lady missionaries, left in 1985 following a joint farewell. (*DN, Church News*, 22 Sep 1985, p. 11.)

Today, British missionaries are serving all over the world. Merthyr Tydfil Stake, for example, had missionaries serving not only in London, Leeds and Scotland, but also in California, Colorado and Winnipeg. Three brothers from the Dewsbury Ward were serving overseas – two in Italy and one in Canada. An elder from Haslingden worked in temperatures of 40 ° below zero, rode snowmobiles and learned to eat grizzly bear meat, elk and moose in Canada, whilst others have gone to Australia, New Zealand, South America, Europe, the Far East and the United States.

An elder from Loughborough returned to the very roots of the Church to serve his mission. When he was baptized at the age of twenty-four, he had a degree in economics from Warwick University and was working as a trainee manager. Nevertheless, within a year he was serving a mission in Ohio, where he had some of the most spiritual experiences of his life. He visited the Kirtland Temple; the Newel K. Whitney store, where the revelation of the Word of Wisdom was received, and where the School of the Prophets met; and the John Johnson farm, where Joseph Smith and Sidney Rigdon saw the vision of the degrees of glory (D&C 76). When he returned home his joy was complete when he found that six weeks previously his parents had joined the Church. Some young people have made considerable personal sacrifice to serve their missions. A couple from Leeds had been engaged only a few months when he was called to a Canadian mission and she to the United States. It was a two-year separation they accepted in order to serve.

There have also been many fine health and welfare missionaries, including a sister from Bradford, Yorkshire, who served for eighteen months in Peru teaching diet and hygiene, and another sister from Parton, Cumbria who, after obtaining her degree in home economics and nutrition from Manchester University, served in the Philippines working to fight disease and malnutrition.

A great step forward was taken early in 1985 when a Missionary Training Centre (MTC), the eighth in the Church worldwide, was opened adjacent to the London Temple. This meant that the missionaries called from Britain and other parts of Europe, as well as from South Africa, no longer had to travel to the United States for training before entering the field. The Elizabethan-era manor house, with its flagstone floors, hand-hewn oak beams and wrought-iron fixtures, provided accommodation for twenty men and ten women. During the three-week orientation, missionaries reviewed gospel principles and learned proselytizing skills. Returned missionaries living in the area assisted in this instruction. No new languages were taught, because all missionaries coming here were assigned to English-speaking missions, mostly in Great Britain. 'We wanted the missionaries going here to be tremendously proud of the British MTC,' explained regional representative Arch J. Turvey. Thus parents of missionaries will also have a greater 'sense of pride and involvement with missionary work, which is a lot stronger when you know your own people will be well trained and well taught'. (*DN, Church News*, 3 Mar 1985, p. 3; 3 Nov 1985, pp. 8–9, 11.)

Religious strife in Northern Ireland has presented a continuing challenge to the Church's progress there. In 1969 meetings of the Belfast Central Branch were moved temporarily to an outlying area because of Catholic–Protestant riots in the city. (*DN, Church News*, 6 Sep 1969. pp. 14–15.) In 1976 headquarters of the Ireland Mission were moved to Dublin, and responsibility for the work in Ulster was assigned to the newly created Glasgow Mission. When this latter mission was dissolved seven years later, the work in Northern Ireland was again supervised from the mission in Dublin.

A recent event which has particular significance for the Church in the British Isles occurred in Ireland in 1985. On the 23rd of October Elder Neal A. Maxwell met Irish Church members and leaders at Loughbrickland, the site where the first baptism in Ireland had occurred some 145 years earlier. Noting that Ireland may have been included in a general way in some of the dedicatory prayers in the British Isles, Elder Maxwell observed that no formal dedicatory prayer had been recorded specifically for Ireland. As a member of the Quorum of the Twelve Apostles, he officially dedicated that land for preaching the gospel and for the expansion of the Church in the Emerald Isle:

We assemble, Father, in near obscurity, but in deep humility, to acknowledge the labors, during decades past, to bring the fullness of the gospel message to the people of Ireland and to establish further Thy Kingdom here, including the first baptism on this island in this very place by one who became a latter-day prophet, John Taylor.

We acknowledge, Father, that we are mere mortals, and so we see nations and we see borders; however, Thou seest but one flock – all of thy children.

We plead with Thee to look with fresh favor upon all of Ireland to the end that this Emerald Isle will know further greening through the fullness of the restored gospel...

Where there has been strife, may there be peace, and if not full peace, enough peace for Thy cause to move forward as never before. May Thy soothing Spirit, Father, encourage reconciliation through the Restoration.

May it be here, as during the mortal ministry of Thy Son, that the common people hear Him and His message gladly. May it occur here also, Father, that Thine elect women and men will be searched out from among the people of Ireland,...to take their place in the Kingdom Thou hast established. We do know Father, that some in Ireland today, were, as the Prophet Alma has said, called and prepared from before the foundation of this world...

May Church members and missionaries alike in Ireland be blessed to bring a hastening to pass – a quiet hastening such as never seen before on this island ...Father, may we now see thy Spirit work upon peoples and governments. May there be changes in attitudes and sufficient tolerance...

May this day and this place mark the dawning of a new era for Thy work on this island. (See *DN*, *Church News*, 1 Dec 1985, p. 3; *Ensign*, Feb 1986, p. 76.)

Shortly after Elder Maxwell's dedicatory prayer, the Irish saints were interested to note new initiatives by government authorities to resolve the conflict in Northern Ireland. Then, in 1986, the Newry Branch was organized to include members both from Ulster and from the Republic of Ireland. Hence it became the first branch ever to span the border. Some members regarded this as an omen of a bright and more peaceful future for Ireland as a whole.

By 1985 plans were well under way to commemorate the Church's 150th anniversary in Britain. The general authorities would conduct six special conferences on the last weekend of July 1987. A 150th anniversary history, *Truth Will Prevail*, would trace a century and a half of progress. Commemorative plaques would be placed at significant sites in British Latter-day Saint history. This milestone would offer an opportunity for saints in Britain to assess what had been accomplished.

It is evident that the Church has at last come of age in the British

The First Presidency of The Church of Jesus Christ of Latter-day Saints. President Ezra Taft Benson, centre; President Gordon B. Hinckley, first counsellor, left; and President Thomas S. Monson, second counsellor, right. (*Photography by Michael M. McConkie, airbrush by George Gruber.*)

Isles. The land is covered by stakes of Zion. British leadership fills almost all the major callings, and important programmes have been instituted. British saints are now ready to move forward, become more outward-looking, and exercise more influence in the broader community. In contrast to early decades when they depended on missionaries from America, they are now contributing their own strength to the Church worldwide. Members in Manchester, for example, collected funds to aid their fellow saints in Utah during 1985 at the time of devastating floods; and in 1976 Elder Derek A. Cuthbert became the first Briton to be called as a general authority while residing in the British Isles.

Still challenges remain. Misconceptions must be dispelled, such as the view that this is only an American church – a foreign organization and philosophy. To bring the Church out of obscurity, it will be necessary for the members to excel in all fields of endeavour. President Brigham Young said:

Elder Russell M. Nelson, Quorum of the Twelve Apostles, left; Elder Carlos E. Asay, President of the Europe Area, right.

Elder Russell C. Taylor, first counsellor, Europe Area, left; Elder Hans B. Ringger, second counsellor, Europe Area, right.

If we will work unitedly, we can work ourselves into wealth, health, prosperity and power; and THIS IS REQUIRED OF US. It is the duty of a saint of God to gain all the influence he can on this earth, and to use every particle of that influence to do good. (*JD 12*:376.)

That is our challenge in Britain today.

Appendix A. *British LDS membership and population*

Years	Membership	Decade change (%)	Population (thousands)	LDS per thousand
1840	3,626	—	20,183	0·21
1850	30,747	748	*c.* 22,250	1·59
1860	13,853	−55	24,524	0·65
1870	8,804	−36	—	—
1880	5,112	−42	31,015	0·19
1890	2,770	−46	—	—
1900	4,974	79	38,237	0·15
1910	8,202	44	42,018	0·20
1920	7,830	−4·5	44,027	0·18
1930	6,491	−17	46,038	0·14
1940	6,481	−0·2	48,183	0·14
1950	6,357	−1·9	50,225	0·13
1955	9,209	110	—	—
1960	16,623	126	52,709	0·32
1965	66,371	299	—	—
1970	67,849	4·5	55,515	1·22
1975	75,692	25	—	—
1980	87,776	35	55,774	1·57

Note. LDS totals before 1910 do not include children. These are stated here as reported, but increased by 15% in calculating ratios and increases.

Appendix B. *Presidents of the British/European Mission*

1837–8	Heber C. Kimball*	1875–7	Albert Carrington*
1838–40	Joseph Fielding *et al.*	1877–8	Joseph F. Smith*†
1840–1	Brigham Young*†	1878–80	William Budge
1841–2	Parley P. Pratt*	1880–2	Albert Carrington*
1842–3	Thomas Ward	1882–5	John Henry Smith
1843–5	Reuben Hedlock	1885–7	Daniel H. Wells*
1845–6	Wilford Woodruff*†	1887–90	George Teasdale
1846–7	Orson Hyde*	1890–3	Brigham Young, Jr*
1847	Franklin D. Richards, *pro tem.*	1893	Alfred Soloman, *pro tem.*
1847–8	Orson Spencer	1893–6	Anthon H. Lund
1848–50	Orson Pratt*	1896–8	Rulon S. Wells*
1850–2	Franklin D. Richards*	1898–1901	Platte D. Lyman
1852–4	Samuel W. Richards	1901–4	Francis M. Lyman*
1854–6	Franklin D. Richards*	1904–6	Heber J. Grant*†
1856–7	Orson Pratt	1906–10	Charles W. Penrose*
1857–8	Samuel W. Richards	1910–13	Rudger Clawson*
1858–60	Asa Calkin	1913	E. Taft Benson, *pro tem.*
1860	Nathaniel V. Jones, *pro tem.*	1913–16	Hyrum M. Smith*
1860–2	Amasa M. Lyman and Charles C. Rich	1916–19	George F. Richards*
1862–4	George Q. Cannon*	1919–21	George Albert Smith*†
1864–5	Daniel H. Wells*	1921–2	Orson F. Whitney*
1865–7	Brigham Young, Jr.	1922–4	David O. McKay*†
1867–8	Franklin D. Richards*	1924–7	James E. Talmage*
1868–70	Albert Carrington*	1927–33	John A. Widtsoe*
1870–1	Horace S. Eldredge	1933–6	Joseph F. Merrill*
1871–3	Albert Carrington*	1936–8	Richard R. Lyman*
1873–4	Lester J. Herrick, *pro tem.*	1946	Ezra Taft Benson*†
1874–5	Joseph F. Smith*†	1946	Alma Sonne*

* General authorities at the time of serving as mission president.
† Future presidents of the Church.

Appendix C. *Highlights in the history of the Church in Britain*

1836	April	Heber C. Kimball prophesies missionary work in Canada and Britain by Elder P. P. Pratt
	April/May	Parley P. Pratt baptizes many in Canada
1837	4 Jun	Heber C. Kimball called to England
	19 Jul	Elders Kimball and Hyde arrive in Liverpool
	30 Jul	First baptisms in British Isles (Preston)
	6 Aug	First branch organized in England (Preston)
1838	20 Apr	Elders Kimball and Hyde return to America
1839	20 Dec	First missionaries arrive in Scotland
1840	1 Jan	Elders Taylor and Woodruff arrive in Liverpool
	26 Jan	First preaching in Liverpool (Elder Taylor)
	6 Mar	First converts from United Brethren
	6 Apr	Elders Young, Kimball, Smith and the Pratts arrive in Liverpool
	14 Apr	Willard Richards ordained an apostle (in England)
	17 Apr	First British patriarch ordained (P. Melling)
	4 May	First apostle arrives in Scotland (Orson Pratt)
	8 May	First Scottish branch organized (Paisley)
	19 May	Orson Pratt's prayer on Arthur's Seat
	20 May	Elders Young, Woodruff and Richards hold conference on Herefordshire Beacon
	27 May	*Millennial Star* first published
	6 Jun	First Church-approved emigration from England
	28 Jul	First apostle arrives in Ireland (John Taylor)
	31 Jul	First baptism in Ireland
	September	First branch in Ireland (Hillsborough)
	16 Sep	First apostle arrives in the Isle of Man (John Taylor)
	6 Oct	First missionary arrives in Wales (Henry Royle)
1841	21 Jan	The Book of Mormon published in Liverpool
	21 Apr	The apostles return to the United States
1844	27 Jun	Martyrdom of the Prophet Joseph Smith (in Illinois)
1845	December	Dan Jones appointed to preside in Wales
1849	26 Feb	First Welsh Saints leave for the United States
	September	Perpetual Emigration Fund Company organized
	October	Tabernacle Choir organized
1850		More Saints in Britain than in North America
1851		Pearl of Great Price published in England
1853	1 Nov	*Journal of Discourses* first published
1856–60		Ten handcart companies cross the American plains
1860–69		Church Trains used by saints to cross Plains
1863	June	Charles Dickens inspects the *Amazon*
1869		USA transcontinental railroad completed
1870		Steamships replace sailing ships

Appendix C. (*cont.*)

1894	June	LDS emigration to America discouraged
1898		Elder James E. Talmage lectures in Britain
1906	26 Aug	First Prophet visits Britain (Jos. F. Smith)
1934–37		Meetinghouse acquisition programme
1937		Centennial of the Church in the British Isles
1939		Beginning of World War II; American missionaries recalled
1945		End of World War II
1946	January	Ezra Taft Benson appointed president of European Mission; missionaries return
1948	8 Mar	First Church property in Ireland dedicated
1952	June	First chapels in Scotland dedicated
	10 Aug	London temple site dedicated
1955		Tabernacle Choir tours Britain
1958	7 Sep	London Temple dedicated
1960	17 Jun	First English stake organized (Manchester)
	5 Aug	Groundbreaking for Belfast chapel
1962	January	Deseret Enterprises, Ltd. established
	26 Aug	First stake created in Scotland (Glasgow)
	17 Nov	First chapel dedicated in Ireland (Belfast)
1968		LDS Student Association (LDSSA) organized in Britain
1968	May	First British temple president (Dougald McKeown)
1970		First Institute of Religion in Britain
1971	August	First area conference in Britain
1972		Administrative offices moved to Lichfield
1974	9 Jun	First Irish stake organized (Belfast)
1980	7 Jul	First Bishop's store house in England (Birmingham)
	16 Oct	First multi-regional conference (London)
1985	23 Oct	Dedication of Ireland (Elder Neal A. Maxwell)
1987	25–26 Jul	Commemoration of 150th anniversary of the Church in the British Isles

Appendix D. *Missions in Great Britain*

(1)	British (now England London)	1837
(2)	North British (now England Leeds)	1960
(3)	Scottish–Irish (now Scotland Edinburgh)	1961
	Central British (later England Birmingham)	1961–83
(4)	Southwest British (now England Bristol)	1962
(5)	Irish (now Ireland Dublin)	1962
	Northeast British	1962–5
	North Scottish	1962–5
(6)	British South (now England London South)	1964
(7)	England Manchester	1976
	Scotland Glasgow	1976–81
	England London East	1978–83
(8)	England Coventry	1980

Appendix E. *Stakes in Great Britain*

(1)	Manchester	1960
	London	1961–78
(2)	Leicester	1961
(3)	Leeds (now Huddersfield)	1961
(4)	Glasgow	1962
(5)	Sunderland	1963
(6)	Birmingham	1969
	London North	1970–8
(7)	East Anglia (now Norwich)	1971
(8)	Nottingham	1973
(9)	Southampton	1973
(10)	Hull	1973
(11)	Bristol	1973
(12)	Thames Valley (now Reading)	1973
(13)	Belfast	1974
(14)	Romford	1974
(15)	Merthyr Tydfil	1975
(16)	Newcastle-under-Lyme	1975
(17	Dundee	1975
(18)	Liverpool	1976
(19)	Hartlepool	1976
(20)	Preston	1976
(21)	Leeds [new]	1976
(22)	Northampton	1977
(23)	Lichfield	1977
(24)	Crawley	1977
(25)	Plymouth	1977
(26)	London Hyde Park	1978
(27)	London Wandsworth	1978
(28)	Maidstone	1978
(29)	Staines	1978
(30)	St Albans	1978
(31)	Aberdeen	1980
(32)	Edinburgh	1980
(33)	Paisley	1980
(34)	Cheltenham	1982
(35)	Cardiff	1982
(36)	Poole	1982
(37)	Ashton	1982
(38)	Chester	1982
(39)	Sheffield	1982
(40)	Ipswich [new]	1983

Index

Colophon

Type for the text is 12-point Monotype Photina, 1 point leaded, set to a measure 28 picas wide. Photina was chosen because it digitizes well and because it is a Transitional face (to use the terminology of B.S. 2961), and as such is between Garalde and Didone. The prototype of the Transitional faces was Romain du Roi, cut by Grandjean in 1694 and based on a report by the Académie des Sciences, wherein each letter was mathematically based on a square having 2,304 sub-squares. Perhaps this curious precursor of digitization contributes to its success when Lasercomp-set. Photina was designed by J. Mendoza for the Monophoto filmsetter and as such was one of the first faces designed especially for filmsetting.

Printing is by offset lithography. The ink is Cranfield Pantone black, a soft black, chosen to compliment the ivory paper. The halftones are scanned in order to get the best printed image from the often faint, flat nineteenth-century images. The paper is Newtone shade 316 Opaque, 80 grams per square metre. The endpapers are Colorplan maize. The book cloth is Snowdon 4046. The design of the book is based on imagery found in D&C 93.

Among the many people who have helped to make this book possible and to whom I am grateful for advice and assistance are: Tamara Hinckley, who undertook the task of sub-editing; Thomas Kent Hinckley, MIOP, AMIRT, responsible for the design; and Terry R. Hardaker of Oxford Cartographers, who supplied the map artwork. At Cambridge University Press the production team were Trevor Dunkley, Robert McKeown, David Sheppard and David Tiplady. My thanks go to these and many others.